Canada's Unions

ISBN — 0-88862-097-7 (cloth)
— 0-88862-096-9 (paper)

Cover design by Don Fernley

Cover photograph courtesy of CUPE

James Lorimer & Company, Publishers
Egerton Ryerson Memorial Building
35 Britain Street
Toronto, Canada M5A 1R7

Printed and bound in Canada

Typeset by Prompt Graphics Inc.
Printed by Charters Publishing Co. Ltd.
Bound by Reliable Bookbinders Ltd.

Canadian Shared Cataloguing in Publication Data

Laxer, Robert M
Canada's unions

ISBN 0-88862-097-7; 0-88862-096-9 (pa.)

1. Trade-unions — Canada. 2. Labour and labouring classes — Canada.
I. Title.

HD6524.L37   331.88'0971

Canada's Unions

Robert Laxer

With the Assistance of
Paul Craven and Anne Martin

James Lorimer & Company, Publishers
Toronto 1976

Contents

Tables

Acknowledgements

The author is particularly indebted to three people: Anne Martin who was tireless and enthusiastic in her research efforts; Leah Fitzgibbon who, as secretary, ploughed her way cheerfully through numerous drafts; and Paul Craven who was merciless in his editorial rewriting, and who with Anne Martin contributed many new ideas and formulations.

Publisher Jim Lorimer was an incisive editorial critic. Shirley Petgrave and Alice Nagami typed some of the final drafts. Peter Martin provided computing assistance.

Thanks are due to Jean Newman and Dorothy Newman of the Centre for Industrial Relations library of the University of Toronto who helped to locate many primary source materials, and to several readers who made numerous suggestions for improving the book.

Preface

The myth of Canada as a quiet society that exists mainly through careful and conservative borrowing from more dynamic societies is still a strong one. Observers of the Canadian scene almost automatically picture Canada as a country on the outside watching the rest of the world — the world where the real action is. In a sense, this picture is a legitimate reflection of Canada's historical dependence on the outside world, particularly on the United States. In another sense, though, the picture results from the narrow perspective of most observers of the Canadian scene.

Canadian scholars and media are too prone to regard the society's élites as the only source of activity worth their interpretation. The Canadian working class is the last place they would expect to find a new consciousness and a movement with the momentum to shake Canadian society.

And yet it has been among Canadian working people that such a new movement has taken shape. This new movement has been all the more difficult to identify easily because it has emerged not from the level of the top leaders of the nation's trade union movement, but from many thousands of activists in white and blue collar jobs.

That something was indeed happening in Canada is suggested by two outstanding facts: in 1974 Canadian workers staged more man-days on strike per capita than workers in virtually any other western country except Italy; and, Canadian wage increases following contract disputes ran at nearly twice the level of American contract settlements in 1974.

The enormous wave of strikes that hit Canada in 1974 was widely discussed in the media. Usually it was dealt with as an alien and unpleasant phenomenon that somehow caused inconvenience to "the public" but did not involve large numbers of Canadians. The strike wave contradicted the image of quiet, conservative Canada. It was clearly not a response to some larger North American movement centred in the United States. It was a Canadian phenomenon. The renewed vitality in English Canada's union movement in the mid-1970s ranked with three earlier periods in the stormy history of Canadian labour. The first wave had come in the 1870s when the movement for a nine-hour day won unionism its first broad following in Canada. The second surge had come after the First World War, finding its most dramatic expressions in the 1919 Winnipeg General Strike and the One Big Union movement. Then, in the decade of 1937 to 1947, industrial unionism became the focus of a third wave of large-scale organization and militancy.

In English Canada the confidence and enthusiasm of the 1940s slowly gave way to the quiescence of the 1950s and the 1960s. But just at this time Quebec saw a new level of union activity. The movement which culminated with the Common Front of 1972 had its roots in widely-supported strikes at Valleyfield in 1947, Asbestos in 1949, Murdochville in 1957 and in the series of teachers' strikes in the 1960s.

In English Canada, however, trade unionism was quiescent during those two decades. Membership growth was relatively slow. Unions had developed a pattern of long contracts with inadequate provisions for safeguarding the real incomes of their members. When inflation struck with a vengeance in 1973 it brought with it a redistribution of wealth away from working people in favour of corporate profits and incomes from investment. The national railway strike of August 1973 which failed to counter this redistribution marked the end of twenty-five years of relative passivity in the union movement in English Canada.

When the storm broke, its centre was Ontario just as it had been a century earlier during the nine-hour movement, and sixty-five years after that with industrial unionism.

This book emphasizes labour events in Ontario, where over fifty-five per cent of union members in English Canada work, and which experienced most man-days on strike of any of Canada's provinces during eight of the twelve months of 1974. Ontario was a focal point of the change in the national mood of English Canada's unions during 1974-1975.

But there was a difference in the 1970s from earlier periods. This time the upsurge came not from manufacturing workers or others in the mass industrial unions. The leadership came from teachers and hospital workers.

The first substantial move came on December 18, 1973 when 105,000 Ontario school teachers walked off their jobs to defeat legislation which would have destroyed their right to bargain collectively. Then, in January 1974, hospital workers in ten Toronto locals, organized in the Canadian Union of Public Employees, announced their "catch-up" campaign and threatened to strike illegally if necessary to win their demands.

The hospital workers and teachers, together with other groups of public employees who were soon to follow their lead, touched a raw nerve in the structure of the Canadian economy. As in other countries, Canada's service industries, including the public sector, had been expanding rapidly. But unlike other industrialized countries, the Canadian economy was increasingly concentrating on resource development rather than on secondary manufacturing. This had meant that there were relatively fewer workers in the goods-producing sector of the economy to create the wealth to support relatively more workers in the public and private service industries. The result was a "fiscal crisis" which Canadian governments attempted to solve, not by strengthening Canada's manufacturing base, but by holding back the pay and working conditions of public employees. Hospital workers and nurses, for example, proved that their wages were twenty-five to forty per cent lower than those of comparable workers in other fields.

While groups like the teachers and hospital workers were falling behind relative to workers in manufacturing or the building trades, corporate profits and investment incomes were increasing at a very high rate. By 1974 public opinion polls indicated that people were less often placing the blame for inflation on union wage settlements, which had by this time fallen behind rises in the consumer price index (CPI). Huge corporate profits were seen to be closely related to the inflationary pressures.[1]

In this context, the campaigns of the hospital workers and teachers received wide public support. Their claims carried social legitimacy sufficient to override the obstacles of restrictive legality. When Ontario teachers staged their miniature general strike on December 18, 1973, and followed up with strikes in York County, Windsor, Thunder Bay, Ottawa and elsewhere, there was some doubt as to whether these actions were strictly legal. In the case of the hospital workers and the nurses, there was no doubt at all — a strike would be illegal.

The moral force of social legitimacy over technical legality was not the only feature of labour's new mood. In the late 1960s, English Canada experienced a growing nationalism, equivalent in many ways to developments in Quebec earlier in the decade. The new nationalism was founded on pride in Canada, in being Canadian and on the realization that Canada's very survival was threatened by its economic dependence on the United States. It included a heightened confidence in Canada's ability to stand by itself, independent of its increasingly onerous relationship with the United States. The anti-Americanism sometimes involved in this sentiment was not, however, directed at American workers. Its chief targets were American foreign policy, the American military, U.S. government infringements of Canadian sovereignty in trade, and most directly, the giant American corporations that were increasingly in control of the Canadian economy.

One expression of this new attitude was public response to the "energy crisis" of 1974 which many people saw as the creation of the mainly U.S.-based multinational oil companies. Increases in the price of oil and gas — when Canada was potentially self-sufficient in petroleum and could maintain a low price structure — added fuel to feelings of nationalism. Some unions began to press for an alternative policy based on public ownership of the petroleum industry. At its 1974 convention, the Canadian Labour Congress received a large number of resolutions calling for a new industrial strategy for Canada based at least partly on public ownership and committed to creating jobs in manufacturing.

Canadian labour's new nationalism turned in other directions as well. One of the most important questions on labour's agenda was the performance of the "international" unions headquartered in the U.S. in meeting the needs of their Canadian memberships. Some activists within many international unions were beginning to feel that their organizations had proven inadequate. A record number of thirty resolutions at the CLC convention in 1974 dealt with the issue of increased autonomy for the Canadian internationals.[2] A new excitement about the potential of an autonomous and eventually independent Canadian union movement was in the making.

The broad nationalist movement in Canada contributed substantially to this new mood of labour, but labour's new activism also strengthened the nationalist movement. For example, the emergence of a widespread nationalist consensus on the need for a tough stand in the area of energy policy was to no small degree a consequence of unionists' pressure for a publicly-owned industry.

There was a time during the rise of Quebec nationalism in the 1960s when English-Canadian commentators asserted that nationalism could never become a force in the Quebec working class. In the late sixties and early seventies, Canadians heard the same kind of pronouncement about the nationalism of English Canada. The proponents of this view included some top officers of the international unions. "Nationalism," said one in 1973, "never put a penny in a worker's pocket."[3] By the mid-1970s this view was less commonly heard.

As the militant mood of Canadian labour continued into the spring of 1975, when almost a million Canadian unionists were approaching contract talks, the federal government tried to intervene. Finance Minister John Turner proposed a plan of voluntary income restraints based on a consensus of business and labour. But the country had rejected the wage and price controls proposed by the Conservatives in the 1974 federal election and labour leaders and union members were no more eager to accept them in 1975. While wages and salaries are relatively simple to monitor and control, profit figures are far more open to manipulation through the calculation of costs, capital expenditures, depreciation allowances and other items. In May 1975 the Canadian Labour Congress turned down the Turner proposals, countering them with a nine-point programme of economic reforms designed to strengthen the Canadian economy and provide for a more equitable distribution of wealth.

Despite the failure of the wage control proposals, or perhaps because of it, the federal government continued to try to place the blame for inflation at labour's door. Although the finance minister's budget of June 1975 contained no wage control provisions, it contributed to a further redistribution of wealth away from working people by granting higher prices and other benefits to the oil companies. At the same time, the Trudeau government stepped up action against strikers, both legal and illegal, with back-to-work orders to grain handlers and Quebec's dockworkers, and charges pressed against federal public workers for "illegal" strike actions. Labour was to be made the scapegoat for Canada's economic problems. In the days of union passivity, labour might have been induced to buckle under. But those days seemed over.

The two currents of nationalism and labour militancy continued to merge in 1974 and 1975. The rapid growth of independent Canadian unions clearly illustrated the vitality of this new period in Canadian labour history.

The new Canadian unionism of the 1970s was at least in part the result of changes in the economic relations between Canada and the United States. As the United States found itself in increasing difficulty, and in danger of losing its control of the corporate world, Canada's "special status" vis-à-vis the United States disappeared. American unions, responding to the decline of the American economy, naturally made it their first priority to safeguard and if possible increase jobs in the United States. This brought them into sharp conflict with their Canadian members.

The protectionism of the U.S. unions often meant taking jobs away from Canadians employed in U.S.-owned branch plants. This conflict heightened the Canadian demand of greater autonomy from their U.S. head offices, and in some cases led to moves for complete independence from the American unions. While Canadian unionists' approaches to greater control of their own union affairs were many and various, all seemed to be leading toward a fully independent Canadian labour movement.

This book examines the development of this new Canadian unionism in the 1970s, highlighting its two merging components — nationalism and militancy.

The first chapter, "Branch Plant Workers and International Unions", takes Hamilton, Ontario for its focus, as it sketches two events involving international unions and the problems which the American union connection has produced for Canadian workers.

Since the starting point for union activity is the economic well-being of the members, and because inflation and recession in 1973-1975 produced much of the impetus for the new Canadian militancy, Part I outlines the state of the Canadian political economy in the mid-1970s. It opens by describing the substantial decline in labour's share of the gross national product in contrast to the rising profits of corporations. It then examines the role and nature of the work force, with particular emphasis on women and immigrants and how corporations plan the use of labour and technology for maximum profitability. Then, the special problems of Canada's economic dependence on the United States are summarized. Part I ends with an examination of the strength, structure and role of unions as labour's response to the corporations within the adversary system of labour-management relations.

Part II moves beyond the immediate effects of inflation and recession to study the emerging conflict between international unions and Canadian labour. It begins with an examination of the philosophy and practice of the American labour movement and then considers the effects of the internationals' new protectionist policies on their Canadian memberships. After examining the conflict of economic interest between American and Canadian workers in the auto industry, Part II concludes with examples of control of Canadian labour by international unions, including the case of the Seafarers' International Union.

Part III takes up the first major theme of the book. The section begins with a brief summary of the century-old struggle to build a Canadian union movement. It then describes the response of Canadian leaders of international unions to the growing nationalism and the demand for union sovereignty in Canada. The six subsequent chapters cover the wide spectrum of the movement for union autonomy and full Canadian independence. The discussion ranges from the conservative craft unions in the building trades to CUPE and the new Canadian Paperworkers Union.

Part IV focuses on the Quebec unions as the most distinct and radical wing of the broad movement for independence. As organizations expressing the aspirations of the Quebec working class, these unions have developed an analysis, a programme and a strategy which together constitute an alternative model for unionism in Canada.

Part V, "The Surge of Labour Militancy in English Canada", takes up the book's second major theme — the new militancy among unionists in the public sector and within Canadian unions. The first chapter provides a background to the policies of "restraint" advocated by some top union leaders in Canada. The next five chapters describe some of the major developments among public employees and the effects they have had on workers in international industrial unions.

Part VI, "Unions and Political Action", opens with the history of Canadian labour's concern with more than bread and butter — with the broad economic, political and social life of the country. The second chapter deals with the unions' relations to the NDP and projects from the evolving Canadian unionism a potential solution to the crisis in labour's "political arm".

The final section of the book begins with a chapter dealing with one hundred years of national unionism followed by a chapter which summarizes the arguments which have been made regarding the international unions in Canada. The last chapter of Part VII, "New Options for Canadian Labour", projects the main strategy which the younger leaders and union activists are likely to pursue in realizing their objective—a fully revitalized Canadian union movement, strong enough to challenge the rule of the American corporations and their Canadian junior partners, and to reshape Canada's future as an independent country.

---

1. For example, *The Gallup Report*, January 15, 1975, showed that 50 per cent of Canadians considered increased profits to be the main cause of inflationary food prices; *The Gallup Report*, November 12, 1975, showed that 48 per cent of Canadians blamed profits of business and industry for rising prices.

2. Canadian Labour Congress, *Resolutions on Constitution and Structure*, 10th Constitutional Convention, Vancouver, May 1974.

3. For example, Larry Sefton (director, District 6), Canadian Policy Conference, USWA, *Directors' Reports*, 1973, p. 83. This statement was repeated by I.W. Abel, international president, USWA, at the 1975 Canadian Policy Conference.

CHAPTER 1
Branch Plant Workers and International Unions

We are in fact an international union serving the North American market. We like the arrangement we have with the international union because we take far more out of it than we put into it. It is very gratifying. . . . We must remember that the labour movement is above nationalism. . . .

Dennis McDermott
Regional director in Canada, UAW
Interview, 1968[1]

As an international union, we can do a better job in bargaining . . . with strength flowing both ways across the border . . .

Lynn Williams
Director, District 6, USWA
Steel Shots, November 1973

In 1975 Hamilton was the most important industrial city in Canada — the heart of the nation's steel industry and the site of electrical products, metal fabricating and rubber manufacturing.

The symbol of industry in Canada, Hamilton was also the symbol of international unionism. No other major city in the country could boast such a concentration of members of international unions. Hamilton was the heart of the industrial unionism of the Congress of Industrial Organizations (CIO) in Canada — forged in the organizing drives of the late thirties and forties.

Nor had any other city in Canada a more developed sense of the traditions of international unionism than Hamilton. For the city's senior labour leaders, international unionism had long been a way of life. For the generation of labour leaders who built the city's large locals, the assumption that international unions provide a strength and power that no Canadian union could ever match was almost automatic.

Yet two recent events in Hamilton suggest that the international unions in Canada are more international in name than in deed. These incidents highlighted the emerging conflict of interest between the American headquarters and the Canadian memberships of international unions.

In February 1974, Local 113 of the United Rubber Workers (URW) at Firestone in Hamilton went on strike. The local had every reason to be confident of success. It had behind it a powerful tradition of militant unionism on both sides of the border, stretching back to the huge "industrial valley" strikes at Akron, Ohio, in 1937. The local was led by president Leo O'Rourke, an experienced unionist and a supporter of international unions. The workers at Firestone could count on the support of their fellow workers at Goodyear in Toronto and Uniroyal in Kitchener.

If there is a classic case of an industry dominated by multinational corporations which essentially control the entire production of one of the satellite countries in which they operate, it is the tire industry. With its headquarters in the United States and its branch plants in Canada, American control of the car tire industry in Canada is virtually complete. Between them, the "big four" U.S. tire companies — Firestone, Goodyear, B.F. Goodrich and Uniroyal — have a stranglehold on the Canadian tire market. Goodyear alone, in 1968, controlled almost fifty-five per cent of the original equipment market, and thirty per cent of the replacement market. The old European companies which had had branch plants in Canada had been swallowed up by the U.S. companies; thus Dunlop is owned by Firestone and Sieberling by Goodyear.

The economic situation was ideal from the point of view of the workers on strike. Canadian car sales in 1974 — and thus the market for tires — were at a record high.

The principal issue of the strike was the workers' demand for a cost of living adjustment clause (COLA), a demand which had not been won in U.S. rubber plants. Local 113 demanded a COLA because the rate of inflation was running at 1.0 per cent per month, reaching a total of 12.4 per cent in 1974. In the previous year, the rate of inflation had been 9.1 per cent.

The Canadian rubber workers' locals, particularly those at Firestone in Hamilton and Goodyear in Toronto, have a long tradition of militancy. The Firestone workers had been involved in Hamilton's 1946 strike wave, when Stelco was successfully organized for the first time and substantial gains were won at Westinghouse and other plants. Both the Firestone and Goodyear workers have fought a number of strikes since. In 1974 the workers were militant and their ranks were solid. They had shut the plants down, and a substantial victory seemed to be on the horizon.

But instead of a relatively quick triumph, the rubber workers had a gruelling struggle. They remained on strike from February to November 1974. In the course of the strike, in order to exert more pressure on the companies, they were joined by their fellow unionists at Goodyear in Toronto from April to October, and at Uniroyal in Kitchener from September to October.

But others on whom they banked for support — the U.S. members of the international union — let them down seriously. The American workers continued to work, producing extra tires for the Canadian markets. Tires produced in Akron, Ohio and other U.S. centres poured into the country, enabling Firestone, Uniroyal and Goodyear to supply their Canadian buyers as if nothing had happened.[2]

After the strike was over the president of the Firestone local attributed the long delay in reaching a settlement to the fact that Firestone "could import all the tires it wanted".[3]

Because car sales had dropped in the United States (as opposed to Canada, which experienced continued strong sales), the American plants had an inventory of unsold tires. There were threats that American workers might have to go on short weeks or lay-off because of the slow-down in U.S. sales. O'Rourke pointed to this when he said:

> During the strike they [the U.S. plants] weren't operating at peak production; they had enough tires banked. They flooded this country with those tires — a sort of dumping. . . . Actually, we were kept out for eight months to supplement the work of the U.S., because it kept them working. Before Goodyear went out, for instance, they [in the U.S.] were contemplating shutting their plants down for a week or two weeks in certain places. . . . But then Goodyear and Firestone in the States stopped their lay-offs. Actually, it is one country robbing another. Really it is, and our government going along with it.
>
> And every time I approached the government on this they said, "What can we do? They can retaliate in so many different ways." You mean if the U.S. decided to bomb us, we are not going to bomb them back because they may retaliate on us?[4]

Aware of these difficulties, Hamilton union leaders developed a three-pronged strategy. They decided to put pressure on the Canadian government to limit tire imports; to try and get support from Goodyear and Firestone workers in the United States; and to appeal for general support from the Canadian labour movement.

A union delegation was sent to Ottawa with an appeal for higher tariffs on tire imports. Under the Auto Pact, original equipment tires were imported duty free. On all other tires, the tariff, which had been dropped to 12.5 per cent in February 1973, was to be readjusted to the statutory level of 17.5 per cent on July 1, 1974.[5] Government officials told the union delegation that this was the most that could be done, for fear of U.S. retaliation.

O'Rourke was very disappointed with the government's attitude. He believes the government could have acted differently, saying to the U.S. companies, as he put it, "Look, we have got plants on strike here that are keeping Canadian people out of work. We don't want you to import those tires." If the government had imposed an extra tariff, he claimed, "the Firestone strike would have been over four or five or six months earlier".[6]

The strike in Canada had provided the U.S. companies with a market for their American over-production. As URW Canadian Director William Punnett suggested:

> Our big problem is that we got into a strike position at the worst possible time. The energy crisis in the U.S. led to a surplus of tires there. . . .[7]

In addition, there were large imports of radial tires which were to be standard equipment on 1975 model cars. There was not sufficient radial tire production in Canada to supply the Canadian market because most of the new radial tire plants had been established in the United States.[8] So this double-barrelled rise in imports, on top of the record level of imports in 1973, seriously undercut the bargaining position of the Canadian rubber workers. In 1973 Canada imported tires and tubes worth $92 million compared with $36 million in 1971.[9] The trade deficit with the United States on tires and tubes reached $155 million in 1974, up $131 million over 1973.[10] According to Punnett, there would have been 2,700 additional rubber industry jobs in Canada if all tires sold in the country had been made in Canada.[11]

The second aspect of the strike strategy, an appeal to the U.S. rubber workers, failed badly. The aim was to get direct support from workers in the U.S. Firestone and Goodyear plants. It was not a question of getting financial support toward strike pay or resolutions offering moral support. Instead, the Canadian rubber workers, particularly those at Firestone, wanted the American locals to try to stop the importation of tires into Canada. Since the Canadian government refused to help, only the American rubber workers could have taken action to stop the flood of imported, strike-breaking tires.

In early July the Firestone local invited all U.S. local presidents to come to Hamilton to discuss shutting down the Firestone operation continent-wide if a settlement was not reached by July 15. A story by labour reporter Peter Slee in *The Hamilton Spectator* of July 10 echoed the local's hopes:

> In strong, visible demonstration of international union solidarity, the presidents of the Firestone local unions throughout the U.S. are expected to arrive in Hamilton over the weekend for a meeting Monday that could force a quick end to the lengthy Hamilton Firestone strike. . . . The U.S. leaders will be asked to organize some kind of disruption of production — a slow-down, a series of study sessions, even wild cat strikes, to halt production altogether. Already workers

at Firestone's Canadian tire operations are solidly behind the Hamilton workers.

"If the U.S. local leaders are willing to stick their necks out to provide substantial assistance to the Hamilton strikers," Slee commented, "no one will have to convince the members of Local 113 of the value of international unionism."

On July 15 *The Spectator* reported that the URW Local 113 president, Leo O'Rourke, was to meet that day with officials of U.S. locals "in an apparent attempt to enlist further support for the continuing strike at Hamilton's Firestone plant".

The newspaper the following day carried the result:

Leaders of the United Rubber Workers of America's U.S. Firestone locals did not appear at the meeting in Hamilton as planned. . . . There have been no work stoppages in the U.S. plants and surplus from these plants is still being imported into Canada to help Firestone meet its commitments to the automobile manufacturers.

After the strike was over, the president of Local 113 was interviewed about this non-event. O'Rourke said:

I would have loved to have seen them shut down. In fact I even went over there to get them to do it — for one day. . . . They [the U.S. locals] would have gone along with it for one day until they bumped into the laws of the land, that said it would have put the blame right on the [international] president . . .[12]

O'Rourke was asked whether the U.S. membership could have found itself in difficulty by complying with the Hamilton workers' requests:

They could have been charged, sure. But look at all the unrest there was in labour in Canada, the U.S., and all over during the last couple of years due to inflation. If anybody was going to take illegal action and have the public sympathetic to them it was in these last two years. They did it here in Canada, didn't they? How did Stelco get a wage increase? They threatened to walk out.[13]

It was difficult to explain why the U.S. local officers did not come to Hamilton. O'Rourke did not want to blame the American union, yet he could not avoid it either. Pressed as to what would have happened had the American workers supported the strike, he admitted:

Well, sure, it would have quickened things up a bit. *But if they had gone out on strike with us, and let's say we settled our strike, they would have had lay-offs there*. You have to consider that too. Actually we were kept out for eight months to supplement the work of the United States. *Because it kept them working*.[14] (emphasis added)

It was on their third front that the strategy of the Canadian rubber workers really paid off. Their own ranks remained solid throughout the strike, and they received strong support from fellow rubber workers and some other unionists in Canada, particularly the Hamilton workers.

Until the beginning of June, the Firestone strike had been very quiet. Firestone then started shipping tires from its warehouses and this led to a confrontation.

On Thursday, June 6, two hundred pickets gathered and dared the office workers to try entering the plant. The picket line consisted not only of Firestone strikers, but also of representatives from almost every major local in Hamilton.[15]

When Firestone began shipping tires, the union interpreted the move as a company response to auto industry demands that either Firestone supply the tires they had contracted for, or the business would be taken elsewhere. The rubber workers' Canadian contacts in the United Auto Workers (UAW) had been telling them that while there was a tire shortage in the auto industry, it was not a serious one. Enough Firestone tires had been coming from the United States to keep auto production going. According to these UAW contacts, every kind of tire was being shipped from the United States to Canadian auto plants.[16] Ford's Oakville factory was among the heaviest users of U.S.-built Firestone tires.

Since a federal election was scheduled for July, federal labour minister John Munro, with his seat in Hamilton, got into the act. On June 6, he described the shipping of tires through the picket lines as a provocative gesture sponsored by Firestone's U.S. head office. *The Hamilton Spectator* reported that the parent company refused to answer Munro's charge.

In contrast to recent experience in other Ontario towns, Firestone did not follow up the first appearance of mass picketing and the stopping of tire shipments with an application for a court injunction. This was attributed to the strength and support of organized labour in Hamilton.

In the context of such militant support by organized labour in the Hamilton area, O'Rourke announced:

> If an agreement is reached with the company before Monday we will go back to running an orderly, sane strike like we had for the past three months. If not, we want all our brothers and sisters from the other locals to come to our picket line on Monday to prevent the police from breaking the picket line.[17]

He indicated that his local was prepared to defy injunctions to prevent the tires from being shipped out of the plant: "We will win even if it means some of us will go to jail."[18]

The support of the local labour movement was impressive. Even more impressive was the contrast between Canadian and American workers within the Firestone chain. The rubber workers at Joliette, Quebec — who had already been on strike for ten months, ending in January 1974 — joined their co-unionists for a two-week illegal strike. So did the Firestone workers in Calgary. Both strikes were illegal, but neither local allowed this to deter their support. Local leaders of all Firestone plants in Canada agreed to back the Hamilton workers with a week of slow-downs, but there was no similar response from the Firestone locals in the United States.

When thirty rubber workers picketed the St. Thomas Ford plant to protest the importation of U.S. tires, 1,800 members of the UAW refused to cross their picket line. The plant was shut down for the day.[19]

By October the tire companies were finally willing to settle, first at Goodyear and then at Firestone and Uniroyal. For the first time, the rubber industry agreed to a cost of living adjustment. Although it was not a good one (it offered one cent for every .45 per cent rise in the cost of living, and only began to apply after a 3.5 per cent rise in the Consumer Price Index), it was nevertheless a breakthrough in the face of tremendous odds. In O'Rourke's assessment:

> We broke the back of the rubber industry when we got a cost of living, such as it is, built into the contract. They said 1,330 people here in Hamilton weren't going to do what 184,000 couldn't do in the U.S. But we did it. They said the tail wasn't going to wag the dog. Well, I don't know whether we are the tail or not, but we wagged something.[20]

O'Rourke has been a long-time member of the URW, and he expressed justifiable pride in the achievement of the Firestone, Goodyear and Uniroyal workers. He was proud of the support he had won from other rubber worker locals, and from the labour movement in Hamilton. He, like other older members, remained a supporter of the international and was reluctant to publicly express any direct criticism of it.

For some Hamilton unionists, lack of support for Canadian rubber workers from their co-unionists in the United States could be seen simply as an isolated and unfortunate example. For others, though, what happened to the Hamilton rubber workers in 1974 was the very essence of international unionism for Canadian workers.

Behind the proud face of the international unions in Hamilton fissures and strains have been evident. At Stelco, the city's largest company, there have always been some members of the United Steel Workers of America (USWA) who believed that international unions were American unions whose first loyalty was to the American membership.

Serious attempts to pose Canadian unions as an alternative to the internationals have often drawn a strong response from the city's union leadership. In 1966, in Local 1005 of the Steelworkers at Stelco, the largest basic steel local in Canada, a group known as the Autonomy Group was active in the union's affairs and critical of the union leadership. The central plank in the platform of this group was a higher degree of "autonomy" for the Canadian sections of international unions.

During the 1966 election of delegates to the International Convention, the Autonomy Group circulated a leaflet criticizing a proposed increase in union dues. They pointed out that in the past such increases had been accompanied by a rise in the salaries of top officers and staff members. In making this point, the leaflet contained the following confused sentence: "A Canadian Strike Fund is desirable but in the past strike funds have been used as a means to increase the salaries of the international officers."[21]

This statement was inaccurate because international officers' salaries were not drawn from a "strike fund". However, the need for a larger strike fund had often been used to justify a dues increase and such dues increases were often followed by an increase in officers' salaries.

An international representative of the USWA in Hamilton, Stewart Cooke, on the basis of this statement, began proceedings against the members of the Autonomy Group for violations of the union constitution. The trial committee, recommended by the local president, found nineteen members of the group guilty of "publishing or circulating among the membership false reports or misrepresentations," and "slandering or wilfully wronging a member of the international union," on the basis of the statement in their leaflet. The trial committee recommended a four-year suspension of membership. The convicted members included six chief stewards, two assistant chief stewards, and nine stewards.[22]

Following this trial decision, a membership meeting was held in the local. The Commission of the International Executive Board of the union reported what occurred there:

On November 9, 1966 . . . extended debate ensued during which the accused vigorously contended once again that the charges were intentionally laid against them to eliminate the possibility that such "Canadian Autonomist" candidates would be eligible to unseat the incumbent Union Executive in the elections scheduled for this summer. The Trial Committee on the other hand argued in support of the acceptance of its report. At the end of the debate a vote was taken in which the membership defeated the recommendation of the Trial Committee.[23]

This, however, was not the end of the matter. The following week Stewart Cooke filed a notice of appeal with the International Executive Board asking that the decision of the Local 1005 membership be reversed. The Pittsburgh office of the USWA then proceeded to overturn the local's decision. A commission was set up which suspended the nineteen members for one year. During that time they were not allowed to visit the Steelworkers' Centre in Hamilton. Moreover, because the international's constitution provided that steel workers be members in good standing for two years to run for executive office in the union, these activists were effectively barred from running for office until 1970.[24]

Subsequently, several of the suspended members have been elected to various committees, the executive board, and grievance committee chairman.

The actions taken by the International Executive Board against these local activists contradicted the notion that the USWA enjoyed autonomy in deciding matters relating to the Canadian membership.

These two incidents in the long history of international unions in Hamilton point to difficulties in the structures of international unionism.

A worker at Goodyear posed the vital question at the end of the long rubber workers' strike:

> I can't understand, in an international union, that the workers over there wouldn't say, "No way ... our brothers are on strike, why should we be working to help the company in Canada keep them out?" ... They don't show good faith, do they?[25]

In 1975 international unions were as prominent as they ever had been in Hamilton, yet a certain unease surrounded their future in Canada. Much of this book is about the place gained in Canada by international unions, and why there are now questions about the future of the international structure in a country alive with a new nationalism and a new labour militancy.

---

1. *The Windsor Star*, May 28, 1968.

2. *The Hamilton Spectator*, June 7, 1974.

3. Anne Martin, taped interview with Leo O'Rourke, president, Local 113, URW, Hamilton, November 14, 1974.

4. Ibid.

5. Letter March 11, 1975. Director of research, the Rubber Association of Canada, to D. Newman, Centre for Industrial Relations, University of Toronto.

6. Martin, op. cit.

7. *The Globe and Mail*, July 30, 1974.

8. *The Toronto Star*, September 18, 1974.

9. *Statistics Canada Daily*, April 11, 1975, p. 6; a URW brief submitted to the Ontario Ministry of Industry and Tourism stated that the value of tire imports jumped 134 per cent in 1973 over 1972. *Labour Review*, January-February 1974; a leaflet distributed during the strike by the URW stated that the number of passenger tires imported in 1973 increased by some 80 per cent.

10. *Statistics Canada Daily*, April 11, 1975, p. 6.

11. *The Globe and Mail*, August 15, 1974.

12. Martin, op. cit.

13. Ibid.

14. Ibid.

15. *The Hamilton Spectator*, June 7, 1974.

16. Ibid.

17. Ibid.

18. Ibid.

19. *The Hamilton Spectator*, May 23, 1974; *The Windsor Star*, May 24, 1974.

20. Martin, op. cit.

21. *Report of Commission of the International Executive Board* on the Appeal of F. Stewart Cooke, Local Union 2853 vs. (19) Members of Local Union 1005, District 6, p. 3.

22. Ibid., p. 4.

23. Ibid., p. 6.

24. To be eligible for office, a member must have attended or have been credited with eighteen of the last thirty-six membership meetings.

25. CFGM Radio, 1310, Toronto, "International Unions in Canada", Ron Knight (host), December 3, 1974, 9-12 a.m.

PART I
Labour in the Canadian Political Economy

CHAPTER 2
The Myth of Affluence

In any community 100 of the leading capitalists possess as much as all the rest put together. . . . A wrong has been committed somewhere in the distribution of production.

John Hewitt
President, Toronto Typographical Society
Ontario Workman, March 13, 1873

A hundred years after these words were written Canadian workers were to experience the age-old "wrong" in a new form. In 1973 the "distribution of production" shifted sharply away from working people's pay toward increased corporation profits. Workers' real income declined because in spite of increases in pay, prices rose more sharply — reaching an overall figure of 12.4 per cent in 1974 and over 20 per cent in the case of food.[1]

This swift reduction in purchasing power first resulted in stunned passivity in Canada's unions; but by the end of 1973 labour's mood had changed. Because unions at first seemed powerless to stop the decline in labour's living standards, workers began to examine the reason for this failure. Since the economic change of 1973-74 served as the spark to Canadian union militancy and nationalism, analysing it is the starting point of a study of Canada's unions in the mid-1970s.

"A wrong has been committed somewhere in the distribution of production," wrote Hewitt in 1873. In 1971 the richest 20 per cent of all individuals received almost half — 49.2 per cent — of all income paid to Canadians. This was two and a half times the national average. A share that had actually increased since 1951 when the figure was 45 per cent. By contrast, the poorest 20 per cent of the population received only 2.0 per cent of the total income for 1971 — just one tenth of the national average. This group's share of the total had declined from 1951 when it received 3.2 per cent of all incomes.[2]

Although the average weekly wage for manufacturing workers rose from $74.45 in 1961 to about $170.00 in 1974, inflation took its toll. The purchasing power of the 1961 dollar had declined to 57 cents by the end of 1974. Wages in manufacturing which had a purchasing power in 1961 of $74.45 were worth about $100.00 in 1974 — $70.00 a week less than the unadjusted figures indicate.[3]

But in spite of inflation, average wages increased substantially between 1961 and 1974: the average manufacturing worker had about $25.00 more purchasing power per week in 1974 than in 1961. This increase amounted to about $2.00 a week per year on the average until 1972.

Taking the effects of inflation into account, the $74.45 of 1961 had become $100.76 by 1972.[4] Then things began to level off, and, in 1973, to decline. Although the average worker found a few more dollars in his pay envelope in 1973, he soon discovered that they would not buy any more than they had in 1972 — and sometimes they would not buy as much.

In 1973, for the first time since the Great Depression of the thirties, average wages and salaries fell behind the increase in the cost of living. Wages and salaries rose by 7.5 per cent while the Consumer Price Index (CPI) was up 9.1 per cent.[5] The gradual growth in real incomes — that is, incomes adjusted for inflation — that had been taking place at the rate of about 2.0 per cent per year since the Second World War was now over.

Support for unionists who claimed a loss in real income during 1973-74 came from Montreal's C.D. Howe Research Institute. Writing in *HRI Observations* in March 1975, Barbara Goldman, assistant economist, and Judith Maxwell, director of economic policy analysis of the Institute, said that labour income "has been significantly eroded by rapidly escalating prices since 1972". Many Canadian workers, they wrote, "are trying to catch up for past losses in purchasing power and to protect their future earnings against inflation. Such wage demands are not only normal for this stage of the business cycle but also a rational response to past inflation." They pointed out that "the share of net national income going to wages and salaries decreased from a peak of 73 per cent in 1971 to 69.8 per cent in 1974, while profits as a share of national income increased from 11.4 per cent to 13.5 per cent".[6]

An examination of contracts between locals or broader bargaining units of major unions and their respective employers showed what happened economically to unionized workers in various manufacturing industries during the three-year period from 1972 to 1975. In general there was a substantial decline in real purchasing power for the workers involved because of the rise in the cost of living. (See Appendix.)

Lower-paid workers were hit especially hard by inflation. For one thing, many did not receive even the "average" increases in wages. Also, their "personal" consumer price index went up much more than the official 9.1 per cent between 1972 and 1973.

The average wage or salary earner and his or her family, far from riding the escalator of "affluence", was actually falling behind in living standards. This occurred within a relatively booming economy.

While many more Canadians were finding it tough to get by, the corporate élite did not face a similar drop in real income, as Table 1 shows. Interest and investment income increased by 111 per cent between 1970 and 1974, while corporate profits increased by 137 per cent.

TABLE 1
Profits and Income from Interest and Investments, 1970-1974

	Corporation profits before taxes	Income from interest and investments
	$ Billion	$ Billion
1970	7.730	3.449
1971	8.983	3.767
1972	10.836	4.160
1973	14.275	5.180
1974	18.330	7.281

Source: Statistics Canada, *Canada Year Book*, 1973, p. 856; *Canadian Statistical Review*, April, 1975, p. 20.

While workers were falling behind the rising cost of living, a smaller group of Canadians was doing very well. The average increase per year was about forty to fifty per cent. Who were these people?

In 1968, forty-two per cent of all shares of Canadian companies were held by the top one per cent of income earners in Canada. The top ten per cent owned seventy-two per cent of all shares. Less than ten per cent of shares were owned by the bottom fifty per cent of income earners.[7] So the enormous returns from corporate profits and other investment income went to a tiny fraction of the population.

Not all of the corporate profits went to this small group of Canadians. Foreign-owned corporations (mainly American) had the largest profit increases. Take the oil industry, for example. Three of the big four companies are U.S.-owned, while the other — Shell — is European. Table 2 shows the annual profits of these companies between 1970 and 1974.

TABLE 2
Oil Company Profits in Canada 1970-1974

	Net profits (after taxes) — $ Millions			
	Imperial Oil	Shell	Gulf	Texaco
1970	105.0	51.2	39.2	24.5
1971	136.0	61.5	53.8	31.3
1972	151.0	79.0	64.4	42.4
1973	228.0	112.5	101.7	55.4
1974	290.0	142.0	161.0	55.0

Source: *The Financial Post Corporation Service,* Data and information cards.

The years 1970 to 1974, then, actually saw a redistribution of wealth away from wages and salaries in favour of corporate profits. One way of demonstrating this is to take the ratio of corporate profits to all wages, salaries and fringe benefits paid in those years as shown in Table 3.

TABLE 3
Distribution of Wealth: Profits to Wages 1970-1974

	Corporate profits	Total wages, salaries and benefits	Ratio of profits/wages and salaries
	$ Billions		%
1970	7.7	46.7	16.3
1971	9.0	51.3	15.6
1972	10.5	57.0	18.4
1973	14.3	64.0	22.3
1974	18.3	74.9	24.4

Source: Based on Statistics Canada, *Canada Year Book,* 1973, p. 856; *Canadian Statistical Review,* April 1975, p. 20.

Thus the corporations' share of incomes, relative to the share going to wage and salary earners, increased by about half during this four-year period.

Another way of looking at this is to ask what kind of wage increases would have been necessary for workers' incomes to keep pace with increases in profits. Between 1970 and 1974, average pay per worker (wages and salaries) increased by approximately 39 per cent overall — without taking inflation into account — while corporate profits increased by 137 per cent. In order to keep up with the rate of profit increase, the 1970 average weekly wage of $126.82 should have been about $317.00 by 1974. Instead, it was about $180.00.

Canadian workers were clearly not getting their share of the benefits of a growing economy between 1970 and 1974. Instead, they were paying the price of increased profits with a decline in real wages.

This "wrong" and how it was perceived by working people provided much of the fuel for the new mood in Canadian labour which began to emerge at the end of 1973.

---

1. Statistics Canada, *Prices and Price Indexes* (Ottawa: Information Canada). This publication of the Prices Division appears monthly.

2. Statistics Canada, *Perspective Canada* (Ottawa: Information Canada, 1974), Table 7.3, p. 156.

3. Statistics Canada, *Prices and Price Indexes*, November 1974.

4. Ibid.

5. Ibid., monthly.

6. *The Globe and Mail*, April 15, 1975.

7. Leo A. Johnson, "The Development of Class in Canada in the Twentieth Century", Gary Teeple, ed., *Capitalism and the National Question in Canada* (Toronto: University of Toronto Press, 1972), p. 156.

CHAPTER 3
Work and Wages

Relations between labour and management, the main area of union activity, focus on the division of the wealth produced within the corporate enterprise. As the H.D. Woods Committee in Manitoba observed, "the search for gain in the form of profits and wages provides the principal motivating force in the private sector".[1]

In the last few decades it has been fashionable to refer to "big business" and "big labour" as the two giants who exercise relatively equal power in determining the course of the economy. However, the corporations in Canada, the largest of which are often American, decide how many workers they need, when they will hire employees or lay them off and how the enterprise will organize the work process for maximum efficiency. These corporate prerogatives show where the basic economic power lies.

Although union seniority establishes procedures and priorities for lay-offs, the corporation has the power to decide whether a particular plant or branch will stay in business. The decision to shut a plant (of which there were many hundred in Canada between 1965-1975) on the basis of profitability illustrates the reality that the worker's labour-power is a commodity for hire at the will of the corporations. An employee is useful only so long as his or her labour produces a surplus for the corporation above the cost of wages and salaries.

Making a profit involves selling goods or services for more than was paid for them at the outset. In 1948 J.S. McLean, founder of Canada Packers, put it succinctly: "We buy cattle as cheaply as we can and sell beef for as much as we can get."[2]

More recently, there have been similar descriptions of the corporate system. In June 1974 Keith Rapsey, president of the Canadian Manufacturer's Association, countered criticisms of the "improved profit performance of leading companies and industries".[3] He referred to "politically motivated attacks" which "distort the record". Although he was "not complaining that profits are not performing well," he had explained at an earlier point that "profits and the hope of profits are the key to the achievement of noble objectives". These noble objectives were "standards of education, health and welfare unknown to history".[4]

In contrast to profits, he named the "annual increase of wage and salaries at a rate not supported by increases in productivity" as one of the "major villains".[5]

In the same month, Ralph Sultan, chief economist of the Royal Bank of Canada, said that "investment spending in Canada will probably have to get a bigger piece of the gross national product pie". This would mean "at least twenty-five per cent of the GNP" in contrast to the past two decades where it had averaged slightly less than twenty-two per cent. "Where are the investment dollars going to come from?" Sultan asked. "Logic seems to lead one back to the corporate sector as the most likely source of increased savings," was his answer.[6]

In what was a record year for corporate profits Rapsey and Sultan were demanding an even larger share of the GNP for the corporations, a share which would go beyond the "productivity" criterion. In effect, this meant a redistribution of wealth toward the corporations. In fact, John Turner's federal government budgets in 1974 and 1975 gave investment from corporate profits as the major rationale for tax reductions to the oil companies and other private sector industries.

Over the past two centuries there have been two direct ways to increase the rate of profit: lengthening the working day, which increases the ratio of product price to wages; and paying workers a lesser share of the products of their labour.[7]

In the 1970s it is not easy for companies to increase the length of the working day. A hundred years of unionism have won legislation governing maximum working hours, and unionists have been able to win increased wages for overtime work. However, this did not eliminate overtime labour as a means for corporations to boost their profits, even at time and a half.

The second and most practical way of increasing profit per worker — reducing the relative size of wages to the overall price of the final product — can be accomplished in two ways: by technological change, and by maintaining a large labour force that will work at relatively low pay. In the seventies, as in earlier decades, corporations are using both methods.

Companies have increasingly turned toward technological change and automation to reduce the amount of labour needed to produce commodities or services, especially as unions have become more resistant to capital's attempts to reduce real income. In this way industries become capital-intensive as opposed to labour-intensive. They are often ready to pay a much smaller work force somewhat higher wages than previously because of greatly increased profitability.

Technological change is made possible by the work of scientists and innovative engineers. The level of technology determines working conditions, how goods and services are produced, how men and women are brought together in the workplace, and ultimately how they relate to management and to each other in the productive process.

Moves toward reducing the labour force through automation, or partial automation, and the use of computers and business machines have been evident in banks and insurance companies, in steel operations, in the auto and petrochemical industries, and in mining. The petrochemical industry is one of the most capital-intensive — with one of the highest rates of return on capital invested. Stelco's new automated plant at Nanticoke, Ontario was expected to double production per worker within a decade.

On an immediate basis, particular workers oppose automation because they stand to lose their jobs, security or particular levels of pay. In the long run, however, there remains a broader social issue concerning the division between "necessary labour", that is the amount that goes to wages, and "surplus labour" which is the amount that goes into expanding private capital through profits. Workers and unions, in pressing for a large share of the corporations' income, have increasingly insisted that technological changes and automation should result in shorter hours and higher purchasing power for labour. In raising these issues of technology unions have touched fundamental questions about the nature of corporate capitalism.

The corporations' resistance to union involvement in issues of technological change shows how crucial an area this is in management's overall strategy for increasing profits. Virtually every union contract has a clause which confines the union's area for negotiations to wages or salary rates, pensions, holidays, medicare, dental care, workmen's compensation, hours of work, shift or premium pay, and other such monetary matters. Most contracts stipulate that all areas not specified in the contract are the prerogatives of management.

Even the Freedman Report of 1965, which recommended that railway unions should have the right to negotiate changes in the technical operations of the railways which affected worker jobs, has been opposed by corporations as a matter of principle.

The success of the corporations in their profit strategies is reflected in the fact that Canadian workers' incomes, taken as an average, fared poorly in comparison to corporate profits and returns on investments in the early 1970s. Behind this "average" income was a wide and obvious variation in pay, ranging from skilled workers to those on unemployment insurance, welfare, or the minimum wage. The 1970 annual incomes of male wage-earners in a few selected occupations appear in Table 4.

TABLE 4
Average Annual Male Incomes in Selected Occupations: Wage Earners, 1970

Occupation	Number of wage earners	Income ($)
Farm worker	74,620	1,888
Service station attendant	31,180	2,426
Construction labourer	69,115	3,929
Timber cutter	19,395	4,457
Longshoreman	44,470	4,758
Hospital orderly	19,765	4,839
Shipping clerk	63,085	4,979
Carpenter	94,965	5,372
Truck driver	195,810	5,592
Mail carrier	17,225	5,722
Bookkeeper	69,135	5,828
Auto mechanic	105,300	5,833
Auto assembler	18,045	6,173
Welder	59,860	6,654
Miner	17,880	6,735
Machinist	37,410	6,842
Pipefitter	44,785	6,962
Insurance salesman	28,715	8,625
High school teacher	63,155	9,152

Source: Compiled from: *Census of Canada, 1971.* "Income of Individuals; Employment Income by Sex, Occupation and Class of Workers, for Canada", Publication 94-765, Vol. III, Part: 6 (Bulletin 3.6 - 7), March, 1975, Table 14.

Beyond pay differences in various jobs, there are also differences in pay for the same job. The differences may be by region, by sex, by industry, or by individual employer.

For example, provincially, the average production line welder in a Quebec machinery plant received $3.76 an hour in October 1973. In the city of Montreal, he received $4.09. In Ontario the hourly wage was $4.10; in Manitoba, $3.73; in Alberta, $5.31; and in B.C., $5.66. A finisher in a steel mill at this time received an average $3.52 an hour in Nova Scotia; in Quebec, he received $4.89; and in Ontario, $6.35.[8]

As well as these regional differences, industry itself is distributed unevenly across Canada beyond the relative distribution of population.

TABLE 5
Regional Distribution of Manufacturing Workers, 1970

Region	Number of manufacturing workers (thousands)	Per cent of all manufacturing workers	Per cent of total Canadian population
Atlantic	75.8	4.64	9.6
Quebec	514.2	31.41	27.9
Ontario	806.6	49.27	35.7
Prairie	114.7	7.01	16.4
B.C.	125.1	7.64	10.1

Source: Compiled from: Statistics Canada, *Manufacturing Industries of Canada: Geographical Distribution, 1970,* Table 2.

As shown in Table 5, Ontario, with about a third of the Canadian population, had almost half the country's manufacturing workers in 1970. The Atlantic and Prairie provinces had only half as many manufacturing workers as their share of the national population might suggest. Quebec had a slightly larger proportion of manufacturing than of the general population, while B.C. had a slightly smaller proportion.

As far as pay differences for the same job in different industries are concerned, a truck driver working in the bakery industry received a national average hourly rate of $3.01 in October 1973, while a truck driver in the brewery industry received $5.40. Pay for truck drivers also varied greatly from region to region.[9]

TABLE 6
Average Earnings of Full-Year Workers in Selected Occupational Groups, 1971

Occupational Group	Male Earnings ($)	Female Earnings ($)
Clerical	7,226	4,610
Sales	7,896	2,947
Service and recreation	6,379	3,000
Transport, communication	7,571	4,672
Miners, craftsmen, etc.	8,077	3,966

Source: Statistics Canada, *Perspective Canada*, 1974. Table 6.30, p. 139.

The most important single factor in determining the pay scale for a given job is the worker's sex. Although they made up 33.2 per cent of the labour force in 1972, the three million women in the Canadian labour force, on the whole, are paid less than men, even when they are performing similar or identical jobs. Table 6, showing average earnings for male and female full-year workers in selected occupational groups in 1971, demonstrates a startling gap on the basis of sex.

On the whole, women in these occupational groups earned about half as much as men. In the sales category women earned only slightly more than a third of what men earned.

There are two aspects to this differential. First, women generally are paid less even when they are in identical job classifications. The differences in pay when men and women are in identical job classifications is evident from an examination of Table 7 in which 1970 annual earnings in selected occupations are detailed according to sex.

TABLE 7
Average Annual Incomes, Selected Occupations; Wage Earners by Sex, 1970

Occupation	Average male income ($)	Average female income ($)
Fish canning, curing, etc.	2,277	1,260
Waiters, waitresses, etc.	2,995	1,442
Tellers, cashiers	3,811	2,326
Library and file clerks	3,855	2,849
Sales clerks	4,276	1,807
Telephone operators	4,463	3,108
Textile knitting occupations	4,609	2,453
Sewing machine operators	4,680	2,681
Shipping clerks	4,979	3,079
Tailors and dressmakers	5,124	2,489
Office machine operators	5,254	3,630
General office clerks	5,357	3,331
Bookkeepers, account clerks	5,828	3,675
Electrical equipment fabrication and assembly	5,859	3,444
Motor vehicle fabrication and assembly	6,173	3,506
Beverage processing	6,800	3,325
Secondary school teachers	9,153	6,765
Pharmacists	11,173	5,937

Source: Compiled from: *Census of Canada, 1971*. op. cit.

Second, and more important, the proportion of men and women varies greatly between occupations. Women are not only paid less than men in the same jobs, but the majority of women workers are in lower paid occupations. There is a group of occupations which has come to be "women's work", where pay is below the lower limits of the male range. Often this is temporary or casual work. Women are excluded from certain areas of work, typically the most highly paid, and concentrated in the service and clerical jobs.

One sometimes hears the argument that most women in the labour force don't really have to work; that work is a form of relief from child-rearing and the tedium of housework. The reality, however, is that almost twenty-six per cent of women working are single and support themselves, while married women — sixty-two per cent of the female labour force — are in most cases permanently at work to supplement their husbands' incomes.[10]

Exclusion of women from key productive sectors of the economy, particularly from heavy and medium industry, construction, transportation and the primary extractive industries, has been an important factor in maintaining their separate work force status. Interestingly enough, these exclusions were reduced considerably during the Second World War, and women demonstrated their ability to perform well in the jobs that had always been considered "men's work". After 1945 their separate status was quickly re-established. Many male workers supported the policy of keeping women out of "men's" jobs, on the grounds that they represented potential competition and that the presence of large numbers of women in those jobs might drag pay scales down to the levels prevailing in the more traditional area of "women's work".

Like women, immigrants form a special group in the work force. For 130 years, groups of immigrants had been brought to Canada to form a cheap, unskilled labour pool along with French-Canadians, Métis and Native Peoples. More recently this pool had come to include Maritimers and Newfoundlanders who had moved, primarily to the provinces of Ontario and Quebec. This special cheap labour force had always been predominantly male, but it had also included immigrant women working in textiles, clothing, hospitals, service industries, harvesting and other unskilled, low-paid jobs.

Difficulty with the language, lack of familiarity with Canadian society, and the fact that they are often not unionized are among the contributing factors that have caused immigrants to accept what is often less than a living wage.

The situation of immigrant workers has been used to demonstrate to native-born workers how much better off they are by comparison. To "move up" the labour ladder implies that there are lower rungs to fill. Immigrants, people from deprived areas of Canada, particular ethnic groups, and women have generally filled those lower rungs. When large numbers of immigrants become unemployed — as happened in 1975 — governments and business have used the situation to combat organized labour's demands for increases in real incomes, shorter hours, longer holidays, and higher pensions. The existence of a large group of unemployed tends to depress wages for those who do have jobs, thus indirectly contributing to increased profits.

The corporations have realized, as well, that it usually takes some time for immigrant workers to move into the trade union movement. Unions themselves have often been guilty of superior attitudes. Even in locals made up largely or even predominantly of immigrants, they have often had little voice, and union leaders in immigrant-dominated industries — particularly in the building trades craft unions — are often English-speaking and native-born.

But bad as the situation is for first-generation immigrant workers, it is worse in many respects for women workers, be they immigrants or native-born. Immigrants occupy some of the lowest-paying, least skilled, most strenuous jobs, but they are involved in nearly all industrial sectors. As part of the male work force, and increasingly part of the union movement, their wages tend to fall within the general range of male workers in their industry, although usually at the lower end of the range.

Females, by contrast, are largely isolated from the best paying sectors of the work force completely. Women in Canada constitute a cheap labour force more than twice as large as that of post-1945 immigrants. According to 1974 estimates, women in Ontario alone lost three billion dollars annually in potential wage and salary income due to male-female wage inequalities. The figure for the whole country was close to seven billion dollars, representing a major gain for corporations.[11]

While technological change leading to automated processes is the most dynamic means to reduce the relative cost of human labour, the large percentage of women and immigrants in the labour force illustrates that employment of these "reserve" groups of "cheap" labour is crucial to the overall profitability of corporations.

1. *Public Sector Employee-Employer Relations in Manitoba*. Prepared by the Manitoba Labour-Management Review Committee, July 1974.

2. Speaking to a parliamentary committee on prices in 1948, *Maclean's*, October 1, 1951.

3. *The Financial Post*, June 8, 1974.

4. *The Globe and Mail*, March 22, 1974.

5. Ibid.

6. *The Financial Post*, June 8, 1974.

7. Karl Marx, *Capital*, Vol. I (Chicago: Charles H. Kerr and Company, 1906), Chapters X, XII, XV.

8. Compiled from: Labour Canada, Economics and Research Section, *Wage Rates, Salaries and Hours of Labour*, Final Report, October 1973, Vol. II, Industry Rates.

9. Ibid.

10. Labour Canada, Women's Bureau, *Women in the Labour Force, Facts and Figures 1973* (Ottawa: Labour Canada, 1974), p. 31. The remaining 12 per cent of the female labour force is widowed, divorced or separated.

11. "Estimated Discrimination Bill" figures were calculated by socialogist Lynn McDonald using Statistics Canada, *The Labour Force*, May 1974, pp. 80-81; *Income Distributions by Size in Canada*, preliminary estimates, pp. 14-15. Presented to the conference on Women and the Law, Winnipeg, February 1, 1975. The "estimated discrimination bill" does not estimate the pay loss for strictly female occupations, but is a "same job" male-female differential in pay.

CHAPTER 4
Foreign Ownership and Canadian Jobs

The twin problems of inflation and growing unemployment which plagued Canadians in the 1974-75 economic recession had their origins in the United States. For instance, the high level of unemployment in the southern Ontario auto industry early in 1975 was a direct effect of the American recession and the drop in U.S. car sales. The United Auto Workers in Canada recognized the general effects of foreign ownership on the economy in a submission to the federal government in February 1975. The Independent Automotive Parts Manufacturers' Association in Canada similarly noted the effects of the $1.94 billion trade deficit with the United States in auto parts in 1974.[1]

Inflation in Canada had been imported mainly from the United States. Although the United States had financed its Viet Nam War largely out of domestic taxation, the war had also been paid for to the tune of some sixty billion dollars by the rest of the world which during this period found itself accumulating largely non-convertible American dollars.

The United States, by virtue of its political and economic power in the world, was able since 1971 to pay for its foreign trade with paper dollars no longer redeemable in gold. Other nations were unwilling to challenge this situation, since it could undermine the whole world monetary situation. Canada had accumulated nearly four billion of these U.S. dollars, representing a "fourth level" of taxation for Canadians, and a factor pressing Canadian prices upwards.[2]

A second major cause of inflation in the United States and the rest of the world was the sudden steep rise in the world price of oil. This rise was the outcome of the alliance of seven major oil companies and the Organization of Petroleum Exporting Countries (OPEC). As a result of this alliance both groups amassed an increase in revenue amounting to approximately seventy billion dollars in 1974.[3]

Both the imported inflation from the United States and the oil price revolution had tremendous effects on the purchasing power of the Canadian dollar and the real incomes of Canadian working people. By the last quarter of 1974 the Canadian economy had stopped expanding. Despite record profit levels, the economy was actually shrinking. Unemployment was on the upswing and by March of the next year approximately 850,000 Canadians were out of work.[4]

Canadians paid for inflation and recession on a proportionately larger scale than most countries because of Canada's major economic dependence on U.S. corporations.

It is not necessary here to describe in detail the extent of Canadian economic dependency on the United States. Over the past ten years, this issue has been studied and documented many times.[5] In summary:

1. By 1963, foreign (overwhelmingly American) corporations controlled seventy-four per cent of petroleum and natural gas, sixty per cent of manufacturing and fifty-nine per cent of mining and smelting in Canada.[6]

2. In gas and oil it was the U.S. companies (which constitute thirty per cent of total U.S. investment in Canada) that were ultimately responsible for the change in the price of Canadian oil from $3.70 a barrel in June 1973 to $8.00 a barrel in June 1975. Any other inflationary rise pales in comparison to this 116 per cent increase.

3. In manufacturing industries, foreign corporations (almost all of them U.S.-owned) controlled ninety-seven per cent of the automotive and auto parts industries, ninety-seven per cent of the rubber industry, seventy-eight per cent of chemicals, seventy-seven per cent of electrical apparatus, seventy-eight per cent of other transportation equipment, including the aircraft industry, fifty per cent of the agricultural machinery industry and forty-seven per cent of pulp and paper in 1971.[7]

4. One of the forms of U.S. investment has been through the take-over of Canadian firms. Such take-overs added nothing to the productive capacity of the Canadian economy. Between 1958 and 1967 from 60 to 93 Canadian firms were taken over every year. In 1968 this jumped sharply to 163, and has remained at a high level up to 1975. Much of the money needed to finance these take-overs was generated in Canada.[8]

5. In the 1960s and early 1970s the outflow of Canadian money to the United States and other foreign corporations in the form of dividends, payments for patents and other revenue was larger than the inflow of foreign investment to Canada. The continuing take-over of the Canadian economy was being financed by Canadian resources and production.[9]

American multinationals have valued Canada primarily as a place to buy raw materials and sell finished products. Since the Second World War the export of Canadian primary products to the United States has increased steadily. Far from becoming more diversified and broadly-based, Canadian trade has increasingly focused on the United States. Between 1950 and 1970, the proportion of Canadian exports going to the

American market increased from sixty to sixty-eight per cent. Canadian imports from the United States increased from sixty-seven to seventy-one per cent in the same period.[10]

There is a direct link between Canada's role as a major exporter of raw materials and semi-fabricated products to the United States and the underdeveloped state of Canadian manufacturing. Canada has been a net importer of most kinds of manufactured goods and has paid for those imports with raw materials. This has meant that Canada re-imports its raw material exports at much higher cost in the form of finished products.

Canada was the world's leading importer of manufactured goods at $463 per capita in 1969. This compared to $279 in the European Common Market, $116 in the United States and only $31 per capita in Japan.[11]

Imports of manufactured goods to Canada in 1970 amounted to almost twenty per cent of the value of manufactured goods produced in Canada. In the United States the ratio was about four per cent. Significantly, American business and government considered the four per cent figure high enough to merit special measures to protect U.S. industry. By contrast, Canadian governments have not regarded the much greater invasion of Canada's manufactured goods market to be sufficiently serious to warrant action.

The weakness of Canadian manufacturing is reflected in the small proportion of the work force that it employs. In 1965 only 24.5 per cent of the paid non-agricultural work force had jobs in manufacturing. By 1971 this had dropped to 21.3 per cent. Among western countries, only Greece and Ireland had a lower percentage of their work force employed in manufacturing.[12]

Qualitatively, Canada's economy was much weaker in the early 1970s than at any earlier time in the twentieth century. The era of American control had progressively undermined Canada's capacity to produce commodities independently. American companies had a stranglehold on the supply of machinery for Canadian industry, and Canada was increasingly dependent on imported technology.

During the 1950s and 1960s — a time when many Canadians thought U.S. investment was the key to growth and prosperity — Canada's manufacturing industries were being steadily reduced to warehousing and assembly operations within huge integrated American corporations.[13]

In the mid-sixties, Canadians began to take the effects of U.S. control of the economy and government policy more seriously. By that time, more profits and dividends were flowing south than were being replaced by new investment funds from the United States. By the end of the 1960s, American corporations were financing ninety per cent of their investment in Canada by reinvesting profits made in Canada and by borrowing from Canadian banks and financial institutions.[14]

Since the mid-1960s the multinationals had taken advantage of special tax write-offs, Domestic International Sales Corporation (DISC) and other incentives offered by the American government to shift jobs to factories in the United States where there are longer production runs, thus further weakening the Canadian manufacturing base.

In 1973 the U.S. Senate produced a study of the behaviour of American corporations abroad.[15] It looked at seven countries: Canada, the United Kingdom, Belgium-Luxemburg, France, West Germany, Mexico and Brazil. The only one of these countries to experience a decline in manufacturing employment in U.S.-owned plants between 1966 and 1970 was Canada. As the study concluded, the presence of U.S. corporations in Canada had a negative effect on manufacturing employment in Canada in the years studied.

This U.S. Senate study acknowledged that U.S. firms displace jobs from the countries in which they have branch plants. It concluded that the major role of American corporations abroad was to foster the sale of parts and components manufactured in the United States to branch plants abroad. It placed the net employment gain to the United States from these activities at about half a million jobs.

Since 30 per cent of U.S. world investment is concentrated in Canada, it can be estimated that a gain of half a million jobs in the United States amounts to an approximate loss of 150,000 manufacturing jobs — many of them highly-skilled and well-paid — in Canada. Another way of viewing the loss of potential employment by Canadians is to estimate the job equivalence of the $9 billion trade deficit in manufacturing with the United States in 1974. At $45,000 average production per worker, this would amount to 200,000 jobs. Taking into account the multiplier effect of manufacturing jobs on employment in the service industries and transportation, the total loss of jobs to Canada would be closer to 500,000.

An example of how U.S. firms can reduce the number of jobs in the host country was reported in *Fortune* magazine in April 1972:

> When Kimberly-Clark built a 23 million dollar paper mill in Huntsville, Ontario to serve the Canadian market, it purchased enough equipment in the U.S. to supply 51 man-years of employment. Had Kimberley-Clark not built the mill a Canadian competitor would have captured the market and bought less equipment in the U.S. (resulting in only 16 man-years of employment). As for the balance of payments, the investment resulted in no net outflow of capital [from the U.S.], and as soon as Kimberley-Clark pays off a Canadian bank loan, the subsidiary expects to pay 2.8 million dollars a year in dividends to the parent company in the U.S.[16]

By 1974 many unionists in Canada had identified the link between extracting and selling resources to the United States and the loss of potential jobs in manufacturing. Numerous resolutions sent to the 1974 convention of the Canadian Labour Congress reflected this analysis.

For example, the Canadian Union of Public Employees submitted a resolution which read in part:

> ... Whereas exports of our resources are nothing more than an irresponsible and short-sighted sell-out which transfers employment potential to other countries ...[17]

In January 1975 the Canadian UAW Council adopted a brief presented to it by the UAW Auto-Tariff Committee. It asserted that "the crisis in the auto industry stems from the decline in the U.S. economy ... and the past and present policies of the auto companies".[18]

The statement went on to show the specific effect this had on the Canadian economy: "The Canadian demand for cars has, over the past two years, been growing relatively faster than demand in the United States, and we expect this trend to continue. If the corporations don't respond by increasing the share of investment going to Canada, our trade deficit will continue to grow and we won't be getting our fair share of jobs." The UAW statement demanded "assurance that corporate investment in Canada match the relatively faster growth in our market".

"If it does not," the statement warned, "we will call for the renegotiation of the Auto Pact to guarantee that jobs in the auto industry grow according to the growth of consumption in each country."

Since there was a $1.9 billion deficit in auto parts trade with the United States in 1974, the UAW Council concluded that the "Big Four have concentrated their investments in Canada on assembly operations and Canada is therefore under-represented in their manufacture of parts". The Council urged that "to reduce our deficit in parts and to better balance the structure of the Canadian auto industry, the government must act to locate more manufacturing in Canada".

Under the heading, "A Development Strategy to Create Manufacturing Jobs for Canadians," the brief said:

> In terms of natural resources — oil, gas, copper, zinc, lead, uranium, nickel, hydro, electric power, wood, etc. — Canada is amongst the richest nations in the world. While private enterprise has been willing to develop these resources to reap the fantastic profits available, they have not been interested in using these resources to develop a strong manufacturing base in Canada.
>
> Along with the above, the branch-plant nature of much of the Canadian economy has meant a reliance for our technology on the U.S. With the long-run prospects for the U.S. looking bleak, it becomes all the more important for Canada to develop an independent technological base.
>
> Since private enterprise has failed to create this manufacturing-technological base which is so vital to the long-run interests of Canadians, government involvement — up to and including public ownership — is essential.

This amounted to opposition not only to the corporations' economic and technological manipulations of UAW members but also to the distortion of the Canadian economy by U.S. multinationals. In this, the Canadian UAW was expressing a viewpoint contrary to that of big business; a viewpoint which many unionists had voiced since labour was first organized in Canada.

1. *The Globe and Mail*, April 24, 1975.

2. *The Globe and Mail*, January 4, 1975.

3. This calculation is based on an OPEC daily production of 25 million barrels of oil × $8 price rise × 365 days = approximately $70 billion.

4. Statistics Canada, *Canadian Statistical Review*, April 1975, p. 43.

5. Kari Levitt, *Silent Surrender* (Toronto: Macmillan of Canada, 1970); R.M. Laxer, *(Canada) Ltd.* (Toronto: McClelland & Stewart, 1973); Canada, Privy Council Office, Task Force on the Structure of Canadian Industry, *Foreign Ownership and the Structure of Canadian Industry* (The Watkins Report) (Ottawa: Information Canada, 1968); Government of Canada, *Foreign Direct Investment in Canada* (The Gray Report) (Ottawa: Information Canada, 1972).

6. Government of Ontario, *Report of the Interdepartmental Task Force on Foreign Investment*, November 1971, p. 4.

7. Ibid.

8. John Fayerweather, *Foreign Investment in Canada* (Toronto: University of Toronto Press, 1974), p. 8, from The Gray Report.

9. See C.W. Gonick, "Foreign Ownership and Political Decay", Ian Lumsden, ed., *Close the 49th Parallel* (Toronto: University of Toronto Press, 1970), p. 43.

10. Jim Laxer, "Canadian Manufacturing and U.S. Trade Policy", R.M. Laxer, op cit., p. 128.

11. Pierre L. Bourgault, *Innovation and the Structure of Canadian Industry*. Background study for the Science Council of Canada, October 1972, Special Study No. 23 (Ottawa: Information Canada, 1972), p. 30.

12. Jim Laxer, op. cit., p. 129.

13. Ibid., p. 145.

14. W.H. Pope, *The Elephant and the Mouse* (Toronto and Montreal: McClelland & Stewart, 1971), pp. 65-66, from Canada, Department of Industry, Trade and Commerce, *Foreign-Owned Subsidiaries in Canada 1964-67* (Ottawa: Queen's Printer, 1970), pp. 40-41; U.S. Department of Commerce, Office of Business Economics, International Investments Branch, Balance of Payments Division, letter to W. H. Pope, November 16, 1970.

15. Committee on Finance, United States Senate, report of, *Implications of Multinational Firms for World Trade and Investment and for U.S. Trade and Labor* (Washington, D.C.: U.S. Government Printing Office, 1973).

16. Jim Laxer, op. cit., p. 143.

17. Canadian Labour Congress, *Resolutions*, 10th Constitutional Convention, Vancouver, May 1974, p. 50.

18. UAW Policy Statement on Economy, brief prepared by UAW Auto-Tariff Committee for presentation to Canadian UAW Council, January 26-27, 1975.

CHAPTER 5
Union Organization in Canada

Monopoly above and competition below are the upper and nether millstones between which the toiler is crushed.

T. Phillips Thompson, 1887[1]

Trade unionism first developed over one hundred years ago in response to what Phillips Thompson termed "monopoly above and competition below". A handful of employers had a monopoly of jobs available; a multitude of workers competed to win them. Either of these processes alone would have forced down wages and the quality of working conditions. Together, they helped to create the widespread exploitation and misery of the early years of industrialization in Canada.

Working people could do little in the short run to end the "monopoly above", although from the beginning Canadian workers were interested in long-run political solutions to the problems of a corporate economy. They could do more about the "competition below", however. By combining into trade unions and bargaining collectively, workers could protect their existing wages, hours of work and job conditions, and press forward to improve them. By overcoming wholesale competition between workers for the jobs available, thereby "regulating" the job market, unions were able to modify the pressures on the lives of working people.

These first unions were usually "craft" unions. They were organizations of skilled workers such as printers, cabinet makers, plumbers and machinists, which tried to lessen the competition for jobs by restricting entry into the trade. This was done largely by requiring long apprenticeships, but also by charging fairly high initiation fees. The craft unions were committed to maintaining high skill levels among their member-ship, retaining the pride in workmanship that had characterized the craftsmen of pre-industrial days.

As Canadian industrialization progressed, with the growth of large factory industries and an increase in assembly-line work and machine fabrication of products, craft workers became a smaller minority of the work force. More jobs were filled by unskilled or semi-skilled workers. A good example was the development of the automobile industry. Previously a highly-skilled carriage-maker, who had undergone a long apprenticeship, built an entire carriage or automobile body from start to finish by himself or with a small group of other workers. Now the assembly line, with a mulititude of workers each carrying out a specific and relatively simple task, reigned supreme.

For the most part, the trade unions continued to be restricted to skilled workers. There had been several attempts to organize unskilled and semi-skilled workers but few of them had been successful in the long run. In the decade between 1937 and 1947, however, a new form of trade unionism emerged on a very broad scale and soon outpaced the craft unions in membership and rate of growth. The new industrial unions organized all the workers in a given industry, from the least skilled to the most skilled. All non-managerial workers (those without the authority to hire, fire and set working conditions) were eligible for membership.

The craft unions had relied on the restriction of entry into the trade to minimize competition for jobs. The industrial unions relied on the mass power of their membership and their potential to halt production to exert their power during negotiations over wages, hours and working condi-tions.

In the 1970s, craft and industrial unions existed side by side in Canada. The construction industry was the most important stronghold of craft unionism. The bulwark of industrial unionism was the mass-production industries: steel, automobile, rubber, chemical and electrical products, but also included mining and forestry. The new "white-collar" unions, particularly the public sector, were mass industrial unions in their own right. They had organized all workers in the government service into one union: the Public Service Alliance of Canada (PSAC) in the case of the federal public service; the Canadian Union of Public Employees (CUPE) in the case of many municipal workers, including workers in hospitals, universities and other public institutions; and ten organizations of pro-vincial public employees.

The newly emerging union organizations of teachers, nurses and other groups which had traditionally been considered purely "professional" were taking shape as a blend of the craft and industrial forms of organiza-tion. Conceivably, teachers could join with other education workers and nurses with other health-care workers to form true industrial unions in these fields. However, in 1975 it was too early to predict what model would become predominant.

Unions are usually organized in "locals" which are the connection between the individual member and the central organization. In industrial unions, locals may represent all the workers in a given factory or institution, although frequently a number of small plants are grouped together to form a composite local. Craft union locals are usually based on a geographical area: all the plumbers in a given city or large territory, for example, will belong to one local.

Unions vary in the amount of autonomous decision-making power they delegate to their locals. Typically, however, strike votes must be ratified by the central office, as must contract settlements. Most if not all unions reserve the right to put locals under trusteeship if they infringe the union constitution. There is a great deal of variance among unions as to the frequency with which trusteeships are imposed, and the reasons for them when they do occur.

All unions operating in Canada have constitutions setting out the powers of the locals and the central office, the control of finances, the rights and obligations of the membership, and the manner by which officers and representatives are chosen. Unions hold conventions at regular intervals, at which delegates from the locals determine such matters as union policy, membership dues, constitutional changes and the election of officers.

Most unions are affiliated to one or another of several "union centrals". These are organizations of unions, intended to facilitate common action and policy in areas of mutual concern. Their most typical role in the Canadian union movement is to act as the legislative voice of the unions, formulating policies and briefs for presentation to the various levels of government. They also play an important role in setting out the jurisdictions of the various member unions, determining which groups of workers each member union has the right to organize and represent. As an extension of this role, the union centrals become involved in mediating jurisdictional disputes between their affiliate unions.

The largest union central in Canada is the Canadian Labour Congress. In 1973 it had about 1.8 million union members organized in 108 separate unions, affiliated to the CLC.[2] The various provincial federations of labour are sub-units of the CLC. Area labour councils, in turn, are sub-units of the federations. Affiliation between member unions and the CLC is purely voluntary, and a great deal of debate took place at conventions in the 1970s concerning the extent to which the CLC can set minimum standards for the behaviour of its affiliates, particularly in the area of "autonomy" for the Canadian sections of international unions.

In Quebec the Confederation of National Trade Unions (CNTU) is an important central, bringing together the independent Quebec unions with a total affiliation of 164,492 members in 1973. Another union central in Quebec is the Centrale des syndicats démocratiques (CSD), with about 41,000 members, made up of unions which broke from the CNTU in 1972.

The Confederation of Canadian Unions is a much smaller labour centre of about 17,455 affiliated members, made up both of locals that have broken away from the international unions, and some new locals organized by the ccu. About fifteen per cent of the organized workers in Canada belong to unions that are not affiliated to any central organization.[3]

The distinction between craft and industrial unions is a common one in the labour movements of the advanced industrial countries. However, Canada's labour movement contains another distinction which is not present anywhere else in the world. This is the distinction between the international and Canadian or national unions. International unions, despite their name, are not world-wide organizations. Rather, they are predominantly American unions which have locals in Canada as well as the United States. Canada is alone among industrialized nations in having a labour movement with a large number of members belonging to unions headquartered in another country.

For three-quarters of a century, the U.S.-based international unions have dominated the Canadian labour movement,[4] both in force of numbers and in terms of their philosophy. Until late 1974, the largest union in the country was the United Steel Workers of America — an international union. Since then it has been overtaken by the Canadian Union of Public Employees — one of the Canadian unions. Membership figures and growth rates of the two forms of Canadian unionism in recent years are shown in Table 8.

TABLE 8
Union Growth in Canada

Year	Union membership as percentage of all non-agricultural paid workers	Percentage of total membership in international unions	Percentage of total membership in national unions
1921	16.0	72.8	—
1931	15.3	69.5	—
1941	18.0	62.4	—
1951	28.4	70.5	—
1961	31.6	71.9	—
1965	29.7	70.8	—
1971	33.6	62.0	34.9
1972	34.4	59.6	37.7
1973	36.3	55.3	42.1

Source: Compiled from: Labour Canada, *Labour Organizations in Canada, 1972;* Labour Canada, *Labour Organizations in Canada, 1973;* Canada Department of Labour, Economics and Research Branch, *Union Growth in Canada, 1921-1967.*

The Canadian unions have, on the whole, been growing much more rapidly than the internationals. If one adds the developing organizations of groups such as teachers, nurses and provincial civil servants — all of which are fully Canadian and engaged in forms of collective bargaining — the growth rate is phenomenal. Canada's labour movement had a high rate of growth relative to that of the United States in the 1970s, mainly as a result of expansion in the Canadian organizations.[5] This trend was producing a major shift in the balance between membership in the internationals and in the Canadian unions.

In addition to the differences in the rate of growth of Canadian and international unions there are significant differences in the degree of union organization in various industries. Overall, about 36.3 per cent of the total non-agricultural work force was organized in 1973.[6] Table 9 shows how union membership grew as a percentage of non-agricultural paid workers.

Union membership by industry in 1972 is shown in Table 10.

TABLE 9
Union Membership as Percentage of Non-Agricultural Paid Workers

1965	29.7
1970	33.6
1971	33.6
1972	34.4
1973	36.3

Source: Labour Canada, *Labour Organizations in Canada, 1973*, p. xxv.

Women workers are less likely to be union members than men; "women's work", as discussed in chapter three, has remained largely unorganized. In 1971, 22.6 per cent of female "paid workers" were in unions, compared to 39.8 of male "paid workers".

This has been changing in the past decade. Between 1962 and 1972 female membership in national unions increased by 219 per cent, and by 79 per cent in international unions. In 1972 women constituted 42.3 per cent of total membership in the national unions and 15 per cent of membership in the international unions.[7]

How have unions in Canada carried out their task of challenging "monopoly above and competition below"? Historically, the unions — influenced by American business unionism — concerned themselves primarily with bread-and-butter issues. They tended to concentrate on wages, hours, pensions, holidays and "fringe benefits". While they concerned themselves with labour and social legislation, these areas were in practice regarded as specialized activities to be dealt with by the union centrals and provincial federations of labour.

At times, however, unions have been involved in broader labour campaigns such as the movements for a nine-hour working day in the

TABLE 10
Union Membership by Industry, 1972

Industry	Percentage of workers unionized			Distribution of membership of all labour organizations in Canada by industry group
	All Unions	International Unions	National Unions	
Forestry	36.6	26.4	10.3	1.0
Mines, Quarries, & Oil Wells	37.6	34.8	2.8	1.8
Manufacturing	43.5	38.9	4.5	32.7
Construction	65.8	61.0	4.8	11.0
Transport, Communication & other Utilities	51.1	27.4	23.7	15.0
Trade	7.3	5.7	1.6	4.0
Service	21.3	5.8	15.5	18.1
Public Administration	61.2	3.9	57.3	14.2
Finances	1.3	.6	.7	—

Source: Statistics Canada, *CALURA*. Report for 1972, Part II, Labour Unions, pp. 68, 73, 76.

1870s, and for a forty-hour working week in the mid-1940s. Periodically, too, unions in English Canada have thrown their weight against a particular piece of anti-labour legislation by lobbying governments or staging mass demonstrations on Parliament Hill or before the provincial legislatures. In Quebec and British Columbia, unions played an important part in bringing down the stridently anti-labour governments of Premiers Duplessis and Bennett. Some unions have affiliated directly to the New Democratic Party and in the mid-1970s this involved about eleven per cent of Canada's union membership.[8]

However, the main energies of union activists are devoted to everyday grievances at the work place. At this level, unions depend on the unpaid voluntary work of union stewards who are elected by their fellow-unionists at their place of work to represent them and their union in day-to-day dealings with management. Union stewards are the unions' most direct contact with their members. One important function is to make official complaints — known as grievances — to management concerning management practices which violate the collective agreement or contract which has been made between union and management.

The issues over which grievances are filed and fought are the kind that seldom make press headlines. Grievances have to do with fines, suspensions or firing over absence or lateness at work; with attitudes of foremen or supervisors; with anomalies in pay for individual workers; and with a myriad of other irritations. The stewards have no control over the larger structure of the system and its implications for workers; they are limited to dealing with the most obvious inequities. While this makes their work routine, they are important to their fellow workers; the stewards are the union in the plant.

Labour-management relations under private enterprise has set definite limits to the scope of union negotiations. Among the items typically excluded are: technological changes; rates of work; work loads and their effects on jobs; decisions to shut down or move the firm's plant or operations; permanent and temporary lay-offs or the hiring of new workers; the choice of foremen or supervisors, or their removal; the company's books, profits and investment plans.

To a large extent these limitations on union power and bargaining have not been subject to serious debate and action. Until unions in Quebec decided to challenge and even "break the system", unions across Canada, most of them affiliated to U.S. unions, accepted this notion of management rights.

Under such circumstances, it is all to easy to denigrate the work of the unions as mundane and lacking in broad perspective. However, within the adversary system where workers and corporations fight over division of the pie, there has always been the potential for outbursts which go beyond the scope and formal procedures of individual grievances or the collective agreement. Such outbursts have expressed an underlying discontent with the entire system. The new wave of strikes and trade union activity that swept Canada in 1974 and 1975 was partly the product of such frustration. Canadian worker militancy has always been more than the demand for bread-and-butter, although it has been that too. It has also been a demand for human dignity; an attempt to establish a new status in society for workers who produce the wealth, but who have little power.

---

1. T. Phillips Thompson, *The Politics of Labor* (1887) (Toronto: University of Toronto Press, 1975), p. 22.

2. Labour Canada, *Labour Organizations in Canada*, 1973 (Ottawa: Information Canada, 1974).

3. Ibid., p. xxvii.

4. H. A. Logan has defined international unions as "branches of organizations with headquarters in the United States". *Trade Unions in Canada* (Toronto: Macmillan Company of Canada, 1948), p. 83.

5. Labour Canada, op. cit., p. xii. In 1973 the international unions in Canada showed an increase in membership of 2.2 per cent over 1972, whereas national unions showed an increase of 23.1 per cent in the same period.

6. Ibid., p. xi.

7. Laurence Kelly, ed., *The Current Industrial Relations Scene, 1975* (Kingston, Ont.: Industrial Relations Centre, Queen's University, 1975), p. s-u-10.

8. Donald MacDonald, York South MPP, stated that 275,000 unionists were affiliated to the NDP at NDP Symposium, University of Toronto, March 4, 1975; *The Globe and Mail*, May 30, 1974, reported fewer than 270,000 NDP union affiliates.

PART II
The Growing Conflict: International Unions and Canadian Labour

CHAPTER 6
American Business Unionism: The AFL

The American trade union movement should fit into the American system.

Samuel Gompers
Founding president of the AFL[1]

We didn't want [to organize] the people that were on the job, we merely wanted the work. So far as the people that were on the job were concerned, for our part they could drop dead.

George Meany
President, AFL-CIO
Referring to his background in the plumbers' union.[2]

For seventy-five years the economic and political outlook of American unions has been a major determinant of the nature of the union movement in Canada. A study of Canada's unions must therefore include an examination of the philosophy and practice of the internationals to which a majority of Canadian unionists still belonged in the mid-seventies.

This chapter describes the basic attitudes and practices of the craft-dominated American Federation of Labor (AFL) during its ninety-year history, while the next chapter deals with the industrial unions of the Congress of Industrial Organizations (CIO) and their integration during the 1950s and 1960s into the mainstream of American union philosophy.

Ever since the founding of the AFL in 1886, the ruling philosophy of the U.S. labour movement has been "business unionism". Against the militancy and political unionism of groups such as the Knights of Labour and the Industrial Workers of the World, the AFL championed what was termed "pure and simple trade unionism" or "bread-and-butter unionism". This was based on three "practical" beliefs:

— that workers are able to improve their position without challenging the economic and political system of American corporate capitalism;

— that the purpose of trade unions is simply to defend the immediate economic interests of their own members;

— that the interests of workers and employers can be compatible.

Samuel Gompers, the father of American business unionism, summed up this view when he said that "the American trade union movement should fit into the American system".[3]

The consequences of this belief have been manifold. It led to U.S. labour support for American policy in Viet Nam and Latin America. It encouraged a craft-dominated union movement with little inclination to organize the unorganized. It produced a union movement whose political credo was "reward your friends and punish your enemies" respecting the two main U.S. parties, making the U.S. union movement the only one in the industrial world which does not support a social-democratic or labour party. And it has led to a labour movement that has largely disavowed the strike weapon.

The three beliefs listed have been the stock in trade of the AFL, and thus of the mainstream of U.S. unionism since the days of the AFL's founder, Samuel Gompers.

The only bona fide political party Gompers ever joined — and that for a short time in his youth — was the Republican Party. In 1903 Gompers stated his political views at an AFL convention:

> I want to tell you socialists that I have studied your philosophy, read your works upon economics, . . . watched the work of your movement the world over. . . . I know too what you have up your sleeve. And I want to say that I am entirely at variance with your philosophy.[4]

In his opposition to "socialism" Gompers opposed legislation regarding unemployment insurance, public health, old age pensions, industrial safety and workmen's compensation. Legislation in these areas would, he felt, infringe on union benefits, and thus weaken members' loyalty to their unions.

This opposition to "socialistic" welfare measures did not die with Gompers. His successor, William Green, told the 1932 Convention of the International Ladies' Garment Workers' Union (ILGWU) that the AFL was on record against unemployment insurance because it did not want to exchange its birthright for a mess of pottage.[5]

This lack of concern for protection for the vast mass of unorganized workers was not altered by the merger of the AFL and CIO in 1955. Asked in the early 1970s why the proportion of U.S. workers organized in unions had declined from 33.1 per cent in 1955 to 27.4 per cent in 1971, George Meany told a *U.S. News and World Report* writer, "I don't know, I don't care. . . . We never had a very large proportion of the work force in this country . . . nothing like Britain . . . the Scandinavian countries . . . the Germans. . . ."[6]

By far the most powerful figure in American unionism after 1940 has been Meany. By 1975, the eighty-one year old labour leader had been president of the AFL-CIO for twenty-three years, and secretary-treasurer of the AFL for thirteen years before that. The embodiment of conservative craft and business unionism, Meany has displayed all the strengths and weaknesses of that union philosophy.

Meany's outlook has basically been that of the upper ten per cent of American workers who are in the highly skilled trades — the plumbers, electricians, bricklayers, sheet metal workers, tool and die makers, printers, pressmen and railway engineers who make up the "aristocracy of labour".

In Meany's eyes, American unionism — particularly the craft variety — had brought its members to the pinnacle of "affluence" compared to workers in other countries. He traces this belief back to his days in the plumbers' union. The plumbers' union, squarely in the business-craft tradition, felt more closely allied to the contractors who employed its members than to the unorganized workers. The plumbers' union, Meany has recalled, made it very difficult for "outsiders" to become members:

> We even went so far that we wouldn't take clearance cards. We shut the union to other union members of our own craft from other cities. I am not bragging about it. I am not proud of it. I am telling you that is what we did.[7]

This attitude to the majority of American workers was a constant theme in Meany's leadership of the American union movement. Asked whether he would prefer to see a larger proportion of the work force organized, he replied, "Not necessarily. We have done quite well without it. . . . Why should we worry about organizing groups of people who do not appear to want to be organized?"[8]

In common with other leaders of the AFL, Meany was for a long time opposed to social legislation like the minimum wage: "We were very skeptical on the minimum wages. We just didn't see the minimum wage situation the way we saw it later."[9]

Meany's attitude toward strikes has long been negative. Speaking to businessmen at a New York meeting of the National Industrial Conference Board in 1966, he expressed the position of the craft workers who are able, because of the scarcity of workers with their high skill levels, to command high wages without resort to strikes. "Where you have a well-established industry and a well-established union," Meany observed, "you are getting more and more to the point where a strike doesn't make sense."[10]

When Meany described his union constituency, he presented as typical the union member who is, "determined to secure the good things of life for himself and his family, and hopeful of accumulating enough to provide reasonable security".[11]

This was probably an accurate description of most craft workers, highly skilled and highly paid, with their own home and perhaps a couple of cars, but it did not fit the concerns of the unorganized, the blacks, the Puerto Ricans and the Mexicans. Nevertheless, part of the reason why American workers have supported business unionism for so long is the privileged position of the U.S. working class — this includes workers in mass production unions — *vis-à-vis* workers in other countries. American workers on the average have had far higher incomes than workers in other industrialized countries. Even in 1974, a year of recession in the United States, there were the following differentials in average hourly compensation in U.S. dollars for all manufacturing including unionized and non-unionized workers:[12]

United States	— $6.55
Canada	— $5.40
West Germany	— $5.25
Italy	— $4.35
France	— $3.96
Japan	— $3.01
Britain	— $2.77

Trade union members, on the average, have had substantially higher incomes than unorganized workers. Since the proportion of the work force that is organized is much higher in many countries than in the United States — Britain, for instance, has a work force some sixty per cent of which is organized by contrast to less than thirty per cent in the United States — it follows that the differential between what the American trade unionist has been paid and the income of his counterpart in other countries was even larger than the differential between average wages in the United States and other countries. Thus while the U.S. working class as a whole was privileged in world terms, the American trade union members were very much so.

The 1974 figures showing the higher income of American workers in manufacturing compared to workers in other countries did not begin to tell the story of the relatively much higher incomes of skilled craft workers. Rates of pay for electricians, plumbers, sheet metal workers, cabinet makers, pressmen, railway engineers and various other highly skilled categories have traditionally been much higher than that of the average worker in manufacturing.[13]

Moreover, U.S. Bureau of Labor Statistics showed that in 1971 American white-collar, salaried employees on the average received sixty per cent more in pay than blue collar workers, while in Canada the difference between the two groups was only thirty-seven per cent.[14] This indicates that apart from a small group of very high salaried managers and directors there is a sizeable section of white collar (along with craft blue-collar workers) whose pay is more than double or triple that of the average American worker. These two groups — highly-paid white collar and highly-paid craft workers — constitute a wide social basis for political conservatism and business unionism in the United States.

But if specialized craft workers have received at least double the income of the average semi-skilled and unskilled worker, the top leadership of American unions have doubled, tripled or even quadrupled the salary of the privileged craft worker. With salaries ranging from $60,000 to $130,000 a year, not including private cars, chauffeurs, expenses and travel, it is not surprising that leaders of the AFL-CIO unions have thought of themselves as parallel to corporate management, as managers of "labour corporations" in their own right. The salaries they receive put them much more on a par with top corporate executives than with their own rank and file membership. Frank Fitzsimmons, president of the Teamsters, received $131,000 in salary allowances and expenses in 1972, while his secretary-treasurer, Murray W. Miller, received over $114,000 in the same year.

Hunter Wharton, president of the Operating Engineers, received $103,000 while Joseph Curran, president of the National Maritime Union, and C.L. Dennis, president of the Railway Clerks, were paid $91,000 each.[15] I.W. Abel, president of the Steelworkers, was voted a $90,000 salary in 1974.[16] In 1971, AFL-CIO president George Meany was voted a salary increase — to $90,000 a year.[17]

It is not surprising, then, that top U.S. union officers have not given up their posts easily. Although by 1975 many unions had set a retirement age of sixty-five, there have been numerous cases of leaders who have held office for forty years or more. One example is the AFL itself, which has had only three presidents in its ninety-year history (with the exception of a single year when Gompers was defeated).

Meany's heyday came with the rise of the United States to the height of its power in the 1950s and 1960s. As America rose to a position of unchallenged economic and military supremacy in the corporate world, providing support to U.S. foreign policies and activities on all continents became an important component of AFL-CIO activity.

From its earliest days the American union movement has had international interests, including Canada, and has sought close relations with union movements all over the world. These relations have, however, differed from the traditional internationalism of labour, and of socialist and liberation movements of the last hundred years. Since 1945, for example, the AFL has had only sporadic affiliation with international union federations of labour, such as the International Confederation of Free Trade Unions (ICFTU). They preferred to operate their own variety of international union relations and here, as abundant evidence has shown, they have received CIA and other governments funds as support for these international activities.[18]

Although their success as world ambassadors of U.S. policies diminished with the exposures of the role of the CIA and its links to many American organizations, including the AFL-CIO, the social basis of support in American unions for U.S. foreign policy, particularly among the better-paid craft workers, has shown little sign of diminishing.

As the experience of the Viet Nam War graphically demonstrated, the craft unions have been an important base of support for U.S. foreign policy. The union movement's leadership gave their official sanction to the war, and many rank and file members — for example, the New York "hard hats" — followed suit.

One of the AFL-CIO's foreign policy concerns has been focused on safeguarding American business abroad. In its 1964 platform proposals to the Republican and Democratic parties, the U.S. labour body called for action to secure American investment abroad against threats posed by national liberation movements or attempts at nationalization by foreign governments. [19]

In warning against wars of national liberation the platform said: "Here is the key of our age with its cold war and local wars of so-called national liberation, communist subversion and the danger of a nuclear conflagration."

The labour body explained why it was advocating these measures:

> In sharp contrast to the position taken by all communist powers and parties, our country and its democratic allies do not seek to conquer or subvert any country or to impose their social system on any people. [20]

However, twenty years earlier, in 1944, the AFL had set up its Free Trade Union Committee (FTUC) to influence unions in other countries toward pro-American policies. The FTUC was in liaison with the Office of Strategic Services, later to become the CIA. Much of the funding came directly from these sources.

According to Thomas W. Braden, who ran the International Organization Activities division of the CIA after the war, the CIA provided American union organizations abroad with funds to support certain foreign unions starting in 1947. Braden estimated that the CIA had used American union channels to pay out nearly two million dollars a year to unions in France and Italy alone. [21]

On one occasion Braden delivered $50,000 in fifty dollar bills to Walter Reuther at the United Auto Workers' "Solidarity House" in Detroit. The money was to be used to bolster unions in Germany and other parts of Europe. Walter Reuther later acknowledged receipt of these funds with the explanation that it was an "emergency situation". [22]

Many of the American unions' activities abroad were carried out by "labour attachés". With the co-operation of the AFL, American trade unionists were attached to U.S. embassies. As a former employee of the International Ladies' Garment Workers' Union described it, their work was marked by:

> (a) the use of a trade union card . . . to secure information which would normally be regarded as the fruit of espionage; (b) the use of trade-union member attachés and/or government funds in supporting or even buying up trade union centres so that they follow policies formulated not by trade unions but by a government . . . and (c) . . .

selling government policy and finding it impossible or difficult to represent an independent trade union point of view.[23]

Meany, who described himself in the 1950s as "the most rabid anti-communist" in America next to Richard Nixon,[24] had a central role to play in support of U.S. policy in Latin America. In the early 1960s Meany contacted President Kennedy concerning the "Alliance for Progress" then being set up:

> So we convinced him that we had a part to play, that instead of all this money being channelled to business institutions or through banks, or through governments, some of it should be channelled through trade unions, that trade unions should sponsor projects, which [were] to be financed under the Alliance.[25]

The AFL-CIO set up the American Institute for Free Labor Development (AIFLD) as its operating arm in Latin America. During the 1960s, the AIFLD was largely sponsored by the U.S. government's Agency for International Development (AID). AID provided sixty-two per cent of the AIFLD operating budget in 1962, and increased its share to ninety-two per cent in 1967. Much of the AIFLD work paralleled the interests of the CIA, but as Meany pointed out, "when you can get that kind of money [from AID], why do you have to run to the CIA?"[26]

Although Meany was president of the AIFLD, a good number of its other officers were not recruited from labour. The chairman of the board was J. Peter Grace, president of the W.R. Grace shipping company. The vice-chairman was the Rockefeller family's expert on Latin American affairs, Berent Friele.

In 1965, this business-dominated board of directors came under fire from Victor Reuther, head of the UAW's international department. Reuther charged that its structure was "a propaganda gift to the enemies of free trade unions who effectively characterize these businessmen as symbols of Yankee imperialism and enemies of social programs in Latin America".[27]

Meany responded to such criticisms, saying that considerable thought had been given to the matter.

> The Executive Council finally decided unanimously that we should bring American business into this institution on the theory that they should have the same stake . . . in the building of free societies in Latin America as we do. They want to do business there, they certainly want to do business with countries that have viable economies.[28]

O.A. Knight, president of the Oil Workers Union, told the CIO Executive Board that in helping to overthrow the Arbenz government in Guatemala, the Eisenhower administration was giving "aid and comfort to the United Fruit Company, which was doing all it could to set aside . . . some of the decent legislation that had been passed down there recently".[29] Emil Mazey, secretary-treasurer of the UAW, said, "we have been supporting the wrong people".[30]

The AFL-CIO's support for the Viet Nam War — dating back to 1952 when Meany urged U.S. intervention on the side of the French — is well known. Associating wars of national liberation with "communist subversion", the AFL-CIO pledged its support to "all measures which the [U.S. government might] find necessary for safe-guarding the independence and freedom of South Viet Nam and the other peoples of South-East Asia".[31]

In 1969 Senator William Fulbright of the Senate Foreign Relations Committee presided over hearings into the activities of the AIFLD. Noting that more than twenty million dollars had been transferred from AID to the AFL-CIO's AIFLD Institute between 1960 and 1968, he commented, "I have wondered if this represented the price we paid for Meany's support in Viet Nam".[32]

Whether or not Fulbright's hypothesis was correct, the AFL-CIO never broke its promise to let "all of the people know that they have a responsibility to support the Commander-in-Chief,"[33] as Meany had put it in 1965.

Meany's role as defender of private enterprise, labour disciplinarian and U.S. foreign policy supporter has been a complex one. Although he has headed an organization which he has regarded as one of the most important corporations in the United States, he is certainly not just another corporate spokesman. The view that Meany — or Abel, or Woodcock — is just another agent of U.S. corporations, the State Department and the CIA is an overly simplistic one. Meany could not have thrust U.S. labour onto the front lines of support for the Viet Nam War or for American repression in Latin America simply by speaking the language of the corporate élite. He could not have advocated the replacement of the strike weapon by voluntary arbitration or long contracts had he not been able to phrase his position in the language of labour opposition to corporate power. Meany may regard himself as a corporate executive, but it is a "labour" corporation, and its most important "shareholders" are the American craft-workers, many of whom share Meany's political and economic views.

Meany's role, like that of other business unionists, has been a contradictory one. Although he supports the general principle of corporate capitalism, he is forced on occasion to confront corporations, to direct actions against individual businesses, although never against "the system" as a whole.

U.S. business union leadership has consolidated its power by its ability to use anti-corporate rhetoric in strikes and the occasional foray against anti-labour legislation to cement its credibility with a sufficiently large section of the "middle Americans" in its membership. The alternative explanation — that the gap between Meany and the thirteen million members of the AFL-CIO is huge, and that he is kept in power solely by his control of the "union machine" — fails to take into account the circumstances and interests of the top ten per cent of the American working class, the craft union members whose annual income was over $20,000 in 1975. Leaders like Meany are adept at representing and manipulating this constituency, combining the objective economic interests of the better-paid workers with ideological appeals that parallel those that flow from the media, the government, the corporations and the unions themselves.

This is not to say that there are no "machines" in the U.S. unions. The Teamsters, the Seafarers' International Union (SIU) and many of the building trades unions are notorious for their methods of control. With thousands of full-time union officials, and perhaps another two hundred thousand unionists (assuming one in fifty is active) who devote much of their time to union business, there is scope for extensive machine politics. But even this large "machine" would not be enough to keep leaders like Meany in power if there was majority rank and file opposition to their philosophy and strategy.

During the Viet Nam War, millions of American workers in the defence and related industries directly benefited from the huge war contracts through regular pay and overtime work at the same time as some of their sons were being killed in Southeast Asia. This conflict was met by U.S. business union leaders with appeals to U.S. patriotism. No army of CIA agents or corporate spokesmen could have matched the effectiveness of Meany and Abel in keeping the majority of the U.S. labour movement solidly behind the war, and in neutralizing and weakening those who were in opposition.

This ability to keep the AFL-CIO "hawkish" on the international front, however, has depended on their ability to deliver the bacon at home. This placed the labour leadership in the quandary of having to combine militant labour rhetoric for protectionist trade policies and against anti-labour legislation, with admonitions against strikes in general, while supporting particular strikes. In accomplishing this, they have been able to retain the support of the best-paid fifteen or twenty per cent of the American working class — and thus a majority of organized labour in the United States.

Some top AFL-CIO leaders, however, have been uncomfortable with Meany's authoritarian and unprogressive leadership. The vice-president of the International Association of Machinists, William Winpisinger, commented on the AFL-CIO president's handling of the 1973 convention:

> It's hard to get over the feeling that we're a bunch of dam sheep. I never saw so many sheep in one hall before. . . . I respect Mr. Meany, but not his leadership. The American labour movement is just standing still under his guidance.[34]

In his position as president of the AFL-CIO, Meany also spoke for the interests of more than a million Canadian workers who are affiliated with AFL-CIO internationals. Meany's view of the position of Canadians in the internationals has been that "Canadian districts" are identical to districts like California or Texas in the international unions.

Meany summarized the significance of membership in American unions for Canadian workers when he commented on the demand for autonomy in 1971:

> They can't have it both ways, belong to a U.S. union and have a system different than the American union. . . . I don't think you can have two organizations in one. There has to be one organization. I feel if it makes sense from a practical point of view to have a separate organization it should be distinctly separate.[35]

---

1. Joseph C. Goulden, *Meany* (New York: Atheneum, 1972), p. 61.

2. Ibid., p. 20.

3. Ibid., p. 61.

4. H. W. Morgan, *American Socialism 1900-1960* (New Jersey: Prentice-Hall, 1964), pp. 41-42.

5. Goulden, op. cit., p. 31.

6. Ibid., p. 466.

7. Ibid., p. 20.

8. Ibid., p. 466.

9. Ibid., p. 31.

10. Ibid., p. 58.

11. Ibid., p. 465.

12. *The Globe and Mail*, April 29, 1975 (U.S. Bureau of Labor Statistics).

13. According to *Datagraph*, The Bureau of National Affairs Inc. (Bureau of Labor Statistics), electricians received $10.25 per hour and plumbers $9.82 on an average in Chicago in the fourth quarter of 1974. The average wage in Philadelphia for these occupations was $10.82 and $10.42 respectively. In contrast, the earnings of production or non-supervisory workers on total private non-agricultural payrolls in October 1974 was $4.35. (U.S. Department of Labor, *News*, Bureau of Labor Statistics, January 21, 1975.)

14. *The Globe and Mail*, April 29, 1975 (U.S. Bureau of Labor Statistics).

15. *Business Week*, August 18, 1973.

16. *The Hamilton Spectator*, September 26, 1974.

17. *Business Week*, August 18, 1973.

18. See Goulden, op. cit.; Ronald Radosh, *American Labor and United States Foreign Policy* (New York: Random House, 1969).

19. AFL-CIO, *Platform Proposals*, 1964.

20. Ibid.

21. Thomas Braden, 'I'm Glad the CIA is 'Immoral' '', *Saturday Evening Post*, May 20, 1967.

22. Ibid., p. 10.

23. Goulden, op. cit., p. 136.

24. Ibid., p. 220.

25. Ibid., p. 328.

26. Ibid.

27. Ibid., p. 330.

28. Ibid., p. 331.

29. Ibid., p. 225.

30. Ibid.

31. AFL-CIO, *Platform Proposals*, 1964.

32. Goulden, op. cit., p. 358.

33. Ibid., p. 354.

34. *The Globe and Mail*, October 25, 1973.

35. "Continentalism: Gain or Drain?", Labour Council of Metropolitan Toronto *Yearbook*, 1973, quoted from *The Globe and Mail*, February 1971.

CHAPTER 7
The CIO Marries the AFL

The union and the company, they are more or less business partners.

Archie Walker
American rank and file member, UAW[1]

A new note was sounded in the American trade union movement with the rise of the CIO in the late 1930s. Beginning with the almost invincible sit-down strikes of this period, the Congress of Industrial Organizations (CIO) established a new tradition of confrontation.

From the outset, however, the CIO included some top leaders who called for a policy of non-confrontation and labour-management co-operation. Although the early tradition of militancy carried right through into the early 1950s, the CIO has since joined the mainstream of business unionism as developed by the AFL. The merger between the two centres to form the AFL-CIO in 1955 crystallized the CIO's opting for the business union approach.

The gradual transformation of CIO union policy from confrontation and militancy to business unionism paralleling that of the AFL appears to have affected the relative incomes of its members according to research conducted by two U.S. economists.

For example, there was at least one major U.S. strike involving ten thousand workers or more by one key CIO affiliate, the United Steel Workers, every year from 1949 to 1960. These included five nation-wide strikes and seventeen major local work stoppages. On the average, one-third of all steel production workers were involved in stoppages in each of those years. According to a study by David M. Gordon and Joseph J. Preskie at the New School for Social Research, the average annual rise in real wages — taking into account increases in the cost of living — was almost 3.6 per cent during this period. Steel workers who had earned real wages of $2.32 per hour in 1949 were earning real wages of $3.43 per hour by 1960.

This was in sharp contrast to the "no strike period" between 1961 and 1970. During that nine-year span there were only two local work stoppages, one in 1968 which did not involve the major steel companies, and another in 1969.

In comparison to the "strike period" when steel workers made real gains of 3.6 per cent a year, during the "no strike period" the average increase was only 0.44 per cent, one-ninth the previous average gain. Gordon and Preskie show that even when factors such as productivity and the "health" of the American economy are taken into account, the higher level of increases in the earlier period is a result of the strike weapon's effectiveness.[2]

The policy of avoiding strikes found an early exponent in the CIO in the person of Philip Murray. Just four years after the Committee for Industrial Organization was founded, Murray, who was then chairman of the Steelworkers Organizing Committee and vice-president of the United Mine Workers of America, and soon to become president of both the USWA and the CIO, co-authored a book explaining his views on labour.[3]

The book argues that unions should be concerned with increasing the productivity and efficiency of the industries they were in:

> Now as management and labour through strong labour unions, become more nearly equal in bargaining power, they can either wage war to gain the spoils of production restriction and scarcity prices, or they can together devise improved production practices that increase the social income. The second is more in keeping with the potential age of plenty ... For organized workers to come face to face with management's problems will have both an educational and sobering influence, just as management will be both educated and sobered by insight into the problems of unions.

"Sobering" the workers was an important step toward the consensus that workers and employers have similar interests:

> Power, wherever it lies, cannot in the long run be disassociated from responsibility. If the labour movement fails to develop an adequate sense of responsibility for output, the alternative will be increasing tension and bitterness over "wages, hours and working conditions," reducing the opportunity for constructive accommodation and community of interest between management and union.

Outlining four stages in the developing relations between employers and unions, Philip Murray and Morris Cooke proclaimed the highest stage to be one of "labour-management collaboration for greater gross production in which both may share ..." In order to bring this about, they called for "labour leaders who are production conscious and who are ready and able to co-operate with management in furthering the common enterprise."

These ideas which were formulated in 1940 have twenty-five years

later achieved full acceptance in the policies of the two largest industrial
unions, the UAW and the USWA. Two major events, the General Motors
strike by the UAW in 1970, and the Experimental Negotiating Agreement
(ENA) of the USWA in 1974, demonstrate how Murray and Cooke's ideas
have become CIO or industrial union practice.

The union which in many ways was most symbolic of the new industrial organizations of the 1930s was the United Auto Workers. Its dramatic sit-down strikes at General Motors in Flint, Michigan were the signal
for rapid organization everywhere and when, in 1940, Ford Motor suc-
cumbed, the victory of the organizing drive was almost complete.

Despite factional struggles within its leadership, the UAW remained a
strong and militant organization during most of the forties. In 1947
Walter Reuther took control as president and a year later he launched his
new policy. It was to be a switch from militant industrial unionism to the
business union philosophy rooted in the old craft mentality.

By 1948 management of General Motors had come to realize that the
union could offer the company "predictability in labour relations".[4] The
company's president ("What's good for General Motors is good for the
country") Charles E. Wilson proposed a new contract formula which he
hoped would change relations between the company and the union from
confrontation to co-operation. He proposed that wage increases be tied
to productivity and to changes in the cost of living. These two innova-
tions were to be incorporated in a proposed five-year contract.

This proposal appealed to Reuther, and he and the UAW bought it in
1950. The agreement was one of the first important precedents in industrial unions for the long contract. *Fortune* magazine called the contract
the "treaty of Detroit" and commented that "G.M. may have paid a
billion for peace [but] it got a bargain".[5] The union was guaranteeing
stability for company operations, and agreeing to tie its wage increases
to increases in productivity. Business unionism had come to the UAW.

The close relationship between the company and the union was carried a step further in 1955. The UAW entered into a "gentlemen's agreement" with the auto companies that the union would strike only one
company in any given contract year. The other companies would match
the agreement arrived at following the strike.[6] After 1955 strikes were
increasingly to become ritual affairs, whose purpose was not so much to
defeat the companies as to satisfy the residual militancy of rank and file
unionists.

The year 1967 saw the UAW leadership once again more strongly
embracing a craft-union mentality. In that year Reuther traded away the
UAW's unlimited cost of living agreement with Ford in exchange for a
thirty cent extra settlement for the skilled tradesmen over and above the
twenty per cent across the board settlement for all workers. This was the
UAW leadership's response to pressure by the skilled trades for pay
comparable to that in the AFL craft unions. In giving in, Reuther was

aligning himself with the craft traditions of the AFL, against the militant industrial unionism of the CIO.

The auto executives realized that Reuther was willing to make his union structure increasingly dependent on the companies. For instance, Henry Ford took particular delight in giving in to the UAW demand for a dues check-off. He said to his chief negotiator, "That will make us their bankers, won't it? Then they can't get along without us. They will need us just as bad as we need them."[7]

As Reuther's friend and advisor, Morris Adler, put it, "In his own way, Walter is the head of a corporation".[8] Continuing, Adler commented, "I think Charles E. Wilson [head of General Motors] understood that".[9]

Responding to the rank and file's image of a militant union, however, Reuther and his lieutenants showed a degree of militancy during strikes when they would denounce the corporations, describing them as "gold-plated sweatshops", "God", "arrogant" and "smelling of greed".[10] Since, it was only the "target company" for that particular year which would come under the rhetorical fire of the leadership, the industry as a whole, or the system within which it operated would be left unscathed.

The 1970 General Motors strike, as documented by journalist William Serrin in his book, *The Company and the Union*, clearly illustrates the degree to which UAW strikes had become rituals staged between union and management. This strike was led by Leonard Woodcock, who had succeeded Reuther as UAW president following the latter's death in a plane crash some months previously.

Woodcock began the strike by hurling some mild epithets at the G.M. corporation, calling it, for instance, an "octopus". Halfway into the negotiations, however, he began to refer to the company negotiators as "civilized" and "gentlemen". At the first important bargaining meeting on nation-wide issues, he announced that he had "nothing but the kindest feelings" for G.M.[11] Woodcock's explanation of why he took a much gentler line in describing G.M. revealed that in his view one of his main responsibilities during the strike was to set the stage to "win over" the rank and file to the kind of settlement the union leadership and the corporate executives could agree on:

> ... when you indulge in inflammatory rhetoric, you delight the people who are with you in the first place; you don't do much to the people who are in the middle; the people who are against you anyway you offend, and you also tend to alienate *some* of those in the middle whom you have to convince in order to win.[12]

A similar attitude underlay the leadership's approach to picketing. Emil Mazey, secretary-treasurer of the union, said that picketing could cause problems because the men might start drinking and harassing management as they enter the plant. "The picketing we do now," he explained, "is to maintain tradition and let people passing by know we are on strike."[13]

United Auto Workers locals had submitted hundreds of bargaining demands, many of them centred on issues of work control, hours and working conditions. The UAW leadership, however, was looking for an agreement that would give a wage increase sufficient to convince the membership, after several weeks on strike pay, to go back to work without having to deal with these complicated and detailed issues. This meant avoiding questions of working conditions on the assembly lines. To this end, the top UAW leadership managed to exclude the locally-elected negotiating committee from the bargaining sessions, on the grounds that the presence of these twelve representatives would make negotiations too difficult. The union and the company set up a special "probing committee' which in the end made the real decisions without the elected bargaining committee, except for its formal stamp of approval.

Union officers like Mazey and Irving Bluestone justified this by claiming that the elected negotiators really play a very small role, and in any case the top union leaders could meet more "comfortably" with the corporation executives if the rank and filers were not there. In the absence of the rank and file representatives, they admitted frankly, they could explain to the company why they "must" get certain concessions in order to win ratification.

The partnership between the UAW leadership and the company was cemented by a financial arrangement worked out at the beginning of the strike. G.M. agreed to pay the $23 million a month insurance costs for the striking workers, and to hold off billing the union for it until after the first of the new year. In effect, the company was floating a gigantic loan on behalf of the union, to finance a strike directed against itself. As Earl Bramblett, G.M.'s chief negotiator, explained it — "we have to live together".[14]

In this atmosphere of mutual confidence and respect Bramblett and Woodcock agreed to keep their target date for settlement secret. The date — November 10 — was not to be announced publicly or even mentioned to the union's elected negotiating committee. As Mazey explained, "the basic decisions are not made by the committee. We make the decisions, the top leaders of the union. And the decisions are conveyed to the committee and they agree."[15]

The company negotiators were happy with this arrangement. As Bramblett put it, it is best to deal with "people that you have confidence in so that if the thing blows up, you are not caught with a lot of things you said in a big crowd".[16] The negotiations were kept so secret that the elected negotiating committee only learned of the company offer and of the likely settlement by reading the Detroit newspapers.

As William Serrin points out, the final settlement was one that the company would have accepted without a strike. But a strike was nevertheless essential. Mazey explained that, in his view, "strikes make ratification easier. Even though the worker may not think so, when he votes on a contract he is reacting to economic pressures. I really believe that if the wife is raising hell and the bills are piling up, he may be more apt to settle than otherwise."[17]

Following the settlement, both the company and the union leadership took pains to overestimate its economic impact. Bramblett talked to reporters using what he later described as "carefully chosen words". When asked whether he considered the agreement to be inflationary, he replied, "I would say the cost of the settlement is substantially more than the anticipated increase in productivity of the country". Asked whether this meant it was inflationary, he replied "that's the definition — the general definition — of inflation".[18]

Two months later G.M.'s negotiator was asked again whether the agreement was inflationary. "If you're just talking about the money," Bramblett said, "it exceeded the projected productivity increases of the country."[19] But, he added, "take the cost of living out of the settlement and it's three per cent per year ... And three per cent a year plus six cents is not really a big earth-shattering settlement." In response, Serrin said, "What worker, after two months on strike, would have voted for a settlement that General Motors called not a big earth-shattering settlement?"[20]

The 1970 strike at G.M. demonstrated the extent to which top union leaders identify with corporate leaders, and the extent to which they are prepared to support the corporate system. Mazey, with customary frankness, pointed out that he had become friends with "most of the corporation officials" through such organizations as the United Foundation.

> So I know all those people ... you simply get to know them. You are involved in community problems or something, and you are having a cocktail before lunch with the guys and the first thing you know, you are talking about a problem you have in the plants.[21]

Although the UAW claims that the Canadian section of the union enjoys autonomy, the Canadian settlement in 1970 awaited the outcome of the events in the American union. Following the conclusion of negotiations in the United States, George Woodcock and the G.M. negotiator, George Morris, arrived in Toronto to get an agreement in Canada. After a little while, Woodcock abruptly left Canada and returned to Detroit where he met with G.M. chairman, James Roche. It was only at this point that movement towards settlement began.[22]

The demand of the local union at G.M. in Ste. Thérèse, Quebec, that French become the official language in the plant, was ignored by both the company and the international union. The UAW's Canadian director, Dennis McDermott, had supported this demand, complaining:

> We cannot get G.M. to comprehend what the problem is in Quebec.

The French language question is no longer a private squabble between the UAW and G.M. There is great social unrest in Quebec.[23]

Despite this, the settlement totally disregarded the issue. UAW leaders had agreed, in a private session with management, to withdraw their Quebec local's demand. George Morris later described how the language dispute was settled. "I just told them there was no fucking way that plant was going to speak French."[24]

****

Philip Murray's philosophy of co-operation between management and unions reached a new level in 1973 with the signing of the Experimental Negotiating Agreement (ENA) between the USWA, another major CIO union, and the U.S. steel industry.

This agreement was founded on a no-strike pledge, originally for a period of three years and then extended by the union for a further three. Thus the leadership of the Steelworkers had effectively promised the industry in this agreement that there would be no strikes until at least 1980. Under its terms, were negotiations to reach a deadlock by April 15, 1974, outstanding issues would be sent to an arbitrator. In effect, the USWA had renounced the strike weapon in favour of voluntary arbitration in its attempt to boost productivity and efficiency in the steel industry.

In a speech made in December 1974, "We Must Face the Challenges of Imports and Productivity", the Steelworkers' president, I.W. Abel, commented on the productivity provision of the ENA:

We have reached that stage in life where we of the United Steel Workers of America and the leaders of the American steel industries ... have developed a mutual understanding and respect to the point that we can take on this kind of task in a mutual, co-operative effort. And it will take co-operation.

Abel observed that, "the new agreement not only provides for additional wages and benefits for employees, but will also provide an opportunity for the companies to increase production through stability of operations and enhance the steel industry's competitive position".[25] The United States had imported a total of 18.3 million tons of steel, leading, according to Abel, to a loss of some 108,000 full-time jobs in steel.[26] He summarized the ENA as follows:

It provides certain guaranteed preliminary benefits for our members in the basic steel industry. It protects certain existing employee benefits and rights.
It safeguards certain management rights.
It allows the parties to negotiate freely in almost all economic and fringe benefit areas.
It eliminates the possibility of a nation-wide strike or lock-out in the steel industry.
It provides for voluntary arbitration of any unresolved bargaining issues.[27]

The USWA leadership has since made much of this "better way" in the basic steel industry, seeing it as a model for the trade union movement generally. The views of ordinary USWA members on the agreement are, however, not known as it was never referred to a vote among the steel union membership. It was decided at a special meeting of local presidents, without reference to a regular union convention. In fact, two thousand USWA members in 1974 filed suit against the union in U.S. District Court for the Western District of Pennsylvania, complaining that the agreement was made following secret negotiations, and that the no-strike pact violated the interests of the steel workers.[28]

The ENA, with its policy of no strikes and voluntary arbitration, was undertaken in 1973 — a year in which the unions might have used a strike threat to particularly good effect in negotiations for it saw the U.S. economy at the height of productive output. The steel corporations were operating near capacity, and steel profits were breaking all barriers. It might be argued — and Abel argued this way — that the rising tide of steel imports threatened U.S. jobs, and thus a productivity increase agreement was the most important item on the union agenda. Ironically, by pledging itself not to strike, the USWA was assuring the steel companies greater profits than they could have earned if there had been a major strike. These profits could then be used to buy the very technology that would increase efficiency and productivity — and displace American workers from their jobs.

The ENA, and its no-strike agreement, which was expected to last at least until 1980, was the logical culmination of Murray's version of CIO philosophy. It brought the USWA fully into line with George Meany's approach to business unionism. The UAW, particularly under the presidency of Woodcock, had also moved very close to the AFL's outlook, and with Reuther's personality clashes with Meany removed as an obstacle, the UAW was moving toward reaffiliating to the AFL-CIO.

By 1975 the CIO had fully merged with the AFL — in basic philosophy as well as in union organization.

---

1. William Serrin, *The Company and the Union* (New York: Alfred A. Knopf, 1973), p. 169.

2. United States Court, Aikens vs. Abel, 373 S.F.upp 425 (W.D. Pa., 1974). Factual Appendix prepared by David M. Gordon and Joseph J. Preskie for brief presented at trial.

3. Morris Cooke and Philip Murray, *Organized Labor and Production* (New York: Harper and Brothers Publishers, 1946, revised), p. 211.

4. Serrin, op. cit., p. 169.

5. Ibid., p. 170.

6. Ibid., p. 18.

 7. Ibid., p. 131.

 8. Ibid., p. 177.

 9. Ibid.

10. Ibid., pp. 177, 61, 168.

11. Ibid., p. 190.

12. Ibid., p. 191.

13. Ibid., p. 139.

14. Ibid., p. 202.

15. Ibid., p. 212.

16. Ibid., p. 213.

17. Ibid., p. 4.

18. Ibid., p. 276.

19. Ibid., p. 277.

20. Ibid.

21. Ibid., p. 46.

22. Ibid., p. 292.

23. Ibid., p. 293.

24. Ibid.

25. I. W. Abel, "ENA — A Better Way", USWA pamphlet PR-217, 1973, p. 8.

26. Ibid., p. 7.

27. Ibid., p. 3.

28. The suit was filed January 7, 1974, at the U.S. District Court for the Western District of Pennsylvania.

CHAPTER 8
From Free Trade to Protectionism

U.S. jobs, therefore, depend on imports in many ways. . . .

AFL-CIO, 1961[1]

Our trade in some areas has been virtually a one-way street. As Maurice Stans, the Secretary of Commerce, said in the *New York Times* on June 25, 1970, "In many respects we have been Uncle Sucker to the rest of the world. It is time to say, 'Let's play fair.' "

Peter Bommarito
International president, URW
Referring to the U.S., 1970[2]

In the late 1960s the deteriorating world position of the U.S. economy was producing economic difficulties in the United States, difficulties which led many Americans, including U.S. union leaders, to make a dramatic switch in their attitude toward foreign trade. This switch has important implications for the relations between Canadian workers and the international unions.

At the beginning of the decade, the economic and military power of the United States had built a vast commercial and industrial empire covering much of the world. For most prominent Americans there appeared to be no end to this "manifest destiny", to Galbraith's "affluent society" and the "Pax Americana". Union leadership in the United States shared in the prevailing optimism.

A pamphlet published by the AFL-CIO in 1961 called for a free trade programme based largely on the import of raw materials to feed American manufacturing and create jobs for U.S. workers. This would more than balance any loss of jobs through imports of finished goods.

As the AFL-CIO put it:

Americans cannot make cars or steel or manufacture other articles without imports. ... These jobs, stemming from imports, do not change the fact that imports of some goods have injured some U.S. businesses and eliminated some jobs. But it *does show the lack of reality* of the "we ought to stop trading with those foreigners" position.[3]

The pamphlet ended with a statement that America's continued world supremacy depended on a policy of free trade: "The world has changed and America must recognize its need to buy overseas to keep expanding its industrial might." Such a policy was appropriate for U.S. unions at the height of American supremacy, so long as their chief goal was to benefit U.S. workers economically.

The turning point came in 1966. Japanese and West European industries, which had just begun to flex their trading muscles in the late 1950s and early 1960s, could now compete seriously with the United States. The automobile markets of the world, so long the exclusive preserve of General Motors, Ford and Chrysler, were flooded with Volkswagens, Fiats, Renaults, Toyotas, Datsuns and Volvos. In the electronics industry, Japanese radios, televisions and stereos competed strongly with U.S. brands. This was happening not just in foreign markets but in the United States as well.

The American economy found it difficult to respond to this new threat. It was already overextended with the war in Viet Nam. The finances and factories required to meet the threat of Japanese and European trade competition were tied up in producing war equipment. By 1969 the value of the U.S. dollar, the standard currency of the world since 1945, was declining in international money markets. Unfavourable balances of trade were beginning to appear. Drastic surgery was required to slow down the relative American decline, and on August 15, 1971 President Nixon announced a new set of economic policies.

In announcing these new policies, the president condemned what he called the "unfair trading practices" of other countries. By this he meant Japan and Western Europe, who had stopped playing by the economic rules laid down by the United States. Nixon proceeded to change the rules. The U.S. dollar was taken off the gold standard, and devalued twice. A temporary ten per cent surcharge was levied on imports entering the United States. Wage controls were imposed on American workers. Various programmes gave special tax credits to U.S. corporations that increased capital investment at home, and that produced goods in the United States for export. One of these programmes, known as DISC (Domestic International Sales Corporation), was an attempt to get the multinationals to shift production from their foreign branch plants back to the United States. The package was labelled "Nixonomics" by commentators.

Nixonomics was a move away from free trade toward protectionism. It steered an uneasy course between the demand of the multinational corporations for continued free trade, and a more extreme form of protectionism. In this new economic situation, the AFL-CIO had become the most passionate advocate of protectionism in the United States. With the decline of American control in world markets and the flooding of the U.S. market by foreign-made goods, the American union leadership had begun to call for import restrictions. In 1967 the AFL-CIO adopted proposals to restrict imports of wool and man-made fibre textiles and clothing; to restrict imports of foreign-made goods that threatened "sensitive" industries in the United States; to restrict foreign investment by American corporations; and to prevent tax concessions to encourage U.S. exports of capital.[4]

As the crisis in the American economy deepened, U.S. trade union leaders increasingly pressed their case for protection. In 1969 a delegation from the Amalgamated Clothing Workers of America (ACWA) met with Nixon to stress that imports posed a threat to U.S. jobs, wages and working standards.

The president responded with a letter which received wide publicity in the American union movement. Written to Jacob S. Potofsky, ACWA president, it said:

> We recognize the disruptive nature of excessive imports. The working future of those millions of Americans involved in the textile and apparel industry cannot be jeopardized.[5]

Although ACWA claimed that it wanted "merely to regulate the flow [of trade], to keep it within limits that will not hurt domestic industry or damage the economies of other nations," Potofsky himself gave a much tougher interpretation of the union's position. He warned that without a satisfactory and effective international agreement to limit imports, unions would find it necessary to press Congress for "appropriate legislation to check the flow of imports to our shores".[6]

Potofsky was not alone. The presidents of three other apparel-textile unions, Louis Stulberg of the International Ladies' Garment Workers' Union; William Pollock of the Textile Workers' Union of America; and George Baldazi of the United Textile Workers of America, all supported his stand. These four unions, hardest hit by foreign competition, were among the most insistent advocates of protection.

Other U.S. manufacturing unions were not far behind. Paul Jennings, president of the International Union of Electrical Workers, called for a top level IUE committee to consult with other U.S. unions and report back in September 1969 on the need for mandatory import quotas. I.W. Abel, president of the United Steel Workers of America, joined with steel corporation spokesmen in urging some form of relief against imports of Japanese and European steel.[7]

By the fall of 1969, the AFL-CIO had taken a definite step in the direction of protectionism. Spokesmen from several unions pointed to massive job losses in the United States:

— IUE claimed a loss of 48,000 jobs between 1966 and 1968 in plants building radios, televisions and components. This was despite the fact that overall sales in the United States were increasing in this period;
— The textile and clothing unions claimed that even with an international cotton textile agreement of 1962, imports continued to increase. The same trend was noted by unions in the shoe, hat and fur industries;
— The steel union claimed that tens of thousands of steel mill jobs had been lost due to imports.[8]

Among major American unions, however, the United Auto Workers still supported free trade in 1969, despite increasing imports of foreign cars.

By 1971 the voice of protectionism in the U.S. trade union movement had become a roar. The *American Federationist* in an article entitled "The Call for New Trade Legislation" outlined AFL-CIO Executive Council policy. This included new tax measures to prevent the export of jobs and production from the United States; legislation to permit the president to supervise and restrict American investments abroad; and legislation to regulate the export of American technology.[9]

A special committee of the AFL-CIO Maritime Trades Department concluded that by 1980 five million U.S. jobs would be lost and argued that:

Ideally, imports should be of two types: raw materials and finished products that are not available in the United States at all. . . . [The] items imported in recent years compete directly with U.S. manufactured items; textiles and apparel, shoes, leather goods, china and glassware, toys, autos and electronics.[10]

In February 1972, the Maritime Trades Department met to consider a document entitled "The Economic Report 1972: The Crisis Deepens". It explicitly supported the Burke-Hartke Bill ("Foreign Trade and Investment Act of 1972"). Although the bill was sponsored in Congress by Representative James Burke (Democrat, Massachusetts) and Senator Vance Hartke (Democrat, Indiana) the AFL-CIO had been rumoured to be its true author.

In the words of the Maritime Trades Department the act called for:

— The removal of special advantages for American corporations which own plants overseas by making U.S. taxes payable on income from foreign as well as domestic sources in the year they are earned. This will be a deterrent against foreign investment which has resulted in the export of United States patents and technology.
— A method to regulate the massive rise in imports which has already cost hundreds of thousands of U.S. jobs. The bill aims at maintaining future imports at the same percentage they represented in the 1965-69 period — Obviously this would not apply to commodities not produced or grown in the United States. Also excused would be those goods already under quotas and those under voluntary agreements.

— Sections 807 and 806.30 of the tariff code would be repealed, ending an abuse whereby U.S. companies assemble products in foreign countries and ship them into the United States as "Made in USA", paying only a minimum duty on the so-called "value added", the cost of the cheap foreign labour.[11]

In May 1972 the AFL-CIO announced a "major educational and lobbying campaign"[12] to gain grass-root voter support for the protectionist trade bill. The "Task Force for Burke-Hartke" set out to pressure Congressional candidates to commit themselves to the bill through the use of the AFL-CIO's political campaign apparatus. The AFL-CIO Executive Council named the presidents of some of the hardest-hit unions to this task force.[13] These included the United Steel Workers of America; United Rubber Workers; National Maritime Union; Seafarers' International Union; International Union of Electrical Workers; Textile Workers of America; International Association of Machinists; and the International Ladies' Garment Workers' Union.

A good part of the "educational and lobbying campaign" involved dramatically portraying the dismal future that awaited Americans if the Burke-Hartke Bill or something very similar did not immediately become law. The Maritime Trades Department published a memorable document, "The Dimming of America", which simultaneously waved the flag and prophesied disaster:

> The greatest industrial power in the world's history is in danger of becoming nothing more than a nation of hamburger stands — a country stripped of industrial capacity and meaningful work ... a service economy ... a nation of citizens busily buying and selling cheeseburgers and root beer floats.[14]

By this time even the UAW, which had disaffiliated from the AFL-CIO in 1968, was firmly in the protectionist camp. At its 1972 Atlantic City convention, the auto union called for "fair trade" rather than "free trade".[15] Without specifically endorsing the AFL-CIO stand in favour of Burke-Hartke, the UAW called for legislation to:

— Require licenses for foreign investments proposed to be made by U.S. corporations, including reinvestment of profits made in foreign operations.
— Tax on a current basis, whether or not repatriated, profits made by foreign subsidiaries of U.S. corporations, and close the tax loopholes favouring production in foreign countries at the expense of the U.S.
— Impose upon corporations making excessive profits in the face of substantial invasion of the domestic market by imports in their line of production a competitive promotion tax which will penalize them heavily for refusal to compete with imports.[16]

The UAW also called for "phased tariffs"; for an amendment to the General Agreement on Tariffs and Trade to enforce "international fair labour standards"; and for stronger anti-dumping laws.

The auto union had effectively joined forces with the AFL-CIO. The language was different, but both sought to eliminate the tax benefits enjoyed by multinational corporations operating abroad. Both sought a move from "free trade" to "fair trade" — or protectionism. In calling for a "competitive promotion tax," the UAW was demanding even stronger measures than the AFL-CIO to force the production of domestic commodities to compete with foreign imports.

But the UAW was walking a political tight-rope. Most of its American membership would benefit from protectionism, while another part would almost certainly suffer. The automobile industry was hit by *imports,* and the grass-roots pressure there was for protective legislation to step up home production to save jobs. However, a sizeable portion of the UAW membership worked in the defence and agricultural implement industries. There, jobs often depended on *export* sales, and that part of this membership was opposed to stiff quota regulations on imports for fear that other countries would respond in kind, shutting off the export markets.

Thus the UAW was a house divided and this explains why the UAW wording in 1972 differed from that of Burke-Hartke and the AFL-CIO. But in both cases the basic intention was to create a "Buy American" policy within the U.S. economy. Both the AFL-CIO and the UAW sought to do this by making it more profitable for American-based multinationals to produce at home than abroad.

As the crisis grew in the U.S. auto industry, the UAW took a harder line on protectionism. In January 1974 the union called for quotas on imports.[17] A nod was made in the direction of members in the defence and implement industries by hanging the work "temporary" onto the call for quotas. This new proposal went much further than anything suggested in Burke-Hartke.

Claiming to be "realists" rather than "doomsayers", Leonard Woodcock announced that "the unemployment picture in some sections of the auto industry is worse than it has been at any time since the Great Depression of the 1930s," and that "there is a potential of catastrophic unemployment for workers in general and automobile workers in particular".[18] The UAW statement went on to say that in 1964 "there were 484,100 imported automobiles sold in this country: a figure that grew in ten years to 1,773,779. . . ." The answer? *We must institute temporary quotas on automobile products imported from outside America."* (emphasis added)

The UAW sought to restrict imports according to a formula based on the ratio of imports to sales over the preceding three years. It would remain in force "only long enough to prevent hardship in this country [the U.S.]".[19] The proposal would apply equally to cars made by foreign companies and to cars made in the foreign branch-plants of American multinationals.

Following the UAW statement, the situation in the auto industry worsened. By January 1975 the number of U.S. auto workers on temporary or permanent lay-off had reached 200,000, some 30 per cent of the automobile work force.[20] As the crisis continued to deepen, the UAW continued to press its campaign.

This change of the AFL-CIO and the UAW to protectionism was to have a large impact on Canada and its union membership.

---

1. AFL-CIO, "Why More Trade?", booklet, 1961.

2. Address of the President, 27th Convention, URW, *Proceedings*, Miami Beach, 1970, p. 11.

3. AFL-CIO, "Why More Trade?", 1961.

4. *The Financial Post*, January 6, 1968.

5. *Christian Science Monitor*, August 15, 1969.

6. Ibid.

7. Ibid.

8. Ibid.

9. AFL-CIO, *American Federationist*, June 1971, p. 13.

10. *The Globe and Mail*, March 12, 1971.

11. Executive Board Meeting, AFL-CIO Maritime Trades Department, February 10-11, 1972.

12. *Business Week*, May 20, 1972.

13. Ibid.

14. *The Globe and Mail*, February 23, 1973.

15. *Business Week*, May 20, 1972.

16. Ibid.

17. *The Windsor Star*, January 31, 1974.

18. *John Herling's Labor Letter*, February 9, 1974, p.3.

19. Ibid.

20. *The Globe and Mail*, February 12, 1975.

CHAPTER 9
Canadian Labour's Response to U.S.
Union Protectionism

If it was low-wage competition you were intending to restrict, you were taking a swing with a sledge-hammer to crack a peanut. [Canada is] not a low-wage country. Most of you have members in Canada and you know better.

Jean Beaudry
Executive vice-president, CLC
Addressing AFL-CIO Executive.
October 1973[1]

Before 1966, while the American economic empire continued its growth, the "special status" relationship between Canada and the United States was relatively harmonious. Most Canadian unionists found little to disagree with in U.S. union trade policy. Thus relations between the U.S. head offices of the international unions and their Canadian memberships were relatively stable.

These years were not completely free of conflict, however. The early 1960s saw the beginning of a crisis in the Canadian auto industry which foreshadowed the larger economic conflicts between Canada and the United States that were to emerge in later years. Canada was experiencing increasing deficits in its auto trade with the United States. However, within the context of America's continuing economic strength, short-term concessions were feasible and this crisis was patched up. The Canada-U.S. Auto Pact was signed in 1965 in exchange for a guaranteed supply of Canadian raw materials to the U.S. economy. The relatively peaceful ties between corporations in the United States and their Canadian branch plants were mirrored in the relations between American unions and their Canadian branches.

Even the United Auto Workers' demand for import restrictions beginning in 1972 was not meant to apply to vehicles manufactured in Canada since trade in automobiles and parts between Canada and the United States was regulated by the Auto Pact.

For the first three years of the seventies the balance of trade under the Auto Pact had been in Canada's favour — that is, Canada was exporting more automobiles and parts to the United States than it was importing. By 1973, however, the balance of trade had shifted sharply to the United States, and by 1974 Canada had a $1.3 billion trade deficit with America under the Auto Pact.[2] This deficit was the biggest in the history of the pact and the Canadian auto industry.

Because the Auto Pact's safeguards would not come into effect until the annual trade deficit against Canada had reached some three billion dollars, the UAW leadership in the United States could still afford to "exempt" Canada from their import restriction policy. The UAW supported "exemption" for Canada, but the auto companies shifted their production from Canada to the United States.

By 1974, Canada's overall deficit in trade of manufactured goods with the United States had reached nine billion dollars. The actual and potential loss of jobs to Canadians involved in this deficit was the underlying reason for the response of Canada's union leadership to the protectionist policies of their U.S. headquarters beginning in 1970. Canadian members of international unions — a large percentage of whom were in industrial unions based on manufacturing — were naturally angered by American union protectionism.

Canada's union leadership argued against American protectionism on two grounds. The first was the moral principle which they thought should govern trade relations. The second was the more pragmatic argument that Canada's economic relationship to the United States was substantially different from that of other countries.

One of the first responses to the earlier protectionist rumblings came in a speech made by William Dodge, then secretary-treasurer of the Canadian Labour Congress. Speaking in July 1970, Dodge said that Canada was watching the trend toward protectionism in the United States with increasing alarm.[3] The CLC, Dodge said, "favours trade liberalization on a world-wide basis".

Despite the CLC's concern, the AFL-CIO was preparing for even more stringent protectionist recommendations. Thus in 1971 the U.S. president's programme of "Nixonomics" was accomplished by the even stronger protectionist stand adopted by the U.S. union centre. When the Executive Council of the CLC met in September of that year, it passed a strongly worded statement calling for Canadian exemption from the import surcharge provisions of Nixonomics, but made no reference to U.S. labour's growing protectionism. The CLC statement relied on Canada's "unique relationship to the United States" to produce "exemption" for Canada:

> We have a unique relationship to the U.S. because of the very close economic ties with that country. ... It can scarcely be called

economic chauvinism to remind the United States that it is highly dependent on Canada for primary and other resources, without which its economy would falter badly. ... It follows therefore that the Canadian government has considerable bargaining power and we strongly urge the latter to exercise this power in seeking to bring about an exemption under the surcharge.[4]

The growing concern of the CLC can also be seen in the Memoranda to the Canadian Government that it presents every March. Thus, the 1971 Memorandum expressed the hope that "your government will endeavour to do everything in its power to curb the current protectionist trends in international trade".

The 1972 Memorandum enlarged upon this, and for the first time identified U.S. unions as driving forces behind the growth of protectionism:

We are disturbed that strong groups in the United States, including groups within the U.S. trade union movement, are pushing hard to get the Burke-Hartke Bill passed through Congress. As you are well aware, this bill would impose a restrictive quota on nearly all exports to the United States, including those from Canada. ...

The 1972 statement went on to attack DISC. But concern over Burke-Hartke was further escalated in the March 1973 Memorandum:

We are particularly concerned with protectionist developments in the United States, for the obvious reason that over two-thirds of Canada's total exports go into the American market. As we stated to you a year ago, we view with serious apprehension the fact that powerful groups in that country, including elements within the American trade union movement, are exerting strong pressures to get the Burke-Hartke Bill through Congress. ... Its effect could result in the unemployment of many Canadian industrial workers. ...

The 1974 Memorandum saw this problem exacerbated by the "energy crisis". It concluded its section on trade policy with the following warning:

No rhetoric and high-sounding phrases of how wealthy we are in natural resources would save us. Should we resort to that kind of complacency, we shall do so at the expense of sharp dislocations of our economy, especially that of secondary manufacturing, and the unemployment toll could be of such magnitude as to cripple us as an economically viable society.

Public expressions of concern over growing U.S. protectionism were not limited to the CLC. Thus the Ontario Federation of Labour, in its 1971 submission to the Ontario Cabinet, expressed concern that American protectionism "would have a serious effect ... in particular on Ontario, a highly industrialized province dependent on export to the U.S."[5]

The OFL based its "moral" argument for Canadian exemption from protectionist restrictions on the close economic ties between the two countries.

Both the CLC and the OFL were calling for a return to the old status quo before protectionism had reared its head. By contrast, the British Columbia Federation of Labour perceived the issue in much broader terms: the role of the United States in Viet Nam and in Canada; Canada as a resource base for the United States; the need to change this toward secondary processing in Canada; and the reactionary role of the U.S. union movement.

The B.C. Federation attacked Nixon's "outrageous and arrogant" economic measures, claiming that they meant that Canadians would be "asked to help pay for the war in Viet Nam and to finance the purchase of our country by American corporations".[6]

It proposed a programme for "an independent Canada with a mature and full employment economy" under complete Canadian control. This programme had some of the features of an alternative industrial strategy for Canada. It included:

— An immediate and aggressive search for new trade with the European and Asian countries;
— The rejection of B.C. Premier Bennett's call for an economic union and free trade with the United States: "We will not sell our souls for an increase in trade with the U.S."; and,
— Real bargaining over natural resources to insure a properly mixed economy with a wide range of Canadian-owned and operated secondary industry: "We must take measures to insure that raw materials extracted from Canada be processed by Canadians."

The B.C. convention adopted a committee report which, unlike the CLC and OFL positions, severely criticized the U.S. labour movement's role in supporting the Viet Nam War, Nixonomics and protectionism:

It [is] especially saddening that President Nixon had the support of the AFL-CIO Executive Council for these restrictive measures. We believe that like the AFL-CIO support for the war, this reflects the tendency under George Meany's leadership to adopt easy policies rather than to provide genuine leadership. . . . We believe that U.S. society is heading for a crisis and that labour there will have to bestir itself to avoid being aligned totally and permanently with forces of reaction.

Most of the leadership of the international unions in Canada inclined more to the CLC/OFL "moral" and "Canadian exemption" stands than to the alternative industrial strategy advocated by the B.C. Federation.

If the exemption campaign were to work anywhere, it should have been in the United Steel Workers of America. The USWA president, I.W. Abel, had probably been the most influential U.S. unionist with respect to the protectionism issue, since he heads the powerful Industrial Union Department of the AFL-CIO. The Steelworkers is by far the largest

industrial union in Canadian manufacturing, and the Canadian membership makes up about thirteen per cent of the total membership — higher
than in most internationals.[7]

That the Canadian leadership of the union was embarrassed by the
active protectionism of their co-unionists in the United States was
shown at the Canadian Steelworkers Policy Conference in 1973. The
policy statement recommended by the union establishment and adopted
by the delegates failed to indicate to the international executive how
strongly the Canadian delegates at their conference had spoken out
against the Burke-Hartke Bill or the AFL-CIO's sponsorship of it.[8] This is
not to say that the Canadian steel workers were unaware of what their
American counterparts were doing. The 3,500-member local at Inco's
Thompson, Manitoba plant had forwarded a resolution demanding that
the international union reverse its stand on Burke-Hartke.[9] During the
debate that followed, all but one of the delegates who spoke expressed
concern that the legislation would hurt Canadian jobs.[10] But the policy
recommendations did not even touch on the widespread concern of
Canadian steel workers over Abel's support of protectionism.

In February 1973 William Mahoney, Canadian director of the USWA,
claimed that "I.W. Abel, International Steelworkers president, last fall
assured Canadian members that the union would press for an exemption
for Canada from the bill's provisions".[11] Mahoney did not mention that
only a few days previously, Abel had presided at a session of the AFL-CIO
Executive Council's meeting at Bal Harbour, Florida, where the very
idea of Canadian exemption was laughed down.

When the AFL-CIO met in convention at Miami Beach in October 1973,
a confrontation with the CLC was in the offing. Jean Beaudry, executive
vice-president of the Canadian Labour Congress, addressed the convention and attacked the idea of protectionism in general and Burke-Hartke
in particular:

> I don't believe it comes as a surprise to you that we are opposed to
> your position on this infamous bill, and I use that word "infamous"
> advisedly. ... As you are aware, the United States is Canada's best
> trading partner ... the trade between our two countries is more
> beneficial to your labour force than to ours since much of our export
> trade to you is represented by capital-intensive raw materials and
> your export trade to us is largely represented by labour-intensive
> finished goods.[12]

Beaudry pointed out the extensive damage Burke-Hartke would bring
to the Canadian economy:

> It has been estimated by official American figures that had the bill
> been effective in 1970 it would have cost Canada 3.6 billion dollars in
> exports. If it were enacted this year (1973) our CLC economists cal-
> culate it would cost the Canadian economy 3.7 billion dollars to 4
> billion dollars. The cost in jobs would be astronomical.

Beaudry ended his speech with a lengthy plea for sympathy from the AFL-CIO. It began with an account of the difficulty experienced by Canadian members of the internationals in justifying their allegiance to the protectionist unions:

> Some of our most active and dedicated trade unionists are being roasted by their critics, both inside and outside the movement, over the possible repercussions for Canadian workers if Burke-Hartke were to be adopted by the U.S. Congress.

Pleading with the delegates to empathize with the dilemma he and his counterparts faced, Beaudry asked the AFL-CIO members to "try to place yourself in the position of a Canadian elected officer, international representative or shop steward of an international union whose international executive board is actively supporting the bill".

In making these and other remarks, Beaudry may well have remembered a pamphlet issued by the AFL-CIO in 1972. Entitled, "The Multinational Corporation", the pamphlet described the operations of American companies abroad as "modern-day dinosaurs which eat the jobs of American workers". Canada headed the list of thirty-three foreign countries or regions where branch plants had been established. Of the 1,568 foreign facilities of the top 50 U.S. corporations, the pamphlet showed, Canada had 175 — the highest score. Canada was the only country with at least one branch plant of every one of the companies shown. The pamphlet deplored the "giant multinational subsidiaries of U.S. corporations" which "roam the world in search of profits by using cheap labour abroad while our own workers starve for jobs". It called for support of Burke-Hartke, and made no reference to Canadian exemption, nor to the fact that Canada is not a "cheap labour" country like many of the others listed.[13]

Pleas by Beaudry and others for Canadian exemption were answered directly a few months later by the president of the AFL-CIO. George Meany had two things to say: first, that he had not heard any demand for Canadian exemption, and second, that such exemption would be impossible under the General Agreement on Tariffs and Trade.[14]

The CLC's president had apparently known for some time that the U.S. union leadership intended to take this position. When asked why the CLC had not carried its campaign for exemption to the AFL-CIO Executive Council meetings in 1973, Donald MacDonald said: "We know they aren't even interested in giving such considerations. It would be a waste of time. They are fully familiar with our position."[15] Russell Bell, CLC research director, echoed this belief: "It wouldn't be worth a twenty-five cent streetcar ride. They've made up their minds solidly."[16]

This recognition by the CLC leadership that the Canadian exemption proposal was mainly rhetoric for the ears of the Canadian membership probably explained why Beaudry did not press it at the October AFL-CIO convention. Instead, he chose to pursue a moral argument against the idea of protectionism in general, with special reference to the dilemma of Canadian officers of international unions. For, as MacDonald had concluded, "there is no doubt whatsoever that the AFL-CIO position on the bill is aggravating existing tensions in the international union movement".[17]

At the same time, some American officers of international unions were still insisting to their Canadian members that exemptions could be made. James Griffin, international bargaining head for the USWA, was saying as late as February 1973 that exemptions would be made for Canada, and that Congressman Burke had agreed to such a clause. He did not point out, however, that Senator Hartke — along with the AFL-CIO — remained opposed. Griffin referred to Canadians who sought the separation of their sections from the internationals as "so many crack-pots" who "don't understand what this ball game is all about".[18]

Russell Bell had a different perspective. "I don't think they [the American union leaders] give a damn, because I don't believe they ever think about it. ... We talk about nationalism in Canada but they have outdone us."[19] Bell had just been involved in an illuminating exchange with Nathan Goldfinger, chief economist for the AFL-CIO, who had been insisting that Burke-Hartke's effects on Canada would be negligible.

In 1971, Goldfinger claimed in an interview with *Globe and Mail* reporter Wilfred List that he did not have the import trade figures on Canada.[20] When List interviewed him again in February of 1973 Goldfinger conceded that there would be "some small adverse effect" on Canada, but that this could be outweighed by the prosperity accruing to the United States. He claimed Canada needs a prosperous United States: " ... Otherwise, what happens to Canadian trade?"[21]

While he admitted that no study had been made of the effects of imports from specific countries, like Canada, he insisted that there was no real foundation for the dispute between American and Canadian trade unionists. "I'd like to know what our Canadian friends are objecting to." And despite the fact that many U.S. union leaders, including those who opposed Burke-Hartke, had by now admitted that Canadian exemption was impossible, Goldfinger claimed that some exemptions could still be considered by the AFL-CIO.

Russell Bell's response to these equivocations and denials about the effects on Canada and the possibility of exemptions was abrupt. He said that further discussion with the AFL-CIO on this matter would be useless. As to Goldfinger's contention that the effects on Canada would be minimal, Bell called it sheer unadulterated nonsense. "There is no provision to exempt Canada or any other country from being subjected to highly restrictive quotas on manufactured goods."[22]

Donald MacDonald, Russell Bell, and many others in the Canadian union movement acknowledged the objective conflict between U.S. unions and their Canadian sections. This conflict had nothing to do with morality or with the goodwill of U.S. union leaders. It was instead the result of an inescapable conflict of interest between U.S. unions and Canadian workers arising from the ownership and structure of the Canadian economy and the nature of Canada-U.S. trade relations. More jobs for the American workers in U.S. corporations with branch plants in Canada would mean fewer jobs for Canadian workers, and vice-versa.

Victor Feather, then general secretary of the British Trade Union Congress, attended the 1973 AFL-CIO Convention as a fraternal delegate. Remarking on the difficulties of international co-operation between trade unions, he said, "there's a strong affinity between unions when jobs are not at stake, but when jobs are at stake unions look after their own — that's the system".

Clearly enough, the leaders of the U.S. unions were "looking after their own". Canadians might belong to the international unions, but when the chips were down, international policy protected the interests of the ninety-two per cent American membership, not the eight per cent who were Canadians.

The problem was not a simple domestic union matter which could be solved by rational negotiations between American and Canadian unionists. It was deeply rooted in Canada's political economy, and, far from going away, could only be aggravated by the growing disparities between the interests of American multinational corporations, government and unions, on the one hand, and Canadian workers on the other. The fact that Canada's business élite is now highly integrated as junior partners of U.S. corporations in Canada does not lessen the conflict. It adds another political dimension and has meant that in confronting the U.S. government, U.S. corporations and international unions in attempts to solve their problems, working people in Canada also confronted Canada's business leaders.

In countering the protectionist drive of the U.S. union leadership, Canadian workers had found themselves facing the consequences of the fact that Canada's manufacturing industries were largely owned by U.S. corporations. These corporations and the U.S. government have assigned Canada the role of resource base and consumer market for American domestic production. It has become evident that U.S. protectionism could only step up the de-industrialization process in Canada. Since over one-quarter of U.S. global foreign investment is in Canada, a drive for the return of production to the United States would have incomparably greater effects on manufacturing workers in Canada than anywhere else in the world. The implications within the confines of Canadian dependency on the United States are that either Canadian or American workers would bear the brunt of unemployment, particularly in recession.

The sympathy of Canadian unionists for the plight of American unionists who were also losing jobs through no fault of their own, and who faced similar problems when they were unemployed, did not alter the objective reality. Sympathy could not overcome the conflict between the dominating American and the dependent Canadian economies, and between the policies of U.S. unions and the interests of Canadian workers.

This new situation had weakened the claim by supporters of international unions that multinational corporations require multinational unions to deal with them. Since the American international unions, if they had their way, would drastically reduce the manufacturing activities of these same multinational corporations in countries such as Canada, they were undermining rather than protecting the interests of Canadian workers.

The issue as it shaped up for Canadian workers required exploring the possibility of an alternative industrial strategy for Canada — and another kind of relationship with the U.S. economy — as indicated by the B.C. Federation of Labour and the 1975 UAW brief.[23] Such a strategy would be designed to guarantee jobs for Canadians independent of the multinational corporations and safe from the potentially very damaging effects of U.S. protectionism.

---

1. *The Globe and Mail,* October 23, 1973.

2. *Statistics Canada Daily,* "Canada-United States Trade In Automotive Products", April 11, 1975.

3. Canadian Labour Congress, *Press Release*, July 28, 1970.

4. *Canadian Labour*, October 1971, p. 14.

5. Ontario Federation of Labour, *Legislative Proposals to the Government of Ontario,* 1971.

6. *The Dispatcher,* December 7, 1971, p. 4.

7. USWA Convention, *Report of Officers*, Atlantic City, New Jersey, September 23-27, 1974, p. 55.

8. *The Hamilton Spectator*, June 5, 1973; USWA Canadian Policy Conference, *Policy and Resolutions*, Montreal, 1973, p. 84.

9. *The Hamilton Spectator,* June 5, 1973.

10. Ibid.

11. *The Toronto Star,* February 26, 1973.

12. *Canadian Labour*, October-December 1973, p. 8.

13. Industrial Union Department, AFL-CIO, "The Multi-National Corporation", pamphlet, 1972.

14. *The Globe and Mail,* February 23, 1974.

15. *The Globe and Mail,* February 20, 1973.

16. Ibid.

17. Ibid.

18. *The Hamilton Spectator,* February 28, 1973.

19. *The Globe and Mail,* February 20, 1973.

20. *The Globe and Mail,* March 12, 1971.

21. *The Globe and Mail,* February 20, 1973.

22. Ibid.

23. See Chapter 4.

CHAPTER 10

The Auto Industry: A Case Study of the Effects of American Ownership and Protectionism

Chrysler is a U.S. corporation. We are a good Canadian citizen. But blood is thicker than water. I didn't like the decision on the six-cylinder engine plant ... if a Canadian doesn't like it, there's not a damn thing he can do about it.

Ronald Todgham
President, Chrysler Canada Ltd., 1975[1]

The auto manufacturing industry is a classic case of industrial branch plants in Canada under the control of huge American multinational corporations. With the recent and minor exception of the Bricklin plant in New Brunswick, car manufacturing in Canada is confined to the four U.S. companies, General Motors, Ford, Chrysler and American Motors. (The Volvo plant in Nova Scotia is an assembly operation.)

Yet Canada's automobile industry has almost as long a history as that of the United States. Noteworthy is R.S. MacLaughlin who began producing cars in his Oshawa carriage factory, using Buick engines imported from Flint, Michigan, about seventy years ago.

The story of how Canada's fledgling auto manufacture passed into American hands typifies the integration of American corporations into the Canadian economy. It also demonstrates the role of Canadian financiers as middlemen in the sale of Canada to U.S. interests.

Until the Second World War, the American companies found it useful to produce cars in Canada not only for sales in Canada, but also as a way of gaining cheaper access to British Empire countries with which Canada had a preferential trade agreement. In 1929 Canadians produced 263,000 vehicles, of which 102,000 were exported. Canada was in that year the second largest manufacturer of cars in the world — a position it never regained.

Following the Second World War, and throughout the early 1950s, the economic boom led to high levels of auto production in Canada as well as in the United States.

By the late fifties and early sixties, foreign competition was cutting into both the Canadian and U.S. markets on a large scale. The earliest competitors were the Volkswagen and a number of British models. As the period wore on, Canadian and American consumers increasingly turned to the Japanese Toyotas and Datsuns, the French Renaults, the Italian Fiats, various British makes and the Swedish Volvos.

During this period, the U.S. auto manufacturers began to shift production out of Canada, into the United States. Canadian production was no longer necessary as the means to break into the British Commonwealth market. The American companies had established branch plants in many of the old British Empire countries, and had initiated their own models in Britain. Canada's trade deficit in cars and auto products began to reach alarming proportions.

By 1960 Canadian production had dropped to 396,000 vehicles; 180,000 cars were imported while exports had dropped to a mere 20,000. Germany, in comparison, produced two million cars in 1960. Since 1929 Canada had experienced a decline in the number of auto industry jobs relative to the size of the work force, in spite of larger relative sales of cars within the country. Within three decades, the Canadian auto industry had dropped from second to seventh position in world terms.[2] The federal government responded by setting up a Royal Commission on the Automotive Industry, under economist Vincent Bladen.

From the perspective of the early 1960s, the choice facing the Bladen Commission was either to integrate Canada's auto production into the American industry on a continental basis, or to rationalize it to produce primarily for the Canadian market. The Bladen Commission attempted to avoid this choice and its recommendations were never implemented. However, several of the briefs to the Commission opted for one or the other alternative.

Not surprisingly, the U.S. auto manufacturers favoured increased integration of Canadian production into the American industry. On the other hand, the Canadian parts producers — generally small Canadian-owned firms — opposed integration, and advocated greater protection for themselves.

The United Auto Workers were split internally on the issue. The Canadian District of the UAW, headed by George Burt, with the support of the Canadian Labour Congress, submitted a brief in favour of continental integration: "In essence, we suggest that the Commission examine the feasibility of an international agreement which would permit free trade in the products of any motor vehicle manufacturing company . . ." The brief added a provision that each company would produce in Canada, or have produced for it in Canada, "a quantity of motor vehicles and parts sufficient to assure maintenance of current levels of employment at current production volume and future increases in employment parallel with the growth of the company's Canadian market".[3]

This approach was precisely the kind adopted through the Auto Pact a few years later — a fact which led the UAW to claim credit for the pact once it had been achieved.

But Local 444 of the UAW (Chrysler, in Windsor) and the UAW General Motors Council rejected the approach of their national office and the CLC. They struck out against a continentalist approach, and called instead for an immediate increase in the Canadian content of cars produced in the country as "a step in the direction of an all-Canadian car".[4]

The crisis in the auto industry in the early 1960s made necessary an immediate choice between the continentalist and the nationalist course. Canada's balance of payments deficit in auto trade with the United States was mounting rapidly. In 1965 it reached a record level of $711 million.[5] In that year Lester Pearson signed the U.S.-Canada Auto Pact and the option of continental integration became a reality.

The Auto Pact contained three safeguards designed to protect a minimum level of auto production in Canada:[6]

1. *A base level of production in Canada below which Canadian production would not be allowed to fall.* The level was calculated in terms of 1964 production by two provisions. First, it provided that Canadian production could not fall below the dollar value of autos and parts produced in the country in 1964. Second, it provided that the ratio of production in the auto industry to the sale of North American cars in Canada could not fall below that of 1964. In that year Canada's share of North American automotive production and sales was roughly 5.3 per cent and 9.1 per cent, respectively. Whichever amount calculated from these two provisions was higher in any given year would determine the lower limit of Canadian production.

2. *An agreement that as sales of North American cars in Canada increased, so would Canadian auto production.* Increases in sales of cars were to be matched by an increase in production equal to at least sixty per cent of the increase in sales. In the case of commercial vehicles, the increase was to be at least fifty per cent.

3. *A commitment by the U.S. corporations to increase production in Canada over and above the other two safeguards, by certain fixed amounts.* This aspect of the pact was not an agreement between the two governments, but between the four U.S. corporations and the Canadian government. By the end of 1968, General Motors was to increase production by $121 million, Ford by $74.2 million, Chrysler by $33 million, and American Motors by $11.2 million. This commitment was achieved by the end of 1968, and has expired.

Under the Auto Pact, Canada's auto industry was rationalized to produce fewer lines of cars for the entire North American market. This rationalization meant increased Canadian productivity, and the transfer of management functions from Canada to the United States. "Continental integration", in other words, meant increased American control.

The first four years of operation under the pact saw a continued trade deficit for Canada. And then, in 1970 and 1971, the balance shifted slightly in Canada's favour. Far from being a normal consequence of the Auto Pact provisions, this was an accident resulting from misjudgements on the part of the U.S. corporations.

The American car companies had resisted large-scale production of compact cars on a purely economic basis. Since the amount of labour involved in building either a small or large car is substantially the same, profits on small car sales are lower. The corporations tried to convince consumers to stick with the bigger cars, and thereby retain eighty to eighty-five per cent of the market for the larger North American-made cars.

As the small foreign-made cars sold increasingly well, however, the U.S. corporations began to produce their own sub-compacts on a limited scale to avoid a permanent loss of customers who preferred the small cars. In time, they thought it would be possible to gradually increase the size and price of the sub-compacts, in line with previous policy.

The U.S. corporations did not expect production of the Vega, Pinto or Dart to be particularly successful. Consequently, they located some of their sub-compact production in Canada, to meet the minimal requirements of the Auto Pact. But to their surprise, the sub-compacts turned out to be successful on the U.S. market. For a short period production in Canada escalated in the area of sub-compact production, thereby causing the favourable trade balances of 1970 and 1971.

TABLE 11
U.S.-Canada Balance of Trade in Automotive Vehicles and Parts

1965	$ −711 million
1966	−601 million
1967	−522 million
1968	−389 million
1969	−90 million
1970	+204 million
1971	+224 million
1972	+67 million
1973	−440 million
1974	−1,328 million
(1st half) 1975	−997 million

Source: *Statistics Canada Daily*. "Canada-U.S. Trade in Automotive Products", October 12, 1973, April 11, 1975; *The Globe and Mail*, September 13, 1975.

But this was not to last. World-wide, the car industry was over-producing on a huge scale. And in the early 1970s American spokesmen, both in and out of Congress, began to press for protectionism and an end to the Canada-U.S. Auto Pact.

Nixon's new economic policies of August 1971 had opened this new stage in the undermining of Canada's auto industry. The DISC tax programme invited multinational corporations to move production back home and to write off fifty per cent of the taxes on their export sales. This was an enormous inducement to the auto companies to export more to Canada from their U.S. plants. While the list of companies making use of DISC has not been made public, the Ford Motor Company acknowledged that it was taking advantage of the programme.

In 1972 Canada's auto trade with the United States still showed a small surplus. But the following year Canada returned to a deficit position, amounting to $440 million. In 1974 this tripled, reaching the staggering figure of $1.3 billion — by far the biggest deficit Canada has ever had. This was made up of a deficit of $2.0 billion in auto parts and a $900 million surplus in assembled vehicles.[7]

The Auto Pact has been one of the major bridge-heads by which U.S. control of Canada is maintained, because it is crucial to Canada's economy. Cancellation of its safeguards could deny Canada access to seventy per cent of its present auto market, and could cut off the flow of parts which is currently essential to Canadian auto production.

It is not surprising that domestic American politicians who have not been housebroken as diplomats often demand that the United States use the threat of cancelling the Auto Pact to bring Canada to terms on other issues, such as oil. For instance, Senator Hartke, co-sponsor of the AFL-CIO protectionism bill, told a Canadian television audience in 1973 that the Auto Pact was a bribe offered by Lyndon Johnson to get Canada into the Viet Nam War — and that the whole pact should be scrapped:

> The Prime Minister of Canada was taken down to the [Lyndon Johnson] ranch and the president talked to him about the value of getting involved in there and saving democracy and helping the Americans out in Viet Nam. And there were some statements that there might be a change of thought, so they gave the Canadian automobile agreement, in my judgement, as a direct trade-off, just as we gave the Philippines $38 million to go ahead and send a thousand troops to Viet Nam.[8]

Later in the programme, Hartke referred to the Auto Pact as "foreign aid".

In July 1975 Hartke was still critical of the pact, claiming Canada has used "virtual blackmail" in negotiating it in 1965. He told the U.S. Senate that the United States had settled for "a lop-sided arrangement which threw open our foreign trade doors in response to only a partial opening on the part of the foreign power". Hartke complained that

Canada, the "foreign power", had extended the "transitional provisions", which established a minimum ratio of domestic production, to sales in Canada. He explained the request by the Senate Finance Committee that the U.S. International Trade Commission "investigate" the terms of the Auto Pact and suggested that the commission "evaluate the effects of repealing the agreement". He urged consideration of the United States negotiating a "truly" free trade area by removing "the Canadian restrictions".[9]

But the Auto Pact has actually been a large plus for the U.S. auto companies. They have been able to use Canada as a surplus production area. When times were good, production would take place in Canada, but when the U.S. car market slumped, Canadian production would get cut back.

By 1974 and 1975 capital investment in the Canadian auto industry had dried up. The trade deficit with the United States continued to rocket, and Canadian auto workers became the victims of the American recession — despite record sales in Canada in 1974.

It should have come as no surprise that the United States would take full advantage of the pact at the expense of Canadian auto workers. In February 1973 a U.S. Senate study on American multinational corporations states that the United States entered into the Auto Pact to prevent the evolution of a Canadian auto industry.[10] The United States could invest less in Canadian manufacturing and at the same time corner a larger share of its market.

In 1970 Canada's share of the North American capital expenditures of the U.S. auto firms peaked at thirteen per cent. By 1973 only five per cent of the industry's North American investment was in Canada. In the winter of the following year Canada's industry minister pleaded with the auto makers to throw a little more capital investment Canada's way. In a speech to Detroit's Economic Club, Alistair Gillespie said:

> If Canada were to continue, over the longer term, not to receive an "equitable portion" of the industry's North American investments, the result would be a reduction in the level of activity in the Canadian industry and increased pressure on the automotive agreement.[11]

As the 1974-75 period of recession developed in the United States and spread to Canada, automobile production was shifted to American plants. Although sales in Canada remained strong in 1974, Canadian workers were laid-off to supplement work in the United States.

As the previous chapter has recorded, by 1972 the UAW in the United States had changed its trade policy from "free trade" to "fair trade". In the face of increasing U.S. protectionism, the Canadian UAW passed a series of resolutions reaffirming support for the Auto Pact, and they received verbal support from Solidarity House, Detroit headquarters of the union.

At the same time, there was a movement in the Canadian UAW in favour of stronger measures to protect production of cars in Canada, and to retain the temporary increase in the number of Canadian jobs in the industry.

One expression of this viewpoint came in 1972 at a conference called jointly by the Ontario Waffle (at that time part of the provincial NDP), the five presidents of the largest UAW locals, and the president of the Windsor Labour Council. The conference adopted a policy statement calling for an all-Canadian car. It also concluded that in the Canadian context, public ownership was the only mechanism by which an independent auto industry building cars for Canadian needs could be developed.[12]

The UAW protectionist demands which emerged strongly in the United States in 1973 and 1974 excluded Canada. But the union's campaign for quotas and protectionism in general had the effect of endorsing the withdrawal of auto production from Canada to the United States. Because of the inadequacy for Canada of the Auto Pact safeguards, the UAW could continue its support of the pact while pressing generally for more auto production in the United States.

Perhaps the clearest indication of the position of the American UAW in relation to the auto production and jobs of its membership in Canada came in June 1975. The UAW had applied to the U.S. Labor Department for special unemployment benefits for 39,000 laid-off employees at Chrysler Corporation under provisions of foreign trade laws. The argument the UAW used for the benefits was that "in recent months, Chrysler has tranferred substantial production from its U.S. plants to its Canadian plants and has imported cars from Canada to the United States".[13]

Douglas Fraser, UAW vice-president, argued the case for the UAW before an American Labor Department hearing. Chrysler argued against the UAW petition, and disputed the union's assertion that "many of the corporation's Canadian plants have been producing at or near capacity whereas U.S. plants making like or competitive products have been closed or operating at substantially reduced levels."[14]

The effect of the UAW's claim, if successful, would be to step up U.S. government and Congressional pressure on the auto manufacturers, as reflected in Senator Hartke's position, to shift popular car lines out of Canada to the United States.

In late 1974, Canadian auto plants began to experience mass lay-offs. Insecurities forgotten since the 1930s returned to the streets of the big auto cities as lay-offs mounted: Windsor, Oshawa, St. Catharines, Talbotville, Bramalea, Ste. Thérèse, Oakville. The auto parts plants, particularly the smaller, Canadian-owned ones, were also hit hard, affecting Toronto, Chatham, London, Kitchener, Guelph, Hamilton and other centres.

In May 1975 McDermott showed an ambivalence toward the effects of the pact on Canadian auto workers. On the one hand, he said that "by and large the Auto Pact has delivered on its goals as they were set when it was established — it has been a plus for the economy and the Canadian industry".

On the other hand, McDermott said that the pact's faults "were there from the beginning". He explained that "the deficit" in the Auto Pact stemmed mainly from the fact that Canadian plants are essentially final assembly while the U.S. plants are manufacturing parts. "We thus continued to buy parts from them while they reduced their buying — relatively — from us." He continued: "The Auto Pact should have given Canadians some design, research, engineering and tool and die work. We argued for it at the time but Ottawa was either deaf or dumb or both."[15]

This 1975 statement was an important modification of earlier positions taken by McDermott, which were in strong defence of the Auto Pact. In January 1972, for example, McDermott was scathing in his denunciation of critics of the pact. He pointed to the "renovations that have gone up in Canada [auto industry] as a result of the pact". The UAW director was scornful of the "critics of the Auto Pact in our union" who were being "political because the pact happens to be with the Americans". McDermott showed his impatience with nationalist critics of U.S. control of Canada. "If it [the Auto Pact] were with say, Argentina or Soviet Russia or Timbuctu, they would not object. They object purely on the basis that it is an economic arrangement with the Americans and therefore they dredge up a lot of nightmares and mental pictures of economic, political and other forms of domination."[16]

While in mid-1975 McDermott was still partially defending the Auto Pact, Patrick Lavelle, president of the Automobile Parts Association, was less sanguine about relations between the United States and the Canadian sections of the auto industry. In late 1974 he warned that the U.S. auto companies were beginning to switch some of their orders from Canadian parts manufacturers to American ones. He predicted, "if the slump in the United States continues — and there's every indication that it will — then it will have a marked effect in Canada . . . We can anticipate lay-offs and plant shut-downs [in the auto parts industry] . . . The effects could be dramatic."[17]

The effects were dramatic. In 1974 Canada had a $2.0 billion deficit in auto parts with the United States, up from $1.3 billion in 1973.

In his 1975 report to the Automotive Parts Association (Canada), Victor Van Der Hout, outgoing chairman, challenged the federal trade minister's explanation that even with the auto trade deficit, the Canadian industry was better off than its U.S. counterpart. He said, "we are not sure that this is so," and added that, in any case, "when twenty per cent of our labour force in our parts industry is unemployed, we can take little consolation from someone else's misery".[18]

Van Der Hout said that one of the contributing factors to the deficit had been a change in buying practices by Detroit which was concentrating more parts purchases in the United States.

We have knowledge that, because of available capacities in the U.S., some jobs that have historically been placed in Canada have gone into the U.S. If this continues further, and I can't see any improvement throughout 1975 and into 1976, our potential volumes will continue to decline and the lack of volume will make us less and less competitive.

The $1.3 billion deficit in total auto trade that Canada experienced in 1974 represented an estimated 22,000 jobs lost in auto vehicle and parts production by Canadian to American workers.[19] Counting jobs created in other industries as a direct effect of auto production, this would total an estimated 50 thousand jobs — jobs lost by Canadians as a result of the auto trade deficit with the United States.[20]

The conflict of interest facing Canadian workers could not be solved within the confines of the branch plants of U.S. corporations. Increasingly, discussion of an alternative industrial strategy, and an all-Canadian car came to the fore as it had in the early 1960s and in 1972 — as the only means of securing jobs for Canadian auto workers and turning back the tide of de-industrialization.

Such a solution for Canadian auto workers' problems was far from the mind of the American president of the UAW, Leonard Woodcock, when he spoke in Toronto in November 1974. On that occasion Woodcock announced his decision to sponsor advertising which would convince consumers to buy American-model cars.[21]

Although Woodcock's fellow UAW board members turned down his proposal for an advertising campaign, this did not bring them closer to supporting the idea of an "all-Canadian car" or to replacing the U.S. auto companies by a Canadian industry.

As 1975 limped on, the Canadian UAW leadership began to abandon the passive belief that you have to take the good times with the bad. Pressures and resentments were building in the union over the lay-offs in auto plants in Canada when Canadian car purchases were still at record levels.

In January 1975 the Canadian UAW Council adopted a brief which had been prepared by its Auto Tariff Committee. This brief, described in chapter four, pointed out the direction toward an alternative strategy for manufacturing in Canada. In calling for the development of a strong manufacturing base in Canada, pointing out the necessity for an independent Canadian technological base, and proposing government involvement in industry — "up to and including public ownership".

Canadian auto workers were seeking a clear alternative to the continentalist policy toward their industry reflected by the Auto Pact. Implicitly, they were also recognizing that the policies of the UAW in the United States were quite different from the policies which represented the interests of Canadian auto workers.

1. *The Financial Post*, January 25, 1975.

2. *Ontario Report*, January-February 1975.

3. Ibid.

4. Ibid.

5. *Statistics Canada Daily*, "Canada-United States Trade in Automotive Products", October 12, 1973.

6. *Ontario Report*, January-February 1975.

7. *Statistics Canada Daily*, April 11, 1975. The $1.3 billion total also includes the deficit balances on tires and tubes and trucks in 1974.

8. *The Globe and Mail*, March 9, 1973.

9. *The Globe and Mail*, July 30, 1975.

10. *Ontario Report*, January-February 1975.

11. Ibid.

12. *The Windsor Star*, January 10, 12, 13, 1972.

13. *Wall Street Journal*, June 2, 1975.

14. Ibid.

15. *Financial Times of Canada*, May 19, 1975.

16. *The Windsor Star*, January 14, 1972.

17. *Ontario Report*, January-February 1975.

18. *The Globe and Mail*, April 24, 1975.

19. The deficit of $1.3 billion, at an estimated average production per worker of $56,000, represents 22,000 jobs.

20. There are almost four workers in non-manufacturing to every worker in manufacturing in Canada.

21. *The Globe and Mail*, November 22, 1974.

CHAPTER 11
International Unions and Autonomy:
The Douglas Case

The American party in Canada is always at work.

Ralph W. Emerson, 1872[1]

The last three chapters highlighted the economic difficulties in America's empire which had strained relations between the international unions and their Canadian memberships. Since American unions first came to Canada a century ago, they have been dominant in Canada's labour movement. Since the last world war, however, this dominance had been softened in some industrial unions by moves toward what is termed "Canadian autonomy".

This has meant that locals of international unions in Canada are granted the right to establish a national council or conference with authority to discuss and determine general policies affecting Canada. In most cases Canadian autonomy has not meant Canadian control over finances, a separate Canadian convention which elects all its own officers, a separate Canadian constitution formulated by the Canadian membership, or the right to merge with other unions in Canada, regardless of the situation in the United States.

Unions such as the United Steel Workers of America and the United Auto Workers are the best known advocates of Canadian autonomy. They have argued that with this autonomy the U.S. union connection has carried benefit without liability for Canadian workers.

This chapter recounts one example of the limits to autonomy in one major international union, the UAW. Many examples of the limitations placed by U.S. headquarters on the freedom of action of Canadian locals could be given, but this case — the Douglas case, involving UAW Local

1967 in the Toronto suburb of Malton — illustrates clearly how union autonomy is often restricted.

The Douglas case of 1971 involved 4,000 members of UAW Local 1967 who had been on strike at Douglas Aircraft Company of Canada Ltd. at Malton. The U.S. employees of McDonnell-Douglas had already accepted a wage settlement that fell within the guidelines set in President Nixon's economic policy of August 1971. In Canada, the Douglas workers saw no reason why they should accept a settlement based on American economic policy.

The Malton plant built wing assemblies for DC 9 and DC 10 airplanes, which were then shipped to the American parent McDonnell-Douglas plants for assembly to U.S.-built fuselages. It became evident that before the end of December, the strike in Canada would threaten the ability of the U.S. plants to turn out airplanes, as no wings were being produced. Thus the pressure from the company for settlement of the Canadian strike mounted. Douglas sent a letter to all the strikers, outlining the possibility that the Malton plant would be closed and production shifted to the United States. Such company statements had become commonplace at Douglas, and they were of no avail in stopping the strike.

As the strike continued, another source of pressure appeared. Just like the parent company, the UAW in the American aircraft industry became increasingly anxious to settle the Malton strike so that production could go ahead in the United States. A shortage of wings for the DC planes could eventually mean lay-offs of American aircraft workers. The UAW leadership began to move to end the work stoppage.

On November 15 the UAW's International Executive Board, meeting in Detroit, ordered Local 1967 to submit the company offer to a secret ballot of the union membership. The telegram to the local was signed by president Leonard Woodcock, vice-president Kenneth Bannon and vice-president Dennis McDermott, also UAW Canadian director. It was addressed to local president Tom Johnson, plant chairman Archie Wilson and financial secretary George Szkavar. In a move to end the five-week old strike, the UAW executives ordered that a meeting be called within two days, and that the Canadian public relations officer, Jerry Hartford, distribute a written summary of the company offer to the membership meeting.[2]

The local was also instructed to afford representatives of the international union "their constitutional right to share in the reporting to the membership".[3]

On November 18 the 3,000 Douglas workers meeting in Toronto's O'Keefe Centre booed Dennis McDermott and Kenneth Bannon, director of the UAW Aerospace Department, when they spoke in defence of the company's offer. Wilfred List of *The Globe and Mail* reported the next day that the meeting, "was an emotionally charged affair" with plant chairman Archie Wilson "emerging as the local hero in opposition to the battery of high-ranking outside international officers."[4] The vote by secret ballot was 1,965 against and 1,029 in favour of the company offer backed by the international office.

After the meeting Wilson sent a telegram to Detroit headquarters in which he said that "the membership rejected the company and international union offer".[5] In speaking of the international's order to take the company's offer to the local membership Wilson told *The Globe and Mail*: "They made me take something to the members I thought was inadequate. . . . Unionism has lost all concept of its purpose. It's like big business. You have to bargain with the company as well as with the union."[6] Wilson accused the international of trying to "pull the wool over the eyes of the members. I don't consider myself a mathematical genius," he added, "but I know what the men want."

The two-to-one vote in a turn-out of seventy-five per cent of the membership might have been expected to satisfy Detroit headquarters about the feelings of the Douglas workers. But pressure from supporters of the American headquarters' stand in the local, encouraged by the international representatives, began to build up again soon after the November 18 meeting. They demanded another meeting and another vote. The steward body, the backbone of the local and the strike, refused to concur in the calling of another membership meeting unless it was confined to offering information.

The local executive called another strike meeting for December 10, 1971. Again a large number of UAW international representatives appeared at the meeting and once more tried to convince the strikers to accept the company's offer — a 5.5 per cent wage increase plus some minor benefits — which fell within the Nixon wage guidelines.

This time, too, by a show of hands, a majority of the two thousand strikers attending the meeting turned the offer down. Within a few hours of the meeting, the strike leaders once again received instructions from the UAW headquarters in Detroit. They were ordered to appear before the executive board of the union at Solidarity House in Detroit the following day.

At Solidarity House, UAW president Leonard Woodcock and his American executive board ordered the local leadership to take their members back to work. They were informed that henceforth strike pay would be cut off.

Without the funds, the strike leadership was faced with a difficult decision. About one-third of the membership had voted to accept the settlement and to end the strike, so that an effort to continue without strike pay would probably result in a deep split in the local. Direct interference of the American union headquarters had created the possibility of a major split in the local — something which the company had been unable to engineer. Reluctantly, the strike committee decided to take the workers back into the plant on the following Monday morning.

The international leadership of the UAW insisted that it had acted in the interests of democracy and the majority of the workers in the plant when it ordered an end to the strike. They contended, at the time, that a minority of radicals in the local, headed by Archie Wilson, had obstructed the will of the majority.

Three succeeding elections in the Malton plant contradicted this claim. Five months after the strike, in May 1972, Wilson was re-elected to the position of plant chairman with a majority of some 600 votes. In the 1973 elections, the following year, the local president and his supporters, who had backed the return to work and campaigned against the "useless strike", were defeated by the strike leadership. And in 1974 Wilson was again re-elected as plant chairman. By this time, however, he was no longer working in the Douglas plant. He, along with the four other members of the union bargaining committee, had been fired by the company.

In fact, in the two years immediately following the strike and Detroit's strike-breaking interference, the company had on various occasions suspended dozens of union activists in the seriously weakened Local 1967. Archie Wilson had been suspended three times.

The sequel to the split in Local 1967 came in October 1973. Douglas suspended three workers who had reported late following their participation in a picket line at a Toronto plant, Artistic Woodowrk, where a hard-fought strike was under way. In response, several hundred Douglas workers had reported "sick" on a particular day. By three o'clock that afternoon the company had announced over the P.A. system that the whole five-man bargaining committee had been fired. The company stated that it would only remain in Canada if there was co-operation from the workers.

The weakened state of the local in the aftermath of the 1971 split was now evident. Normally, the Douglas workers would have responded with an immediate mass walk-out in defence of their bargaining committee. Instead, the local, prodded by its international representatives, decided to take the "legal" route of arbitration. The Douglas company then used all the legal angles of the arbitration process to keep the committee members out of the plant for a year and a half after they were fired.

The international union offered little support for the fired workers. While it had only taken a few hours for the executive board to be called together in Detroit to call off the 1971 strike, it now took three telegrams from Local 1967 over a three-week period to get a response from international headquarters concerning this firing. This reply simply stated that the executive board was not planning to meet, and therefore could not hear the appeal of the Douglas workers for support.

Eighteen months after the firing of the "Douglas Five" in October

1973, an arbitrator upheld the firing of four of the members of the five-man bargaining committee.[7] The precedent of a bargaining committee being fired en masse had been set. The local had lost its former power and solidarity.

This account reflects the experiences of just one local of one international. Of course most locals of the UAW and other U.S.-based unions have not experienced such direct intervention — with such damaging consequences — as in this case. But the U.S. headquarters of these unions, even those which have made a point of Canadian autonomy, are not afraid to intervene in the affairs of Canadian locals where they consider this to be called for.

Indeed, had U.S. headquarters not stepped into the 1971 strike at Malton, American UAW members would probably have criticized their union leaders for refusing to protect the large number of American UAW members in Douglas Aircraft plants from suffering as a consequence of a strike by the numerically smaller group of UAW members in Local 1967. No doubt it was this consideration which lay behind the UAW leadership's action. But this situation demonstrates the real limits placed on the autonomy of Canadian members of international unions when a conflict of interest develops between the needs of Canadian and U.S. workers.

1. Robert M. Hamilton, comp., *Canadian Quotations and Phrases* (Toronto: McClelland & Stewart, 1952), p. 4.

2. *The Globe and Mail*, November 16, 1971.

3. Ibid.

4. *The Globe and Mail*, November 19, 1971.

5. *The Globe and Mail*, November 20, 1971.

6. Ibid.

7. *Ontario Report*, May-June 1975, p. 17.

CHAPTER 12

American Unions in Canada: The Special Case of the Seafarers' International Union

> I am with Seafarers' International Union, SIU, 272 King Street, Toronto. We had a strike and when that strike was over, myself and 16 other men were blacklisted. . . . I have lost my livelihood . . . I can't fight this alone.
>
> Letter from a Canadian seaman to Morton Shulman, Ontario MPP.
> Read in Ontario Legislature, November 1974.

When Morton Shulman, NDP member of the Ontario Legislature, brought the Seafarers' International Union into the headlines in 1974 with a demand for a public inquiry into its corruption, it was the third time in as many decades that this American-based union had attained such wide notoriety.

The story of the SIU, as it unfolded first in the late 1940s and again in the 1960s, constitutes an extreme case of U.S. union interference in Canada's labour movement. Its history demonstrates the lengths to which the AFL-CIO and some international unions would go to maintain control over their Canadian branches. This special case also illuminates the role of the federal government in the 1960s when, like the leadership of the Canadian Labour Congress (CLC), it buckled under the dual pressure of the U.S. government and the AFL-CIO. The SIU's presence in the CLC, except for the years 1960 to 1966, and its continued affiliation into 1975 in spite of the numerous charges of corruption against it, provides some useful insights into the extent and nature of American influence in Canada's labour movement.

This chapter first traces the role of the American unions, including the AFL, in the destruction of the Canadian Seamen's Union despite the strong resistance of leaders of the Trades and Labour Congress of Canada and the seamen themselves in the late 1940s. It then details the events of the late 1950s and early 1960s which brought all the chief actors into dramatic focus — the American government, the AFL-CIO, the American-based SIU and the Maritime Trades Department, the Canadian government, the Canadian Labour Congress, the SIU in Canada, and several other unions in Canada including the Canadian Brotherhood of Railway Transport, the United Steel Workers of America and the National Association of Marine Engineers.

Before 1936 when the Canadian Seamen's Union (CSU) was formed, Canadians working on the Great Lakes and the St. Lawrence had no union, and their position suffered greatly during the depression years. Following a disastrously-led strike in 1935, they began to lay the groundwork for the CSU. In the beginning, they received help from organizers of the Communist-led Workers Unity League and then from the All-Canadian Congress of Labour.

The newly-formed CSU was a militant union which rapidly achieved a substantial improvement of wages and conditions aboard ship. In the late forties, economist H.A. Logan described the role of the CSU:

> It has brought the industry up from a condition of long hours, low pay, lack of ventilation and safety inspection ... It has won collective bargaining rights for the crews of the majority of Great Lakes vessels and of some on the Atlantic and Pacific seaboards; it has obtained improved feeding and sleeping conditions, and brought the four-hour watch system to the merchant fleets ...[1]

This achievement did not endear the CSU to the shipping companies and during a 1948 strike they made their first move to break the union. The shippers recognized a rival organization, the Canadian Lake Seamen's Union, as bargaining agent for the seamen in an attempt to force seamen to abandon the CSU. This was later described by Mr. Justice Norris as a "failure to respect basic principles and legal obligations".[2]

At the same time, a number of the shipping company owners, together with some top officials of international unions in Canada, approached the head of the SIU in the United States. Alleging that the CSU was dominated by Communists, they asked that the SIU send an organizer to Canada to break the CSU. Seafarers' president Paul Hall obliged by sending in Hal Banks, a former San Quentin inmate.[3] Accordingly, in September 1948, the Canadian district of the SIU was officially formed by a merger between Hall's union and the Canadian Lake Seamen's Union (CLSU). The merger was in line with official AFL policy. As early as 1944 the American Federation of Labor had decided to ignore the existence of the CSU — which was an affiliate of the Trades and Labour Congress of Canada, forerunner of the CLC — and granted jurisdiction over Canadian seamen to the SIU. At its convention that year, the AFL had passed a resolution giving Hall's organization "jurisdiction over seamen and fishermen in all waters of North America and Canada".[4]

At the time, the Canadian TLC condemned the American action as dual unionism, giving two unions jurisdiction over the same workers. Congress president Percy Bengough told AFL president William Green in July 1945 that the resolution conflicted with the existence of a TLC affiliate, the CSU.

The TLC leadership was, at first, prepared to defend the CSU, but the shipping companies and some international unions were determined to see it go. Late in 1948 their opportunity arose. When the CSU rejected the recommendations of a conciliation board, the newly-formed Canadian district of the Seafarers' stepped in by accepting the board's report and signing agreements with the companies on behalf of the seamen who were still members of the CSU. In March 1949, during the CSU dispute with Canadian National Steamships, the same process was repeated. Finally, in December 1950, the CSU received its death blow. On the grounds of alleged Communist domination, the Canadian Labour Relations Board revoked its certification.

One of the most serious conflicts of the TLC's history developed over these raids. The Congress leadership called an emergency conference in Ottawa in 1948 to support the CSU. Many of the "roadmen" — full-time, paid representatives of international unions — opposed the TLC's action. They set up a picket line at the entrance to the conference hall to examine delegates as they arrived.

The TLC executive council, infuriated by the roadmen's behaviour, condemned this "direct and flagrant violation of the Congress constitution".[5] They suspended the Brotherhood of Railway and Steamship Clerks which, under Frank Hall's leadership, had played a leading role in the roadmen's action. The executive council's statement said, "we must always condemn the actions of the Sullivans and Halls in siding with the employers where workers are out on strike".[6] Pat Sullivan had been a president of the CSU and when he undertook to organize the CLSU, he resigned as secretary-treasurer of the TLC.

When the Trades and Labour Congress met in convention that September, the suspension of the Steamship Clerks was the focus of debate. An attempt by the roadmen to overturn the suspension was soundly defeated by the rank and file delegates, with a vote of 545 to 198.[7] In most cases, the international representatives were unable to win the support of delegates from their own unions.

After this convention the TLC executive councillors journeyed to Miami to meet with the leaders of the American Federation. The AFL, alarmed at the weakening power of the international representatives in Canada, tried to force the TLC executive to change the TLC constitution to permit "each international union to deliver a block vote at the convention" through its representatives.[8]

This attempt to undermine the internal democracy of the TLC was condemned by Congress leaders as a move to make their organization a mere appendage of the AFL. Led by Percy Bengough and John Buckley,

the executive council issued a statement, "Co-operation yes, domination no!" Characterizing Frank Hall and the roadmen as "international
representatives discredited by the convention delegates from their own
organizations,"[9] the TLC leaders announced that they had had enough of
international union dictation. If the American unions wanted to secede
from the Congress over the suspension of the Steamship Clerks, the
statement said, they could go ahead. The TLC would take over their
jurisdictions and charter full Canadian unions to represent the workers
involved.

This outburst of national determination was not to last. As the internationals, the AFL, the shipping companies, and the Canadian government
brought increasing pressure to bear on the TLC, its leadership buckled.
Enemies of the CSU used the threat of communism to gain their ends and
by the summer of 1949 the TLC leaders had expelled the 9,000-member
CSU and accepted the SIU under Hal Banks, in its place.

The group of Canadian international union leaders that had been
instrumental in bringing Banks to Canada, had also sponsored his Canadian citizenship. One important character witness for Banks' citizenship
in 1957 was Claude Jodoin, president of the CLC, and a former international union representative of the ILGWU.[10] Within two short years
Jodoin was to lead the fight for the expulsion of Banks and the SIU from the
Congress.

With his union snugly ensconced in Canada, Banks turned to raiding
other unions to increase the Seafarers' memberhsip and help cover the
high administration costs of the SIU and his own personal expenses.
Among his targets in the late 1950s were the CBRT, National Association
of Marine Engineers (NAME), the Canadian Merchant Service Guild
(CMSG), the USWA (representing seamen on several ore carriers), and the
Brotherhood of Maintenance of Way Employees.

Banks' tactics were modelled on those he had used successfully
against the CSU a decade earlier. The SIU conducted negotiations with
employers on behalf of workers belonging to other unions, without
regard for existing contracts or certifications. Banks also guaranteed the
shipping companies that his organization would cover the employers'
legal costs if they were sued for breach of contract by the unions being
raided.   After a first attack on NAME had been repulsed, Banks mounted
a second assault in 1958. The union responded by bringing charges
against the SIU to the CLC. Following hearings before the executive
council of the Congress, the result was SIU suspension from the CLC in
June 1959. On its failure to appear before the 1960 CLC Convention
Banks' union was expelled.

In October 1960 the SIU reached an agreement with the Association of
Lake Carriers, representing the ship owners, to negotiate on behalf of
their unlicensed seamen. Banks pressured the same companies to revoke
their contracts with NAME, covering licensed seamen, in favour of his
union.

Its agreements with the shipping companies concluded, the SIU applied for certification. The Labour Relations Board refused the application on the grounds of fraud. The Supreme Court of Ontario upheld the existing contracts with NAME. Banks was not slowed down by these set-backs; he went ahead and signed additional agreements with the shipping companies. By June 1961 all the companies except Upper Lakes Shipping had signed with the SIU.[11]

Upper Lakes concluded agreements for its unlicensed employees with the bargaining agents recognized by the Labour Relations Board: the CBRT and the Canadian Maritime Union (a new Canadian Union set up in opposition to the SIU with the CLC's backing). The SIU responded by withdrawing its licensed members from the company's vessels, and began a campaign of terror and harassment that eventually led to the appointment of the Norris Commission.

One of the most infamous incidents occurred when the Northern Venture crew was attacked by SIU goons upon arrival at the port of Marquette, Michigan. The Seafarers' had the full backing of the AFL-CIO in this harassment. When CLC president Jodoin contacted AFL-CIO president George Meany to ask him to intervene, to stop the violence, Meany made no response. He was apparently influenced by SIU international president Paul Hall and other powerful members of the Federation's Maritime Trades Department. Later requests for AFL-CIO intervention also went unanswered.

Instead, the executive board of the AFL-CIO's Maritime Trades Department adopted a resolution fully supporting the Seafarers' raids against Canadian affiliates of the CLC. This same resolution also condemned the CBRT, a Canadian union, for "conspiring with the owners of the Northern Venture to undermine the rights of Canadian seamen to man Canadian-owned ships".[12]

This event moved Jodoin to reopen his correspondence with Meany. The CLC president condemned the resolution and warned the AFL-CIO not to intervene in Canadian affairs. He corrected eight "falsehoods" in the Maritime Trades Department statement which, he said, was "clearly based on the fictitious version of the incidents spread in the United States and Canada by representatives of the Seafarers' International Union".[13] The letter concluded with the following warning:

> Any action by the Maritime Trades Department, as outlined in the "resolved" portion of the resolution adopted, will be vigorously protested by this Congress to the AFL-CIO, if necessary by retaliatory action in Canada, and by protest through the Canadian government to the U.S. government.[14]

Still the AFL-CIO refused to act to prevent the harassment of Upper Lakes vessels. The CLC decided its only recourse, in line with Jodoin's letter, would be to ask for government intervention. Accordingly, Jodoin wrote to Prime Minister Diefenbaker in May 1962 describing fourteen instances of harassment, violence and intimidation within the preceding forty-two days. He asked that a full-scale inquiry be undertaken into the activities of the SIU.

In June Jodoin informed the CLC's legal counsel that "through External Affairs, the United States government has received a note on the subject matter. I am recommending to some connections I have that the president of the AFL-CIO, Mr. George Meany, be approached by a high ranking official to the U.S. government, no less than Dean Rusk, Arthur Goldberg or President Kennedy himself, to call a stop to this illogical attitude."[15]

That the CLC would feel compelled to act through the American State Department and the U.S. government to influence the AFL-CIO was an indication of the powerlessness of the Canadian union movement in dealing with U.S. headquarters.

In the same month, Jodoin received a letter from the director of USWA District 4 in the United States informing him of Meany's latest move. The AFL-CIO central body in Duluth had asked Meany whether its members should load ships manned by the Canadian Maritime Union. Meany's response was characteristically blunt:

> I see no reason why a national policy decision is necessary to point out the simple fact that the Seafarers' International Union is an affiliate in good standing with the AFL-CIO while the Canadian Maritime Union is not.[16]

The CLC's options were running out in the face of Meany's continued intransigence. The request for an official inquiry had been turned down on the grounds that it was a provincial, not a federal matter. The exchange of communications between the Department of External Affairs and the American State Department had also brought no results. A boycott was the only option left. On July 5 the CLC issued a press release announcing that "A boycott of ships manned by crews from the Seafarers' International Union was undertaken in the Great Lakes and St. Lawrence River areas at 8:00 a.m. today".[17]

This move forced the Canadian government's hand. Mr. Justice Thomas G. Norris of the British Columbia Appeal Court, one of Canada's few admiralty judges, was named to head the Industrial Commission of Inquiry into the Disruption of Shipping.

The CLC was caught between two fires. On the one hand, it was opposed in principle to government intervention in the affairs of the labour movement. On the other hand, it was evident that, despite the fact that Canadian ships manned by Canadian seamen belonging to a Canadian union were being harassed by members of an American union, a one-time affiliate of the CLC, the Canadian labour movement had little or no power to control the activities of this international union operating in Canada so long as the AFL-CIO refused to help.

The CLC was forced to ignore its long-standing opposition to government intervention in union affairs and welcome the government inquiry. The boycott was called off, and the CLC negotiated with the government to restrict the inquiry to the activities of the SIU. The CLC had recommended to the Commission that it determine the SIU to be "not a bona fide trade union"[18] and that negotiations take place with the American government to ensure an end to the harassment of Canadian ships and seamen in U.S. ports.

Instead, the Commission recommended that "special federal legislation be passed as an immediate interim measure putting the maritime transportation unions in Canada or the maritimes transportation section of the unions . . . under government trusteeship".[19] Thus even Canadian unions such as the CBRT and the Canadian Maritime Union were liable to trusteeship. This upset the CLC leaders who were also unhappy with the inadequate safeguards Norris proposed regarding the harassment of Canadian crews in the United States.

A long series of negotiations with the Department of Labour followed. Although the CLC was unable to have the trusteeship restricted to the SIU, it did manage to win concessions. A trusteeship would be set up " on the understanding that [it] would be of temporary duration, and that the legislation providing for it would contain other safeguards including the progressive removal of the trusteeship . . ."[20] But the battle over this poin was still not complete. The Americans had yet to get into the act. Theii move came from the Maritime Trades Department of the AFL-CIO when it passed resolutions condemning both the CLC and the CBRT, terming the Norris Commission a "union-busting program instigated by the Conservative government of Canada for the purpose of destroying the Seafarers' International Union of North America, Canadian District, at the behest of the Canadian ship owners unwilling to pay decent wages . . ."[21]

Telegrams were sent to the heads of all international unions by SIU president Paul Hall, informing them of the resolutions. In reply, CLC president Jodoin sent telegrams to the same leaders, advising them that any attempt by American unions to influence the course of Canadian legislation would be deeply resented in Canada, and would prove harmful to the future of international unionism.[22] As it turned out, the Americans were willing to take this risk.

In the meantime, the CLC executive had attempted to end the harassment of Canadian union members in U.S. ports. In August 1963 a delegation of officers from the Canadian Department of Labour fruitlessly met with the American Secretary of Labor to try to win U.S. government co-operation. The Canadian union leaders were once more thrown back on their own resources. When a Canadian ship was dynamited in Chicago, Jodoin decided to have another try at winning Meany's co-operation. He wrote to the AFL-CIO president about the incident. Meany's reply merely asked for "information".[23]

Despite insults and let-downs, the Congress was trying to negotiate a private, as opposed to governmental, trusteeship. This was to be administered jointly by the CLC and the AFL-CIO, thus giving the American unions a substantial say in what happened to the SIU in Canada. The CLC's eagerness to involve the AFL-CIO in a trusteeship arrangement, after the long history of its indifference to the Canadians' calls for help, was based on the hope that such involvement would gain AFL-CIO enforced protection of Canadian seamen in U.S. ports.

One of the Canadian unions involved, the CBRT, was understandably perturbed by this CLC proposal. Its president warned the CLC that the union would be forced to make an "agonizing reappraisal" of its affiliation with the Congress if such an arrangement was made.[24]

The Canadian government was not willing to go along with the idea of a private trusteeship, so in September 1963 Jodoin co-operated with the Deputy Minister of Labour in drawing up a draft memorandum of understanding, laying out the principles of government trusteeship. The following day a meeting was held in Boston. It was attended by the Canadian Minister and Deputy Minister of Labour, the American Secretary and Assistant Secretary of Labor, CLC secretary-treasurer Donald MacDonald, and Lain Kirkland, executive assistant to George Meany, later to become secretary-treasurer of the AFL-CIO.

The Americans withdrew to hold a private discussion on the draft plans. When they returned, the U.S. Secretary of Labor, Mr. Willard Wirtz, emphasized that "if it [the memorandum of understanding] raised the question of government versus private trusteeship of the SIU in Canada, that they favoured the latter, private trusteeship, and regarded the former with complete disfavour".[25] Wirtz went on to say that the sections of the memorandum that dealt with Canadian government involvement were unacceptable. The fact that what was "unacceptable" consisted of a trusteeship to be imposed by the Canadian government on a union representing Canadian seamen and employed by Canadian companies on ships of Canadian registry did not deter the American government officials.

Furthermore, Kirkland, on behalf of the AFL-CIO, insisted on the SIU's right to veto the trusteeship. Thus, both the American government and the American trade union centre were determined to dictate the decisions of Canadian labour and the Canadian government. As the account of the meeting put it, "their position was that neither the U.S. government nor the AFL-CIO could be party to a document that provided for the imposition of a trusteeship on a union by the Canadian or any government".[26]

Not only did Wirtz and Kirkland insist on changes at the Boston meeting, but even after the memorandum had been redrafted according to their demands they wanted to alter it further. Kirkland discussed the meeting with Paul Hall and then telephoned the CLC offices to offer further amendments. Apparently, Hall had demanded that two of the three trustees should be appointed directly by the AFL-CIO. This astonishing proposal would have given Hall and the U.S. union officials the choice of the majority of the trustees.[27]

Political scientist David Kwavnick summarized these negotiations as follows:

> ... the United States government and the AFL-CIO had been made parties to the settlement of a Canadian problem in order to obtain freedom from harassment for Canadian ships in American ports. As a result of their involvement, the U.S. government and the AFL-CIO had been able to obtain concessions which implied acceptance of their major objective — that the trusteeship be non-governmental and, with respect to the SIU, voluntary. This meant that the success of the trusteeship would be dependent upon the co-operation of Paul Hall.[28]

Again the CLC was caught in a bind. If it continued to insist on AFL-CIO involvement the trusteeship would be meaningless. On the other hand, there was no other way of guaranteeing the safety of Canadian workers and the integrity of Canadian unions. After a week of deliberations, the Congress decided to accept a government trusteeship, which came into effect after passage of the Maritime Transportation Unions Trustees Act.

The trusteeship did not in fact curb the SIU. It did not end the harassment of Canadian ships in U.S. ports. As Kwavnick described it:

> In the end, the policy of violence paid off for the SIU of North America. While the United States government, at the behest of the AFL-CIO, condoned the violence of the SIU, the SIU leadership was able to use this violence as a bargaining counter to protect their interest in negotiations with the Canadian authorities.[29]

Nor did the trusteeship fundamentally change the organization of the SIU. Banks had already moved on, skipping bail in Montreal and returning to New York after being convicted of conspiracy in the assault of a rival union officer. When Canadian law enforcement officers failed to locate him, Banks was found living on a luxury yacht in New York by a *Toronto Star* reporter. As it turned out, the American authorities refused to extradict Banks. The rest of the SIU leadership in Canada was not changed.

The victory of the SIU, the AFL-CIO, and the American government was practically complete. The CLC was impotent in the face of the AFL-CIO, just as the Canadian government was impotent in the face of the American government. Canadian management authority John Crispo summed up the outcome of the trusteeship along precisely these lines:

> In return for an undertaking on the part of the SIU to end the boycott of ships manned by Canadian Maritime Union crews in American ports, the trustees agreed to maintain the affiliation of the SIU of Canada with the SIU of North America and would further appear to have agreed to remove no other leading officers of the SIU of Canada except its

president, whom they had already ousted. Because of the international ramifications of the dispute and the renewed disruption of shipping which would easily have occurred on the St. Lawrence Seaway, this may have been the only way out in view of the imminent opening of a new shipping season.[30]

The SIU's victory was complete when in 1966 it was readmitted to the CLC over the protests of the B.C. Federation of Labour, the CBRT, and two top officers of the Canadian Maritime Union. Two years later calls for the expulsion of the Seafarers' were heard again when Jack Staples, president of the CMU, warned, "they haven't changed since 1962 ... [from being] a gangster movement. They'll come in here and take over if we don't watch out."[31] The CLC leadership, firmly under the influence of AFL-CIO internationals, disagreed. The SIU had become a bona fide union, they insisted, with democracy and no violence.

So the SIU still operated in Canada in 1975, facing yet another official government investigation of charges of violence and blacklisting. Back in 1963, the *Economist* commented on the findings of the Norris Commission in words that could have been written with even greater conviction in 1975. The article spoke of the dispute as one "which in many American eyes is primarily a trade union affair," but "is seen by most Canadians as a question of national independence. [Canadian] resentment concentrated on the AFL-CIO's apparent tendency to treat the CLC merely as a troublesome subsidiary. The dispute will hasten the day when the Canadian labour movement severs all ties with its sister movement in the United States."[32]

1. H. A. Logan, *Trade Unions in Canada* (Toronto: Macmillan Company of Canada, 1948), p. 289.

2. David Kwavnick, *Organized Labour and Pressure Politics* (Montreal: McGill-Queen's University Press, 1972), p. 145. *Report of an Industrial Inquiry Commission relating to the Disruption of Shipping on the Great Lakes, the St. Lawrence River System, and Connecting Waters* (Ottawa: Queen's Printer, 1963), p. 48. (Hereinafter cited as Norris Report.)

3. Ibid., p. 146.

4. Charles Lipton, *The Trade Union Movement of Canada 1827-1959* (Toronto: NC Press, 1973), 3rd edition, p. 276, from Trades and Labour Congress of Canada, 63rd Annual Convention, 1948, *Proceedings*, pp. 156-157.

5. Lipton, op. cit., p. 277, from *Searchlight*, September 30, 1948; *Canadian Tribune*, September 20, 1948.

6. Ibid.

7. Ibid., p. 278, from *Trades and Labour Congress Journal*, March 1949, pp. 12-13.

8. Ibid., p. 279.

9. Ibid.

10. Peter Gzowski, "Hal Banks: The Fight to Break Canada's Waterfront Warlord", *Maclean's*, May 18, 1963, p. 51.

11. The sequence of events is described in detail by David Kwavnick, op. cit.

12. Kwavnick, op. cit., p. 150, *The Maritime Register* (official publication of the Maritime Trades Department, AFL-CIO), October-November 1961, p. 2.

13. Ibid., Letter January 25, 1962. Jodoin to Meany, CLC files.

14. Ibid.

15. Ibid., p. 151, Letter June 13, 1962. Jodoin to CLC Legal Counsel, CLC files.

16. Ibid., Telegram June 5, 1961. J. P. Maloney, director, District 4, USWA to Jodoin, CLC files.

17. Canadian Labour Congress, *News Release*, July 5, 1962.

18. Kwavnick, op. cit., p. 154, CLC, *Submission by the Canadian Labour Congress and Certain Affiliated Organizations to the Industrial Inquiry Commission*, March 1963, p. 65.

19. Ibid., p. 155, Norris Report, pp. 304-305.

20. Ibid., p. 156, Letter July 31, 1963. George V. Haythorne, Deputy Minister of Labour, to Jodoin, CLC files.

21. Ibid., p. 161, Affixed to letter September 12, 1963. P. M. McGavin, executive secretary-treasurer, Maritime Trades Department, to Meany, CLC files.

22. Ibid.

23. Ibid., p. 159, Telegram September 10, 1963. Meany to Jodoin, CLC files.

24. Ibid., p. 160, Letter October 3, 1963. W. J. Smith, CBRT national president, to Jodoin, CLC files.

25. Ibid., p. 162, *Minutes of Meeting, September 28, 1963, Hilton Statler Hotel, Boston, Mass.* (typescript).

26. Ibid.

27. Ibid., p. 163.

28. Ibid.

29. Ibid., p. 164.

30. John Crispo, *International Unionism: A Study in Canadian-American Relations* (Toronto: McGraw-Hill, 1967), p. 130.

31. *The Telegram* (Toronto), May 7, 1968.

32. *Economist*, November 30, 1963.

PART III
The New Nationalism in Canadian Labour

Introduction

Events of the first half of the 1970s highlighted the difference of opinion between an increasingly nationalist membership and a largely continentalist leadership in Canada's international unions. The existence in 1975 of some 100 American-based unions embracing an estimated 1.5 million Canadian unionists alongside an estimated 1.3 million unionists in about 95 Canadian unions (excluding about 250,000 teachers and nurses) had created tensions between these two groupings over the structure and strategies of Canada's union movement.[1]

Canadian unions had tended to be more nationalist in their broad concerns and in their attitudes to Canada's union movement in particular. The new protectionism of the American unions added a new and pressing economic consideration to the other problems of the international union structure and the business union approach.

This gap between an increasingly more nationalist union membership and the majority of the Canadian leadership in American-based unions had produced conflicts, too, in labour's political arm, the New Democratic Party. This had important implications for labour's future role in independent political action.

These conflicts within the union movement occurred in the broader context of the growth of nationalism in Canada. Public opinion polls in Canada have shown a continuing and sometimes dramatic trend toward increased nationalism over the past twenty years. While only twenty-seven per cent of Canadians thought their way of life was being too heavily influenced by the United States in 1956, fifty-three per cent expressed this opinion ten years later.[2] Eighty per cent of Canadians thought that relations with the United States were good or excellent in 1955; by 1974 this had declined to fifty-four per cent.[3] In 1972 almost as many Canadians considered their country to be a "colony" of the United States as thought it to be a "partner".[4]

In 1972, five times as many of the Canadians polled thought that American investment in Canada should be screened as thought it should not,[5] and in 1974 only eighteen per cent opposed the idea of legislation restricting or controlling further foreign investment.[6] In a 1963 poll, forty-eight per cent thought Canada's dependence on the United States to be a good thing; ten years later, only thirty-four per cent held that opinion.[7]

The shift in public opinion over the years is shown in the summary of Gallup Poll results in Table 12.

TABLE 12
Canadian Public Opinion on U.S. Investment in Canada

"Now thinking about U.S. capital invested in Canada — do you think there is enough now or would you like to see more U.S. capital invested in this country?"

	Enough Now	Like to See More	Don't Know
1964	46%	33%	21%
1967	60%	24%	16%
1970	62%	25%	13%
1972	67%	22%	11%
1975	71%	16%	13%

Source: *The Gallup Report,* July 19, 1975.

By 1975 the number of Canadians who believed Canada had "enough" U.S. capital was over four times as numerous as the number that wanted "more" capital.

Polls like these try to measure the attitudes of Canadians in general. More specialized studies, looking at particular segments of the population, have shown that there are differences in the degree of nationalism among various groups. For example, John Fayerweather, an American social scientist, studied the attitudes of four "elite groups" in Canada in 1971 and 1972: members of parliament, permanent government officials, heads of business firms and labour union leaders. He compared these groups with other sections of the general population.[8]

He found that blue-collar workers — many of whom were members of trade unions — along with students and teachers had the most unfavourable attitudes toward the activities of foreign corporations in Canada and their effects on the Canadian way of life. Businessmen were, on the whole, continentalist in their outlook; they tended to view the activities of foreign corporations in Canada favourably.

One of Fayerweather's questions dealt with attitudes toward the

Canada-U.S. Auto Pact of 1965. All four of the "élite groups," including trade union leaders, tended to take a favourable view of the automotive agreement. While the businessmen showed themselves most favourable, the trade union leaders, members of parliament and civil service officials were all close behind. In sharp contrast to these groups, the blue-collar workers were shown to have a decidedly unfavourable view of the Auto Pact. White-collar workers and teachers responded similarly.

Fayerweather commented that the labour leaders, "despite negative public statements about foreign investment . . . took a rather pragmatic, essentially favourable view of foreign firms. . . . Their negative opinions were related more to specific actions like plant shut-downs than a general desire to check foreign investment."[9]

Many union leaders in Canada claimed to be "ahead" of their membership on national economic and political issues. But as Fayerweather's questions showed, they were "ahead" of rank and file workers only if "ahead" meant tolerating or favouring U.S. control of the Canadian economy.

Continentalism, the belief that the United States and Canada are basically so similar that the border is an unfortunate accident of history, is often expressed in the view that the North American economy should be fully integrated; that the "artificial" trading barriers between Canada and the United States should be replaced by "free trade". Canadians have historically rejected this position — most notably, perhaps, in the famous "reciprocity election" of 1911 when Sir Wilfrid Laurier's Liberal government was defeated on precisely this question.

Yet in July 1975 the Economic Council of Canada released a report advocating a policy of free trade between Canada and the United States, and also between Canada and Western Europe and Japan.[10] There were prominent labour representatives on the ECC: among them were Joe Morris, president of the Canadian Labour Congress, Donald Taylor, assistant to the Canadian director of the Steelworkers, and Canadian Union of Public Employees president Stanley Little.[11] These leaders had thrown their weight behind free trade with the United States and further continental integration.

Asked about the free trade policy, Donald Taylor defended the ECC report and declared that the labour representatives had been able to modify it by including Western Europe and Japan in the free trade package. Stanley Little also voiced support of this continentalist proposal.[12]

It is within the broad context of this burgeoning Canadian nationalism that many Canadian unionists have been pressing for increased autonomy within the internationals, and for complete independence from them.

On the whole, Canadian leaders of the internationals resisted this trend. Although some accepted the direction of their members and pressed hard for autonomy and even for independence, as the first chapter in this section shows, the majority of them have defended the international tie.

Some international union officials have fought a rear-guard action against the growing strength of Canadian unions. One of the threats they perceived has been the rise of the Canadian Union of Public Employees to a powerful all-Canadian organization that might one day swing the balance of power in the Canadian Labour Congress toward Canadian unionism. Through the CLC, the internationals tried to limit CUPE's jurisdiction in the early seventies and thus postpone its rise to power in the Congress.

The Canadian Union of Public Employees, along with other Canadian unions, responded by pledging itself to reform the CLC and replace its international leadership at the 1974 CLC Convention. The mild guidelines for autonomy that the convention finally adopted antagonized the leaders of the most thoroughly dominated internationals in the country — the craft unions in the building trades. This served to bring a series of conflicts between their nationalist membership and continentalist officers into public view.

One example of an international union which enabled its Canadian members to vote on whether to become independent — and which then did so — is the Canadian section of the United Paperworkers International Union, which severed its ties with the international union in 1974 and went on to form a fully independent union. There were similar developments in some smaller international unions. And although it seldom made headline copy in the press, within the largest and most important American unions in Canada, like the USWA, rank and file pressure for greater autonomy and independence mounted steadily.

As this undercurrent gained strength in the American-based unions, the local break-aways that once seemed a major vehicle for gaining Canadian union independence lost their former significance.

This section examines the new nationalism of Canadian workers in the early 1970s, and their attempts to change their union organizations to reflect this new national awareness.

---

1. These estimates are derived from a projected 10 per cent growth rate for the union movement for 1974 and 1975 based on the 10.1 per cent growth rate of 1972-1973. Under these conditions, the Canadian union movement would be 3.1 million by the end of 1975.

2. *The Gallup Report*, May 25, 1974.

3. *The Gallup Report*, May 22, 1974.

4. *The Gallup Report*, May 10, 1972.

5. *The Gallup Report*, February 16, 1972.

6. *The Gallup Report*, March 2, 1974.

7. *The Gallup Report*, August 26, 1972.

8. John Fayerweather, *Foreign Investment in Canada* (Toronto: Oxford University Press, 1974), p. 19.

9. Ibid., p. 51.

10. Economic Council of Canada, *Looking Outward: A New Trade Strategy for Canada* (Ottawa: Information Canada, 1975).

11. Ibid.

12. *The Toronto Star*, February 20, 1975.

CHAPTER 13

Canadian Labour Leaders and Nationalism

It is a great tribute to the intelligence and maturity of Canadian workers that they are taking on the full responsibility of their unions in Canada.

Donald MacDonald
President, CLC
Referring to Canadian paper workers, 1974.[1]

Of course we will continue to be harassed by that clutch of self-serving individuals who trumpet their nationalistic and chauvinistic platitudes, setting worker against worker, and thereby dividing and weakening the labour movement.

Donald MacDonald
In the same address, 1974.

The real issue is not whether independence will eventually be gained. I think that it is a foregone conclusion, and that it will take place within this twenty-year span.

William Dodge
Secretary-treasurer, CLC
With reference to the independence of Canadian unions, May 1973.[2]

The rising tide of nationalism among Canadian workers in the 1970s had brought in its wake a great variety of organizational and structural responses in the union movement. Likewise, labour leaders in Canada spanned the spectrum from unbending hostility to the new mood of wholehearted enthusiasm for the cause of transforming Canadian branches of the internationals into fully independent national unions in their own right. There was no simple explanation for particular responses from union leaders. For each of them an intricate weave of diverse elements came into play. These elements included personal commitment to nationalism or continentalism, vested interest in a career with the international union, feelings of loyalty within a particular union and sensitivity to the demands and needs of the rank and file.

That particular responses of union leaders might change dramatically was not an unreasonable prediction given the vitality and rapid growth of the nationalist movement in the seventies. Union members were changing their minds on this important issue; and so might their leaders.

In 1968 Henri Lorrain told Canadian paper workers that it would be tragic if labour's march for "economic, social and political reform was subverted by the ravenous appetite of nationalism".[3] Only six years later, he was to become president of the Canadian Paperworkers Union after he had led 52,000 paper workers out of their connection with the international.

Lorrain's background had been one of deep commitment to international unionism. During the CIO organizing years, the Lorrain home in Gatineau, Quebec had been a refuge for U.S. industrial union organizers. On the surface it seemed that he might always be a champion of the American unions in Canada. Indeed, when in February 1974 the president of Canadian Paperworkers locals voted to call a referendum of their members, Lorrain received a telephone call from his 92-year-old mother, demanding to know what had happened to "la fraternité". He explained that times had changed.[4]

Similarly, Donald Secord of the Canadian Brotherhood of Railway Transport and General Workers advocated in 1969 that his union become part of an international.[5] By 1973 he was predicting that nationalism "will continue to grow until Canada has an entirely self-governing and self-sufficient labour movement. That may take another five years, maybe ten years, maybe longer. But it will come in the lifetime of most of us here."[6]

One of the best examples of an equivocal stance was Dennis McDermott, Canadian director of the United Auto Workers. Since the UAW was no longer a member of the AFL-CIO (it disaffiliated in 1968), McDermott was free to criticize the mainstream of U.S. unionism without implicating his own organization in the process. Always forthright, McDermott had spoken frequently on this subject, enough to provide some insight into his position.

At the January 1973 meeting of the UAW's Canadian District Council, he referred to the "conflict of interest between Canadians and Americans" in unions other than the UAW:[7]

> I am very sad when I view the spectacle of the degeneration of the U.S. union movement with a few notable exceptions, including our own UAW, by their embrace of Nixon. . . .

In the UAW thus far, at least, there has been no conflict of interest between Canadians and Americans on matters such as the Auto Pact, DISC, the Burke-Hartke Bill, the imposition of the ten per cent surtax. . . . But look at a large part of U.S. labour, and you see the diametric opposite. Small wonder there is a sharp reaction among Canadian labour people to that scene.

While emphasizing that "I, for one, do not look forward to that prospect," McDermott insisted that "one day very soon there has to be a wholesale review by labour itself of U.S.-based unions in Canada". Labour would have to face the "simple question . . . is a union genuinely international in scope and structure or is the Canadian section merely a satellite of an American union?"[8] There will be a "moment of truth", McDermott went on to say, which "if it hasn't already arrived is not too far away".[9]

McDermott distinguished between "genuine internationalism, with Canada as a true partner" and "a U.S. union with a branch-plant mentality and Canada treated as an occasional patronizing after-thought".[10]

These comments show McDermott in one of his most perceptive moments. But these remarks were accompanied by an expression of McDermott's apparent lack of confidence in the ability of Canadian workers to make independent unionism viable:

> . . . regardless of any emotional statements we might be inclined to make, very little over here in Canada can be achieved unless we can depend on the united and total support of the international union as a whole.[11]

McDermott had frequently argued that the real criterion for a union was "that it be effective — not that it be Canadian".[12] He was sceptical of the ability of Canadian workers to run "effective" national unions. Beyond this, he feared that the labour movement would "fall into the hands of mickey-mouse all-Canadian unions"[13] under the influence of the "phony nationalism" of the "yahoos on the right and the yahoos on the left".[14]

The core of McDermott's worries about Canadian unions was re-vealed in a speech he made at St. Clair College in Windsor, where he shared the platform with UAW international president, Leonard Wood-cock. "Give us nationalistic unions" in the face of giant corporations like General Motors, he said, and it would be "a great exercise in going down the drain in an all-Canadian fashion".[15] The message was that Canadian unions alone do not have the muscle to deal with giant multi-national corporations:

> I get sick of these people saying we should be fragmented and inde-pendent. Any one of these national unions would keel over in a dead faint if General Motors so much as looked at them.[16]

Jean Beaudry of the Steelworkers, a former vice-president of the CLC, expressed similar opinions in August 1973 when he attacked "two-bit" nationalism. "We had better think twice about trying to feel we're big enough . . . and don't need the help of anyone else."[17] Terry Meagher, secretary-treasurer of the Ontario Federation of Labour, also echoed this sentiment when he said "with multinational corporations it's suicide to talk about nationalism". There is a contradiction implicit here, and McDermott saw it when he talked about the "conflict of interest" between the American and Canadian memberships of the internationals. In 1973 he had observed that in the UAW, "thus far at least" such a conflict had not arisen. But two years later (as seen in chapter ten) the conflict had clearly moved into the UAW.

In the first half of the 1970s the Canadian leaders of the USWA — Canadian director William Mahoney, late District 6 director Larry Sefton, and his successor, Lynn Williams — adopted a defensive posture in the face of Canadian national unionism. A successful break-away by a large local at Kitimat, and an all-but-successful one at Trail, produced violent antagonism. Mahoney called the break-away movement "a clear warning to ourselves and the Canadian labour movement of the growth of a new and insidious form of company unionism,"[18] while Williams said the Kitimat break-away was a result of "illogical nationalism" which had been used "to conceal the real issue: effective unionism".[19]

A few months later, referring to Canadian unions, Larry Sefton, USWA District 6 director, wrote in a similar vein: "We face a dangerous ploy by the bosses and their unwitting accomplices. I am talking of course about nationalism."[20]

This argument that nationalism was in the corporate rather than in the workers' interest, however, runs counter to statements of corporation spokesmen in Canada, warning against the dangers of Canadian nationalism. The corporations and the banks were explicitly continentalist in their outlook and frequently bemoaned the existence of nationalism in Canada.[21] Indeed, spokesmen of American and Canadian corporations and of the banks have often warned against growing nationalism in Canada. In the case of Peter Riggin, vice-president of the giant Noranda industrial complex, anti-nationalism was linked to his assertion that an all-Canadian labour movement could create problems for businessmen. He pointed out that while U.S. labour leaders accepted the free enterprise system, their Canadian counterparts were more ideologically oriented. Riggin was particularly suspicious of Quebec union leaders who, he said, appeared bent on overthrowing the system.[22]

The late Larry Sefton best expressed the suspicions of many top Canadian labour leaders concerning Canadian nationalism:

> Nationalism has never put a penny in a worker's pocket and it never will. Nationalism has never rallied the workers to anything but the trenches for conflicts between the races of people on the earth.[23]

But Sefton's position ignored the fact that Canadian nationalism has always been a *defensive* nationalism, directed against control by imperial powers; England in an earlier period, and the United States after the Second World War. And it also failed to account for the rapidly-emerging connection between Canadian jobs and the need for Canadian-based unions which would fight to protect them.

At the same policy conference William Mahoney took a somewhat different tack. He suggested that "we ought to spend some time dealing with nationalism, because I'm a Canadian nationalist and I am sure that applies to everybody in this room. ... We do not have to decry legitimate nationalism," he continued, "in order to realize that even a Canadian nationalist must operate within a world in which people are becoming more interdependent every day."[24]

This was similar to McDermott's view that Canadian workers would achieve little "unless we can depend on the united and total support of the international union as a whole". But the notion of "interdependence" overlooked the basic problem of a developing conflict of interest between Canadian and American trade unionists.

The 1974 Canadian Policy Conference of the USWA produced another defence of international unionism in Canada. The official policy statement included a passage urging that, "to link together issues of national identity and trade union structure would be most unrepresentative and most suicidal for even the Canadian integrity of our union".[25] The reason they gave for separating "national identity" and "trade union structure" was that "significant numbers of steel workers, in English-speaking Canada and in Quebec, hold different and even conflicting views on where they put their national identity".[26]

The argument is that since English-speaking Canadians often differ with Quebecois workers on their "nationalism", the two could reduce their differences by coming together in an American union. This ignored the fact that workers in Quebec had been able to link their national identity to their trade union structure by building their own unions, in the Confederation des syndicats nationaux (CSN) and the Corporation des enseignants du Quebec (CEQ). English-Canadians have done the same thing, particularly in the public sector. In organizations such as the Canadian Union of Public Employees, the Letter Carriers or Public Service Alliance, English Canadians and Quebecois have reduced their differences while retaining their national identities.

The Steelworkers' leadership and Mahoney were on more solid ground when Mahoney stated in 1973 that it was tragic that "just when corporations are becoming more multinational and more global in nature, the trade union movement is breaking down into regional blocs".[27] However, his conclusion that Canadian workers should remain in American unions ignored the alternative of co-operation on the basis of equality. Thus Mahoney continued to insist that "rampant nationalists" had no solution to this problem.

> It's an historical fact that once an ultra-nationalist gets going and can't find a simple solution to a problem, then he has to find a scapegoat as a substitute for a solution; and international unions have become the scapegoat of Canadian ultra-nationalists.[28]

Mahoney's distinction between "ultra" nationalism, which supported independent Canadian unions, and "legitimate" nationalism, which left the internationals intact, masked the inconsistencies in his position. He would recognize the new nationalism — but only so long as it left everything unchanged. He supported the Canadian USWA's policy in favour of greater "autonomy", saying that there was need for an "evolutionary change that will provide common ties but less organic integration". He never made it clear, however, why co-operation between Canadian and American unionists would not be best carried out between two co-operating organizations instead of within a single international union.

In a continuing effort by the steel union leadership in Canada to convince Canadian workers that nationalism was against their interests, I.W. Abel, American president of the USWA, was invited to speak to the annual Canadian Steelworkers Policy Conference in Toronto in May 1975. This is the body that presumably decides on Canadian policies, without the benefit of international headquarters. Abel referred to Philip Murray in the United States and Charles Millard in Canada as people who had the "good sense to know that Steelworkers on both sides of the border in North America should be united into one, big, strong union. These wise leaders," he said, "knew that national boundaries are nothing but *lines of convenience....*"[29] (emphasis added)

He continued, "but there are those in the United States and Canada who today find fault with our international structure. In the name of nationalism they would ... carve up our union and serve it up to corporate industry wrapped in flags." He warned that "in Canada, there are those who regard international unionism as detrimental to Canadian national identity and they express ridiculous rumours about union attempts to colonize Canadians or exploit members of this country".

Quoting the late Larry Sefton he said, "Nationalism has never put a penny in a worker's pocket, and it never will. ... And there is no all-Canadian union that can match our achievements in bargaining, in social programmes or in political action." Abel's 1975 address to Canadian steel workers was reminiscent of the pro-conscription lectures read to Canadian workers in 1917 by Samuel Gompers, president of the AFL.

One of the strongest opponents of Canadian unionism among union leaders has been Mike Rygus, Canadian vice-president of the International Association of Machinists. His continentalist position, expressed in 1973 with his insistence that "it's complete, sheer insanity to see the Canadian border as the beginning and end of everything,"[30] was reinforced by his refusal to allow the use of French as one of the official languages at the 1975 Montreal convention of his union. This action, together with his characterization of opposing union leaders as escapists into a "hippie cult", led some 7,500 Air Canada mechanics and airport workers to petition the IAM headquarters in Washington for greater autonomy for the Canadian section.[31]

In 1973 Rygus proclaimed that the controversy over Canadian unionism was causing Canadians to "really miss what the real issues of our country are".[32] He argued that even if every union were purely Canadian, there would still be problems of unemployment and trade, concluding from this that Canadian workers needed international unions.

Ironically, the "trade" problems to which Rygus referred are one of the best reasons for an immediate move toward independent unions as a solution to the conflict of interest between American and Canadian workers.

Rygus made the news again in 1974 when he announced that the IAM locals in the pulp and paper industry would not co-operate in upcoming negotiations with the newly-independent Canadian Paperworkers Union. He argued that by breaking off from the international, the paper workers had been seriously weakened.[33] President Lorrain of the CPU sent a blistering letter to Rygus, taking him to task for his "damaging and divisive public utterances".[34] He reminded Rygus that 52,000 Canadian workers had joined the CPU while only 3,000 had stayed with the international, and that his union represented more than five times as many mechanical workers in the industry as the IAM claimed to represent. Lorrain pointed out as well that it was the CPU "which in recent months spear-headed the drive in the paper industry to open contracts in mid-term, to successfully negotiate cost of living escalator protection and interim wage increases".

One of the most dramatic responses to growing nationalism among Canadian workers came directly from the Canadian Labour Congress in 1973 when the CLC Executive Council authorized a one million dollar campaign to combat break-aways of locals from the "internationals". Eighty-seven union officers, representing more than sixty-five unions, held a closed meeting in Ottawa in May 1973 where they worked out a programme labelled as "organizing the unorganized in co-operation with affiliates". Calling for the defence of CLC affiliates against raids by outside groups, it included co-operation of affiliated unions for offensive and defensive action, the planning and execution of specific projects, and a million-dollar fund-raising campaign. The CLC was to be asked for $50,000, with the balance to come from affiliates. A highlight of the campaign was to be a public relations drive "to expose destructive activities" of "break-aways".[35]

The Ottawa meeting had been kept quiet. Apparently, Congress officers did not want to create the impression that they were pushing the panic button. However, the meeting's decisions were leaked to the press, creating the very impression they sought to avoid. *The Globe and*

Mail featured a front page story under a three-line head: "Union officials agree on $1 million programme to fight break-aways". The campaign faded away, however, when the threat of break-aways subsided.

The top leadership of the CLC has always had to straddle an uncomfortably wide fence on the national union issue. Its tendency has been to lean in the direction of the international unions which provide much of the CLC's funds. In May 1974, just before his retirement from the Congress presidency, Donald MacDonald decried those "who want to beat the drums of chauvinistic and jingoistic nationalism," warning that they were "playing with fire".[36]

MacDonald equated the U.S.-dominated international unions with real internationalism. He said that labour should be pushing for internationalism that extended beyond the borders of North America. MacDonald saw the international unions as a step in that direction, the harbingers of internationalism. Yet in his capacity as president of the International Confederation of Free Trade Unions, speaking at the USWA Atlantic City convention in September 1974, he had to urge the American unions to join the international body which the AFL-CIO had left in the 1960s because it was too radical.[37]

Nevertheless, in his final presidential address to the 1974 CLC convention, MacDonald recognized the important step taken that year by the Canadian paper workers:

> It is a great tribute to the intelligence and maturity of Canadian workers that they are taking on the full responsibility of their unions in Canada. We also note the responsible fashion in which one of our affiliates has chosen to separate its Canadian membership from its international. . . .[38]

But immediately after saying that the Paperworkers' decision "is an outstanding and in some regards an historic move," and that the CPU's "members will be well served as a result of their decisions," MacDonald warned the delegates not to "regard that decision as a blueprint for all international unions". In an abrupt turn-about, he launched into an attack on nationalism:

> Of course, we will continue to be harassed by that clutch of self-serving individuals who trumpet their nationalistic and chauvinistic platitudes, setting worker against worker, and thereby dividing and weakening the labour movement.

While MacDonald's speech reflected the ambivalence of many Canadian leaders in international unions to the growth of nationalism, other CLC officers had been more willing to give guarded recognition to the move for Canadian labour independence. When former secretary-treasurer William Dodge was asked whether the Paperworkers' referendum should serve as an example to other internationals, he replied:

It is certainly a democratic model to which no one can take exception. Whether or not moves of a similar nature will be made by other unions remains with them and their members to decide.[39]

Joe Morris, at the time executive vice-president of the Congress, agreed that the Paperworkers' referendum was a "forward-looking approach to the question of Canadian nationalism"[40] and predicted that it would undoubtedly influence the decisions of other international unions although their circumstances might be different. Unions with "autonomy", he suggested, might find it easier to fully separate.

Both Morris and Dodge were at the time eyeing the presidency of the CLC, and it is possible that these statements were influenced by that fact. Nevertheless, their views showed somewhat greater flexibility on the question than former CLC leaders. This was especially significant since the CLC has always been an important barometer of trends among the Canadian leaders of international unions. And it is in the CLC that many of the skirmishes have been fought, particularly around the guidelines on Canadian autonomy. The 1974 CLC convention (see chapter fifteen) provided another episode in the continuing debate over nationalism in the unions.

One of the major underlying causes of these battles was the rapid growth of the Canadian Union of Public Employees to the position of the largest union in Canada.

---

1. Canadian Labour Congress, *Proceedings*, 10th Constitutional Convention, Vancouver, May 1974. p. 4.

2. *The Toronto Star*, May 2, 1973.

3. *The Globe and Mail*, October 2, 1968.

4. *The Windsor Star*, March 9, 1974.

5. See Chapter 18.

6. *The Globe and Mail*, September 18, 1973.

7. Dennis McDermott, *Report of the International Vice-President and Director for Canada*, Canadian UAW Council, Windsor, Ontario, January 13-14, 1973, pp. 5, 15.

8. Ibid., p. 16.

9. Ibid., p. 14.

10. Ibid., p. 15.

11. Ibid., p. 9.

12. *The Financial Post*, March 2, 1974.

13. *The Toronto Star*, February 28, 1973.

14. *The Globe and Mail*, February 28, 1973.

15. *The Windsor Star*, February 2, 1973.

16. *The Telegram*, October 20, 1970.

17. *The Toronto Star*, August 7, 1973.

18. *The Globe and Mail*, October 23, 1972.

19. Ibid.

20. *London Free Press*, May 31, 1973. This speech was read to the USWA Canadian Policy Conference in May 1973 following Sefton's death.

21. In March 1975, R. V. Frastacky, deputy chairman of the Metropolitan Trust Co. of Toronto, told its annual meeting that "Canada must lift itself above the narrow economic nationalism that at present seems to be the fashion in some sectors of Canadian society". (Referring to the Foreign Investment Review Act, Part II.) *The Globe and Mail*, March 22, 1975.

22. *The Toronto Star*, September 1, 1973.

23. Larry Sefton, USWA Canadian Policy Conference, *Directors' Reports*, Montreal, May 31-June 1, 1973, p. 83.

24. Ibid., p. 12.

25. USWA Canadian Policy Conference, *Policy and Resolutions*, Vancouver, May 9-10, 1974, p. 40.

26. Ibid.

27. Jack Williams, "The Steelworkers' Solution is a Constant Move Towards Greater Autonomy", *Labour Gazette*, August 1973, p. 530.

28. Ibid., p. 528.

29. Address by I. W. Abel, USWA Canadian Policy Conference, Toronto, Ontario, May 8, 1975.

30. *The Toronto Star*, March 1, 1973.

31. *The Gazette* (Montreal), March 8, 1975.

32. *The Toronto Star*, March 1, 1973.

33. *The Globe and Mail*, October 25, 1974.

34. Canadian Paperworkers Union, news release to the OFL Convention, October 28, 1974.

35. *The Globe and Mail*, May 10, 1973.

36. Philip Smith, "Labour's Strong Man", *Weekend Magazine*, Vol. 24, No. 18, May 4, 1974.

37. Donald MacDonald, Address to the Seventeenth Constitutional Convention, United Steel Workers of America, *Proceedings*, Atlantic City, New Jersey, September 23-27, 1974, p. 228.

38. Canadian Labour Congress, *Proceedings*, May 1974, p. 4.

39. *The Globe and Mail*, February 6, 1974.

40. Ibid.

CHAPTER 14
CUPE Confronts the CLC Establishment

We believe the [CLC] leadership is blind to the social and political changes that have been occurring right in front of their noses over the past twenty years.

Stan Little
President, CUPE
CUPE convention, 1973[1]

For too long, we have been taking too many orders from the U.S. We are not going to take any more crap from people in the U.S.

Russ Doyle
President, CUPE Local 43
CUPE convention, 1973[2]

The Canadian Union of Public Employees (CUPE) is one of the fastest growing unions in the country. It had doubled its membership between 1963 and 1973 by maintaining the phenomenal growth rate of more than one thousand new members per month,[3] and by mid-1975, with a membership surpassing 210,000, it overtook the Steelworkers and became the largest union in Canada.

The union was born in September 1963 when two older public service unions merged. The National Union of Public Service Employees had roots going back to the formation of the Canadian Electrical Trade Union in 1921, while the National Union of Public Employees dated its beginnings from a 1949 organizational meeting of civic employees.[4]

The 1963 merger of NUPE and NUPSE created a union which was soon to outpace in size and diversity any other organization in the Canadian labour movement. The CUPE locals ranged from the western shores of Vancouver Island all the way to Newfoundland; from Windsor in the south to Yellowknife in the north. It embraced workers in a huge variety of occupations, including helicopter pilots, deep-sea divers, priests, garbagemen, draftsmen, labourers, truck drivers, secretaries, hospital orderlies, cooks and laboratory technicians. Its members worked for school boards, universities, hospitals and nursing homes; municipal public utilities and provincial hydro commissions; the CBC, libraries and parks boards; police forces and ambulance services; municipal, county and regional governments; charity and welfare organizations; health boards and other public organizations.

As well as being large and growing CUPE was an independent Canadian union which took pride in its organizational differences from those of many of the internationals. Its principles of operation, set out at the 1963 founding convention, included a commitment that local unions must have full control over their own affairs. "The democratic functioning of each local union is the corner stone on which CUPE is built."[5]

"As a Canadian organization," CUPE proclaimed, "we must reflect what Canada is. We must be a coast-to-coast bilingual organization." The new union's structures were evolved to provide for these commitments, and while CUPE's record has not been perfect, it has been more open to broad membership participation than have many internationals.

About forty per cent of CUPE's members are women, making it the largest organization of working women in the country. One of its two top officers has been secretary-treasurer Grace Hartman. And Shirley Carr, formerly president of CUPE's Ontario division, was the union's successful nominee for executive vice-president of the CLC in 1974. The union has experienced some problems in developing equal participation for women in union affairs, but CUPE has demonstrated greater concern than many other unions with this problem. In 1968 only one local with a male majority had a woman president. By 1975 there were forty-two such locals. Twenty-eight per cent of all locals in CUPE had women presidents compared to only twelve per cent in 1968. In 1971 and 1975 CUPE produced an official report entitled, *Status of Women in CUPE*, and has made a number of efforts since to improve the situation. But women still have some distance to cover before they achieve full equality in their role as union leaders in CUPE.[6]

The union laid out a further goal for itself at its founding convention, one that was to lead it to the brink of a major confrontation with the leadership of the CLC:

> We must strive for the day when all public employees are part of a strong union so we do not suffer from the pull-down of inferior wages and conditions.[7]

The confrontation came when the CLC Executive Council, wary of CUPE's developing size and militancy, tried to undermine its growth by limiting its jurisdiction.

From the time of its initial Canadian Labour Congress charter in 1963,

CUPE has been designated by the CLC as the organization to which all employees of provincial and municipal governments, with the exception of British Columbia public employees (who were already affiiliated to the CLC), would belong.[8]

On April 20, 1971, CUPE's president Stanley Little, wrote to the heads of all the provincial government employee associations, announcing the union's plan to form a provincial government employees' division within CUPE. The main benefit of such a division, the letter said, would be that it "will form an integral part of CUPE and that the members will therefore have full voice and vote in the determination of overall national policies for public employees".[9] The union announced its intention to call a national conference of all government employee associations interested in this proposal.

Another attempt, parallel to CUPE's initiative, to organize provincial public employees on a national basis was made in 1971. This was a move toward the founding of a Canadian Federation of Government Employee Organizations (CFGEO). A year later, in April 1972, CUPE pledged its assistance to help build this new organization.[10]

A founding convention was called by CFGEO organizers for September and Little, along with the president of the Public Service Alliance of Canada, Claude Edwards, addressed the delgates in support of the new organization.

But on the second day of the convention it became clear that the proposed national union was not going to get off the ground. Seeing what was occurring, Little informed the delegates that he no longer felt any commitment to help them build a national structure outside CUPE.

The union changed its policy to extend assistance only "in the direction of developing a national structure or division within CUPE for provincial government employees. Anything else would be a disillusioning waste of time."[11]

Not long after the 1972 attempt to form a national union of provincial employees, some of the employee associations began to look to direct affiliation to the CLC as an alternative to becoming part of CUPE. What was wrong with this approach, in CUPE's eyes at least, was that some CLC executives seemed to be encouraging them to do this. As early as October 1971, CLC executive vice-president Jean Beaudry had suggested to the British Columbia government employees union that, in the words of the CUPE brief, "no hurdles should be put in the way of any provincial group that wanted to come into the Congress".[12]

In what was a backhand swipe at CUPE, Jean Beaudry continued:

> No affiliate should — either by its attitude or action — try to deprive these people of the opportunity of becoming part of the legitimate union movement.[13]

In October 1971 the executive and senior staff of the CLC had met with representatives of nine of the provincial organizations, including the

B.C. union which was already affiliated to the Congress. According to CUPE, CLC president MacDonald "made a number of questionable statements concerning the building of a national union," and discussed "affiliation and reaffiliation to the Congress of individual associations or groups of associations, and jurisdiction of provincial employee associations (even granting them jurisdiction over employees of regional government)".[14]

At the abortive founding convention of the CFGEO in September 1972, Frank Chafe, head of the CLC Government Employees Department, told the delegates:

> The Canadian Labour Congress is prepared to receive applications from organizations which can present themselves to us in a shape that equates itself with a legitimate union within the terms of the constitution of the Canadian Labour Congress. Every organization in this country, and each province, that represents provincial government employees can do that.[15]

Chafe apparently repeated this position at a meeting of the Newfoundland Association of Public Employees in 1973. According to Stan Little, Chafe told the Newfoundland association that "they could either come marching in proudly through the front door (by direct affiliation) or they could come in through the side door by affiliation through CUPE."[16]

CUPE objected strongly to these statements and activities of CLC leaders. The CLC had in 1963 granted CUPE jurisdiction over provincial government employees (except in B.C.) as well as over most other government employees except federal public workers. This had been reconfirmed in 1967. But when CUPE began serious work to organize provincial government employees, CLC officials were stepping in, attempting to undermine CUPE and to persuade the provincial government associations not to join CUPE but to become unions in their own right and affiliate directly to the CLC.

The CLC also distributed a document entitled "Questions and Answers of Affiliation with CLC". The civil service associations were told that "public employees in all jurisdictions are expected not to participate openly in political activity. [This] means that public employees are advised not to engage in partisan politics, such as becoming a political candidate while employed by government, by publicly supporting a political party or candidate, or by contributing money to a political party or candidate."[17]

This statement served two purposes. It appealed to the conservatism of the civil service association leaders, and at the same time it chided CUPE. In 1971 Shirley Carr, one of CUPE's most prominent members, had been an NDP candidate in Niagara Falls while she was an employee of the municipality.

In response to these CLC activities, CUPE presented a sixty-page brief to the CLC Executive Council on July 11, 1973.[18] The union's position was stated bluntly:

We are opposed to direct affiliation of provincial government employee associations to the Congress. Accordingly, we must state our strong opposition to the officers and staff of the Congress who have compromised themselves and trade union principles in their wooing of these associations.

The union based its stand on a number of points. First, CUPE argued that it was hurt by the weakness of the provincial civil service associations:

The presence of weak organizations at the provincial level has an adverse effect on the activities of public employees at other levels. More particularly, when governments wish to impose wage guidelines it is easier to do so with provincial groups who have no recourse to economic sanctions against such an imposition. Once the pattern is set, public employees at the level of municipalities, hospitals, and school boards find it that much harder to break out of it.

Its second argument was concerned with providing the best possible union for the provincial employees. The brief argued that CUPE offered greater union strength to government employees than was possible with direct association affiliation:

CUPE believes it has far more experience and success in organizing and developing militant trade unionism among public employees than any other group or organization, including the CLC itself. We think it is essential that provincial employees be exposed to the experience of belonging to a strong and progressive trade union. ... [This was preferable to] being sold jurisdictional protection to maintain the status quo, which is all direct affiliation to the CLC would amount to.

The CUPE brief posed five blunt questions about the CLC's encouragement of direct affiliation in contradiction to its own jurisdictional policy:

1. When the Congress officers received "invitations" from CFGEO or individual associations, why did they not refer the subject to CUPE, as the union with the jurisdiction, in accordance with the constitution and established practices of the Congress?
2. Is it right that an affiliate's dues be used by the Congress to undermine the activities of that affiliate?
3. What has the Government Employees Department [of the CLC] done recently except to work against the interests of CUPE?
4. Who gave the officers authority to run counter to established policies of the Congress and even to principles laid down by the Constitution (Article II, Section 2(a), 3.5, 8 and 9, and Article III, Section 2)?
5. If the CLC officers can "organize" for fifteen cents per member per month any kind of unaffiliated group, even management-dominated associations, in opposition to the interest of CUPE, why can the same thing not be done to any other CLC affiliate at some time in the future?

The CLC responded to these charges on several occasions. Its response was summarized in the document Chafe distributed to the Newfoundland Association of Public Employees in May 1973. "Questions and Answers of Affiliation with CLC" responded to a statement of Little's in the Vancouver *Sun* on October 18, 1971, when CUPE's president was quoted as saying:

> We have written documents, adopted by the Executive Council of the CLC in 1967, stating categorically that, with the exception of B.C., all provincial civil servants would be under the jurisdiction of CUPE.[19]

In response, the CLC document acknowledged that CUPE had been recognized for jurisdiction over provincial government employees. But it went on to say that "this will continue to be the case where there are no provincial government unions recognized or affiliated, *or until the Executive Council determines otherwise*". (emphasis added) The document indicated the executive had already "determined otherwise" when it advised the Newfoundland civil servants that their organization:

> ... could seek reaffiliation to the Congress on the same basis as previously. ... This could indeed result in jurisdictional problems within the Congress, but any such problems could be referred to an impartial umpire or otherwise dealt with under the disputes procedure.

The CLC executive consistently put the issue in terms of jurisdictional procedure. More important than the particular legal niceties, however, was the basic policy issue. The CLC leadership was trying to undermine the position of a large Canadian union in its attempts to organize provincial public employees. Since this issue exploded in 1973, eight civil service federations (Quebec public employees are mainly affiliated to the CNTU) have affiliated directly to the CLC, and there was talk of the formation of a Canadian union of provincial public employees.[20]

Feelings within CUPE reached a high point at its Montreal convention in November 1973 when the question of CUPE's continuing membership in the CLC became the main focus of the convention. This issue made the 1973 convention the stormiest in CUPE's history, and the debate reached a point where the top CUPE leadership temporarily lost control.

Three groups were in evidence at the CUPE convention. The sentiment of the great majority of the delegates was for an open break with the CLC. These delegates favoured at least a temporary disaffiliation from the Congress in order to press for a new policy on the status of provincial public employees. This group was led by Shirley Carr, president of CUPE's Ontario Division (later to become executive vice-president of the CLC).

The second group, made up mainly of delegates from British Columbia, represented a conservative or status quo position. They opposed any position that would indicate a threat to take CUPE out of the Congress, even if the CLC refused to make any concessions.

President Stanley Little, along with CUPE secretary-treasurer Grace

Hartman, took a middle-of-the-road position, mediating between the two sides. In the course of the debate, it became clear that the majority group, favouring withdrawal, realized that the real issue was the desire of the U.S.-based international unions to retain control of the CLC. Thus Russ Doyle, president of CUPE's 5,000-member Local 43 in Toronto, supported the withdrawal resolution, saying, "For too long, we have been taking too many orders from the U.S. We are not going to take any more crap from people in the U.S."[21]

Louis Laberge, president of the Quebec Federation of Labour, addressed the convention, and urged CUPE to stay in the CLC:

> Stay in — don't get out. We have never won a fight by running away from it, and you don't win yours if you run away from the CLC. You may not win, but if you try, we will be behind you. . . . Turn it into an organization no longer ruled by Washington and Pittsburgh.[22]

Arguments like Laberge's eventually swung the support of the withdrawal group to a resolution that stopped short of an actual break with the Congress. Even delegates like Shirley Carr, who told the convention that "the CLC has raped the Canadian Union of Public Employees . . . they're out to destroy CUPE because you are too powerful. . . . [CLC officers] are afraid they may have to get out and labour instead of having cushy seats to put their fat bottoms on,"[23] finally went along with the compromise resolution.

The resolution adopted called for CUPE to remain inside the CLC, at least until the Congress Convention in May 1974. If the CLC convention did not adopt a "reform programme" drafted by CUPE, PSAC and CBRT, then CUPE's executive board would be authorized to withdraw the union from the Congress. The resolution said that CUPE would "embark on a programme of reform, revitalization and change in the leadership of the CLC to prevent further breaches of faith and moral responsibility on the part of the CLC". It committed CUPE locals across the country to send delegates to the CLC convention in an effort to have the reform programme adopted.[24]

This programme called for a code of standards for better trade unionism. It emphasized the merger of small unions into larger organizations,[25] elimination of "direct affiliation" to the CLC, increased labour activity against multinational corporations, better CLC servicing for affiliated unions, and, most significantly, "Canadian control".

> Members of unions in Canada are entitled to have control over their unions' policies, finances, services and election of officers. Without neglecting the need for international co-operation, the Congress must promote and protect the rights of members to increased Canadian control as a prime function and responsibility of the Congress.[26]

The reform programme concluded with this warning:

> If these and many other progressive steps are not taken, workers in

Canada will be denied the effectively functioning national labour movement that is becoming more and more essential if their interests are to be properly promoted and served.

Not only was this position a much feebler version of the original militant sentiments shown by the majority of delegates, but it was also to be further watered down by the CUPE leadership in the ensuing months of negotiations with the establishment of the CLC.[27]

Following the 1973 CUPE Convention, a "reform group" of five unions emerged. In addition to the three unions that had drafted the original reform programme, the Canadian Union of Postal Workers and the B.C. Government Employees Association joined the group. The reform programme represented a cautious compromise acceptable to the leadership of these unions, although far behind that of the younger membership eager to challenge the American union domination of the CLC. The reform group stated that it was going to the 1974 CLC Convention with the object of electing a new reform leadership.

The most interesting aspect of the 1973 CUPE debate was the strength of nationalist feeling among the delegates. They saw the fight as a struggle by the leaders of the American unions to block CUPE in its attempts to offer provincial public employees a strong union voice. Underlying the drama of the Montreal convention was the suspicion that CUPE was being thwarted by the international union leadership because it threatened the power of the internationals within the CLC.

But by the time of the 1974 CLC meeting, the militant stance visible at the CUPE convention had all but evaporated among the top leaders. Gone were the militant policies on jurisdictional rights, the demand for a strong national organization of provincial public employees, and the insistence on basic changes in CLC policy, leadership and structure. The guidelines for Canadian autonomy finally adopted excluded the key points of control of finances in Canada and the right of unions in Canada to merge into larger organizations without reference to international headquarters.

---

1. *The Windsor Star*, November 26, 1973.

2. *The Toronto Star*, November 28, 1973.

3. *CUPE Journal*, September-October 1973.

4. CUPE, "CUPE Story", pamphlet, n.d.

5. *CUPE Journal*, September-October 1973.

6. Laurence Kelly, ed., *The Current Industrial Relations Scene, 1975* (Kingston, Ont.: Industrial Relations Centre, Queen's University, 1975), p. s-u-11.

7. *CUPE Journal*, September-October 1973.

8. *The Canadian Union of Public Employees, Provincial Government Employees and The Canadian Labour Congress*, brief submitted by CUPE to

the special session of the Executive Council of the CLC, July 11, 1973, Appendix E.

9. Ibid., Appendix B.

10. Ibid., p. 34.

11. Ibid., p. 35.

12. Ibid., p. 41.

13. Ibid., p. 42.

14. Ibid.

15. Ibid., Appendix D.

16. Ibid., p. 44.

17. Ibid., Appendix E.

18. Ibid.

19. Ibid.

20. *The Globe and Mail*, December 12, 1974.

21. *The Toronto Star*, November 28, 1973.

22. *The Globe and Mail*, November 29, 1973.

23. *The Toronto Star*, November 28, 1973.

24. *CUPE Journal*, December 1973.

25. On mergers, the reform programme said: ''The Congress and its officers must work with determination towards rationalization of the Canadian labour movement.''
    ''Rationalization must be guided by a policy of establishing industrial or other groups of affiliates which have common concerns and/or related jurisdictions.''

26. *The Courier*, January-February 1973, p. 3.

27. See next chapter.

CHAPTER 15
The 1974 CLC Convention

The Ford Motor Company of Canada is not going to fight to preserve the independence of Canada. The Shell Oil Company isn't going to do that. The one force that will struggle to keep Canada independent and to preserve Canada is the working people.

C. Rundgren
IBEW Local 213 delegate
CLC convention, May 1974[1]

We went along with the 1970 provision. I can live with what you put in that document, but I cannot live with compulsion. I say that you are hypocritical, if you come here and say: "The Executive Council has the right, if you don't do what we tell you, to compel you to get out of this Congress.

Ken Rose
International vice-president, IBEW
CLC convention, May 1974[2]

The 1974 Vancouver convention of the CLC provided dramatic evidence of both the growing intensity of nationalist sentiment among rank and file trade unionists, and the resistance to change on the part of the internationals which make up the Congress establishment.

The number of resolutions dealing with "Canadian autonomy" and independence in one form or another was the largest in the history of the CLC. The number of resolutions on autonomy had risen from seven in 1970, to fourteen in 1972, to thirty in 1974.[3] Within the CLC, most of the discussion about Canadian control had been expressed in terms of autonomy. The driving force behind this movement within the Congress had come either from those unions which have always been Canadian, or, more recently, from unions like the Paperworkers which had become

Canadian by withdrawing from internationals. Increasingly, momentum was added by individuals and locals within international unions who advocated the independence of whole Canadian sections.

Despite the number of autonomy and independence resolutions forwarded to the convention, Vancouver was an anticlimax for many of the local delegates who came in the hope of making major steps toward Canadianizing the labour movement. The main problem was a crisis of leadership among the reform group. Various deals and trade-offs made in the months preceding the convention seriously diminished the impact of the fifty per cent of the local union delegates who came from Canadian organizations.[4]

One of these deals concerned the presidency of the CLC. There were two serious presidential candidates in the months preceding the convention, both of them long-time members of the CLC "establishment"; William Dodge who had been secretary-treasurer and Joe Morris, who had been an executive vice-president. The most significant difference between the two lay not in their policy views, but in their union origins. Dodge had been an officer of the Canadian Brotherhood of Railway, Transport and General Workers, while Morris had been president of the Western Canadian Region of the International Woodworkers of America (also retiring president Donald MacDonald's union).

A meeting of the CLC executive in February 1974 was to have considered the question of Donald MacDonald's successor. However, a discussion of the potential threat from the "reform movement" in the wake of the CUPE convention took up most of the meeting's time.

The general expectation in the union movement was that Dodge would get the nod for the presidency at the executive meeting in March. However, in a ten-to-nine vote, Morris was chosen, apparently because he posed less of a potential threat to the internationals in the CLC than did Dodge.

After the executive nominated Morris to their slate, he began to campaign for the support of the "reform group" leadership. Morris is understood to have promised that he would support CUPE's efforts to solve its jurisdictional dispute with the CLC by establishing a separate Canadian union of provincial employees as a compromise measure. In exchange, "reform" leaders like Stanley Little of CUPE and Claude Edwards of PSAC apparently decided to refrain from nominating a "reform" candidate to oppose Morris.

Following this compromise move, the leadership of the reform group seemed to collapse. When the building trades unions threatened to break with the Congress if the autonomy guidelines became compulsory, the reform leaders may have been frightened by a vision of a CLC consisting of only autonomous and Canadian unions. More important, probably, was the deal over CUPE's new relations to unions of provincial employees, substantially changed from the policy adopted by CUPE at its 1973 convention.

Thus the most outstanding feature of the reform movement at the Vancouver convention was not the power, skill or determination of its leadership — for these qualities were not in evidence. What was outstanding was that after several months in which the reformers had gained momentum, with press reports announcing the imminent transformation of the CLC, their leadership became almost passive on the very issues they had been championing a few short months before.

For the first time, fifty per cent of the local delegates came from Canadian unions, due particularly to the huge turn-out of CUPE delegates. In 1972 there had been 414 delegates from locals of all Canadian organizations. In 1974 this figure was 1,057, and CUPE alone sent 569 delegates, some 27 per cent of the total number of local union delegates attending.[5]

The "autonomy" proposals for the Canadian sectors of international unions proposed by the CLC executive at the 1974 convention looked much like a replay of 1970. The most important planks in the reform platform — Canadian control of union finances, and authority for Canadian sections of internationals to merge without regard for the American sections — were referred to the Executive Board for further consideration. In effect, the only new decision made at Vancouver was the provision for enforcement of the guidelines.

This new provision, however, was enough to enrage the top leadership of the building trades internationals, giving rise to a situation where craft union international representatives were denouncing the resolutions from one microphone, while rank and file delegates from the same unions supported the proposals from another.

In fact, the most forceful and the most numerous speeches in support of a strong position on the autonomy question came not from reform group delegates, but from rank and filers in the building trades. Delegate L. Robson, from Local 452 of the carpenters' union, opened the debate by pointing to the "very strong-growing nationalist consciousness among the workers of this country that needs to be answered".[6] He outlined the causes of this new nationalism:

> The AFL-CIO in the United States is supporting the Burke-Hartke Act which, if implemented, is going to cost the jobs of 300,000 Canadian workers. You have the DISC programme that is also being supported by the AFL-CIO. Again, it's going to take thousands of Canadian jobs. There's no doubt that those are the reasons why there's a growing consciousness. When you consider all of these things, along with the fact that inflation is obviously coming from the American quarter, the domination of our economy from that area, there's no question that Canadian workers want some answers on these problems.

Robson attacked the CLC executive's "autonomy" recommendation for not going far enough: "In actual fact, what that calls for is a threat to throw those unions out if they do nothing about a do-nothing policy. That isn't good enough.'' He went on to predict that international representatives from the building trades would argue that the CLC guidelines amounted to interference in the internal affairs of their unions, and that they would pull their organizations out of the Congress if the resolutions were to pass. Then he gave this warning:

> Let me say this to the international representatives. . . . ''Do not put the workers in this country into the position of choosing between our international union and this great Congress.'' Don't do that, because that'll cause some problems that they will be sorry about.

After a few similar speeches, Robson's prophecy was fulfilled. Delegate R. Taylor, an international representative of the Sheet Metal Workers, condemned the autonomy resolution as interference in his union's internal affairs:

> I want to say loud and clear that any issue . . . affecting sheet metal workers will be decided by sheet metal workers, in conventions of the Sheet Metal Workers International Association, and not by a parent labour body, whether it be the Canadian Labour Congress, the AFL-CIO or even a Building Trades Department. . . . [7]

And, as Robson had predicted, he threatened the withdrawal of his union:

> . . . we will then seriously consider our position within the Congress as a union. . . .

One of the building trades rank and filers, D. Jappy of Local 170, Plumbers, summed up the question at issue: ''Do the workers have the right to be master in their own house?''[8] Jappy was asking two questions. First, did Canadians have the right to run their own trade union movement? Second, did the rank and file have the right to speak for its unions, or was that to be left to the international representatives?

When the debate resumed in the afternoon, the same ground was covered again when two delegates from the International Brotherhood of Electrical Workers illustrated the two extremes within the building trades unions.

Ken Rose condemned the convention as ''hypocritical'' for trying to enforce its guidelines. ''I cannot live with compulsion,''[9] the IBEW vice-president told the delegates. For Rose, the issue was one of the Congress trying to forces its affiliates to obey certain basic rules.

A rank and file IBEW delegate, C. Rundgren of Local 213, emphatically answered Rose:

> The international vice-president of my union . . . says the IBEW conforms to the present standards laid down by the CLC. In the opinion of our local that is not true.[10]

Rundgren went on to enumerate the areas in which the IBEW had failed to live up to the guidelines. But his emphasis was on the role of the trade union movement in the broader spectrum of Canadian nationalism:

> The Ford Motor Company is not going to fight to preserve the inde-
> pendence of Canada. The Shell Oil Company isn't going to do that.
> The one force in Canada that will struggle to keep Canada indepen-
> dent and to preserve Canada is the working people. The trade union
> movement, of course, is the key in that struggle. That's why there has
> to be, in my opinion, and in the opinion of my local, an independent
> Canadian trade union movement.

Measured against this speech, the statements of the reform group
leaders were very mild. CUPE's Little, for instance, went along with the
executive's guideline proposals, even though they represented a major
watering down of what his own union stood for. He called for the passage
of the executive recommendations, while noting that there were some
"omissions".[11] These "omissions" were the right of Canadians to ratify
their own collective agreements, the retention of sufficient operating
funds in Canada, and the right of Canadian sections to merge with other
unions of their own accord. Little concluded his speech with these
words:

> This report, I suggest, is a good beginning. I believe we can be proud
> of adopting this section of the Commission's report. In fact, if we pass
> this section, it will be said hopefully that the CLC, as it enters its
> second decade, won't be known as getting older, but getting better.

Little's speech signalled the failure of the "reform" leadership at the
convention to give the hundreds of delegates who had come for that
purpose an opportunity to support a meaningful move toward greater
autonomy and eventual independence.

However, the reform delegates did manage to score secondary victories over the establishment. The first came when the delegates over-
ruled the CLC leadership on the convention floor on the question of the
special status of the Quebec Federation of Labour. The QFL had requested the right to control educational and some other finances within
the province. The executive of the Congress recommended against the
request. Here QFL president Louis Laberge supplied the leadership that
the "reform" group had been so sadly lacking.

In his speech, Laberge played directly on the rank and file delegates'
impatience:

> As far as I'm concerned, I have no more time to lose in discussing
> with people who don't want to understand or people who have made
> promises to us. ... What could be done is a clear decision from the
> delegates to the Committee and the officers to the effect that they
> don't want to accept this any longer.[12]

Following his speech, an overwhelming majority of the convention
delegates voted to overturn the executive recommendations. Laberge
had sensed the frustration and captured the imagination of the delegates.

One CUPE official told a reporter, "In a sense we blew it: Louis Laberge showed us what could be done and how to do it". [13]

Rank and file delegates won a second victory in the executive elections. No serious challenger to Joe Morris had emerged, at least partly due to the deal he had made with the "reform" leadership. At the last minute, however, a relatively unknown trade unionist, a member of Dodge's CBRT, ran and managed to win almost forty per cent of the delegate votes.

More significantly, the delegates scored two important upset victories over establishment slate candidates. Neil Reimer, national director of the Oil, Chemical and Atomic Workers' Union and former Alberta NDP leader, was defeated for the secretary-treasurer's position by Donald Montgomery, a steel worker and president of the Toronto Labour Council. Long-time CLC executive vice-president Jean Beaudry, who had previously been a USWA staff representative, was defeated in his bid for re-election by Julien Major, a representative of the United Paperworkers International Union which was transforming itself into a fully Canadian union. Major was elected with the support of Laberge and the QFL delegation. [14]

The second executive vice-presidency went to CUPE activist Shirley Carr. The Congress executive had included her in its official slate when it became clear that she would win in any event.

The administration slate had played on the fears of "moderates" that a strong reform move would lead to the withdrawal of important internationals from the CLC. The slate leaflet billed the official candidates as the "Unity Team" and put out a strong pitch for this so-called "unity":

> Unity is the backbone of the labour movement. . . . The Unity Team is devoted to working together, because united is the way our labour movement will reach its goals sooner. [15]

The election results were probably more significant as a reflection of rank and file opposition to the establishment of the CLC than as an indication of any profound changes on the way. The four newly-elected executive officers, headed by Morris, were not a "reform" group although there may be a potential for change given a more effective reform movement at subsequent conventions.

Any lingering hopes of reform were soon dashed. In August 1974 president Morris spoke to 2,500 delegates of the Carpenters' Union Convention in Chicago. The carpenters had been among the most vociferous opponents of the mild autonomy provisions passed by the Vancouver convention. In the context of the fierce debate over the autonomy provisions, Morris explained his union philosophy:

> My suspicions about current Canadian nationalism, except in its purely economic dimensions, are very deep and I, for one, will work to see that the Canadian Labour Congress looks in the direction of

true international unionism with links that will span the oceans and the continents.[16]

Ironically, CUPE's leaders, who had dealt away their strong "autonomy" stand in exchange for a jurisdictional settlement, did not fare too well on the compromise they had worked out. The jurisdictional dispute was referred back to the incoming executive for reconsideration. Even the presence of Shirley Carr on the CLC executive was no guarantee that the issue would be decided in CUPE's favour.

The final executive ruling on the jurisdictional question was a compromise along the lines of the deal made with Morris before the convention. Three resolutions on this question had been referred back to the CLC Executive Council. The first, authorizing the establishment of a national organization of provincial employees, was accepted. The second, which called on the Congress to delay the affiliation of civil servants' groups until such a national union existed, and if no such union worked out, to affiliate them only through "the affiliate holding the jurisdiction", was to be given "further consideration". The third resolution, which would have directed provincial government employees, aside from B.C., to join CUPE, was rejected.[17] While this was not total defeat for CUPE, it was not the "tremendous success" Little had proclaimed for CUPE after the convention.

However, the 1974 biennial meeting of the CLC cannot be evaluated entirely on the basis of resolutions passed or rejected at the convention because its effects continued to be felt in the aftermath.

In a meeting in December 1974, the Executive Council of the CLC disposed of the many resolutions which had been referred to it by the convention.[18] Responding with apparent caution it decided to give "further study" or "further consideration" to all resolutions dealing with Canadian autonomy and independence. Significantly it avoided outright rejection of any such resolutions, even the ones which called for full Canadian independence or the holding of referenda to decide the issue.

A typical resolution was C35 which summarized the original intention of the reformers at the convention. It was to be given "further consideration". Submitted by PSAC, the Canadian Union of Postal Workers, CUPE and the CBRT, the resolution read:

> Be it resolved that the policy of the Congress on Canadian union autonomy shall be:
> (a) all Canadian officers of unions operating in Canada be elected from and by the Canadian membership;
> (b) any union policy affecting the Canadian membership shall be adopted by democratically elected Canadian officers, by conventions of Canadian delegates; or by referendum of Canadian members;
> (c) only Canadian officers shall have the authority to speak for the union on matters relating to its Canadian activities;

(d) no collective agreements may be ratified without a vote of the Canadian members affected;

(e) all fees and dues collected from members in Canada shall be retained in Canada and controlled by the Canadian membership, except to the extent the membership agrees to remit funds to an international headquarters; and

(f) union constitutions must guarantee full functional autonomy for Canadian members, as a right, including the right to enter into mergers and affiliations.

This resolution, which goes much further than the CLC guidelines adopted in 1970 and 1974, was in effect left in limbo by the Executive Council. However, the Executive Council did not reject it, thus opening the door to further consideration of such resolutions at subsequent CLC conventions.[19]

It is significant, too, that the Executive Council did not reject but agreed to give further consideration even to resolutions such as C59, which called "for complete autonomy and independence".

It read:

Whereas the sovereign and independent future of Canada is seriously threatened by the degree to which the United States and other foreign corporations have established ownership and control of great areas of our economic life; and

Whereas the trade union and labour movement in Canada must give leadership to overcome this threat, and ensure Canadian independence based on the interests of working people; and

Whereas a united sovereign trade union movement could best fight for the all-sided interests of labour;

Be it resolved that this convention of the Canadian Labour Congress strongly encourage the achievement in all unions of complete autonomy and independence, while maintaining strong fraternal ties with the trade unions of the United States and other countries, including, where appropriate, co-ordinated efforts in collective bargaining, mutual assistance in strike struggles, and solidarity actions in support of each other.[20]

Even more important was the adoption by the Executive Council of resolution C48 as "covering Resolutions C45, C46, C47 and C48".

These resolutions congratulated the Canadian paper workers for conducting a referendum based on their "democratic right to decide on the desired constitutional structure of their organization in Canada". The C48 resolution concluded with the statement "that this convention congratulate the United Paperworkers International Union for their forethought and initiative and urge all other international unions to follow suit if requested by their Canadian membership".[21]

Resolution C45 was even more strongly worded in that it called on the CLC to encourage international unions to hold referenda of Canadian memberships where requested by the membership. It concluded:

Be it further resolved that the Canadian Labour Congress in the interest of all Canadian trade unionists call upon all international unions to:
(a) hold a similar referendum or Canadian Convention on this subject if so requested by the Canadian members; and
(b) to respect the wishes of the Canadian members as shown by such referendum or convention.[22]

Although these resolutions call for the holding of referenda only if requested by their membership, they come close to encouraging Canadian members to consider such requests — a door that could open all international unions in Canada to full Canadian independence.

It could turn out that the reformers had actually gained more in the long run than was evident at the May 1974 convention — especially if they revive the content of these resolutions for adoption at subsequent CLC conventions.

But one ominous note in the proceedings of the CLC Executive Council in December 1974 was to be found in the adoption of Resolution C65.

This resolution calls for changes in the CLC constitution to base its power on "total membership of an affiliate" instead of on direct representation from local unions based on their size. It also called for "implementation of the block-voting system".[23] Carried to its extreme, this block-voting system could enable one union representative to vote for 200,000 members, and nullify the present democratic procedure at conventions of one delegate: one vote. For such a far-reaching change to be made by the Executive Council instead of the convention itself would seriously undermine the CLC's original constitution. It will likely be challenged at future conventions as a retrograde step for the Congress.

The 1974 convention did not differ much from previous conventions in the policies it adopted. Where it did differ was in the unprecedented strength of the delegations from fully independent Canadian unions. With a strong leadership, they had the potential to move the Congress substantially toward greater autonomy and to install a new leadership in the CLC.

Future CLC conventions would inevitably seen the numerical strength of the Canadian unions increase. When Canadian unions would develop a younger and more vital leadership to correspond to their relative strength in the Congress and gain allies among members of international unions in Canada was not certain. The promised transformation of the CLC did not occur at Vancouver because not all the ingredients had yet emerged.

But at least one section of the internationals thought that far too many of the ingredients were already on hand in 1974. The leadership of the building trades unions bitterly opposed the "autonomy" provisions which had been built into the CLC constitution. Tension was mounting even in the traditionally conservative and U.S.-dominated craft unions.

1. Canadian Labour Congress, *Proceedings*, 10th Constitutional Convention, Vancouver, May 1974, p. 69.

2. Ibid., p. 75.

3. Canadian Labour Congress, *Resolutions on Constitution and Structure*, 1970, 1972, 1974 Conventions.

4. Canadian Labour Congress, *List of Delegates* and *Supplementary List of Delegates*, 1974.

5. Calculated from CLC, *List of Delegates*, 1974. Of these, 899 came from "locals of national unions", 143 from "provincial organizations", and 15 from "directly chartered unions".

6. Canadian Labour Congress, *Proceedings*, May 1974, p. 69.

7. Ibid., p. 70.

8. Ibid.

9. Ibid., p. 75.

10. Ibid., p. 76.

11. Ibid., p. 79.

12. Ibid., p. 97.

13. *The Windsor Star*, May 22, 1974.

14. *The Toronto Star*, May 17, 1974.

15. "The Unity Team", Election Broadsheet, 10th Constitutional Convention, CLC, 1974.

16. *Leader-Post* (Regina), August 1, 1974.

17. Canadian Labour Congress, *Disposition of Matters Referred to the Executive Council by the Tenth Constitutional Convention of the CLC*, 1974, pp. 4-5.

18. Ibid.

19. Ibid., Committee on Constitution and Structure, p. 6.

20. Ibid., p. 10.

21. Ibid., p. 8.

22. Canadian Labour Congress, *Resolutions on Constitution and Structure*, 10th Constitutional Convention, Vancouver, May 1974, p. 14.

23. Canadian Labour Congress, *Disposition of Matters Referred to the Executive Council by the Tenth Constitutional Convention of the CLC*, 1974, p. 11.

CHAPTER 16

Canadian Unionism and the Building Trades

Be it resolved that: Any union which does not have effective Canadian autonomy by December 31, 1977 shall not be permitted to join or to remain in this Congress . . .

Resolution C21, submitted to the 1974 CLC convention by PSAC, CUPE, and the Letter Carriers Union of Canada.[1]

[There] is no way that bunch of garbage collectors is going to tell us what to do.

Ronald Taylor
International representative
Sheet Metal Workers' International Association[2]

For the top Canadian officers of most of the American unions in the building trades, the "Canadian autonomy guidelines" laid down by the Canadian Labour Congress in 1974 were all too radical. The construction union leaders might tolerate recommendations, but they were strongly opposed to any attempt by the CLC to enforce the guidelines.

Prior to the CLC convention, John Carroll — Canadian vice-president of the International Brotherhood of Boilermakers, and chairman of the Canadian Advisory Board of the Building Trades Unions — announced publicly that the international building trades officers would challenge the CLC executive guidelines.[3] Concern centered on the enforcement procedures. These procedures, as discussed by the CLC executive before the convention, provided for a series of small steps to be taken over a lengthy period. The steps might include sending a letter to the non-complying unions, setting out the CLC policy and standards; a request for compliance; or a request that the non-complying union spell out how much time it needed to amend its constitution in order to follow the guidelines.[4]

Before the 1974 convention the CLC asked its affiliates to supply information about their degree of compliance with the 1970 guidelines. Of the thirteen affiliates that failed even to reply to this request, five were building trades unions.[5] John Carroll's union, the Boilermakers, was one which did reply. It was among the seven unions that reported complete non-compliance with all the guidelines. This disregard of CLC decisions over a period of four years clearly anticipated the defiance building trades leaders would show to the 1974 CLC decision.

The top Canadian officials of the AFL-CIO building trades unions and members of the Canadian Advisory Board to the AFL-CIO building trades executive called a special strategy meeting of their CLC delegates in Vancouver just prior to the 1974 convention. The Canadian Advisory Board recommended to the delegates that if the CLC executive proposal for enforcement of the guidelines was passed, the international building trades unions should withdraw their Congress affiliation. This recommendation was defeated by a vote of 116 to 98.[6]

The strongest opposition to the Canadian Advisory Board proposal came from the British Columbia construction unions which had been pressing for greater Canadian autonomy. The B.C. representatives made up 95 of the 240 delegates present at the Vancouver conference. The B.C. and Yukon Territory Building and Construction Trades Council had forwarded a "Canadian autonomy" submission to the Building and Construction Trades Department of the AFL-CIO prior to its October 1973 meeting in Bal Harbour, Florida. Thus there was a division of opinion not only between the leadership of the building trades unions and the CLC, but also between the leadership and an important section of their Canadian membership as well.

Signed by Council president J. Kinnaird (who was later to become Assistant Deputy Minister of Labour in B.C.'s NDP government) and secretary-treasurer C. Stairs, the submission was largely the fruit of work done by the carpenters' union in B.C.[7] This proposal, therefore, had a special significance; it came from a section of the union movement in Canada that had long been established, had a tradition of craft as opposed to industrial unionism, and had experienced the most thoroughgoing American control of any section of the labour movement in Canada. The submission represented pro-Canadian union feeling within the most conservative wing of international unionism in Canada.

The document had two thrusts: it combined a demand for greater Canadian control or autonomy with a demand for greater rank and file control of local affairs. It combined appeals to reason with only slightly veiled threats of the consequences if its recommendations were not heeded. These threats, by and large, were directed more against the entrenched Canadian leadership of the American unions, which had become increasingly isolated from the Canadian membership, than against the American unions themselves.

The submission began by outlining the history of American unionism in Canada, saying that, in spite of long association with international unions, "times change . . . history progresses and people and institutions mature". The submission warned:

> Within our unions, the ferment has gathered pace, manifesting itself in different ways — some reasonable and some alarming. The growth of national and nationalistic unions has gathered steam, and has been only too successful in many areas . . . The Canadian Labour Congress . . . has witnessed the constantly increasing attention of our members to the problem of "autonomy" or growing up.

After outlining the 1970 CLC guidelines, the submission described the position taken by the B.C. Federation of Labour at its 1970 convention, which had overwhelmingly endorsed a demand for the establishment of Canadian sections as soon as possible. It then referred to the finding of the all-party Parliamentary Committee on External Affairs of the 28th Federal Parliament, which supported moves toward greater Canadian autonomy.

The B.C. and Yukon Territory Building Trades Council's submission clearly gave continued support to international unions, saying that such unions "have a continuing and important role in the affairs of the Canadian building trades worker . . ." but added that, "we are not so impressed with the policies of our internationals in the social and political fields".

According to these Canadian building trades unionists, Burke-Hartke and U.S. union protectionism were particular thorns:

> Viewed from the point of view of American trade unionists the situation is understandable [but] as international officers, the stand of our leaders is inexplicable. Let it be clearly said — they don't speak for us as Canadians.

Continuing in this vein, the submission emphasized the totally American outlook of the international leadership:

> . . . it is understandable but not sufficient in our view that the policy statements regularly expressed by the international officers should so completely express an American point of view . . . Clearly, constitutional and institutional provisions must be made to enable the members of an international union, but also citizens of a sovereign nation, to conduct their affairs in a manner, at the time, and according to a policy of their own choosing.

They criticized the tendency of the internationals to view the Canadian branches as though they were regions within the United States:

> This is similar to, if not identical with, the experience of many of our convention-goers who return with a standard story to the effect that

when they placed resolutions of Canadian particularism before the convention some highly placed spokesman will exclaim — "This is not acceptable — what if California wanted the same?" [This] argument is irrelevant to a true understanding of the word *international* and moreover has vaguely insulting overtones that do absolutely nothing for the esprit de corps of our people. We don't want to be tedious, but "international" does not mean the same as "interstate" or "inter-provincial".

After a series of explicit proposals for changing the constitutions of the internationals, the submission also considered the problem of "raiding" by national unions:

Frankly, we believe that the raiding of national, or possibly more correctly, "nationalistic" unions is the direct result of an apparent inability of our unions to get the message across to the internationals that a major reform must be made in their structures to allow for the concept of Canadian autonomy ... The current atmosphere in our society, that is exemplified by the slogan "maîtres chez nous" or "masters in our own house" should not lead anyone to underestimate our "international" problem in this regard.

The submission pointed out that so far the internationals in the building trades had opposed any resolutions presented by Canadian affiliates on the autonomy issue:

Not only have they been unsuccessful but in the main the opinions expressed have apparently been swept under the carpet. Certainly, in no cases we know of have there been intimate consultations with the Canadian local to explore, if nothing else, the origins of the problems.

Under the heading, "Internationalizing the Internationals," the brief made a series of recommendations for change. These included:

— setting up a Canadian section within the constitution of each international;
— calling a "Canadian constitutional council" made up of representatives from each Canadian local: "this would create the machinery — constitutional and otherwise — for making real the objectives of self-government";
— paying all per capita dues directly to the Canadian national office, under the control of the Canadian Council. ("Financing, being the gut factor of autonomy, must be closely considered. There is no more touchy area than this with the average Canadian worker."); and,
— maintaining the bulk of the Canadian per capita dues for use in Canada: "We feel ... that the Canadian office in each case should pay an affiliation per capita based on the Canadian membership to the international office based on a negotiated level of involvement. The bulk of the regular per capita would stay in Canada, however, for the expenses of representatives, collective bargaining programmes, general administration, etc., under control of the national executive."

The submission called for a clear definition of the role of the proposed

Canadian Council, including "all matters dealing with legislation, collective bargaining, appointment of representatives, matters of membership or local discipline ... [In addition,] the Council should act at least in a major advisory role in the formation of sub-regional councils," and the Canadian headquarters should "take the initiative for union publications".

Admitting that this represented a major set of changes, the B.C. — Yukon unions went on to urge their adoption:

> We would most earnestly warn, that in our opinion, such change must take place in one form or another. We would hate to think of what might happen over a period of years should there be an adamant refusal to face evolving realities.

The submission concluded by making four points:

> One, the maintenance of the status quo will not be tolerated much longer by the average member — militant or not — of our unions in Canada.
>
> Two, the growing tendency for a true Canadian identity in Canada is a logical progression in a people's march for a recognized national status. The basic thrust of this movement lies in a national pride of achievement in the making of our own laws, our own history, our own parliamentary and political institutions. This high state of national maturity must be matched in our trade union organization.
>
> Three, if full recognition is given to our national requirements then the full measure of international ties will not be lost upon the Canadian membership, even upon the now unorganized worker, as the knowledge that in unity there is strength to deal with international corporations ... will have clear and universal acceptance, unsullied by negative considerations.
>
> Four, international officers of international unions must lead. Action, not reaction, must be the role of our leadership ...

This submission, an appeal to reason on the part of the top leadership of the building trades internationals, was the voice of an important section of the Canadian rank and file. It was not heeded. A resolution forwarded to the Building Trades Department 1973 meeting called for a study committee to explore the entire question of an autonomous Building Trades Organization in Canada in accordance with CLC guidelines. It was referred to the Executive Council because "the Committee did not have a cross-section opinion of the feelings of our members throughout Canada".[8]

But the extent to which the leadership of the construction unions rejected Canadian autonomy only became fully apparent after the May 1974 convention of the Canadian Labour Congress.

Apparently, the AFL-CIO delegates from the United States who attended the CLC convention had reported back to George Meany that "the left" had taken control in the CLC.[9] This alarmist portrait — bearing no relation at all to what actually happened at the convention — may have prompted the hysteria with which some American union leaders in the building trades reacted.

Following the Vancouver convention, fifteen of the eighteen internationals in the building trades began to withhold all or part of their CLC dues in protest against the autonomy guidelines. By October of 1974 this had brought about a serious financial problem for the CLC, which already had debts amounting to some $750,000.[10]

Martin Ward, international president of the plumbers' union, (Canadian membership of 35,000 and a total membership of 320,000) was among the most outspoken. He claimed that the CLC decision ran contrary to his union's constitution. He objected in particular to the guideline calling for the election of the Canadian vice-president by the Canadian membership, and to the CLC decision to increase the per capita tax.[11]

At the August 1974 international convention of the carpenters' union — where Joe Morris voiced his "suspicions" of Canadian nationalism (refer to chapter fifteen) — the delegates voted overwhelmingly to send the resolution on Canadian autonomy to the union's executive committee, thus postponing any action on it. The resolution in question merely called for the union "to recognize the minimum standards of self-government for the Canadian membership of international unions".[12]

In September 1974 when the International Brotherhood of Electrical Workers met in convention in Kansas City, the position of the Canadian members within the international was on the union's mind.

First, eight thousand construction electricians in Quebec had just withdrawn from the IBEW in protest against its handling of finances, especially pension funds.

Second, Canada's postmaster-general, Bryce Mackasey, was the convention's keynote speaker. Because he was "an unabashed friend of the American people," he used the occasion to gently caution American delegates that international unionism was in danger because some U.S. unions "refuse to make it possible" for Canadian members to "do their thing," by "insisting that Canada is not a nation . . ."[13]

Despite both these spurs to caution, the American delegates overwhelmingly defeated three resolutions presented by the Canadian delegates which proposed a degree of Canadian self-government. One of the delegates from the Hamilton local explained that they were calling for "Canadian autonomy" on the model of the steel and auto unions, rather than full independence.[14]

Leading the anti-autonomy fight on the convention floor was Canadian vice-president Ken Rose. He attacked the CLC guidelines and, with apologies to the chairman for his language, told the CLC to "go to hell". He also claimed that his union was not withholding funds from the Congress — an erroneous statement for which he was later censured by one of the Canadian locals.

The international executive offered a "compromise" of tacking on the word "Canada" to the phrase "District 1" in the international constitution. The U.S. delegates accepted this.

There were other responses to the CLC convention from Canadian leaders of construction unions. David Cairns, Canadian director of the Brotherhood of Painters and Allied Trades, charged that the CLC convention had been "packed" by the big national unions, led by CUPE, which, he claimed, had allied themselves with the Quebec delegates to push through their programme.[15]

Ronald Taylor, international representative for Canada of the Sheet Metal Workers, asserted, referring to CUPE, that "[there] is no way that a bunch of garbage collectors is going to tell us what to do".[16]

The rank and file, and lower-level leadership of the building trades unions in Canada reacted strongly to the action of withholding CLC dues. At a meeting in Kitchener in November 1974, fifteen Ontario construction locals adopted a resolution in support of the CLC position, and against their own top leadership. During the debate they particularly criticized the fact that the decision to withhold dues had been made by the top leadership in the United States and Canada without consulting or even informing the Canadian locals.

Jack Donnelly, business representative of the Sheet Metal Workers' local in Toronto and chairman of their Canadian Co-ordinating Committee, said that he had known nothing of the action until he read about it in the newspaper. "There are a lot of things wrong with the CLC," he told the Kitchener meeting, "but I dispute the right of people in a foreign country to tell me what organizations to belong to . . . That was an insult to our intelligence. It is not our intention to pull out of the international, but it looks as though the Americans don't want us."[17]

Clive Ballentine, business manager of the Toronto Building and Construction Trades Council, expressed his resentment at the unilateral action taken by international officers without consulting the Canadian membership. Robert Elwell of the Sheet Metal Workers' Ottawa local accused his international of blackmail in its dealings with the CLC.[18]

In late October 1974, the Ontario Federation of Labour met in convention and decided to lend money to the CLC to help it over its financial crisis — thus, in effect, subsidizing the building trades unions' withholding of dues.[19]

The CLC president visited the AFL-CIO Building Trades Department and the presidents of the international construction unions with a plea for the resumption of dues payments. According to a story in *The Globe and Mail*, Joe Morris reassured the building trades presidents that the CLC was in good hands and that the international unions had nothing to fear. The article went on to suggest that had dues payments not been resumed, the building trades unions would have been expelled from the CLC, and this could have led to local break-aways in Canada.[20]

Whatever the reason — the CLC president's assurances or the threat of break-aways — the building trades unions began to resume payment of dues in March 1975, having withheld $350,000 up to that time.[21]

This settled the CLC's financial problems, but it did not mean the end of discontent within the Canadian locals of the building trades unions. The struggle for Canadian unionism in those locals was in its early stages compared to some other American unions in Canada but this incident was a clear indication of a growing division of opinion between these unions' leaders and their rank and file Canadian membership.

In September 1975 Canadian members of fifteen American-based building trades finally won the right to establish a Canadian Building Trades Council at the convention of the Building Trades Department of the AFL-CIO in San Francisco. A similar request made in November 1974 had been rejected by the AFL-CIO Building Trades Department. Undeterred, Canadian members of the building trades unions met at their first Canadian conference in Winnipeg in July 1975 and repeated their demand for an autonomous Canadian Building Trades Council.

Henry Kobryn, executive-secretary of the Ontario Building Trades Council, said that the decision by the U.S. headquarters of several unions to withhold dues from the CLC in 1974 as a means of sabotaging stricter guidelines for Canadian autonomy had angered Canadian members. "That got a lot of people angry and started the ball rolling towards forming a Canadian Council," Kobryn said.

Kobryn told the press that delegates from 582 union locals and building trades councils representing some 400,000 members of fifteen building trades unions had been invited to meet in Winnipeg in January 1976. Kobryn and other supporters of a Canadian Council hoped it would become the policy-making body for construction unions in Canada while remaining part of the AFL-CIO Building Trades Department.[22]

---

1. Canadian Labour Congress, *Resolutions on Constitution and Structure*, Vancouver, May 1974, p. 4.

2. *The Globe and Mail*, November 4, 1974.

3. *The Globe and Mail*, May 14, 1974.

4. A series of non-compliance procedures, including suspension, was recommended at the 1974 CLC convention but the provisions remained recommendations and were not yet in the constitution.

5. *The Globe and Mail*, May 14, 1974.

6. Ibid.

7. B.C. and Yukon Territory Building and Construction Trades Council, *Submission on Canadian Autonomy for the Building Trades to the executive board of the Building and Construction Trades Department of the AFL-CIO*, 1973.

8. Building and Construction Trades Department, AFL-CIO, *Report of the Proceedings*, Bal Harbour, Florida, October 8-9, 1973.

9. *The Globe and Mail*, October 30, 1974.

10. Ibid.

11. *The Financial Post*, June 8, 1974.

12. *Leader-Post* (Regina), August 1, 1974.

13. *Canadian Tribune*, October 2, 1974.

14. Ibid.

15. *The Globe and Mail*, November 4, 1974.

16. Ibid.

17. Ibid.

18. Ibid.

19. *The Globe and Mail*, October 30, 1974.

20. *The Globe and Mail*, March 6, 1975.

21. Ibid.

22. *The Toronto Star*, October 2, 1975.

CHAPTER 17

Break-aways and the CCU

> ... let it be understood that the American unions in Canada hold firmly to the view that once you join their ranks, voluntarily or involuntarily, *you are forever after their "property"* ... You are a subject, bound by the rules laid down on Miami Beach ... To disobey this imperial law must naturally bring sanctions.
>
> Kent Rowley
> Secretary-treasurer, CCU[1]

No account of Canada's union movement and of the growing nationalism of Canadian workers would be complete without a discussion of the break-away movement and the Confederation of Canadian Unions. The CCU's activities have not been confined to local break-aways, nor has the Confederation been significant in terms of the number of members it has organized. But the activities of the CCU and its most prominent spokesmen, Kent Rowley and Madeleine Parent, have focused public attention on the nationalist debate in the unions.

No union leaders in the country have been so subject to the verbal attacks of certain international officers as Rowley and Parent. More often than not, a stinging attack has been returned by these two union leaders who have had a long history in the Canadian union movement. In the debate over Canadian versus American unionism, they had earned their right to be heard.

Both were associated with the early days of industrial union organization among textile workers in Quebec and other parts of Canada. Rowley was a vice-president of the United Textile Workers of America for some twelve years and Parent was equally prominent in the organizational days of that union. They both led the historic Valleyfield and Montreal strikes of 1946 and the Lachute strike of 1947. Rowley and Parent were also both convicted of "conspiracy" under the infamous anti-labour laws of Quebec's Premier Duplessis. This conviction occurred in the course of their struggles to organize a union in an industry characterized in vivid terms during a 1936 federal inquiry. In testimony to a Royal Commission the textile industry was described as:

> ... a shameful, sickening story of heartless exploitation and whole-sale robbery by men prominent in the public life of Canada. Inordinate barefaced lying, general fraud, characterized the careers of this gang of high placed crooks. These were the leaders in the cotton manufacturing industry.[2]

Rowley and Parent had endured many attacks from the Quebec cotton companies and from Duplessis. But the hardest blows came not from these sources, but from the American headquarters of the union they had done so much to build — the United Textile Workers of America.

In 1952 the Canadian district of the UTWA became embroiled in another of its long series of disputes with the Dominion Textile Company. On the first of April, 5,500 textile workers went on strike legally in Montreal and Valleyfield.[3]

On May 25, when the mills had been closed for seven weeks and pressure on the company was building, the U.S. headquarters of the UTWA entered the picture. Lloyd Klenert, secretary-treasurer of the international, arrived from Washington and attended a meeting of the Montreal-Valleyfield joint strike committee. The members asked him what they might expect from union headquarters in terms of financial assistance, but Klenert refused to commit himself.

Early the next morning, "a person or persons unknown" broke into the Montreal headquarters of the union and stole its records. That same day, the Washington office issued a statement declaring that it had dismissed the entire Canadian staff of twelve organizers, headed by Rowley and Parent. The international announced that it was presenting the Canadian textile workers with a "safe, clean leadership" headed by Sam Baron and Roger Provost.[4]

Sam Baron was not a favourite of the workers at Valleyfield and Montreal. Two years earlier, as Canadian head of the rival Textile Workers of America, he had tried to raid their locals and replace the UTWA as bargaining agent.

But the company and the Duplessis governement clearly appreciated the new leadership. Blair Gordon, president of Dominion Textile, referred to Baron and Provost as "men who understand that the well-being of the workers depends largely on the well-being of the industry". Premier Duplessis said "this is excellent news"; and his Minister of Labour, Antonio Barrette, announced "I am pleased". Hal Banks, of SIU fame, proclaimed that "this news is indeed welcome to myself and the organization I represent".[5]

The negotiators who eventually bargained with Dominion Textile on behalf of the striking workers were Frank Hall — whose union had been suspended by the TLC four years previously for its role in smashing the Canadian Seamen's Union — Bernard Shane, Sam Baron, and Hal Banks.

The UTWA secretary-treasurer's claim that "we are now providing a clean trade union leadership for the textile workers of Quebec" was hardly supported by these facts.

Klenert himself was a dubious character. The Ethical Practices Committee of the AFL-CIO, reporting on September 16, 1957, found that at the same time he was introducing the "clean" leadership into Quebec, Klenert was using union funds to buy himself a house. Testimony before the U.S. Senate Select Committee on Improper Activities suggested that between 1954 and 1956, Klenert had spent $65,000 in union funds for personal purposes.[6]

Kent Rowley added some interesting facts in a personal account of the 1952 events.[7] He recalled that in the middle of the strike Klenert came to Canada and met secretly with the heads of Dominion Textile. He then visited Rowley in his hotel room, showed him the contract he had negotiated with the company, and ordered Rowley to sign it and settle the strike. The contract included the very "bonus" plan the union was striking against. There had been no consultation whatsoever with the membership. Rowley refused to sign. Then, as he tells it:

> . . . the Klenert crowd along with the Montreal police smashed into our national office in the dark of the night, stole records and money, and mutilated our files. The next morning, headlines in the newspapers announced that the entire staff and I in Canada were summarily fired. No vote, no trial, nothing.[8]

Rowley footnotes the union actions by saying "during all the long strike — [we had] not a cent of relief from the Washington headquarters to which we had loyally paid our per capita tax".[9]

There seem to have been no limits to the pressure the "international" leadership of the UTWA was willing to put on Rowley. He recalls one occasion when president Valente came to Montreal and invited Rowley to his room at the Mount Royal Hotel. When Rowley got there, he found an open file on the bed which Valente told him he might find "interesting". Valente went to take a shower, leaving Rowley with the file, which turned out to be Rowley's life history as compiled by the FBI.[10]

By 1952, then, Rowley and Parent had gained a good deal of insight into U.S. business unionism. In the 1950s and 1960s the two union leaders remained active in a small Canadian union of textile workers which had been organized as the Canadian Textile and Chemical Union. Its membership in the early 1970s was about 1,200.

Rowley and Parent founded the Council of Canadian Unions in 1971. Rowley explains its formation and role:

The Council of Canadian Unions finally gave a vehicle and voice for those who believed in a united Canadian labour movement. We began to answer and expose the false propaganda of the American labour bureaucracy. We exposed their domination and exploitation of Canadian workers ...

We published the facts as finally reported under the Corporations and Labour Unions Returns Act (CALURA) — figures that showed clearly that Canadian workers are subsidizing the fat and corrupt leadership of the American trade union movement. In only eight years of reporting (1962 to 1969), the American unions collected from Canada $249,213,000 and spent $159,311,000, leaving them a net profit of $89,902,000.[11]

In the early days of the CCU, the position Rowley took seemed to suggest that the only way Canadian workers could free themselves from bondage to the "internationals" was through break-aways, where a union local breaks away from its parent union body and affiliates with another union. The impression was created that Rowley saw the independence process as a gradual nibbling away of the internationals, slowly adding weight to the side of Canadian unionism. More recently, however, this position was modified. In 1973 Rowley said, "We have no illusions we are going to take over the internationals. But I do think we can act as catalyst ..."[12] The CCU policy, according to Rowley, then, was to see:

That all the existing Canadian unions come together to form one powerful centre. There are already 800,000 members of Canadian unions. That the Canadian members of the American unions develop their understanding to the point where they are able to call conventions of their Canadian members to declare their independence.[13]

The impression formed in earlier days that the CCU was relentlessly hostile to the existing branches of American unions in Canada may partly have been created by the strong terms Rowley used to describe them. For example, when the Alcan workers at Kitimat, B.C., broke away from the United Steel Workers of America and joined the CCU-affiliated Canadian Association of Smelter and Allied Workers in October 1972 Rowley had this to say about the Steelworkers:

I went to Kitimat several times ... The men of the smelters were unhappy, and the torrents of discontent flowed full. For they had turned their backs finally on the United Steel Workers of America — pride of the fleet, dreadnought of imperial union power. They were building a Canadian union — and had thus committed the ultimate offence against "private property" in the business world of American trade union bureaucracy.[14]

In another statement describing the Kitimat break-away, Rowley wrote:

The final act of indignity by the "Steel" bureaucracy against the workers of Kitimat was to rush to secure the local workers' property for their overlords in Pittsburgh. But the whining of the "Steel machine" was drowned by the celebration of workers that lasted far into the night.[15]

In response to the charge that the CCU leadership were "flag-wavers" Rowley said:

> Let me say a word about "flag-waving". The truth is that the top leaders of the American unions in Canada do not really believe in the independence of this country. They accept the colonial status that their situation implies. So long have they been accustomed to rising to their feet before the Stars and Stripes at their "international" conventions, that they consider the Maple Leaf to be an intrusion.[16]

To the argument that international unions were necessary to fight multinational companies, Rowley has stated:

> First, it shows a failure to understand the economy of imperialism. Secondly, it indicates lack of knowledge of true internationalism. Of course, in a way it must be said that the "international" unions in Canada are just as international as Ford. They are American unions with Canadian branches.[17]

This characterization of international locals in Canada as "branches" similar to the branch plants of American corporations has aroused hostility and anger among leaders and activists of those unions in Canada.

But it was not just Rowley's words that earned him the enmity of the leadership of the international unions in Canada. A more important factor has been the willingness of some international locals to break away from their U.S. unions and join CCU affiliates.

The Alcan plant at Kitimat had been organized by the United Steel Workers of America in 1956. Many of the workers there were European immigrants who had belonged to strong national unions in their home countries. Their experience with the Steelworkers led many of them to conclude that the U.S. connection was a liability.

After paying ten dollars each month in union dues, most of which went directly to Pittsburgh, the membership received little service. Even the steel union leadership admitted this after the break-away had taken place. As dissatisfaction in the Kitimat local grew, a group of workers appealed to a new Canadian union which had recently been formed on the west coast, the Pulp, Paper and Woodworkers. They launched an organizing campaign and eventually applied to the B.C. Labour Board for certification. However, under the Social Credit government of W.A.C. Bennett, the Labour Board did not find it necessary to hold public hearings on union applications, or even to give justifications for their final decisions. Amid claims by the Steelworkers that there had been "irregularities" and "fraud" in the attempt to form a Canadian union, the PPWC application was thrown out.[18]

Following the certification attempt, the USWA laid charges against ten activists in the Kitimat local, accusing them of violating the international constitution by aiding and abetting a "dual union". When the charges were brought before a general membership meeting, the ten were acquitted by an overwhelming majority. The steel union headquarters in Pittsburgh then assigned two international representatives to Kitimat. Upon arrival they revived the charges, tried the men, found them guilty and took away their union rights.[19]

The ten disbarred unionists then received a letter notifying them that they could launch an appeal, at their own expense, before the next meeting of the International Executive Board to be held in Washington, D.C. Two representatives were sent to appear before the USWA court, presided over by I.W. Abel. The sentences were upheld.[20] Events like these revealed the extent of the power vested in the international president under the USWA constitution. He has absolute power over union members and locals: "... where, in the opinion of the international president, the best interests of the international union or local union require, the international president is empowered to suspend officers of, and establish an administratorship over, the affairs and property of a local union prior to notice and hearing ..."[21]

Not long after the Washington hearing, the second round at Kitimat began. The workers set up the Canadian Association of Smelter and Allied Workers, elected officers, signed up members, and affiliated to the CCU. This organizational work was done almost entirely by men in the plant.

The USWA responded by sending in large numbers of organizers. The USWA spokesmen belittled the ability of a small Canadian union to take on a powerful world-wide corporation, asking where the money and research would come from. And, as they had done in their attacks and raids on the Mine, Mill and Smelter Workers Union in an earlier period, the steel representatives started to call the workers who wanted a Canadian union "communists". William Mahoney, Canadian director of the USWA, talked about "a new and insidious form of company unionism".[22] When a similar move was taking place in Trail, B.C. shortly afterwards, the Steelworker local's president, Bob Keiver, said that the "so-called union leaders who preach nationalist slogans are in league with the worst racists in the Ku Klux Klan or the Nazi party".[23]

Kitimat received only one television station, and the steel union was able to buy hours of broadcast time to campaign against the "vote Canadian" proposals. However, Kitimat workers proceeded to file their application for certification, and the USWA demanded a hearing to present their charges of "fraud" and "forgery". The hearing was held and the chairman asked the USWA representative to present his evidence of fraud. The steel union's lawyer said he had no evidence to submit. The vote was ordered in October 1972 and the result was 1,112 to 305 in favour of an all-Canadian union.[24]

A similar attempt in 1973 at Cominco in Trail — a USWA local that had originally been part of Mine, Mill before the steel raids — was defeated on a technicality under the B.C. Labour Relations Board.[25]

In presenting a balanced assessment of the CCU, it must be pointed out that despite its success at Kitimat and near-success at Trail, the actual growth of the Confederation had been very slow. By 1975 it numbered some 20,000 members — less than one per cent of Canada's total union membership. The break-away movement had largely been confined to western Canada which had a tradition of local militancy and of willingness to change from one union to another. There had been very little growth in industrial Ontario.

To some extent the latter might be explained by the greater conservatism of Ontario workers. The unions in Ontario had had their greatest strength in the U.S-owned manufacturing industries in the urban centres. By contrast, union strength in B.C. had been in the resource industries, where workers moved more from job to job and hence came into contact with a number of different unions and locals. This may have made B.C. workers more sensitive to the differences that changes in union structure can bring about.

But conservatism is not the only explanation, for Ontario has witnessed sweeping changes in the degree of militancy of workers in 1973-75. This has been seen among previously conservative organizations of teachers, hospital workers, nurses and provincial public employees.

This was also a tendency for workers to hold on to organizations which they had built. And within the international unions there were several locals — particularly the larger, more powerful ones — with a militant and activist tradition, which from time to time had been under a local leadership which opposed the business unionism of their internationals. This had kept alive the alternative of a transformation of the whole Canadian section of various international unions into Canadian unions, from within.

The CCU itself came to recognize that it was not the only, or even the major, route to Canadian unionism. But it had indeed served an important role as a catalyst.

In the course of travelling that road, which Rowley has called "very rocky", the CCU had even managed to antagonize some of its friends. This was most clearly seen in the case of the Mine, Mill local at Falconbridge in Sudbury. This, the only remaining local of the old Mine, Mill union, was one of the founders of the CCU, and its largest affiliate. The first two presidents of the CCU, Roy Scranton and Ed Nitchie, were both members of the Mine, Mill local.

A difference arose between the Falconbridge workers and others in the CCU over organizing tactics. Mine, Mill tended to favour concentration on organizing the unorganized, so that unions affiliated to the CCU would be contributing to the growth of the labour movement in Canada. They opposed what they called "raiding" — the CCU practice of accepting or encouraging the affiliations of locals that would break away from international unions. Mine, Mill, as the last survivor of the Steelworkers raid on their union, was particularly sensitive to this problem. In 1972, Mine, Mill withdrew from the CCU. The separation was not a friendly one, as CCU leaders accused the Falconbridge local of a "below the belt attack".[26] This did not enhance the CCU's reputation.

After 1973 the CCU toned down its language and moderated its goals to some extent but it still looked to the formation of a centre of all-Canadian unions as an alternative to the CLC.

Whatever the roads to a fully independent Canadian union movement, and several had been taken by 1973, only a tiny minority had chosen the CCU path. Since 1973 the potential power of Canadian unions within the CLC has also grown substantially. However, the arguments raised by the CCU in the early 1970s had contributed substantially to the debate and had influenced workers who were searching for solutions to the problem of domination of their unions and the CLC by the American-based internationals.

---

1. R. Kent Rowley, "The Road to Kitimat", *Canadian Forum*, March 1973, p. 6.

2. Charles Lipton, *The Trade Union Movement of Canada 1827-1959* (Toronto: NC Press, 1973), 3rd edition, p. 273, from testimony of E.E. McRuer, counsel to Justice W. F. A. Turgeon, head of 1936 Royal Commission into the textile industry.

3. Ibid., p. 291.

4. Ibid., p. 292, from *The Gazette* (Montreal), May 26, 1952; *The Montreal Star*, May 26, 1952.

5. Ibid., p. 292, from *The Montreal Star*, May 26, 1952; *The Gazette*, May 28, 1952; *The Gazette*, June 4, 1952; *The Montreal Star*, May 28, 1952.

6. Ibid., p. 293, from AFL-CIO, *Proceedings*, Vol. 2, 1957, p. 550.

7. R. Kent Rowley, "Canadian Workers: A Message from R. Kent Rowley", *Canadian Dimension*, March 1973, p. 30.

8. Ibid.

9. Ibid.

10. Ibid.

11. *Canadian Forum*, March 1973, p. 7.

12. *Edmonton Journal*, September 21, 1973.

13. *The Leaflet*, July-August 1973, p. 7, from *Canadian Dimension*, March 1973.

14. *Canadian Forum*, March 1973, p. 6.

15. Ibid.

16. Confederation of Canadian Unions, *Proceedings*, Report of the Secretary-Treasurer, Winnipeg, July 7-8, 1973.

17. *Canadian Dimension*, March 1973, p. 35.

18. *Canadian Forum*, March 1973.

19. Ibid.

20. Ibid.

21. Constitution of International Union, United Steel Workers of America, adopted at Atlantic City, New Jersey, September 27, 1974, Article IX, p. 61.

22. *The Globe and Mail*, October 23, 1972.

23. *The Windsor Star*, February 8, 1973.

24. *This Magazine*, August 1973.

25. *Canadian Union News*, June 1973, p. 1; see also Chapter 27.

26. *The Globe and Mail*, July 10, 1972.

CHAPTER 18
From Autonomy to Independence:
The Paperworkers and the CBRT

Others are watching our progress. We will be the yard-stick against
which will be measured the development of a distinctive industrial
labour union movement in Canada.

Henri Lorrain
President, Canadian Paperworkers Union
Founding convention, 1974[1]

In April 1969 members of the Canadian Brotherhood of Railway Transport and General Workers overwhelmingly rejected a plan of their top
leadership to merge with an international union. In June 1974 Canadian
members of the United Paperworkers International Union severed their
ties with the American union in order to build their own full-Canadian
organization. These two events indicated both how much the thinking of
the labour movement could change in just five years and, at the same
time, how continuous the nationalism of Canadian workers has been. In
1969 this nationalism was expressed defensively, against a plan to take
away a union's national identity; in 1974 it was asserted positvely, with a
decisive separation.

The most surprising aspect of the CBRT leadership's 1969 attempt to
forge a merger with the Brotherhood of Railway, Airline and Steamship
Clerks (BRAC) was that it was done in the name of nationalism.

What lay behind the proposal was a desire to reduce the number of
separate unions representing Canadian railway workers. The discussions among union officials began with the idea of forming a single
independent Canadian union merging the CBRT — an independent Canadian union founded in 1909 — with the Canadian members of an international, the Brotherhood of Railway, Airline and Steamship Clerks. But
the outcome was a proposal that the CBRT be merged into the BRAC. The

idea was defended on the basis of arguments about Canadian independence.

Columnists Douglas Fisher and Harry Crowe commented satirically about the proposal in *The Toronto Telegram:*

> Come again? This is precisely the double-think, double-talk proposal of William J. Smith ... To preserve Canadian autonomy, to achieve the brotherhood's traditional objective of national unionism, CBRT membership cards must be torn up and replaced by union cards of the Brotherhood of Railway, Airline and Steamship Clerks ... A lot can be learned about Canada's American problem by studying this extraordinary case history ...[2]

The merger proposal arose out of a policy decision made at the CBRT's 1967 convention. The delegates had adopted a statement which advocated the unification of the railway unions, and stated that:

> There are unmistakable signs that the desire for national autonomy is growing rapidly among the members of the international unions in Canada. They not only want one union on the railways, they also want it to be a Canadian union.[3]

President William J. Smith and the other top CBRT officers used this resolution as the basis for merger talks with BRAC. As the talks went on, the original idea of consolidating the railway organizations into one Canadian industrial union was submerged in the idea of Canadian autonomy in an international. As Fisher and Crowe remarked, "... we cannot avoid the feeling of resentment that the Americanization of a fine Canadian union is being sold to the rank and file membership as some kind of super-nationalism".[4]

The CBRT leadership called a special convention for Montreal in June of 1969 to vote on the merger proposal. Opposition to the merger quickly developed among union activists.

George Thivierge, chairman of the biggest local in the CBRT, Montreal Local 330, claimed that the majority of union members he had contacted were opposed to the merger, particularly in Quebec. "French-Canadian rank and filers will never buy this," he said. "They don't want their dues and control of their union going to the United States."[5]

Thivierge said that the main source of opposition to the merger was the nationalism of the rank and file, but added that there were suspicions about the leaders' motives:

> Rank and filers aren't getting anything out of this that they don't already have. The only ones who are getting any advantage are the salaried officers and the salaried people who will get higher salaries from BRAC.

This referred to the fact that Smith, then 64, received a $21,000 annual salary as Canadian president of the CBRT, but would receive $30,000 as an international vice-president of BRAC. Compulsory retirement age in

BRAC was 70 compared to 65 in the CBRT, and BRAC had a better pension plan for its top officers.[6]

Thivierge charged that president Smith was trying to stampede CBRT members into approval of the merger with the bigger and richer international by giving dire warnings that railway jobs would be lost due to automation. He noted that for decades the railway brotherhoods in joint negotiations had tried and failed to curb declining employment, and that merging with BRAC could not change that situation in the slightest.

Richard Greaves, business agent for the CBRT's seaway local at Welland, said that the merger proposal was the first step into the quicksand. He said he did not trust the "autonomy" safeguards promised by BRAC since Canadians would have a minority voice at international conventions, "The tail," he pointed out, "doesn't wag the dog." He also warned that the merger would take the leadership even further away from the rank and file:

> I have no desire for a merger with an international union. We can make our own decisions in Canada for Canadians and within the Canadian context. We now have full autonomy and we don't have to bargain for it.[7]

Another leader of the anti-merger movement was Jim Hunter, who later became a vice-president of the union. "To merge with an international union now would be a complete reversal of what is happening in Canada today, both in unions and elsewhere — a cry for more autonomy,"[8] Hunter argued.

Prior to the special convention, president Smith and secretary-treasurer Donald Secord convinced some members of the press that they were invincible. Fisher and Crowe were sure Smith could override the majority and effect a merger. Lamenting the spectacle of a president of a Canadian union and vice-president of the NDP advocating merger with an American union that "takes the straight George Meany-Pentagon line on Viet Nam," they claimed that they had received from BRAC pamphlets originating from the AFL-CIO Allied Western Hemisphere Labour Organization, which according to testimony before a congressional committee is financed by the Central Intelligence Agency.[9]

According to Toronto newspapers, delegates were greeted with "Yankee Go Home" signs and "Canada First" buttons as they entered the convention and tables in the convention hall were draped with Canadian flags. Delegates stood to sing "O Canada", and forced the officers on the platform to rise and join them.[10]

During the debate, anti-U.S. sentiment was evident in many of the speeches. For example, Victoria delegate Haye Anderson said he could live with the Americans, "but I'm damned if I'm going to sleep with them". Thomas Bernett of Local 400, representing Vancouver seamen, won loud applause when he announced that if the convention decided to go into BRAC, the seamen on the west coast would not go with them.[11]

The leadership failed disastrously on the first of three proposed amendments that were to clear away legal obstacles to a merger. This would merely have given the right to a CBRT convention to authorize a merger with any other trade union. But the delegates understood what was behind this innocuous language, and they opposed it from the outset with a vote of 305 to 61 against the proposal.[12] Following the convention, Smith said that there would be no further attempts to continue negotiations with BRAC. At the same time, he forecast that a consolidation of railway unions was bound to occur, although it might be years in the future. He did not indicate clearly whether or not this would be a fully independent Canadian union.[13]

The events of the CBRT's special convention in 1969 highlighted the two sets of factors that have operated together in Canada's labour movement. In rejecting the merger proposal, CBRT members were opting both for nationalism against continentalism, and for rank and file democracy against bureaucratic control from the top. This was similar to the combination of factors leading up to the paper workers' decision in 1974 to separate from their international and form an independent Canadian union.

American pulp and paper unions have existed in Canada since the turn of the century. For fifty years, two AFL-affiliated unions, the Pulp, Sulphite and Paper Mill Workers and the United Paper Makers and Paper Workers, dominated the Canadian industry. Then in 1957 the United Paper Makers merged with the CIO's United Paperworkers' of America and in 1972, this merged union joined the Pulp, Sulphite organization to form the United Paperworkers International Union.[14]

In 1963, a group of British Columbia locals broke away from the Pulp, Sulphite union to form the Pulp, Paper and Woodworkers of Canada (PPWC). In Quebec, the independent CNTU's pulp and paper union — the Federation of Paper and Forest Workers — was growing. Demands for greater Canadian autonomy within the international were being heard, and the international responded quite favourably to these pressures. Canadian members of the pulp and paper unions had had a degree of "autonomy" since 1944, when a separate research and educational unit for Canada was established.[15] By the time of the 1968 convention, the Canadian members had many autonomy rights:[16]

— a bilingual Canadian newspaper;
— a separate research and education department;
— the right to initiate and direct their own legislative programmes;
— a Canadian director with responsibility for communication and information programmes, including editorial control of the Canadian newspaper;
— the right to initiate and direct organizing campaigns in Canada;
— the right of the Canadian director to convene nation-wide collective bargaining conferences;
— the right of the Canadian director to be head of the union in

Canada, and to convene all-Canadian conferences;
— independent representation at international labour conferences;
— a distinctive national symbol of their own choosing;
— the right to nominate their own officers and choose their own "international" representatives; and,
— the right of the Canadian director to approve strikes and collective agreements.

Few American unions in Canada could — then or now — boast a greater degree of "autonomy". But as the 1974 decision showed, this was not enough for the Canadian paper workers. Several factors contributed to the ultimate rejection of such "autonomy" as a permanent status for Canadian paper workers.

There had been serious rumblings within the American membership in the 1960s over charges of poor servicing, lack of democracy and corruption. Some twenty thousand American pulp and paper workers on the west coast left the union over such charges. According the U.S. judge who investigated the charges laid against UPIU president Joseph Tonelli by the Americans who left the union, "the evidence clearly establishes that Tonelli purchased a $45,000 home, with a swimming pool and a new Cadillac car, and financed an extravagent wedding at a time when his modest income would barely provide room and board . . ."[17]

Another case of corrupt activities on the part of the international was a letter circulated in April 1959 to members of the executive board by then-president John P. Burke. The letter concerned an economic report prepared by the union's research and education director, George Brooks, which showed that collective agreements in the pulp and paper industry had fallen behind agreements signed by other unions in other industries. Burke was attempting to suppress the report, and the reason was made clear in his letter:

> If we use the argument suggested by George Brooks in our arguments with the employers this year the delegates attending these conferences may begin to think that some other union perhaps could do a better job for them in the negotiations . . .[18]

Tonelli, while vice-president of the Pulp, Sulphite Union, similarly tried to suppress the fact that other unions were signing better contracts. A passage in one of his letters, written in 1958, said:

> You will notice in the agreement that they are exceptionally high for the industry. I do not think that these rates should be publicized in other corrugated locals we have under contract.[19]

Given such practices, it was not surprising that paper workers in British Columbia decided to break away from the international in the early 1960s.

Another factor leading to the 1974 separation of the 52,000 Canadian members was the UPIU's handling of a series of strikes in the Canadian industry in the summer and fall of 1973. On July 25 of that year, about

3,200 Quebec UPIU members struck the plants of the Canadian International Paper Company at La Tuque, Gatineau and Trois-Rivières. In early July members of the International Union of Operating Engineers (IUOE) and the International Association of Machinists (IAM) struck the Ontario-Minnesota Pulp and Paper Company in northern Ontario and UPIU members respected the picket lines. On July 6 UPIU members in B.C. had struck MacMillan Bloedel.[20]

By August, the strike movement had spread to other plants in the provinces already affected, as well as to plants in New Brunswick and, later on, to Nova Scotia and Quebec.

The Abitibi Paper Company — one of the two largest chains in the pulp and paper industry, employing some six thousand workers — was the pattern-setter in the settlements that ended the strike wave. This pattern established an increase of 8.5 per cent in each year of a two-year contract.[21] Since the cost of living index rose by 9.1 per cent in 1973, the paper workers were actually falling further behind following the agreement than prior to it. The other contract provisions — increased holidays and pension benefits — while significant, would hardly make up for the lack of a cost of living adjustment in the contract.

Yet the settlement was fiercely resisted by some of the paper companies, particularly the Canadian International Paper Company, a subsidiary of the U.S.-owned International Paper Company. Some 4,500 CIP workers were on strike in Hawkesbury, Ontario; Gatineau, La Tuque and Trois-Rivières, Quebec; and Dalhousie, New Brunswick. The Canadian subsidiary was not willing to settle for the Abitibi pattern of 8.5 per cent in each of two years. It wanted to sign an agreement similar to that signed between its parent company and 10,000 American employees earlier in the year. This had been a three-year contract with a 6.9 per cent increase in the first year, 6.5 in the second year and 6.25 per cent on average in the third year.[22]

Members of the UPIU on strike at CIP's Gatineau plant were particularly concerned with job security. Local president Roland Osborne was unhappy with the international's policy, saying that its leaders had not respected local priorities concerning job security and cost of living provisions when they signed the Abitibi agreement. In the middle of the Gatineau strike Osborne submitted his resignation from the local presidency in protest against the Abitibi pattern agreement. "Job security is our top priority," he said. "In 1970 I negotiated for 1,460 men but today my membership is down to 1,061."[23]

The 1973 strikes were costly for the international, not only in terms of prestige with its Canadian membership but also in terms of hard cash. The UPIU spent more than it received in Canada in that year despite president Tonelli's claims to the contrary.[24] This may help to explain the good grace with which Tonelli assented to the Canadian section's move to independence in 1974.

Another important factor leading the Canadian members to adopt a strategy of full independence was the general growth of nationalism among Canadian workers.

In 1974 the Canadian vice-president of the UPIU, Henri Lorrain, requested permission from the international executive board to hold a referendum in Canada on the separation of the Canadian section as a whole. In mid-February Lorrain met with the presidents of most of the 210 Canadian locals, who represented 52,000 workers in every province except P.E.I. He told the local presidents:

> We can and must establish our separate identity, our sense of national pride ... Can we afford to be independent? ... Self-confidence, self-assurance, pride, the ability to walk tall and untrammelled: none of these intangible qualities is measurable. I must answer, therefore: can we afford not to be independent?[25]

The local presidents voted 179 to 5 in favour of holding the referendum.[26]

The question was put to a vote in the week of April 15. The result was conclusive: 86 per cent of the 31,000 Canadian paper workers who voted were in favour of separating from the UPIU and setting up a fully independent Canadian union.[27] Such an overwhelming vote in favour of Canadian unionism by workers who had long associations with their international and who came from virtually every corner of the country was impressive evidence of the strength of nationalist sentiment among Canadian workers.

Lorrain predicted: "Others are watching our progress".[28] He pointed out, too, that international solidarity must follow from the new, independent Canadian union:

> We shall of course have special relationships — of pride of craft or community of interests — with our brothers and sisters in the pulp and paper industry in all countries ... But we shall do this as craftsmen and as Canadians.[29]

Tonelli, the UPIU president, told delegates to the founding convention of the Canadian Paperworkers Union that the change resulted from "a challenge that has been growing over a period of the last ten years reflecting the desire of our Canadian sisters and brothers to have their own national union ... Assertion of a truly Canadian identity became crucial elements in the lives of many Canadians."[30]

In an historic move, the Canadian paper workers had separated cordially from their international union. The outstanding issue that remained to be settled was the division of funds involving between $1.5 and $2.0 million. Settlement of this matter depended on the American UPIU convention in 1976.

While the new CPU had not made a complete break with the practices of business unionism by 1975, its formation was an historic move. The international head office of the UPIU also set a precedent when it acceded cordially to the nationalist demands of its Canadian members.

The forestry industry negotiations of 1975 demonstrated that militancy was challenging business unionism in the CPU. With a demand for a two dollar per hour general wage increase the CPU led the departure among industrial unions from the practice of avoiding "excessive" demands.[31] It helped set the pattern of demands in the B.C. forest industry which led to a giant strike in the summer of 1975.

In August 1975 Lorrain commented in an interview on the new possibilities for participating as an independent union in the International Federation of Chemical Workers Unions. "One of the things that our union is keen about is that we belong to the International Federation of Chemical Workers — a body of unions based in Geneva, which groups together pulp, glass, ceramic and rubber workers. We attended a conference in Geneva in June where we decided very seriously that we were going to attempt to co-ordinate collective bargaining in one or two of the large multinational companies."[32]

"The German unions are keen on this, the Brits and the Scans, and want to make sure our American friends are too. . . . I think we will now be able to play a role in the International Confederation of Free Trade Unions (ICFTU) that we couldn't before because we were part of a U.S.-based organization. We always had to give thought to the fact that the majority of the membership was American. Now we're going to look at what's good for the Canadian membership and we'll play our role and provide leadership."

Asked whether he sees it as one of his jobs to encourage "the growth of nationalism in the Canadian union movement", Lorrain replied yes. "I think that while we've been very careful to say that ours was not a blueprint for everybody else, I think that if we achieve the success that I think we will, by our example, it will lead to people in other industries looking for greater autonomy — autonomy that will lead to independence."

Lorrain explained that they had been "very successful" in their union in utilizing the tools that they had because of their autonomy. "We set goals in Canada. We established certain aims and we co-ordinated the collective bargaining in Canada. We didn't wait to see what Wisconsin or anywhere in the United States was doing. We didn't wait for them to get together. We did our thing and very frankly — I don't think we have to be modest — the fact is, we were very successful in utilizing the tools that we had to such a degree that we just left the Americans behind. . . . From 1965 on we developed momentum and by 1967-1968 they were falling behind [in pay], and by 1970-1971 we were gone!"

Lorrain continued, "We hope to develop, through the ICFTU, far greater co-ordination than existed when we were a continental union — that's a good term, a continental union — as opposed to the international movement we're part of now as a national union".

The CPU's example was the largest and most successful of the moves toward Canadian unionism in the mid-seventies. But it was not the only one; four other examples of parallel, although not exactly similar, developments are noteworthy.

Two years earlier Canadian communication workers set up their own fully independent union, Communications Workers of Canada, in a cordial arrangement with their international. The CWC represented some 5,000 workers.[33]

An interesting sequel to the display of Canadian nationalism by the railway workers in 1969 and the CPU in 1974 was the 1975 decision to establish an independent Canadian structure within the Brotherhood of Railway, Airline and Steamship Clerks, the same international union into which it had been proposed the CBRT should merge. The new Canadian organization in BRAC was to hold its own conventions and executive elections and have its own Canadian president and Canadian secretary-treasurer for a trial period of four years, during which time it was to have full control over its own finances. International president C.L. Dennis told BRAC's May 1975 convention in Washington that this decision was a response to the rising national sentiment in Canada which demanded increased autonomy for Canadian unions.[34] This development provided an interesting historical twist. Instead of the CBRT becoming part of the American-based BRAC in 1969, BRAC in Canada was moving in 1975 to become a Canadian union. This perhaps would open the door to a possible merger of railway unions in Canada on an all-Canadian basis.

A similar move in the direction of full Canadian independence came at the 1974 Atlanta convention of the National Association of Broadcast Employees and Technicians. With about 4,200 Canadian and 5,900 American members NABET was a small international union. Pressure for Canadian independence had built up over the years, especially from the Quebec membership.

A compromise was effected, whereby two parallel organizations were set up within the structure of the international, each with separate executive councils and constitutions. The two executive councils were to make up the "multinational executive council" which would meet every four years and was to have advisory powers only. Its recommendations were to be approved by the American and Canadian memberships separately before they could be adopted.

This structure, which meant almost but not quite full independence, was spear-headed by the Montreal membership, and won the support of the American delegates at the convention.[35]

The brewery workers provided yet another example of Canadian members in international unions separating from American head offices. After the international brewery union announced its intention to merge with the Teamsters in 1973, representatives of Canada's 9,000 brewery workers met to set up their own national organization. This attempt was promised the support of the CLC.

In July 1974 the Canadians won a six-month legal battle when the Ontario Labour Relations Board ruled that the merger of the Teamsters and Brewery Workers was unconstitutional and invalid. By February 1975 a new union, the Canadian Union of United Brewery, Flour, Cereal, Soft Drink and Distillery Workers, had joined the growing family of fully independent Canadian unions.[36]

The movement within the international unions to win independence or greatly increased "autonomy" for the Canadian members was not restricted to those unions that had introduced structural changes. In the 1970s members of locals in other unions had pressed for such organizational changes to be made, and their activities had often taken the shape of resolutions to international conventions and Canadian policy conferences.

For example, in March 1974 the 11,500-member USWA Local 1005 at Stelco's Hamilton plant passed by a narrow margin the following resolution for presentation to the Steelworkers Canadian Policy Conference:

> Whereas there is a growing concern on the part of steel workers to have their own Canadian union; and
> Whereas under the present constitution that cannot be done; and
> Whereas this is causing serious problems, pitting one worker against another, dividing and weakening our organization, draining our energy and resources; therefore
> Be it resolved, that this Policy Conference instruct the Canadian Directors and the National Office to work towards creating a completely independent Canadian Steelworkers Organization.[37]

A similar resolution, generalizing the policy to all international unions in Canada and calling for a referendum among their Canadian memberships, was narrowly defeated at a subsequent meeting of the local.

The significance of these two votes lay in the fact that Local 1005 had had thirty years devoted to building up the international tie, during which time much had been made of the degree of "autonomy" offered by the USWA. But even among the older members who attended local meetings, by the mid-seventies some fifty per cent supported fully independent Canadian unionism. Activists in the local have noted the feeling among members in the under thirty-five age group who constituted a majority in the local in 1974. The younger members, although they did not attend meetings in large numbers, were even more strongly pro-Canadian.

While the older members dominated the 1005 executive, younger workers were taking an active role as stewards. The steward body in the local numbered some three hundred and fifty early in 1975, and the overwhelming majority were under thirty-five.

This new level of activity among younger workers was in evidence at the Lasco Steel local in Whitby, Ontario, whose six hundred members, and local leadership, were on the whole younger than that of Local 1005. They passed the following resolutions to be presented at the USWA's 1974 Atlantic City convention:

Be it resolved: that a referendum be taken . . . to determine whether a majority of Canadian steel workers prefer a fully independent Canadian union retaining fraternal ties with our fellow-workers in America. Be it further resolved: that the international executives of our union be required to abide by the decision of the majority of Canadians in this instance and not put forth any obstacles to the formation of a Canadian union if the majority vote so indicates.[38]

This resolution, like some two hundred others, never reached the floor in Atlantic City. Nonetheless, it was yet another demonstration that the movement for fully independent national unions was gaining strength even in the bosom of Canadian "autonomy", the USWA. These developments have lent credence to Henri Lorrain's claim that the new Canadian Paperworkers Union would be "a yard-stick against which will be measured the development of a distinctive industrial labour union movement in Canada."[39]

---

1. Notes for an address by L. H. Lorrain, chairman, United Paperworkers Union Organizing Committee, to the Founding Convention of a New Union of Paperworkers in Canada, Toronto, June 3, 1974, p. 9.

2. *The Telegram* (Toronto), April 17, 1969.

3. Ibid.

4. Ibid.

5. *The Toronto Star*, June 12, 1969.

6. Ibid.

7. *The Globe and Mail*, June 13, 1969.

8. *Sudbury Star*, June 10, 1969.

9. *The Telegram*, June 6, 1969.

10. *The Globe and Mail*, June 13, 1969; *The Toronto Star*, June 12, 1969.

11. *The Globe and Mail*, June 13, 1969.

12. *The Globe and Mail*, June 17, 1969.

13. *The Globe and Mail*, June 13, 1969.

14. *Canadian Pulp and Paper Worker Journal*, July-August 1972.

15. *The Windsor Star*, March 9, 1974.

16. J. P. Tonelli, address to the Founding Convention of a New Union of Paperworkers in Canada, Toronto, June 3, 1974, p. 5.

17. John Lang, "U.P.I.U. goes Canadian", *This Magazine*, June 1974.

18. *Brief of the PPWC to the B.C. Enquiry Commission*, 1967, p. 3.

19. Ibid., p. 4.

20. *Labour Gazette*, November, 1973, p. 780.

21. *Ottawa Citizen*, September 8, 1973.

22. *The Financial Post*, September 15, 1973.

23. *Ottawa Journal*, September 13, 1973.

24. Tonelli, address, op. cit., p. 9. "Some people have suggested that the matter of finances was instrumental in bringing about the separation. Nothing can be further from the truth."

25. *The Windsor Star*, March 9, 1974.

26. Ibid.

27. *Labour Gazette*, July 1974, p. 456.

28. Lorrain, address, op. cit.

29. Ibid., p. 11.

30. Tonelli, address, op. cit., pp. 3-4.

31. See Chapter 27.

32. Stephen Bingham, conversation taped in Montreal at Canadian Paperworkers Union headquarters, Henri Lorrain, CPU president, Neville Hamilton, CPU public relations director and executive assistant to the president, July 30, 1975.

33. *The Globe and Mail*, August 15, 1972.

34. *The Globe and Mail*, May 13, 1975.

35. *AFL-CIO News*, November 2, 1974; *NABET News*, October 1974.

36. *The Toronto Star*, July 17, 1974; *The Globe and Mail*, February 4, 1975.

37. USWA Canadian Policy Conference, *Policy and Resolutions*, May 1974, p. 99.

38. Resolutions forwarded to the International Convention, USWA, 1974. Letter September 8, 1974. Local 6571 USWA, Oshawa, Ontario to Walter Burke, international secretary-treasurer (photocopy).

39. Lorrain, address, op. cit.

PART IV
Quebec Labour's New Unionism

CHAPTER 19
Quebec Labour in the Seventies

This is only the beginning.

La Presse demonstration slogan
October 29, 1971[1]

Quebec's unique history, language, and traditions have produced a labour movement that is distinct and increasingly separate from that in English Canada. Because of its uniqueness as the first major departure from American business unionism in Canada it offers an alternative pattern for English Canadian unionists to consider. Quebec unionism is the most developed and distinct separation from international unionism in Canada.

Unionism in Quebec has been distinct because nowhere else in Canada did "confessional" unionism — the existence of organizational links between unions and the clergy — take hold for several decades. Nowhere else has an independent national union centre enjoyed such a long life. And nowhere else has working class militancy combined with nationalism become such a powerful force in recent years.

These differences, however, have not erased the parallels between the Quebec and English Canada labour movements. In 1974 well over forty per cent of union members in Quebec belonged to international unions and were affiliated through the Quebec Federation of Labour (Fédération des travailleurs du Québec) to the Canadian Labour Congress. A large proportion of the Quebec work force was employed by American-owned corporations, and the problems of foreign control — exacerbated in Quebec by the presence of an Anglophone financial élite — received a great deal of attention in the union movement. And like English-Canadian workers, the Québécois were subject to intervention by the federal government, as for example, in the 1975 legislation ordering striking Quebec longshoremen back to work.

Nor was the heightened militancy and nationalism of the Quebec labour movement in recent years alien to English Canada. The new mood of the Quebec movement of the 1960s and early 1970s anticipated, and to some extent paralleled, later events in English Canada. Many of the same conditions served to explain the new mood of workers across the country.

Although the most dramatic and profound changes in Quebec unionism have taken place since the "Quiet Revolution" of the 1960s, their roots extend back to the transformation of the Confederation of National Trade Unions/Confédération des syndicats nationaux after the Asbestos strike of 1949 and the militant textile strikes of the late 1940s.

The CNTU/CSN was organized as the Federation of Catholic Workers of Canada at a 1921 convention in Hull. The two hundred founding delegates represented 40,000 members from 89 unions, all of them confessional unions whose locals were given spiritual and often organizational guidance by priests who enforced the conservative Catholic view of labour relations. In the words of the FCWC declaration of principles in 1921, a strike was a "dangerous weapon" to be used only as a last resort. The only legitimate economic demand of a trade union was a minimum living wage for the worker and his family, and sympathy strikes were viewed as immoral. Largely due to this conservatism and failure to develop a militant approach to organizing the unorganized, the FCWC actually had fewer members by the end of the decade than it had had in 1921.

A good part of the FCWC's early appeal was its nationalism. As the founding convention put it:

> The FCWC believes that it is wrong, an economic error, a national abdication and a political danger to have in Canada syndicates [trade unions] depending on a foreign centre. . . .[2]

The Quebec nationalism of the FCWC was offset by a conservative approach to organization of non-unionized workers, which left it far behind while the CIO and other American unions were being established in Quebec. The doctrine of a basic harmony of interest with the employer, and a virtual ban on strikes as a means of making gains, made it a poor competitor to the militancy of the new CIO unions.

The 1940s brought a number of changes to Quebec. During the Second World War, Quebec was further industrialized and urbanized. The Duplessis government sought to attract American corporations, promising a cheap and submissive labour force. Some of the most repressive labour legislation anywhere was subsequently established by Duplessis for the new industrial work force in Quebec. At the same time, the industrial movement of the CIO was setting examples of gains through militancy, and Catholic social thought was undergoing a period of change toward a more humanistic view of the worker's plight.

A new secular leadership began to emerge in the Catholic union movement. The turning point came in 1949, when FCWC asbestos miners in Quebec struck against the Duplessis labour laws and the American-owned asbestos company. When the provincial police were sent in, the support of the Catholic labour movement and even of the Catholic hierarchy swung behind the strikers. Archbishop Charbonneau of Mont-real — later banished to Vancouver for his forthright support of the strikers — warned in a sermon that "the working class is the victim of a conspiracy which seeks its destruction. . ."[3]

The Asbestos strike of 1949 set the FCWC (later called the Canadian and Catholic Confederation of Labour) firmly on the track of militant trade unionism. It hastened the process of secularization. The entire or-ganized labour movement in Quebec, historically split among several rival centres, gradually united in opposition to Duplessis.

By December 1952 the CCCL had reached the point of convening an emergency conference to call for "a general strike which shall take place with the least possible delay"[4] in protest against the Quebec govern-ment's policy. This was the first call for a general strike in Canada since the Winnipeg strike of 1919. Although the action never took place — as the CCCL could not win the support of the other labour centres in Quebec — the conference set the tone for later developments.

In 1956 the by then fully secularized CCCL became the CNTU: a centre for militant nationalist unionism in Quebec. By 1973 the CNTU had some 164,492 members, largely in the public service, but also including in-dustrial workers in asbestos, textiles and clothing, transportation, pulp and paper and other sectors.

The second important labour centre in Quebec has been the older Quebec Federation of Labour, the provincial organization affiliated to the CLC, which was organized in 1956. Its history stretches back to the 1880s, to earlier federations and councils of the Knights of Labour, the Trades and Labour Congress, the All-Canadian Congress of Labour and the Canadian Congress of Labour. The QFL's affiliated membership of 300,000 is mostly in international unions like steel, auto, rubber, pulp and paper, chemicals, aircraft and meat packing, although Canadian unions such as the CUPE, CBRT, and postal and letter carriers were also affiliated. In addition, most building trades unions have been part of the QFL.

The third important labour centre in Quebec has not been affiliated to any federation or congress — the union of the Quebec teachers or Corporation des enseignants du Québec (CEQ), numbering some 87,546 members.

The "Quiet Revolution" of the 1960s, which saw the rapid development of a self-confident Québécois nationalism, had some of its roots in the working class battles against Duplessis in the previous decade. But the Quiet Revolution itself, although supported by the working class, was led by the Quebec professional middle class. Its programme was economic growth for Quebec, culminating in the replacement of English-speaking managers, bureaucrats and professionals by French-speaking ones.

Such growth, according to Jean-Charles Falardeau, would direct the "dreams of the younger and the frustrations of the older . . . through the channels of escapism created by North American culture".[5] With such a policy, the "ever developing bureaucracies of government, business and the Church" played the role of "the improvised agent of an 'administrative revolution' . . ."[6]

Thus, the Quiet Revolution, while it improved the relative position of a small group of French Canadian technocrats and top civil servants, and introduced some long overdue social and educational reforms, did not change the basic power relations of élites in Quebec. The American corporations became even more dominant, while the Anglo-Canadian financiers prospered as before.

The newly-influential Francophone professional middle class attempted to buy off working class militancy. As political economist Daniel Drache has said, "had the new professional classes been able to divide the working class more than they were able to do with wage increases and the lure of consumerism, they might have forced a political stalemate on Quebec unionism".[7]

However, the Quebec working class was not co-opted and instead moved toward further radicalization. Middle-class Quebec nationalism confined its programme largely to a more important role for a French-speaking élite in business and politics while offering some social reforms to win popular support. On the other hand, working-class nationalism, while clearly in support of an independent Quebec (as shown in its conditional backing of the Parti Québécois) pressed for a new social order for Quebec.

During much of the 1960s Quebec trade unionists had hoped that the new Liberal government in the province would prove more amenable to labour's goals than had Duplessis. In October 1970, these hopes were shattered. The CEQ manifesto (discussed in chapter twenty) outlined the reaction of trade unionists to the War Measures Act:

> During the October Crisis, the police and the Department of Justice, whose duty it is to insure that the rights of others are being respected, combined forces to lock up 500 persons who might actually say what they really think. The War Measures Act was applied to divert the attention of the workers from the very lively interest which they took in the FLQ manifesto.[8]

The October Crisis was another turning point for the Quebec labour movement. It was followed by a renewed wave of labour militancy, and by careful reassessments of the movement's strategy by each of the three major centres as expressed in their individual manifestos of 1971. In October 1971 over 10,000 workers demonstrated their solidarity with the striking *La Presse* workers in opposition to the political axis of Mayor Drapeau, Premier Bourassa and Power Corporation, owner of *La Presse*. Their banner read: "This is only the beginning".[9]

And so it was. The *La Presse* demonstration was followed by the Common Front strikes of March-May 1972. The Common Front was organized to include all public employees in Quebec, whether they were affiliated to the CNTU, the QFL or the CEQ. On March 9 the organization announced that eighty per cent of the public employees had voted in favour of a general strike to support their contract negotiations with the Bourassa government. Three weeks later, a 24-hour general strike took place. Two weeks after that, the general strike was resumed on a continuing basis until the Quebec legislature passed back-to-work legislation on April 21.[10]

Large groups of strikers refused to obey the legislation. Some forty union leaders were arrested and sentenced. The three presidents of the labour centres, Marcel Pépin of the CNTU, Louis Laberge of the QFL, and Yvonne Charbonneau of the CEQ were each sentenced to one year in jail for defying the back-to-work order. In Ste. Jérôme defiant strikers took over the radio station and operated it for several hours.[11] In the Sept-Îles area there was a general strike in support of the public employees and their arrested leaders.[12] The Common Front had become a political weapon in which several unions confronted the government as a united force.

One of the most significant features of the Common Front strike was that better-paid public sector workers agreed to accept a lower settlement in order that the lower-paid could win a hundred dollar weekly minimum-wage. This was a break with the traditional sectional emphasis of business unionism.

The union solidarity of the Common Front, however, broke down after 1972. This was largely due to the rivalries between the QFL and CNTU which had their roots in the traditions of business unionism. The struggles between the building trades unions in the two centres were particularly vicious, as in the James Bay disaster of 1974. These rivalries, together with the corruption of some locals of international building trades unions in the QFL, wasted the energies and efforts of the trade union movement in Quebec.

Since 1972 the bitter inter-union conflicts had hampered efforts to set up united campaigns for the reopening of contracts due to inflation. However, the movement toward solidarity and militant unionism began to reopen over the United Aircraft strike, the Bourassa labour legislation of May 1975, and the three-year sentence imposed on Louis Laberge in June 1975. As public employees approached the opening of 1975 negotiations, the idea of a Common Front was reviving.[13]

The 1974-75 Cliche Commission hearings on the construction industry in Quebec revealed numerous examples of corrupt business unionism in international building trades locals, as well as extensive corruption on the part of the companies in collusion with the Bourassa government. During the course of the hearings, the QFL established a trusteeship over twenty-three construction affiliates. However, after three months Louis Laberge admitted that he had been powerless to oust corrupt leaders.[14]

Commissioner Cliche termed the trusteeship a "joke" when he learned that the QFL was committed to respecting the autonomy of its member unions during the effort to eliminate corruption.[15] The Commission recommended a government trusteeship which Bourassa imposed together with other restrictive legislation. The Quebec premier neglected to follow the Commission's recommendations concerning the construction companies and his government.

It is significant that the American craft unions in the building trades proved a major obstacle in the transformation of the Quebec labour movement. Although they had not been able to completely halt changes, these unions weakened the credibility of the Quebec labour movement as a whole, and particularly the QFL, by reproducing their business union mentality and its attendant corruption in the province.

In the spring of 1975 there were clear indications that the mainstream of Quebec unionism was trying to disassociate itself from the building trades internationals. The fact that the independent national construction unions in the CNTU were free of corruption was not lost on Quebec unionists.

Another reminder of the tenacity of business unionism had come when a section of the CNTU broke away as a result of the militancy of the Common Front strikes. With a total affiliation of some 40,000, the break-away Centrale des syndicats démocratiques (CSD) did not grow after it was formed in 1972 and seemed destined to irrelevance and perhaps eventual disappearance.

More serious was the fact that many of the old-style business union leaders remained powerfully entrenched in QFL craft and a few industrial unions. The transition to strong, nationalist, working-class unionism was not developing without strong opposition. The business union mentality seemed likely to remain a force in the Quebec union movement for some years to come.

The strike movement which swept English Canada in the mid-seventies was also widespread in Quebec. In 1974 there was a series of demonstrations, centred in Montreal, demanding the reopening of contracts to make up for the effects of inflation on living standards. Other actions included strikes by firemen, pulp and paper, rubber, public transit, and asbestos workers, illegal strikes by construction workers at the Olympic Games site, by postal workers, and by longshoremen.

The most significant and symbolic action for both Quebec and English Canada was the long strike of the UAW local at United Aircraft (now Pratt and Whitney Aircraft of Canada Ltd.) near Montreal. The strike, which began in January 1974 and which was not settled until August of the following year, has been likened to the Asbestos strike of 1949. The tenacity with which some thousand workers held out for the duration of the strike on strike pay of thirty to forty dollars a week was remarkable.

The parallels in the 1949 strike and the United Aircraft strike included several of the same issues: an autocratic American corporation, a government favourable to the company, the demand for union security and the right to make French the working language in the plant.

Four important features combined to make the 1974-1975 strike an historic and classic Canadian confrontation: an American company, an international union, and involvement of the federal and provincial governments. The employer was a huge American multinational based in East Hartford, Connecticut, which declared a $24.5 million profit in the third quarter of 1974 on sales of $802.5 million. In spite of its profitable status, the Canadian government gave the company $70 million in grants and $200 million in contracts "to create jobs".[16]

During the strike, U.S. unionists paralleled the actions of the American rubber workers during the Hamilton and Toronto strikes.[17] They went along with production boosts in the United States to make up for lost production at the struck plant in Quebec. Much of the company's production equipment, paid for in part by the federal government grant, was exported to the United States during the strike.[18]

This was not the only way that the AFL-CIO related to Quebec workers in this situation. One of the main issues was the local's demand for the Rand Formula — automatic dues check-off for all workers, without compulsory union membership. The company based its refusal to grant this demand on the fact that its American workers did not have such a provision in their contracts. The Quebec government, which had legislative power to make the Rand Formula compulsory, did nothing although Quebec Labour Minister Jean Cournoyer agreed that it was a reasonable demand. "How could I be opposed? My own public employees have it in their own contract."[19]

Although the United Aircraft workers were confronting four adversaries, they did not back down. Instead, they adopted the slogan used by Quebec Firestone workers in their 10-month strike. "Hold on for one minute more."

For the thousand members who stayed on the picket lines (others had taken new jobs, while some had returned to the plant) the strike became a way of life. One activist, André Choquette, described the results:

> There's one thing the company never anticipated in dragging the strike on so long — that the guys would get to know each other. . . . The way the plant was run, you never met anyone. You just sat in your corner. Now we know who's who and when we get back inside we'll be organized. Look, I've got eight years experience at United. How many have you got, Marcel? Sixteen? Marcel's got sixteen. Jean here has got twenty-five.[20]

The United Aircraft strike became a rallying point for militant rank and file unionism in the province. It symbolized the new mood of nationalism and working class activism that was helping to transform the Quebec labour movement.

In the end, the union lost the strike at United Aircraft, particularly in its major demand for automatic dues check-off, just as the asbestos workers had lost in 1949. As in the earlier Asbestos strike, the twenty-month strike at United Aircraft in 1974-1975 was expected to have long-term effects on Quebec's union movement. It was expected to make Quebec labour even more aware of the role of American corporations in the Quebec economy and to raise stronger doubts about the alleged efficacy of international unions in handling multinational corporations in Quebec.[21]

Behind these epic strikes, behind new expressions of solidarity like the Common Front, the three Quebec labour centres were formulating new policies, structures and strategies. The pressure for this came from the activists and the response of the leadership was strong. As a result, the CNTU, QFL and CEQ prepared major statements in 1971 on the role of the trade union movement in building a new Quebec.

In examining the analysis and strategies of Quebec unions in the first half of the 1970s, and how they compared to those in English Canada, it is imperative to begin with the difference between the nationalisms of Quebec and of English Canada. While nationalism in English Canada has been broadly concerned with Canada's dependence upon the United States, Quebec nationalism has focused mainly on the domination of Quebec by the Canadian federal state.

When the CNTU published its manifesto in 1971 a gradual change in focus of some sections of Quebec's nationalist movement began. Some Quebec nationalists, especially in the union movement (as the next chapter demonstrates), were increasingly emphasizing Quebec's economic and political dependence on the United States. The Quebec unions were the first to recognize, too, that American domination of the Quebec economy would in the long run be harder to overcome than that of the historic Anglo-Canadian dominance. Such a convergence of the nationalisms of Quebec and English Canada, however, was entirely in the realm of theory.

Most Quebec nationalists, including many in the labour movement, conceived of a two-step strategy in their political and economic liberation. First would come political independence from the Canadian confederation. This would open the second stage — economic and political liberation from domination by the United States. In 1975 most Quebec nationalists insisted on downplaying an anti-American economic strategy, fearing that this might divert attention from the need for Quebec to achieve political independence from the Canadian federal state as the opening phase in self-determination.[22]

Even nationalists, like those in the labour movement who had recognized the United States as a bigger strategic problem for Quebec's self-determination, were not seriously considering, in 1975, a concerted strategy with nationalists in English Canada to overcome mutual dependence on the United States.

This orientation may partly explain the attitudes and actions, in the CLC debate in May 1974, of labour leaders like Jean Gerin-Lajoie, director of District 5 of the Steelworkers (of which Quebec is the largest section), and of Louis Laberge, president of the QFL. Quebec unionists pressed for the extension of the autonomy and spheres of activity of the QFL in the CLC but downplayed the need for greater autonomous power for unions in the CLC *vis-à-vis* their American headquarters.[23]

Laberge and Lajoie sought an alliance with the English-Canadian reformers in Canadian unions and won their full support on the extended activities of the QFL. The Quebec leaders showed less interest in pressing for tougher autonomy guidelines for Canadian branches of international unions. They were motivated by a Quebec, not an English-Canadian, nationalism. Nevertheless, it was significant that their most natural allies would turn out to be the English Canadian nationalists. This indicated how the two nationalisms might converge, given their common concern over American control of the Canadian economy. All three manifestos of the Quebec labour centrals in 1971 showed the effects of this new analysis on their proposed strategies.

The three "manifestos" or discussion papers that were the product of two decades of growing nationalism and militancy were unique in the Canadian labour movement. They suggest a complete break with the business philosophy of American labour and they indicate the potential for a new national and militant working class unionism — in Quebec and in English Canada.

---

1. Daniel Drache, ed., *Quebec — Only the Beginning* (Toronto: New Press, 1972), p. xv.

2. Charles Lipton, *The Trade Union Movement of Canada 1827-1959* (Toronto: NC Press, 1973), 3rd edition, p. 224. Canada Department of Labour, *Annual Report on Labour Organization in Canada*, 1921, p. 27.

3. Ibid., p. 324, from Renaude Lapointe, *L'Histoire Bouleversante de Mgr. Charbonneau* (Montreal, 1962), p. 56.

4. Ibid., p. 326.

5. Jean-Charles Falardeau, "The Changing Social Structures of Contemporary French-Canadian Society", in M. Roux and Y. Martin, eds., *French-Canadian Society* (Toronto: McClelland & Stewart, 1964), p. 121.

6. Hubert Guindon, "The Social Evolution of Quebec Reconsidered", Roux and Martin, op. cit., p. 156.

7. Drache, op. cit., p. xx.

8. Ibid., p. 135.

9. Ibid., p. xiv.

10. Ibid.

11. *The Globe and Mail*, May 13, 1972.

12. *The Toronto Star*, May 13, 1972; *The Globe and Mail*, May 18, 1972.

13. *The Globe and Mail*, January 22, 1975.

14. *The Gazette* (Montreal), March 8, 1975.

15. Ibid.

16. Brian Johnson, "In Dubious Battle", *Maclean's*, February 1975, p. 36; $73 million in aid was given to United Aircraft between 1960 and 1975. *The Globe and Mail*, January 28, 1975.

17. See Chapter 1.

18. *The Globe and Mail*, January 30, 1975.

19. Johnson, op. cit.; at the time of the settlement in August 1975 there was an indication that the Quebec government was considering legislation which would make automatic dues check-off mandatory.

20. Ibid.

21. *Financial Times of Canada*, August 25, 1975.

22. Recently, there was an indication that this was beginning to change. In August 1975 Jacques Yves Morin, Leader of the Opposition of the Parti Québécois in Quebec's National Assembly, said that Quebec needs to control its economy, not just social and cultural matters: "It is the control of Quebec's economy and natural resources by Ottawa and multinational corporations which constitutes the gravest danger for the cultural future of Quebeckers." *The Toronto Star*, August 27, 1975.

23. Refer to Chapter 15.

CHAPTER 20

Three Union Centrals and their Manifestos

> ... any fundamental change is almost impossible if we play by the rules politics has itself established to insure the system's perpetuation.
>
> "The State is Our Exploiter"
> Quebec Federation of Labour Manifesto, 1971

In the summer and fall of 1971 the three Quebec labour centres each published lengthy documents pointing the way to the future of trade unionism and working-class politics in the province. In the wake of the October Crisis, the three centres had put aside their factional disputes to build the Common Front and reassess the role of the labour movement in the political and economic life of Quebec.

The three documents, published for discussion by their memberships, and often referred to as manifestos, differed in emphasis. Their underlying analysis, however, was similar and together the three stood in striking contrast to the programmes of American business unions operating in English Canada. "It's Up To Us," by the csn/cntu; "Phase One," by the ceq/qtc; and "The State is Our Exploiter," by the ftq/qfl all suggested a radically different alternative for the workers: the possibility of a militant and political trade unionism to replace the conservative policies of the business unions. In this chapter, these three manifestos will be considered.[1]

Any analysis of labour's position in the economy has to come to terms with the fact of U.S. economic and political power and its dominance in English Canada and Quebec. The cntu manifesto was most explicit on this point. In a preface, it posed the question:

What's the nature of capitalism in Quebec? What's American

imperialism? What's the relationship between the federal or provincial state, and American and Anglo-Canadian imperialism?
What's the relationship between the founding and expansion of
multinational corporations, and the development of the industrial
structure in Quebec? Finally, what are the consequences of American
imperialism in Quebec?

The document examined the business class in Quebec, and sub-divided
it by degree of dominance. First, and most important, was the "non-
resident American bourgeoisie". Next came the Anglo-Canadian
business class, spread across the country, but with its centre in Toronto,
followed by the French-Canadian bourgeoisie which had two sections.
The first of these was Quebec businessmen who were at the service of
the American and English-Canadian groups and fully integrated with
them. The second group, according to the manifesto, was "a small
professional and technocratic bourgeoisie, whose ambition was to replace the Anglo-Canadian bourgeoisie in Quebec. . . ."

In identifying as the most important group the heads of the American
multinational corporations, the CNTU manifesto departed from the position of the Parti Québécois and raised a new set of strategic questions for
the labour movement. The Parti Québécois concentrated on the
English-Canadian corporations and the federal government as the
dominating features in Quebec society. The CNTU manifesto dismissed
the idea that English-Canadian corporations were dominant by pointing
out that "the Anglo-Canadian bourgeoisie is today licking its wounds
because it wasn't strong enough for the fight. And it's in this predicament
because it has been directly contributing to the expansion and consolidation of American imperialism in Canada and Quebec since 1926."

The importance of this for Quebec workers was suggested by the
description of imperialism in the manifesto:

> [it is the type of corporate capitalism] that uses multinational corpora-
> tions and the banks to cross borders looking for yet higher profits. In
> Quebec, the major exploiters of local labour are American and Cana-
> dian bourgeois capitalists. These foreign capitalists set up operations
> here that are designed to make profits. Part of this profit will be
> reinvested here in other production, and part will be returned to its
> American and Canadian capitalist owners. This means a lot of money
> leaves Quebec and ends up in the hands of foreign capitalists.

The document illustrated this by tracing the history of American
business in the whole Canadian economy, pointing out that in 1968,
American multinational corporations controlled more than fifty-eight
per cent of Canada's manufacturing industry, sixty-two per cent of the
extracting industry, and one hundred per cent of the refining and
petroleum industry. The consequences of this for Quebec were spelled
out:

> . . . multinational corporations control three-quarters of our mining.

Nor has American capital any interest in refining this mineral and forest wealth here in Quebec. . . .

The domination, first by American and then by English-Canadian business, could be seen in the relative sizes of various kinds of businesses in 1961:

At that time, a typical Quebec business was one-seventh the size of a typical American multinational corporation, and one-quarter the size of a typical Anglo-Canadian multinational corporation. The average value-added of a Quebec business was $792,000; for an Anglo-Canadian business it was $3.3 million, and for an American multinational corporation, it was $5.6 million.

"The important fact in all this," the manifesto suggested, "is that Quebec's natural resource-based industry is being developed to meet the needs of foreign capital. Generally, these resources are exported without being substantially refined, because the refining industry . . . is the one that creates the most economic activity and therfore the most value and profit."

The Quebec teachers' union manifesto had a similar analysis of the importance of multinational companies in turning the province into a resource-based economy for their own private profit:

The imbalance that we have described is worse for Québécois than for other Canadians . . . they see that national wealth uniquely Quebec's passes into the hands of international capitalists who do not care about our feelings and have nothing in common with the workers. . . . They take our minerals, our forests, our natural resources in order to process and make money from them only in the United States.

Similarly, the Quebec Federation of Labour's manifesto argued that "most of our economy is controlled by American or Anglo-Canadian capital". In the political sphere, it said, "both Quebec and Ottawa are agents of economic power which is primarily American, English-Canadian to a lesser degree, and only minimally Québécois."

All three documents describe Quebec's economic system as one dominated by private capital's search for profit at the expense of the workers. "The motivating force of our economic system," said the QFL, "has been profit for the owners, not satisfaction of the needs of those who produce the goods. The latter are forced to sell their labour in order to survive. . . . In the search for maximum profits, anything goes; reduction of labour costs through lowering of salaries or cuts in personnel, speeding up of production, lowering the quality of the product. . . ."

Such a society was said to be made up of two main classes of people. On the one hand, there was the capitalist or dominant class, as the CNTU put it, which consists "of a small number of owners who receive an income (mainly from the shares they hold in the business) simply because they own the means of production. They're the ones who decide the course of these businesses, in fact of the entire economy, and they therefore control business managers and politicians. . . . This class controls economic and political power. . . ."

On the other hand, there is the group consisting of workers, labourers, civil servants, secretaries, housewives and farmers. They own none of the means of production and are forced to sell their labour in order to survive.

Such a system, said the CNTU, is wasteful. "A worker's salary represents only a fraction of the value he has produced. The rest goes to the capitalist, who uses it to consolidate the empire — or just throws it away." The manifesto described this system as an "anarchic" one:

> This search for ever-greater profits results in an unplanned economy, lacking the central direction which would organize resources and production to meet the needs of the people. . . . So the economic system is one of anarchy. "Anarchy" implies the waste of both production energy and the worker's energy.

The same might have been said for capitalism anywhere in Canada. But, as the CNTU manifesto pointed out, it was doubly true for Quebec. Domination by an American and Anglo-Canadian bourgeoisie, as well as a local business class, had had an especially destructive effect on the Quebec economy.

The CNTU manifesto demonstrated this point by comparing the growth of manufacturing in Ontario with that in Quebec. Making use of figures from the Castonguay-Nepveu Report, it showed that "between 1961 and 1965, Canadian manufacturing increased 15.6 per cent; Ontario's grew 21 per cent and Quebec's grew 9.3 per cent". In addition, unemployment in Quebec grew disproportionately to that in Ontario: between 1946 and 1950, unemployment ranged between 2.5 and 4.4 per cent, while between 1966 and 1970 it climbed to between 4.7 per cent and 7.7 per cent. This was a consequence of the underdevelopment of the manufacturing sector. Using the 1961 to 1965 figures, the CNTU concluded:

> If we take the overall Canadian figure of 15.6 per cent as the norm, the growth of Quebec manufacturing in that period should have produced 68,049 new jobs instead of 40,438. That's 27,611 missing jobs. . . . In order to equal Ontario's rate of increase, we would have had to create 100,000 new jobs over the last ten years *in the manufacturing sector alone*.

Within Quebec itself, there had been major regional disparities in manufacturing and in unemployment. Uneven industrial development had been the cause of uneven distribution of unemployment according to the CNTU: "[Therefore] capitalist owners benefit by the cheap labour made available for the manufacturing industry of the major centres in Quebec." The implication was that Quebec bore the same relationship to English Canada, particularly to Ontario, that Canada as a whole bore to the United States. Just as the United States was the beneficiary of an underdeveloped manufacturing sector in Canada, so English Canada benefited from the exploitation of the Québécois by the American corporations and their Anglo-Canadian associates.

All three manifestos recognized that this economic subordination of the Québécois was maintained by the structures of political power. As the QFL put it, "The control of political power by economic power is essential for the maintenance and the development of this regime. Financiers must be assured that their liberty will not be threatened by political powers which might respond to the desires of the people. They, therefore, establish close relationships with political machines and support those governments which serve their interests."

Since this was as true of the Quebec government as it was of Ottawa, the solution could not be a simple one of replacing the domination of the English-speaking business class with that of a French-speaking bourgeoisie. As the QFL explained it:

> French-speaking Quebec capitalists would not show any more consideration for Quebec workers. . . . They would use the *liberal state* in the same way: to protect their privileges and stoke their profit machines.

The real alternative, according to the manifestos, was a socialist society in Quebec with a planned economy. The CNTU outlined the goals of such a society:

> One, furnish goods and services in sufficient quantity and quality for all Québécois. Two, develop a production structure that would continually improve the standard of living and put an end to the exploitation of the people's work by a minority.

Such a society would require "worker control of the economy" and it could only be achieved through nationalization. "Nationalization is the only possible way to reorient production so as to meet the needs of the people."

Furthermore, the CNTU manifesto argued, a combination of nationalization and workers' control of the economy was the only guarantee of improving working conditions:

> History shows that, despite constant battles, capitalists really aren't concerned with working conditions. . . . Workers won't forget their own interests when they run the factories!

The priorities for nationalization followed from the analysis of the importance of various sectors in the Quebec economy:

> The obvious conclusion is that sectors belonging to American imperialists must be quickly nationalized, since these are the sectors that always export their profits and deprive Quebec of important resources. Anglo-Canadian businesses must also be nationalized, especially the financial sector, which has always made huge profits in Quebec.

The CEQ manifesto saw similar goals for Quebec. Defining its objective as "a society which allows every individual to have access to the collective wealth, each according to his needs," the teachers' union posed the choice open to its members:

> Will we be the defenders of the established order . . . ? Or will we join those who believe that the present economic, social and political system requires profound change so that all people can benefit equally from the means of production and each in his way become creative?

The three manifestos implicitly linked the struggle for an independent and socialist Quebec to the need to develop a new kind of labour movement. The process of creating a new society is mirrored, the teachers argued, in building a union that is democratic and controlled by its membership. In this way, the development of a strong rank and file labour movement in Quebec would lay the groundwork for a new socialist society:

> The unions still provide the workers with the securest and freest conditions in which to talk, study, and pave the way for the liberation of all workers. The conditions which the unions can provide are still the most democratic, and it is there that the tools to construct a harmonious, free, and non-repressive society can be fashioned.

The manifestos assumed that the Quebec people already constituted a nation by virtue of their language, their traditions, their history, and their land. What was required to end the domination of Quebec society by American and Anglo-Canadian corporations was political independence for Quebec. This was because the political system in Quebec and Canada was dominated by the corporations so that, in the words of the QFL manifesto, "the state is our exploiter".

But it would be wrong, according to the manifestos, to look to the French-Canadian business class to bring about the new society of an independent Quebec. As the CNTU manifesto put it, one part of this business class was fully integrated into the American and Anglo-Canadian corporate élite, while the other part looked forward to Quebec's independence only so it could replace the American and English-Canadian business leaders in a position of dominance. If an independent and socialist Quebec along the lines proposed by the manifestos was to be built, labour must play the leading role.

For this to take place, business unionism must be replaced by a new kind of labour movement. As the CEQ manifesto said, "unions are a struggle for change and not a business; persons who have as their pivotal point the model of the 'industrial relations' of the bosses are not the agents of mobilization".

The QFL manifesto, like the others, criticized the strategy adopted by unions in the past as inadequate:

> We have tended in the past to deal with issues one at a time, both for reasons of efficiency and because this seemed to make it easier to

zero-in on problems. We thought it was better to defend the workers group by group, factory by factory, because in this way it was easier to look after their particular interests adequately. When we demanded political reforms our objectives were very specific because we preferred making small gains but losing the large battles. . . .

The QFL manifesto argued that simple trade unionism could not correct the problems, because they were rooted in the whole nature of Quebec workers' dependency and domination. Instead, "as a long-term strategy we must give priority to the development of our political power". In the short term, the QFL said, "we must continue to fight with ever increasing militancy to preserve our acquired rights, including our so-called social legislation. We must continue to press for improvements in working conditions and salaries." However:

We must not lose sight of the fact that these short-term measures . . . are not the whole answer. Because these short-term measures may rid us of American and Anglo-Saxon control over our economy only to replace it by that of a technocratic and Quebec bourgeoisie. This is one stage in our move towards liberation which we can do without.

Here was the suggestion for a new strategy — for the elimination of one stage where the Quebec bourgeoisie would be in control of Quebec society.

The CNTU document echoed this sentiment, saying "Quebec workers already know that they can't count on Quebec capitalists. . . ." In its call for workers to reclaim "control of the union movement," it summarized the thrust of all three manifestos:

We are our own strength; let's stop selling ourselves. It's up to us.

---

1. All quotations from the manifestos are taken from Daniel Drache, *Quebec — Only the Beginning* (Toronto: New Press, 1972).

PART V
Labour Militance in English Canada

Introduction

As seen in earlier chapters, Canadian workers took an economic beating in 1973 and 1974. On the whole, unions in Canada responded half-heartedly in 1973 to the challenge of higher costs, lower purchasing power, and record-shattering corporate profits. The American business unionist mentality, with its advocacy of long contracts and "reasonable" wage demands, channelled workers' anger away from militancy, toward feelings of frustration and impotence. As in many other industries, the imported strategy of American unions in steel and auto had tied Canadian workers to three-year contracts.

As workers' purchasing power continued to deteriorate, the union movement was faced with a critical choice. It could continue to live within the strait-jacket of long contracts and restrictive labour laws, or it could discard the baggage of these business unionist practices, and break through to a new strategy. It could force the reopening of contracts, stage walk-outs be they legal or not, and generally raise the level of demands and expectations beyond that condemned by many major union leaders.

In late 1973 Canadian workers began to recover from the dazed impotence with which they had met almost a year of skyrocketing prices and stationary wage rates. The spell was broken when 105,000 Ontario teachers participated in an illegal walk-out on December 18, followed by a six-week teachers' strike in York County in January 1974.

The mood of public employees in Canada had changed rapidly. The old-style "professionalism" and "white-collar" superiority which led many public workers to take conservative positions and to think of themselves as somehow different from "blue-collar" workers and their unions fell by the wayside. It was to be replaced by a growing trade union consciousness, followed by the transformation of public employee staff

associations into genuine unions, engaging in collective bargaining, an
using the strike weapon to press their demands. The new approach wa
symbolized in the CSAO slogan: "Free the Servants."

Despite the frequent claims that public employees are privileged, the
have tended to receive lower wages on the average than workers in th
private sector, particularly organized workers. As their economic pos
tion worsened, public workers came to recognize that getting a "salary
instead of a "wage", having a cafeteria rather than a lunch-pail, c
working for a government rather than a private business, did not mak
them members of an élite. As part of the eighty per cent of Canadians i
the labour force who worked in non-managerial capacities for other:
public employees had begun to associate themselves consciously wit
the union movement.

Part of the reason for this new consciousness was the place of goverr
ment employees in the national economy, and particularly the speci:
difficulties the public sector was now facing. Government expenditure
had grown at a faster rate than the general growth of the economy. I
Canada, expenditures by all three levels of government in 1973 totalle
37.6 per cent of the gross national product.[1]

The expansion of employment in the public sector had outpaced th
overall growth of the labour force. Increasingly, larger numbers c
workers were employed by government and other service employer:
while relatively fewer Canadians were involved in directly producin
goods.

But governments and private employers were financing the wages an
salaries of service workers out of the economic worth of the good
produced by manufacturing and resource workers. As the public secto
expanded out of proportion to basic production, a "fiscal crisis" de
veloped because insufficient wealth was being produced to cover th
wages of all the service workers. It has been estimated that it takes on
worker in primary or secondary industry to support every two worke
in the service sector.

The over-extension of the service sector would be a serious enoug
problem in itself. But in Canada, as in other dependent countries, it wi
complicated by the distorted nature of the productive economy. Sinc
1966 there had been a tendency for manufacturing jobs in the mult
national corporation branch plants — jobs involving the direct produ
tion of goods — to be withdrawn from Canada, either back to the Unite
States or to low-wage countries.[2] The Canadian manufacturing secto
was getting smaller relative to the service sector — the cause of a fisc:
crisis even in metropolitan countries like the United States. In additio
it was being eroded as a consequence of the foreign, mainly America
domination of the Canadian economy.

Canadian public employees began to feel the effects of the fiscal crisi
in the early 1970s. For example, teachers had become accustomed t
regular annual salary increases during the 1960s boom period. Th

squeeze began in most provinces in 1971, when governments started to impose limits on education spending because of insufficient financing.

By the following year the squeeze had become tighter. Governments were trying to reduce the number of teachers they employed by increasing class sizes. This was one of the basic issues of working conditions that, along with the right to strike, aroused a new militancy among teachers and led to the province-wide walk-out of Ontario teachers in December 1973.

After 1972, inflation, and later recession, hurt the living standards of all Canadian workers, not just those in the public sector. As the economic problems deepened, it became more apparent that the interests of workers in the public sector were similar to those of manufacturing and resource workers. Increasingly, they had two choices. Workers could accept the divide-and-conquer arguments used to turn working people against each other, or they could join together in a wide common front.

The divide-and-conquer arguments had been quite effective in the past. Workers in the primary industries and manufacturing had been told that their living standards could not rise because of high taxation required to pay the salaries of public employees. They were told that the wage demands of teachers, hospital workers, civil servants and nurses were unreasonable and inflationary. Public sector jobs had been painted as soft, undeserving of salary increases.

On the other hand, the two-thirds of the work force that is made up of public and service workers had been told that the blame for inflation lies with the blue-collar, manufacturing workers. Allegedly, higher prices are the result of higher wages received by those workers.

By mid-1973 these myths began to vanish. Public opinion polls showed that more Canadians were coming to believe that escalating profits were a primary cause of inflation.[3] Increasingly, workers in all sectors of the economy were undertaking similar kinds of action to defend their living standards and working conditions.

What was new, however, was that the lead in this kind of action came from the public sector. In January 1974 hospital workers in ten Toronto CUPE locals demanded an average increase of thirty-eight per cent in a one year "catch-up" programme. If this demand was not granted by May 1, they declared they would strike illegally in defiance of the Hospital Labour Disputes Arbitration Act. The breakthrough by hospital workers, including nurses, boosted the militancy and morale of the rest of organized labour. The policy of avoiding demands which raised "expectations" had been shattered.

Only a few months previously the railway workers had asked for 38 cents; now the hospital workers were demanding $1.14 an hour increase in one year. By the fall of 1974 Ontario provincial public employees were calling for a 61 per cent increase — an average increase of more than $2.50 an hour in a one-year contract.

In sum, labour struck a new tone in bargaining. A sharp, direct challenge by workers in the public sector — hospital workers, teachers, civil servants — had ushered in a year of unprecedented worker participation in militant demands and strike actions.

A long series of strikes followed, making 1974 the biggest strike year in Canadian history. The 1972 record of 7.8 million man-days on strike was surpassed, so that in 1974 more than 9.2 million man-days were spent on strike, the highest ever recorded.[4] This was a significant barometer of working class feeling and militancy.

This section examines the militancy displayed in this strike wave and its social and political implications, with particular emphasis on the leading role played by Canadian unions in the public sector.

First, however, the section begins with an examination of the business unionist philosophy that was prevalent in the thinking of top Canadian union leaders and their advisors in the early 1970s. It then describes the nation-wide railway strike of 1973 as the critical watershed, the last strike in the old-style tradition before the new militancy.

---

1. Canadian Tax Foundation, *The National Finances 1974-75* (Toronto: Canadian Tax Foundation, 1975), Table 2-12.

2. Committee on Finance, United States Senate, report of, *Implications of Multinational Firms for World Trade and Investment and for U.S. Trade and Labor* (Washington, D.C.: U.S. Government Printing Office, 1973), p. 418.

3. *The Gallup Report*, January 15, 1975, showed that 50 per cent of Canadians felt profits to be a major cause of rising food prices; *The Gallup Report*, November 12, 1975, showed that 48 per cent of Canadians blamed profits for rising prices.

4. Labour Canada, *Research Bulletin: Work Stoppages*, December 1974.

CHAPTER 21
Militance and Canada's Labour Leaders

Extravagant demands raise expectations in the membership which cannot be fulfilled.

David Lewis
Former national leader of the NDP
Miami, 1972[1]

The business unionist philosophy that "extravagant demands" and "expectations" were to be avoided was the conventional wisdom in top Canadian labour circles in the early 1970s.

Charlie Millard, retired District 6 director of the Steelworkers, expressed his view on this matter in November 1974. Speaking to a meeting of the Federation of Engineering and Scientific Associations, he argued that many blue-collar workers were ready to exchange their right to strike for arbitration. Millard insisted that the problem was one of outdated modes of thought in the union leadership. They should consider U.S. Steel's Experimental Negotiating Agreement (ENA), a long-term, no-strike pact, he said, for "only some outdated thinking separates [the leadership] from making real progress".[2]

Lynn Williams had also indicated his support for the Experimental Negotiating Agreement in the U.S. steel industry, saying in a *Financial Post* series article in February 1975,[3] that it was evidence of "a very mature bargaining system". He observed:

We have to forget the old idea I think we have all lived with, that the pie was infinitely expandable so we could get a big settlement and management could pass on a big price increase so everyone would be happy. We're into a world where that's going to change radically.

According to this view, workers cannot go on seeking large wage increases if management is no longer able to pass on higher prices to the public. Williams' views on ENA and his warning against the notion that the "pie was infinitely expandable" were to have an important effect on his union's bargaining strategy in 1975, in Stelco, Algoma and Inco.[4]

Jerry Hartford, publicity director for the Auto Workers, told *The Financial Post* that "collective bargaining per se is part and parcel of free enterprise ... you can't have fully functioning free enterprise without collective bargaining". When asked whether workers would continue to press for a bigger share of the pie even in a depression, he replied, "if you mean by your question, would we agree to a reduction in income if the cost of living goes down, the answer is yes".[5]

Senator Ed Lawson, director of the Teamsters' region in Western Canada, had also echoed the philosophy of avoiding strikes, saying that strikes are "a public declaration that the parties aren't mature, intelligent or responsible enough to settle their problems any other way".[6]

Such ideas had also been expressed by David Lewis, former federal leader of the NDP, in several speeches he made in 1972 and 1973. For example, in a speech in Miami, Florida, he said:

> Union demands must be socially justifiable if they are to gain public support. Extravagant demands raise expectations in the membership which cannot be fulfilled. The dynamics of the situation results in frustration and resentment, and sometimes in strikes which might have been avoided.[7]

In a speech to the National Press Club in Ottawa in March 1972, Lewis said:

> There is one thing I hope Canadians have noticed on a number of recent occasions. . . . The leaders of unions would much rather avoid strikes because they appreciate more keenly the importance of public support for their cause and the union's obligations to consider the public interest as well as that of its members. But the latter [the members], just as you and I and all other Canadians, think of their own interests first, and demand that their union fight for them.[8]

In 1972 Steelworkers' Canadian director William Mahoney pointed out that there had been relatively few strikes in manufacturing industries. Both sides, he said, had learned the rules. He contrasted this to the public sector where the problem was that neither the government nor the unions had had much experience in collective bargaining.[9]

Mahoney's 1972 observations were made in the context of some startling revelations by the union's research director, Gordon Milling. Milling said that real wages in the iron and steel industry had risen by only twenty-one per cent in the ten years preceding 1971, while productivity had risen by thirty-one per cent. In the same period, the wage gain for all manufacturing had been thirty per cent but the overall gain in productivity for manufacturing had only been fourteen per cent.[10] Steel workers had fallen behind the rest of the manufacturing work force in relative wage increases despite the fact that productivity in their industry had increased by more than double the rate for manufacturing as a whole.

These facts challenged Mahoney's argument that strikes were no longer helpful to workers' incomes in the steel industry. He was also urging union leaders to "work like hell" to persuade their members to accept and comply with the contract agreements.[11] This amounted to a warning against attempts to reopen contracts in mid-term — a policy that would lead many workers to lose ground economically during the period of rapid inflation from 1973 to 1975.

In July 1975 Roman Gralewicz, president of the SIU in Canada, called for a ten-year, no-strike pact if the federal government decided to create a Canadian deep-sea fleet. This suggestion was challenged by Donald Nicholson, a vice-president of the Canadian CBRT. Nicholson said that any deal based on a ten-year, no-strike pledge would back-fire. He predicted that seamen would rebel against a union that "tried to increase its membership and revenue regardless of what the union promised the employers". Nicholson said there was no justification for denying seamen basic union rights enjoyed by other Canadian workers and by ships' crews of other countries.[12]

As seen in earlier chapters, business union policy has meant not only avoiding strikes and achieving respectability in the business community, but also promoting long contracts. The one-year contract which typified industrial unions in the thirties and forties was replaced by first two and then three-year contracts. The effect of such long contracts on the living standards of workers in 1973 and 1974 has already been noted in the Appendix.

Business unionism has permitted unions to be co-opted into a restrictive system of labour-management relations which tend to make the unions a quasi-official arm of government. This aspect of business unionism is evident in the whole network of procedures set up by government which are designed to reduce the number of strikes through the "cooling off" periods. Thus there is certification, conciliation, mediation, arbitration, compulsory arbitration, and "designated" workers in the public service. These procedures have replaced mobilization and other actions demonstrating workers' collective strength.

The response of top Canadian leadership stood in contrast to that of British labour in the early 1970s. The British trade union movement when faced with efforts to impose a Labour Relations Bill in 1971, legislation which would have chained British labour to some of the procedures and regulations experienced by Canadian workers, was successful in defeating the bill through a militant, nation-wide strategy of opposition.

By late 1974, however, there were indications that some Canadian leaders of international unions were beginning to "catch up" to their members in supporting bigger demands and breaking with earlier policies of "restraint". This is not to say that the language of business unionism had disappeared entirely. Lynn Williams of the USWA, for instance, was aware of the new mood among younger workers in 1975:

> We have a generation of people who weren't depression kids, who aren't uptight. ... They think they have rights as people and they don't have to put up with a lot of crap, and they aren't going to. In that atmosphere, the [bargaining] committees have to be sensitive to a much broader range of problems — as do the companies.[13]

In the previous year CLC president Joe Morris had said that workers would have to go after big pay hikes, not only to keep pace with inflation, but also to make up for the lost ground of 1973 and 1974. In his 1975 New Year's message, Morris warned that there was "little to be optimistic about" in the coming year, and again pointed to the need for the labour movement to act to protect workers' incomes:

> The challenge to the labour movement is to drive ahead to protect men and women workers against the blight of inflation, to stop the merciless attack on the purchasing power of their hard-earned wages and salaries.[14]

As early as March 1974 Shirley Carr of CUPE had called for an across-the-board twenty per cent wage increase as well as one-year contracts for all workers to combat the uncertainties of inflation.[15]

In that same month, Federal Finance Minister John Turner told a meeting of the Railway Labour Association that workers' incomes were running ahead of prices in the inflationary spiral. The reactions of union leaders were immediate and hostile. Mahoney of the USWA called Turner's comments "absolute claptrap, and he knows it. The only people Turner could not convince is your average Canadian family that's struggling and failing to keep up."[16]

At the beginning of May 1975 Turner moved from criticisms of union wage settlements to a proposal for voluntary or "consensus" restraints on wage and salary increases.[17] This would have placed a 12 per cent ceiling on wage and salary increases for Canadians who had been "below average in previous income boosts. Those who had received an average or above average increase would be limited to an 8 per cent increase or a maximum of $600, whichever was the greater.[18]

In contrast, profits would be unlimited, provided they were based on increased sales volume and not on increased profit margins. There would be no limit to dividends or interest rates. Rents would be allowed to follow their present course although provinces would be encouraged to "attempt to exercise some restraints" in this area. There was no indication as to how profits could or would actually be kept to designated levels, whereas wages or salary increases could be calculated to the nearest cent.

Reactions of the trade union movement to the finance minister's proposals were strong and negative. The CLC Executive Council criticized the government for being "unwilling or incapable of bridging the gap between their concept of equity and ours".[19] The CLC pointed out that whereas wages and salaries had accounted for 73 per cent of the national income in 1971, this had dropped to 69 per cent by the third quarter of 1974. In the previous two years industrial wages had risen by 22.3 per cent compared to a rise of 22.7 per cent in consumer prices:

> Industrial workers, on the average, gleaned no benefit at all from industry's eleven per cent improvement in productivity. Meanwhile, the two-year increase in food prices was thirty-seven per cent — mortgage interest twenty-eight per cent — new house prices (in metropolitan areas) fifty-three per cent. These items made up at least half of the average worker's budget.

The CLC statement continued:

> In the face of these realities, Turner's proposal would freeze the already reduced buying power of wage and salary earners at their present levels and provide no mechanism to protect the public against rising costs of rents, interest rates, professional fees and land speculators.

Nine measures without which "no programme can be considered acceptable," were then listed by the CLC. These included measures to create full employment; a negative income tax; regulation of rents and oil and gas prices; and higher pensions. It made no concessions on labour's wage and salary demands.

The Canadian union movement reacted strongly to attempts to make labour bear the burden of inflation and the 1975 recession. This response stood in sharp contrast to the reaction of U.S. union leaders in 1971, when they either supported or passively tolerated President Nixon's economic policies of wage controls.

In September 1975 Shirley Carr, executive vice-president of the CLC, addressing a Labour Day luncheon at the Canadian National Exhibition in Toronto, answered the rising criticisms of the union movement's economic demands by federal government and corporate spokesmen. A few days earlier, Trade Minister Gillespie had challenged labour leaders to come out "four square for competitive settlements" and to use Labour Day to "tell it how it is".

Shirley Carr said the CLC accepted the challenge and added that economic facts do not bear out "unwarranted attacks on labour. Rather, they suggest that this country has been plagued by irresponsible corporate power which is helped along by paralyzed politicians who jump on the corporate bandwagon in their traditional response to economic difficulty."

Carr pointed out that in 1971 wages and salaries took 72.9 per cent while corporation profits took 12.3 per cent of national income. By 1974 labour's percentage had dropped to 70.5 per cent, while the share going to corporate profits had risen to 17 per cent. She stated that from 1971 to 1974 corporate profits had increased 111 per cent — from $8.6 billion to

$18.3 billion — while average earnings per paid worker climbed by only 25 per cent.

"Where was the government when this was happening? Where were the calls by politicians for price restraints? Where, indeed, were the corporations and those in positions of responsibility within them . . . ?"

She continued: "I would suggest that the corporate community was pursuing its own selfish interests and the maximization of profits. I would also suggest that it was doing this with the blessing of the federal government, for the politicians stand condemned on the issue through their own silence."

After pointing out that labour's share of the national income had dropped between 1971 and 1974 because workers were tied to two and three-year agreements she observed: "While corporations were chasing hard after every dollar they could grab, the workers were being held captive and thus powerless to act as a countervailing economic power".

When the economic cycle turned around and these same workers could exercise their economic muscle through their unions, noted Carr, "the previously deadening silence from the political powers turned into a ridiculous cry for wage and price restraint".

Carr concluded: "The way it is, Mr. Gillespie, is that you, and the government of which you are a part, acted in an extremely irresponsible manner in seeking to protect and to serve the interests of the Canadian people in general and of workers in particular".[20] It was not clear in August 1975 how far labour's leaders would go in their challenge to Turner, Gillespie and the federal government if wage controls were implemented. But a confrontation of major proportions was in the making. Union activists who had evolved a new bargaining stance in 1974-1975 did not seem to be in a mood to abandon Canadian labour's new militancy for previous or current patterns of American unions.

Most of the statements of union leaders up to the spring of 1975 appeared to be "tactical" rather than "strategic". The Quebec experience indicated that when leaders like Pepin and Laberge changed their approach to basic labour strategy they also changed their stance both in collective bargaining and in the struggles of the Quebec working class as a whole. The Quebec labour manifestos and the Common Front were companion developments, the three labour centres joining in strategic objectives and united tactical actions (refer to chapters nineteen and twenty).

Such a movement appears to have begun amongst some union leaders in English Canada. An example was the UAW brief presented to the Ontario cabinet in March 1975 by Dennis McDermott. It included the following passage:

> It is clear to us that a serious programme [to stimulate the economy] cannot be implemented without fundamentally challenging the power of the corporations in our society. It is equally clear that the philosophy of this government, and its links with these same corporations,

have been an effective barrier preventing the introduction of programmes geared to working people rather than the sacred rights of private property. ... In certain circles, we in the labour movement are increasingly asked to show restraint and responsibility. ... But without changes in our social system, restraint means no more than working people being squeezed so as to maintain the status quo. For the corporations, it means they can carry on business as usual, and for the government it means that they can avoid dealing with the difficult problems of changing the nature of our social system. When we see that our society is seriously moving to serve the interests of its working people, we can sit down and talk of restraint.[21]

1. *The Globe and Mail*, August 10, 1972.

2. *Financial Times of Canada*, November 18, 1974.

3. *The Financial Post*, February 8, 15, 22, 1975.

4. See Chapter 27.

5. *The Financial Post*, February 15, 1975.

6. Allan Fotheringham, "Ed Lawson: Senator from the Teamsters", *Maclean's*, August 1972, p. 33.

7. *The Globe and Mail*, August 10, 1972.

8. Remarks from a speech to the National Press Club in Ottawa, *Steel Labor*, March 1972, p. 8.

9. *Financial Times of Canada*, August 7, 1972.

10. Ibid.

11. Ibid.

12. *The Globe and Mail*, July 12, 1975.

13. *The Financial Post*, February 22, 1975.

14. *Canadian Labour Comment*, December 13, 1974, p. 6.

15. *The Toronto Star*, March 20, 1974.

16. Ibid.

17. *The Toronto Star*, May 5, 1975.

18. Ibid.

19. *Executive Council Statement* prepared for meeting of ranking officers of CLC affilates, May 7, 1975.

20. *The Globe and Mail*, September 2, 1975.

21. *The Toronto Star*, March 20, 1975.

CHAPTER 22
The Last of the Old-Style Strikes:
The Railway Strike of 1973

One major event that appears in retrospect to have been the last of the important old-style strikes was the nation-wide railway strike in the summer of 1973.

In August of that year 56,000 "non-ops" — workers who service the railways as clerks, typists, truck drivers and signalmen — went on strike. The unions' bargaining committee had originally demanded an increase of 53 cents an hour in the first year and 13.8 per cent in the second year of a two-year contract. By the time Parliament was recalled to deal with the strike, the unions' demands had been reduced to an immediate increase of 38 cents an hour, plus 10.8 per cent in the second year of the contract. The Liberal government's bill introduced on August 30, offered an interim settlement of 30 cents an hour, pending arbitration. Eight cents an hour separated the unions and the government.

Organized labour was at a crossroad. The railway workers could lead the rest of the union movement in holding out for a settlement that would stop the decline in purchasing power. Objectively considered, the railway strikers had a lot going for them. There was every possibility of getting a substantial settlement with the help of their natural allies in the union movement. And because of the strategic sector of the economy they represented, the railway workers had the potential of standing up for every Canadian wage-earner who was falling behind in living standards.

This potential was not lost on the Trudeau government. The Liberals moved quickly to prevent the railway workers from setting a pattern of substantial wage settlements.

Within a week of the strike's spread across the country, Parliament was convened in special session to legislate the "non-ops" back to work. After two days and sixteen hours of debate in the Commons and the Senate, the Maintenance of Railway Operations Act, 1973, was passed, ordering the strikers to end their walk-out.[1]

Because railway workers could practically shut down the day-to-day operations of the Canadian economy, editors across the country demanded an immediate legislated end to the strike. For instance, *The Edmonton Journal* termed the railway strikes "periodic bouts with chaos" in an editorial entitled "Enough". It continued:

> If the strike is allowed to go on, much of the nation's economy will grind to a total stop. The consequences — while so many other facets of the national and international economy are already unsettled — could be disastrous.[2]

Speeches in Parliament by members of all three parties reflected the same view.

A Conservative MP, Don Mazankowski, told the House that the railways "are not only essential but represent a national life-line". He continued:

> The cost of this disruption and its effect on our economy has amounted to untold millions of dollars. . . . This strike has caused a great deal of suffering, discomfort and misery to millions of people.[3]

Liberal cabinet minister Jean Marchand told the members of Parliament that "the only reason we are here is that this is a national emergency".[4]

NDP leader David Lewis said in the Commons that his party agreed:

> . . . that Parliament has a duty to the people of Canada and to the public interest, and that there comes a point in a strike such as a national railway strike at which members of Parliament must take the responsibility of making certain that rail operations are resumed so that the harm, the difficulties, the hardship, caused by the strike are ended.[5]

The pressure on the railways and on the government, which owns the CNR, mounted daily. As it had done in 1950 and 1966, Parliament could order an end to the strike. Parliament has the formidable weapon of compulsory arbitration, and with it, the power to impose two-year jail sentences and fines of up to $1,000 a day on unions and workers if they violate the law by refusing to go back to work.

The "non-ops" had a choice' to "obey Parliament" or to defy Parliament's edict. In the beginning, even the leaders of the non-operational unions had considered the possibility of defying the back-to-work legislation proposed by the government which would give them the thirty cent increase pending arbitration. On August 30, the day Parliament convened to consider the proposed legislation, the union leaders issued a public statement saying that they would refuse to order their members back to work on the basis of the legislation as it had been introduced.

> We will not send them back to work for the meagre wage increases proposed in the bill. We are still hoping that the bill will be improved sufficiently before being enacted that we can accept it as a fair basis of settlement. But as it now reads, we cannot and will not comply with the directive to us to break our own strike.[6]

Yet two days later, when the bill had been amended to provide for a mere four cents more in the first year and one per cent more in the second, the union leaders agreed to comply.

A brief examination of the context within which the union leaders were operating and the kinds of advice they were receiving from their closest associates provides a useful background to the events which followed. First, however, it is useful to consider the "case" made by the railway workers before the public.

In their pamphlet, "We're Sorry We're Essential",[7] published before the strike, they had contrasted their minimum hourly wage rate of $2.32 with the $4.01 rate at Stelco, $4.04 at International Nickel, and $4.80 for the minimum assembler rate at General Motors. They showed that their increase in output per man-hour between 1949 and 1971 had been almost twice as high as that for manufacturing. The railway workers also showed that their output increases had been higher than that of U.S. railroads. The pamphlet went on to explain the precarious bargaining situation:

> For collective bargaining to work both employer and employees must know — *in advance* — that if they don't work out a mutually acceptable agreement, both sides must risk losing money. But, when one side knows that they run no serious risk, why should they bargain seriously? Our employers know, *in advance,* that if we don't agree to their proposals the law will force us to keep on working for unchanged wages and under unchanged working conditions. ... Under these conditions would you, if you were our employers, bargain with us seriously?

The limitation in the railway unions' argument could be found in the last sentence of their pamphlet:

> Since you have taken away most of our bargaining power, shouldn't you also insist that "essential" employees be guaranteed *better than average* wages and working conditions?

The unions accepted that being "essential" justified the outlawing of strikes, and that there was no serious way this built-in legal bias against the railway workers could be challenged. Thus, on the inside cover of their pamphlet, they suggested that being essential weakened their bargaining position: "We're sorry we're essential. ... We believe that, if we were less essential, we'd be a lot better off."

Earlier defeats had led railway union leaders to adopt a fatalistic attitude toward bargaining. Thus, on April 2, CBRT president Donald Secord recalled the 1950 and 1966 strikes which had ended with special legislation and arbitration: "Strikes followed conciliation and if it goes the same route this time, the government will either adopt legislation preventing a strike or put you back to work following the strike."[8]

Had they been strongly supported by top leaders of the trade union movement, perhaps the railway union officers would have held out. Instead, when the federal government introduced its back-to-work legislation, Donald MacDonald, president of the CLC, advised the railway workers that they should go back to work.[9] From NDP leader Davis Lewis came the same advice. On August 31 he told the House of Commons:

> I can appreciate the frustration and the anger of those who are being affected by this law. . . . I want to emphasize that in our view, and I know in the view of every member of this House, all Canadians have to accept the decision of Parliament. The cause of the strikers and the cause of the employees will not be served by those who set out deliberately to defy the law that has been passed, even though that law is not entirely fair to them. . . .[10]

The advice given to the railway union leaders was that the railway workers should tone down demands and actions. The railway union leaders' demand for a thirty-eight cent an hour increase fitted the strategy of "non-extravagant" demands, as it turned to be only four cents more than the legislated settlement following the Conservative-NDP amendment.

The amendment served its purpose well. A four cents difference did not seem to be enough to cause a strike and consequent jail sentences. The thirty cents proposed in the government bill had been described by the union leadership on August 30 as a "meagre" amount.[11] The following month, Jack Winter, CBRT representative for Northern Ontario, told the CBRT convention that the joint negotiating committee of the unions had "sold out for a lousy four cents an hour".[12]

The binding decision of the federally-appointed arbitrator, Emmett Hall, which affected all railway workers, came down on January 16, 1974. For the "non-ops" it provided an additional fifteen cents to the thirty-four cents passed by Parliament for a total of 13.8 per cent retroactive to January 1, 1973, and a further 9.0 per cent effective January 1, 1974. Increases for other railway workers were slightly smaller. However, Hall had based his award on the estimate that the consumer price index would rise by about 7.5 per cent in 1974. The actual rise in that year was 12.1 per cent. So even with the Hall settlement, railway workers fell behind in their purchasing power by about 5.0 per cent in 1974—and this did not take into consideration what they had lost previously.[13]

Some of the railway workers had realized at the time the settlement was being made that they had been dealt a rotten deal. Many defied the back-to-work order. In B.C.'s Lower Mainland some two thousand stayed out for a full week, disrupting rail traffic substantially. There was similar resistance at Windsor, Thunder Bay, Winnipeg, Cranbrook, St. Catharines, Calgary, Niagara Falls, Welland, Fort Erie, Capreol and Chatham.[14]

Richard Tino, president of the CBRT's Windsor local, commented:

> Even the older men are angry. They remember 1966 when there was compulsory arbitration and they got little out of it. They figure they won't get a damned thing this time, either.[15]

In Vancouver, where six of the strikers were charged with refusing to obey the back-to-work order, union spokesman Roy Head wondered if jails could be built "fast enough" to hold all the railway workers.

> Our people are back at work here but they're certainly not happy about it. With an issue like this I can see they'd be back out ... If the Government is capable of doing this to us — of forcing us back to work under threat — how much longer before they would try it on other labour people?[16]

As late as September 8, railway workers in the New Westminister CBRT local had held five votes on whether to obey the legislation; on the fifth vote, 609 voted against going back to work, with only 177 in favour.[17]

The largest opposition to a return to work came from the CBRT, the only Canadian union in the non-operating group. In contrast to the international unions in the group, where the top leadership ordered the members back to work without even a token attempt at rank and file ratification, the CBRT leaders asked each of their locals to vote on the recommendation, although without offering any leadership themselves.[18]

Twenty-two CBRT locals, mostly in Ontario, turned down the thirty-four cents, but a majority of locals across the country accepted the legislated settlement. This became the basis for the union leadership's advice to all locals to go back to work.

Since there was substantial opposition to the legislation after the leadership's compliance, it is difficult to assess what would have happened had all the railway workers followed the advice of Louis Laberge, president of the QFL, when he urged them to defy Parliament. At a meeting of the Canadian Labour Congress executive, Laberge turned to the press corps after president Donald Macdonald had urged the workers to comply with Parliament's edict, and told them:

> You either have the right to strike or you don't have it. If the only strikes that are permitted are those that don't hurt anyone, you might as well not have the right.[19]

The experience of the British coal miners a few months later in 1974, and of the Quebec workers who fought the Common Front strike in May

1972, has suggested that the railway workers could have held out and won wide support from the rest of organized labour against the legislation. But the structure of unions in the railway industry would have made this extremely difficult to do.

In 1974 there were seventeen unions in the railways: seven in the "non-ops" group; two in the operating or running trades; and eight in the crafts. With the exception of the CBRT, all the unions were branch locals of American organizations. In 1973 the three groups bargained separately.

The very existence of seventeen unions among 110,000 workers in a single industry perpetuates fragmentation, isolation and poor communication. In the smaller railway centres, each of the unions may only have a handful of members belonging to locals with geographical boundaries spanning hundreds of miles. Under these conditions, the opportunity for a member to attend a local meeting is minimized. During the 1973 strike, the fragmentation of the unions had a demoralizing effect on the members.

The logic of their political and economic experience has pressed railway workers to consider the steps required to achieve a single union embracing all railway workers. This idea — which had been the official policy of the only Canadian railway union, the CBRT, since at least 1908, and which CBRT president Secord pressed for again after the 1973 strike — carried with it the necessity for an all-Canadian union.

The decision in May 1975 to form a Canadian structure for the Brotherhood of Railway and Airline Clerks (BRAC), with Canadian conventions and control of all union finances in Canada, was expected to speed the process of unifying the railway unions into one all-Canadian organization. With its 20,000 members in Canada, BRAC joined with the CBRT would constitute close to half of Canada's railway workers.[20]

An all-Canadian union has been seen by CBRT and other workers as the most direct way to achieve a merger in Canada without confronting all the jurisdictional complexities and conflicts of the railway unions in the United States. Such a union would also be the most effective way to deal with Canada's two national railway systems, in protecting future job security and promoting an alternative railway and transport policy for Canada.

The modesty of the demands of the railway unions and the caution of their leaders in August 1973 stood in stark contrast to the wage and salary demands and the vital leadership in the union battles that came only a few months later. While the leaders of the railway unions had fought their strike according to the "book" of business unionism, within months public employees had thrown away these axioms. And while the railway union leaders had carefully gone after goals that were not "excessive", public employees were raising expectations which had seemed fanciful only a short time before.

After the railway strike was ended by order of Parliament, the defeatist mood of the railway workers was reflected in Winnipeg's Labour Day Parade when a group of CNR electricians carried a coffin mourning the "death" of collective bargaining in Canada.[21] The mood of labour was to change soon after this defeat.

---

1. *The Toronto Star*, September 1, 1973.

2. *Edmonton Journal*, August 25, 1973.

3. Canada, House of Commons, *Debates*, 29th Parliament, July 19-September 21, 1973, Vol. VI, p. 6126.

4. Ibid., p. 6104.

5. Ibid., p. 6076.

6. *The Globe and Mail*, August 31, 1973.

7. Associated Non-Operating Railway Unions, "We're Sorry We're Essential", pamphlet, Montreal, n.d.

8. *The Globe and Mail*, April 2, 1973.

9. *The Globe and Mail*, September 11, 1973

10. Canada, House of Commons, *Debates*, Vol. VI, p. 6175.

11. *The Globe and Mail*, August 31, 1973.

12. *The Globe and Mail*, September 19, 1973.

13. *Financial Times of Canada*, January 21, 1974.

14. *The Toronto Star*, September 8, 1973; *The Globe and Mail*, September 8, 1973.

15. *The Toronto Star*, September 8, 1973.

16. *The Globe and Mail*, September 10, 1973.

17. *The Globe and Mail*, September 8, 1973.

18. *The Globe and Mail*, September 4, 1973.

19. *The Globe and Mail*, September 11, 1973.

20. *The Globe and Mail*, May 13, 1975.

21. *Winnipeg Free Press*, September 13, 1973.

CHAPTER 23
Ontario Teachers Set the Pace

I've never before participated in a strike. I've always voted Conservative, but I'll strike, I'll do any other goddamn thing because there is no way I'll stand around and let my rights be legislated away without protest.

R.R. Wilson
Past president, Ontario County District, OSSTF
December 1973[1]

December 18, 1973 was a turning point in Canadian unionism. On that day, 105,000 elementary and secondary school teachers in Ontario stayed off the job. If it is possible to isolate a single event that characterized the last of the old-style unionism, as with the railway strike of August 1973, it is equally possible to identify the emergence of a new militance. Teachers in Ontario provided the leadership in December 1973.

In the fall of 1973 *The Globe and Mail* ran a series of editorials which opposed Ontario teachers' efforts to reintroduce the 1971-1972 pupil-teacher ratio. *The Globe* was calling for greater productivity per teacher in a programme of efficiency, lower costs, and a tough employer-employee relationship.[2] The efforts of the Toronto newspaper and other business-dominated institutions to whip up a campaign against the teachers in Ontario, to turn public opinion against them, to throw them on the defensive, and to prepare the ground for legislation to curb militant teacher action failed. They failed because the teachers responded quickly and decisively.

In the several years prior to 1975, rising inflation, an influx of younger teachers, ever-larger classes, provincial government ceilings on education spending, and the example of their Quebec counterparts had begun to break down the narrow "professionalism" of teachers across Canada. The 75,000 Quebec teachers had formed themselves into one of the most progressive and militant unions in that province. The quarter of a million teachers in English Canada were also becoming part of a broad labour movement.

The notion that teachers were above such mundane matters as rates of pay and conditions of work was replaced by increasing awareness that teachers were working people who need union-like organizations to defend their rights. Nowhere in English Canada was this shift more dramatic than in Ontario in 1973-1974.

As early as 1969, the Ontario Secondary School Teachers' Federation abandoned its twenty-year-old opposition to the tactics of mass resignations in mid-year. Two member districts used this bargaining tool with the full support of the OSSTF.[3]

In May 1970 eight thousand teachers gathered in Toronto's Maple Leaf Gardens to hear the past president of the OSSTF ask for the resignations of all Metropolitan Toronto secondary school teachers. Six thousand resignations were placed in the Federation's hands. As a result of this pressure, the Metropolitan Toronto School Board agreed to hire eighty-three additional teachers.[4]

Concerned with the mounting wave of teacher militancy, the Conservative government in Ontario set up a Committee of Inquiry into the negotiation procedures at the elementary and secondary school level. The Committee's findings, published as the Reville Report in June 1972, described with dismay the "situation [that] developed [in 1969-1970] in Toronto which disrupted negotiations across the province".[5]

Stating that "the right to strike is incompatible with professionalism generally and with the professional status of the teacher in particular," the Report called for:

> a system of negotiations between teachers and their employers which will render unnecessary the degrading techniques of the past and will insure teacher-school board relationships worthy of teacher professionalism and trustee responsibility.

The "degrading techniques" referred to were mass resignations and the use of "work to rule".

The teachers rejected the core of the Reville Report. As the spending ceilings began to cut seriously into the number of new staff hired, teachers were willing to use "degrading techniques" to ensure some say in working conditions and job security. At Christmas, 1972, teachers in Windsor submitted their resignations en masse and in Timmins only four of 244 teachers reported to work after Christmas.[6] A similar action had just been averted in Toronto by a last-minute settlement. A spirit of militant action was spreading across the province.

Toronto teachers' opposition to the education policies of the Davis government was also expressed in the St. George by-election in the spring of 1973. Following the lead of British Columbia teachers who had helped elect the Barrett government, Toronto teachers were active in defeating the Conservative candidate in a long-held Conservative riding.

In May 1973 two teachers organized a protest march demanding that spending ceilings be lifted and for the first time in the recent period won the public support of Ontario's organized labour for teachers.[7]

As November 30, the official deadline for mass resignations approached, it became clear that many boards in Ontario would be without teachers on January 1, 1974. In Metro Toronto, settlements were approved, but by only fifty-two per cent of the membership. The deadline date arrived and across the province seventeen boards received mass resignations. The teachers' negotiating demands included a reduction in the pupil-teacher ratio, together with more control over bargaining and working conditions.[8]

The Ontario government reacted quickly and on December 10, Education Minister Thomas Wells introduced Bill 274 in the Ontario legislature. He referred to it as an interim bill, "designed to bring our basic intentions to bear upon any teacher-board negotiation which has not reached a successful conclusion by January the first, 1974".[9] These "basic intentions" were unmistakable:

> This bill voids any mass resignations, and stresses that all schools must resume normal operations in January. At the same time, a process of binding arbitration will be initiated in those remaining situations where agreements have not been reached.[10]

While the Reville Report had called for a new system of negotiations which would render "degrading techniques" unnecessary, the new system, under Bill 274, would be compulsory arbitration, without the right to mass resignations or to strike.

In an unprecedented move, the five teachers federations, grouped in the Ontario Teachers' Federation, called for a one-day protest strike to signal their opposition to the proposed legislation. On December eighteenth 105,000 teachers in elementary and secondary schools did not report to work.

On the same day, 35,000 teachers from across the province met at a rally at Toronto's Maple Leaf Gardens and then marched to demonstrate at Queen's Park. This was the largest labour demonstration in the city's history.

The Toronto executive of the OSSTF published a newspaper release which included these passages:[11]

> We, the teachers of this city and province, object to these pieces of legislation on the grounds that they deprive the individual citizen of the basic human right to negotiate freely with his employer.
>
> ... What is the meaning of this repressive legislation to the students and parents of Ontario? These measures on the part of the government could possibly set the stage for the implementation of future

legislation directed against the collective bargaining rights of labour and professional groups.

The Canadian Labour Congress, the Canadian Union of Public Employees, the Ontario Medical Association, the United Auto Workers, the Civil Liberties Association, the United Steel Workers, the Metro Toronto Labour Council, and others see great danger in these ill-conceived bills and have thrown their support behind the teachers.

As a result, we challenge the Conservative government's assumption that it represents the views of the majority of the citizens of Ontario in this matter . . . Your future should be in your hands.

The atmosphere at Maple Leaf Gardens was electric. The Travellers, a Canadian folk-singing group, led the teachers in old union songs like "Hold the Fort" and "Solidarity Forever". Then, wave after wave, teachers shouted: "Go Wells Go — Go Wells Go!" This was followed by another chant: "No Wells, No Wells — Down with the Bill he's trying to sell!"

As the demonstrators marched across downtown Toronto, thousands of placards portrayed the anger of the teachers: "Withdraw 274", "Jingle Bells — to Hell with Wells", "The Tories Must Go", "All's Well that Ends Wells".[12] R.R. Wilson, a teacher for twenty-five years and past president of the Ontario County District of the OSSTF, was carrying a sign reading "Kill 274, Bury Davis". He explained his involvement:

I'll strike, I'll do any other goddamn thing because there is no way I'll stand around and let my rights be legislated away without protest.[13]

The province-wide walkout was clear evidence of the newly developing labour consciousness of many teachers. It represented an unprecedented spirit of unity among French and English-speaking elementary and secondary teachers from both public and separate shcools.

In the face of these demonstrations, Wells withdrew Bill 274 and brought in Bill 275 in its place. The new bill was supposed to be a compromise, but it still gave the government the right to impose compulsory arbitration. Bill 275 was withdrawn in turn because of continued teacher opposition.

The success of the December 1973 demonstrations raised the teachers' morale for the coming negotiations. Early in 1974 some 660 of York County's 850 secondary school teachers staged a seven-week strike. Besides straight pay matters, they were demanding the right, eventually won, to discuss the pupil-teacher ratio and other working conditions.

The Ontario provincial government drafted another bill — Bill 12 — to order the York County teachers back to work and refer their dispute to compulsory arbitration. On March 13, 1974, this bill was passed by the legislature, with both the Liberal and NDP members opposing the imposition of compulsory arbitration.[14]

But NDP provincial leader Stephen Lewis then told the teachers that they should obey the new law. "I hope the teachers will accept it and return to the schools . . . Even if the law is an ass people should observe it."[15] This kind of statement, as events were to show, was out of keeping with the new mood of militancy, the conviction that social legitimacy superseded narrow legality.

The three-man arbitration panel in the York County strike reported on June 6. In addition to offering salary increases ranging from fifteen to twenty-four per cent, it gave the teachers increased job security and a guaranteed maximum pupil-teacher ratio. It included, for the first time in Ontario teacher-trustee agreements, a no-discrimination clause against teachers who had been active in the strike.[16]

Among the most militant of Ontario teachers were those in the industrial city of Windsor. In November 1974 the Windsor teachers became involved in straightforward strike action. Unlike the York County walk-out, or the previous walk-out of Windsor teachers for three weeks in January 1973, this strike was not preceded by the tactic of mass resignation. From the outset, the Windsor strikers made their position clear. As Bill Lozinsky, head of their negotiating committee, put it, "We won't accept arbitration in any form, and provincial involvement [of other teachers' groups] comes in if the minister tries to interfere".[17]

The Globe and Mail, in its continuing crusade against teacher militancy, commented:

> So here we are at the picket line stage; the debate-by-placard level of dialogue. It brings no enlightenment, injures the innocent, feeds bitterness, and sets a dismal example . . .[18]

The Windsor Board of Education tried to break the strike by applying for a court injunction to order the teachers back to work. Mr. Justice John Osler of the Ontario Supreme Court denied the application, giving as his main reason the absence of violence on the teachers' picket lines. He pointed out that while there was no doubt that the teachers were on strike and in breach of their contracts, the Ontario Labour Relations Act made no provision for teachers' strikes.

After an eight-week strike period (which included the Christmas break) the strike was finally settled. In a breakthrough agreement, the Windsor teachers accepted a twelve-month contract providing for inflation-proof salaries and an average increase of about twenty-nine per cent.[19]

Teachers in Thunder Bay's ten high schools began a series of rotating strikes in late November 1974, five weeks before their mass resignations were scheduled to take effect.[20] By January 1975 this had turned into a continuing strike with the resignation of 524 high school teachers. Secondary teachers in Timiskaming also went out. Both of these groups won settlements similar to the Windsor pattern.[21]

While the York County teachers had won the right to be consulted on a wide range of school board policies, the Windsor teachers had won the right to actually negotiate a number of such policies. Shortly after the Windsor victory, a conference of four hundred school trustees and senior administrators from across Ontario met to lick their wounds. Peter Bargen, executive director of the Ontario School Trustees Council, commented on the settlement: "Windsor represents a great extension of what was so hard-fought a year ago in York County."[22]

Harvey Nightingale, director of economic and legislative services for the trustees' group, told the conference that the Ontario government had abandoned enforcement of its own laws:

> By its failure to respond to the teachers' illegal strike activity, the government has given *de facto* recognition to illegal actions that do not provide a process which school boards can address and cope with. In essence, if the government will not enforce the spirit and intent of its laws, how can one expect the school boards to do so?"[23]

He ended his speech by complaining that "the absence of an orderly process through legislation severely restricts every school board's ability to counter teacher power".

The key word was "power" because teachers were learning to use it. No sooner had the trustees arrived home from their conference (where, among other things, they had been urged not to negotiate at all with teachers in 1975 unless legislation was enacted), than 1,600 high school teachers in Ottawa went on strike. The Ottawa high school teachers strike gained additional significance because it was the largest in Ontario, but even more because it occurred in the nation's capital in the midst of intermittent strikes by blue-collar workers in the federal public service.

The Ottawa board retaliated by threatening to fire the strikers, and to black-list the striking teachers. The Ottawa board chairman said, "we are leaving it up to the minister to decide what should be done".[24] Education Minister Wells was on the defensive this time and commented:

> It isn't an illegal strike. The teachers in Ottawa are obviously breaking their individual contracts. I'm sure they'd be the first to acknowledge that. They aren't breaking any provincial law.[25]

Well's interpretation of the Ottawa teachers' strike as "legal" in contrast to Nightingale's denunciation of "the teachers' illegal strike activity" illustrates the elasticity in concepts of legality as modified by social legitimacy. Had public opinion been clearly against the teachers' strikes, and thereby deprived teacher militancy of social legitimacy, Wells might have stretched a prevailing attitude of illegitimacy into a declaration that the strikes were "illegal".

A week later, responding to a strike plan by Metropolitan Toronto high school teachers to win salary increases of up to seventy-three per cent, Wells reverted to his previous style. The demands were "nothing more than public blackmail, pure and simple". The teachers were "holding a gun to the public's head," he said.[26]

Teachers' new activity was not all directed toward winning wage gains and more say in negotiating working conditions. Much effort also went into building more effective vehicles for the new-found militancy and trade union consciousness of their members.

District 5 (Brant County) submitted a brief to the Commission on Restructuring of the OSSTF.[27] This brief showed broad concern with the questions of public financing, and the role of teachers in society. The brief warned that the developing recession in Canada would put pressure on the government to limit education spending:

> Recent figures show that auto production for the 1975 model year is already down thirty per cent. Canadian branch plants will be under tremendous pressure in Ontario. Teachers and other public employees in Ontario should realize what implication this has for us. The fiscal squeeze on government will continue.

It recommended that the OSSTF develop a "close working relationship" with the following groups in Ontario: 1) other teacher groups; 2) other workers in the education field; 3) public sector employees; 4) organized labour in the private sector. It explained these last two alliances as follows:

> Workers in the public sector are our natural allies in any major battle we may have to face. People employed by municipal, provincial and federal governments are all facing similar problems. The taxation system in Canada is the common basis of financing government and paying our wages and salaries . . .
> Teachers can no longer afford to isolate themselves from the vast majority of workers in this province. These workers are the taxpayers who support the public sector. Ultimately all of us depend on a healthy and viable manufacturing base . . . Can we expect trade unionists to support our battles . . . if we do not a) support them when they face difficulties in collective bargaining or b) work for changes in the taxation structure and economic system?

The brief provided a glimpse of the possibilities such an alliance would create:

> In time of major conflict of any one of the groups, all could react quickly and effectively in common support. Teachers would gain hundreds of thousands of natural allies if we followed this course, and the "divide and rule" game played by the government would not be effective.

At the 1975 annual meeting of the OSSTF James Forster, president of the 34,000-member organization, spoke about the gains teachers had made in the past year, and the goals they had yet to attain. Referring to Ontario Premier Davis' contention that it was the OSSTF leaders who were "militant" while the membership was "responsible", Forster charged that this was "an attempt to interfere in the internal democracy of this federation".[28] His remarks summed up the new role Ontario teachers were playing:

> There is no militant leadership and docile membership, Mr. Davis. There are militant teachers. And they are militant because they demand a fair and equal share of the good life for themselves and for their families. And they are militant because they demand their full professional role in the planning of their own school programmes.

Their militance forced the Davis government to back down on its no-strike position. In July 1975 the Ontario Legislature approved Bill 100 which gave teachers the right to strike after a series of compulsory steps. A five-man Education Relations Commission would enforce these steps prior to a strike. They would include: a fact-finding inquiry and report, a secret ballot by teachers in which a majority rejected the board's last offer and a five-day notice prior to launching a strike.[29] The bill gave principals and vice-principals the right to participate in a strike ballot but not the right to join teachers in strike action.[30] Definition of a strike included voluntary extra-curricular activities of teachers. This would rule out the widely used technique of "working to rule".

The Canadian Teachers' Federation at its annual meeting in July 1975 passed a resolution sponsored by the Ontario Teachers' Federation that said this Ontario legislation "restricts the right to full and free collective bargaining".[31] Teachers' federations were particularly concerned about the outlawing of strike activity by principals and vice-principals, a move which would tend to split schools and force principals into a position of opposition to teachers' collective bargaining.

Viewed from the stance of the Ontario Government in December 1973 with its intent to outlaw teachers' right to strike, the July 1975 legislation represented a substantial if not complete retreat in recognition of the reality that Ontario teachers would henceforth act like unionists in full-fledged collective bargaining.

Ontario teachers, one of the latest groups to join the labour movement, had set an example with their new-found militancy and social consciousness.

1. *The Globe and Mail*, December 19, 1973.

2. R. M. Laxer, "Address to Conference of District 15 of the OSSTF", Toronto, November 1973.

3. *The Toronto Star*, November 29, 1969.

4. *The Report of the Committee of Inquiry into Negotiation Procedures Concerning Elementary and Secondary Schools of Ontario* (Reville Report), June 1972, p. 11.

5. Ibid.

6. *The Toronto Star*, January 4, 1973; *The Toronto Star*, January 3, 1973.

7. *The Toronto Star*, May 17, 1973.

8. *The Globe and Mail*, December 1, 1973.

9. Intercom *Epic*, OSSTF, No. 2, "Bill 274 — The Great Debate", January 1974, p. 7.

10. Ibid.

11. "An Open Letter to the Students and Parents of Toronto", *The Toronto Sun*, December 18, 1973.

12. Compiled from photographs in Intercom *Epic*, January 1974.

13. *The Globe and Mail*, December 19, 1973.

14. *The Toronto Star*, March 14, 1974.

15. Ibid.

16. *The Toronto Star*, June 7, 1974.

17. *The Windsor Star*, November 4, 1974.

18. *The Globe and Mail*, November 21, 1974.

19. *The Globe and Mail*, January 9, 1975.

20. *The Globe and Mail*, December 7, 1974.

21. *The Globe and Mail*, February 4, 1975.

22. *The Globe and Mail*, February 15, 1975.

23. Ibid.

24. *The Globe and Mail*, February 28, 1975.

25. Ibid.

26. *The Toronto Star*, March 7, 1975.

27. David Neumann, Lorne Foerter, Fred Philips, Paul Massicotte (ad hoc committee, Brant District 5, OSSTF). Brief to the Commission on Restructing OSSTF, excerpted in *The Brant Connection*, November 1974.

28. *The Globe and Mail*, March 22, 1975.

29. *The Toronto Star*, June 16, 1975.

30. *The Toronto Star*, July 19, 1975.

31. Ibid.

CHAPTER 24
Legitimacy or Legalism:
Hospital Workers and Nurses

Court action might nail a few of us, but they can't jail all 40,000 of us, though the government is welcome to try.

> John Askin
> President, Local 220 SEIU,
> London (Hospital workers)
> April 1974[1]

We are looking closely at what we can get if we go on strike because if nurses don't get a fair deal this year I am sure they will come to the conclusion that a strike is the only answer.

> Anne Gribben
> Chief negotiator, Ontario Nurses Association
> April 1974[2]

Nurses and other hospital workers, like the teachers, were joining the Canadian union movement in the 1970s. Their militancy, free of American business unionist traditions, was to contribute to a major change in the stance of that movement.

Just as the teachers were up against provincial government ceilings on education spending, the hospital workers were facing ceilings on hospital expenditures. The real battle, then, was with the provincial government. As one CUPE spokesman pointed out, the hospitals were merely acting as "a front for the provincial government".[3]

While high school teachers in York County were preparing for a strike and workers at United Aircraft near Montreal were entering their epic siege, CUPE locals at ten Toronto hospitals had joined in a committee to present a "Common Front" to their hospital boards. Early in January

1974 they issued a demand for a $1.14 an hour increase in a one-year contract.[4] Their demands immediately attracted public attention.

Non-medical hospital workers such as cleaners, orderlies, laundry and kitchen staff were being paid at a much lower wage than comparable workers in boards of education, organized plants and private industry. *The Toronto Star* ran a feature story on January 5 entitled "Hospital Worker Would Break Law to Win 'Justice'" in which Emmanuel Bourdos, a Riverdale Hospital orderly, was quoted as saying, "I am ashamed to go to work and come home to see my kids do without".[5] He went on to state that he would be glad to go to jail just to put more food on the dinner table and clothes on the backs of his children.

The ten Toronto CUPE locals held a series of strike votes in which majorities of eighty-five to ninety-nine per cent declared that they would strike illegally on May 1, defying the Ontario Hospital Labour Disputes Arbitration Act, if their "catch-up" demands were not granted.[6]

Arbitration, CUPE said, would be unacceptable. Tom Edwards, co-ordinator of the union's hospital division, called on the hospitals to join with the union in asking provincial Health Minister Frank Miller to appoint a responsible representative to meet with the union and hospital officials. The alternative was an illegal strike:

> Failing this, reluctantly but with a sense of rectitude, the union members will withdraw May the first in order to compel the government to intervene and eradicate poverty wages.[7]

The Toronto CUPE locals received support from fellow hospital workers in the Service Employees' International Union. John Askin, president of SEIU's 4,000-member Local 220 in Southwestern Ontario announced that the 14 bargaining units in his local would all take strike votes within two weeks. At a meeting in early April, Askin told 150 CUPE stewards and officers:

> If CUPE decides to strike, and even if it's against the law, a bad one at that, our union will strike to support them, even if some of our contracts haven't expired at the hospitals. . . . A dirty game is being fought right now and we are not going to back away from it. The day of paternalism is over, when a few can decide for the many.[8]

When asked what would happen if the government ordered the strikers back to work Askin replied:

> That's always possible. Court action might nail a few of us but they can't jail all 40,000 of us; . . . the government is welcome to try.

Public support for the "catch-up" campaign grew, spurred by revelations of the extremely low wages hospital workers were being paid. Even *The Toronto Star* gave guarded editorial support to the CUPE campaign. On April 13, it said:

> No one can condone a hospital strike, for precisely the reason the

government gives. But neither can one condone a policy that dooms essential workers and their families to live their lives in poverty, not only never catching up with workers elsewhere, but falling further behind as food and shelter costs keep rising.

The editorial concluded: "The government must find the money to pay hospital workers decent wages. There are just seventeen days left."

At the last minute the government agreed to an increase of $1.50 an hour, to be paid in stages over a two-year contract. In the words of Health Minister Miller, the government was agreeing to pay the hospitals "forced costs" over which they had no control.[9] The mood of the workers in Toronto was shown in the fact that only sixty per cent of those who voted favoured ratification of these terms.[10]

Expecting the worst, hospital administrations in Ontario hospitals had sent letters to their employees, predicting bitter clashes resulting in suffering to patients, were a strike to take place.[11] Such a situation never materialized as the threatened strike of 2,600 SEIU members was called off when the workers received a similar $1.50 increase.

The settlements with CUPE in Toronto and the SEIU locals in southwestern Ontario had repercussions for workers in other hospitals. At Woodstock General Hospital 150 non-medical workers illegally walked off the job on May 24, 1974, demanding reopening of their contract. Management handed a notice to the union, informing it that "withdrawal of services . . . is illegal. We demand you arrange a speedy and orderly return to work by your members."[12] Askin commented:

> We realize it is an illegal action and we are prepared to suffer any consequences that may result through injunctions, or any other action. . . .[13]

The Woodstock strike was eventually settled on the patterns of the Toronto and London settlements. This took place after ninety-five workers at St. Mary's General Hospital in Kitchener walked out for twenty-four hours in support of the Woodstock strike.[14]

Other hospital administrations resisted adopting the Toronto and London pattern settlements for their employees. Hamilton was a case in point. For a time it appeared that the city's hospital workers would have to strike to achieve the pattern. The Hamilton District Labour Council, together with many Hamilton area locals, supported the hospital workers' cause.

In July Elizabeth Brokman of the Hamilton Civic Hospital local warned that a hospital strike would be even more unpleasant than the garbage strike of the previous summer. "We are able to take out garbage to an emergency dump," she commented, but "sick people can't be disposed of that easily."[15] She said the very idea of a hospital strike was shocking to Hamilton hospital workers. "But if management leaves the strike route as the only way out for us, then we'll go."

Similar developments occurred in New Brunswick during 1974. In

March 6,500 angry non-medical workers, represented by CUPE, disrupted hospital operations across the province, locking out directors of nursing, taking over cafeterias, holding study sessions, or walking out. The workers were calling for a mid-term opening of their contracts. At first the government refused. Later, when it attempted to pacify the workers by offering a one-time cost of living bonus of $125.00 they demanded an across-the-board increase of $25.00 a week, retroactive to the beginning of December 1973. They also sought a cost of living escalator clause, to give them a one per cent increase in wages for each one per cent increase in the consumer price index.[16]

M.A. Hughes, CUPE's Atlantic Region director, commented:

> The spirit of militancy is there and has been amply demonstrated. The mood of the workers is one of frustration as they watch inflation eat up the salary increases they earned. Unless this government is prepared to bargain realistically, it would be a great surprise to me if one member of our union across the province wasn't prepared to go all the way. We have taken a beating on this thing and can't afford to wait around much longer.[17]

The New Brunswick government was finally forced to reopen negotiations in July, five months before the contract was to have expired.

The drama of the hospital workers' actions, their threats of illegal strikes, and the carrying out of those threats had a profound influence on the development of trade unionism among Ontario and New Brunswick nurses.

In April 1974, at the height of the confrontation between Toronto hospital workers and the government and hospitals, the Ontario Nurses Association announced it would consider strike action if necessary to win its demands. Anne Gribben, chief negotiator for the newly-formed joint bargaining organization, expressed the dissatisfaction nurses felt with the modest gains that compulsory arbitration had brought them in the past. She expressed her awareness that the fortunes of Ontario's 14,000 bargaining registered nurses were tied to the battle CUPE was waging with the Toronto hospitals.

If the registered nurses did not gain raises equivalent to those won by the CUPE members, Gribben said, they would consider an illegal strike to press their demands.[18]

By June some thirty-four local nurses' associations had joined the new province-wide union. The Association had sent telegrams to forty-eight hospital administrations in every area of the province demanding a joint bargaining session in June. The nurses' associations across the province suspended all scheduled arbitration, conciliation and mediation proceedings and demanded that employers wishing to talk contracts come to a June 21 meeting in Toronto.[19]

The RNAO, the nurses' professional organization, presented a brief to an Ontario government inquiry into hospital wages and working conditions in June. Noting that "passiveness is changing through years of frustration," and that "the situation is becoming explosive," the brief declared:

> It is totally unacceptable that nurses' salaries be determined on the basis of what is the going rate in a neighbouring hospital. . . . It is just as unacceptable that nurses be paid wages below many workers who have less education, [fewer] qualifications, [fewer] skills and [fewer] responsibilities simply because they are women.[20]

According to this brief, the average Ontario worker earned $8,814 in 1973, while nurses were starting at a rate of $7,740. Ambulance drivers, whose qualifications consisted of a driver's license and a first-aid course, were paid about $9,600.

Early in July *The Globe and Mail* published a letter by Linda Deyarmond, a registered nurse who, as she put it, had become "frustrated with the working conditions and salary discrepancies to the point where I left this dedicated service for a nice clean office job with better pay and weekends off".[21] Outlining these stresses and frustrations she asserted:

> True, we believe in the sanctity of living and dying and we agree that it takes a special kind of personality to be a nurse. But we are also a strong and very large working force of women and men who can no longer tolerate the pressures of our jobs for the salaries we are receiving. . . . To those leaders of our most honourable profession who are bucking the traditional passiveness we nurses are noted for, I say "bravo".

Of the 45,000 registered nurses employed in Ontario at the time, about 34,000 worked in hospitals. At the end of June, the Ontario Nurses Association rejected an offer made by hospitals employing about 10,000 nurses. The association announced that July 22 was the date set for an illegal strike challenging the Ontario Hospital Labour Disputes Arbitration Act. A caucus meeting of about 500 nurses approved the strike deadline.[22]

As the confrontation neared, Boris Mather, president of the Canadian Confederation of Communications Workers, wrote a stinging letter to the editor of *The Globe and Mail*.[23] He referred to an article published in the newspaper on June 11, which had said "if the employers do not come to the June 21 negotiations meeting . . . Ms. Gribben does not know what the nurses will do". Mather wrote:

> The inference is that Anne Gribben and the people she represents are simpering idiots who will stand around wringing their hands. I know what they will do, you know what they will do, and the hospital administrators know what the nurses will do if rebuffed by the hospitals — they will raise absolute hell all across the province in one way or another. . . . Don't think that the demands of the nursing profession can be laughed off with cheap jokes. That day is past. The nurses' drive for equality and justice has to be recognized and respected.

Results of nurses' strike votes began to come in as the strike deadline neared. Nurses at Sarnia General Hospital voted 98 per cent in favour of a walk-out. At Kingston General Hospital 150 nurses voted overwhelmingly to strike if necessary. Stratford nurses were to meet July 22, either to ratify a settlement or prepare for a strike.[24]

A week before the deadline, nurses began to set up picket lines at many Ontario hospitals. These were "to show management we want to be taken seriously and that we are not fooling about the deadline of midnight July 22,"[25] one spokesman said.

Just five days before the July 22 strike deadline, the reopening of negotiations was announced. The Association adopted a new set of demands, based on the settlement won by one thousand nurses at Ottawa Civic Hospital in a June arbitration decision. Most of the major demands were won. Following the basic pattern established at Ottawa Civic Hospital, the ten thousand nurses involved in the settlement received pay increases of between forty-five and fifty per cent by April 1975.[26]

Nurses in British Columbia won similar increases and nurses in other provinces were watching closely. One Nova Scotia nurse told a reporter for The Financial Post, "We've been underpaid for years. You can certainly expect a lot more militancy from this end of the country."[27] A Manitoba nurse echoed these sentiments: "If the government does not match the Ontario and British Columbia settlements, we are eventually going to have an illegal strike on our hands."[28] And similar moves toward a strong nurses' union were taking place in Newfoundland.

In January 1975, 1,300 of 1,600 nurses in 21 New Brunswick hospitals handed in their resignations collectively as a way to force the granting of higher salaries. Although these resignations were later withdrawn, the protest made a great impact.[29] In early February, 150 of the 190 nurses at Victoria Public Hospital in Fredericton voted not to return to work in spite of a New Brunswick Supreme Court injunction ordering them to do so.[30]

In September 1974, 2,100 federally employed nurses voted in a referendum to shift from the arbitration route to the hard-line system of conciliation and strike in their upcoming negotiations with the Treasury Board.[31] In May of the following year nurses at federal hospitals across the country went on strike to protest a conciliation board report that did not give them parity with provincially employed nurses.[32]

The Ontario nurses' threatened strikes and subsequent settlements also had an influence on other medical technicians and professionals. Although they were just beginning to get organized, laboratory technicians, X-ray technicians, and other workers with specialized skills were also asking for forty-five or fifty per cent increases. An Ontario union official commented that after the nurses got their raise "we received hundreds of calls from these groups. Settlement has been a real asset in convincing these people to sign up with a union."[33]

The theme of social legitimacy as a higher order of morality tha legality ran through the statements of hospital workers and nurses a they found a language to express their newly-won freedom to act as powerful force in society.

---

1. *London Free Press*, April 6, 1974.

2. *The Toronto Sun*, April 29, 1974.

3. *The Globe and Mail*, April 4, 1974.

4. Ibid.

5. *The Toronto Star*, January 5, 1975.

6. *The Globe and Mail*, March 22, 1974.

7. *The Globe and Mail*, April 4, 1974.

8. *The London Free Press*, April 6, 1974.

9. *The Toronto Star*, May 4, 1974.

10. *The Globe and Mail*, May 2, 1974.

11. *The Globe and Mail*, April 4, 1974.

12. *London Free Press*, May 25, 1974.

13. Ibid.

14. *London Free Press*, May 28, 1974.

15. *The Hamilton Spectator*, July 26, 1974.

16. *The Toronto Star*, April 26, 1974.

17. Ibid.

18. *The Toronto Sun*, April 29, 1974.

19. *The Hamilton Spectator*, June 12, 1974.

20. *The Toronto Star*, June 24, 1974.

21. *The Globe and Mail*, July n.d., 1974.

22. *The Globe and Mail*, June 27, 1974.

23. *The Globe and Mail*, June 24, 1974.

24. *London Free Press*, July 11, 1974.

25. *London Free Press*, July 16, 1974.

26. *The Financial Post*, July 27, 1974.

27. Ibid.

28. Ibid.

29. *The Globe and Mail*, February 12, 1975.

The Toronto Star, February 7, 1975.

The Ottawa Journal, October 4, 1974.

The Globe and Mail, June 5, 1975.

The Financial Post, July 27, 1974.

CHAPTER 25
Freeing the Servants

> This is the last year ever for compulsory arbitration. This is the end of
> CECBA. This is the beginning of free collective bargaining for all
> Ontario government employees.
>
> Charles Darrow
> President, CSAO
> September 1974[1]

In 1974, after sixty-two years of existence as a "tea and crumpets"
organization, the Civil Service Association of Ontario (CSAO) became a
union. It proved to be a dramatic example of the widespread transformation to union consciousness amongst formerly conservative associations
of provincial, municipal and federal government workers.

Delegates to the Ontario Federation of Labour's convention in October
1974 gave unanimous support to a request by the CSAO for demands
which could lead to a strike by Ontario's civil servants. Addressing the
convention, CSAO president Charles Darrow outlined the changes that
the association was undergoing. "For far too many years our organizations was in limbo. We were neither a social club nor a union. . . . We are
fast emerging as a union and we hope to have a delegate at the OFL
convention next year."[2] Shortly after this, the CSAO affiliated to the CLC.

For some fifteen years, former general manager Harold Bowen had
run the CSAO, disbanding the regional districts and reorganizing the CSAO
along occupational lines. With members spread from Kenora in the
northwest to Cornwall in the southeast, Bowen's reorganization had
ensured that members in each of the new occupational divisions would
rarely have the opportunity to get together and discuss policy. And
under Bowen's rule, a system of cozy relationships between the association and the government had developed.

In 1973 Bowen was replaced by Ron Morse. Then in July 1974, Jake Norman, who had been on staff since September 1973, became general manager. A new leadership which saw the association as a potentially powerful trade union began to emerge.

The CSAO's new style first appeared in its campaign against the Ontario government's 1972 labour legislation, the Crown Employees Collective Bargaining Act, or CECBA. Under this act provincial government workers in the CSAO jurisdiction, numbering more than fifty thousand, were denied the right to strike. Its compulsory arbitration provisions gave the government two representatives to the association's one, and the grievance board it set up had fourteen government seats, with none for the CSAO. In addition, civil servants were denied the right to bargain over many working conditions and were prohibited from participating actively in politics.

Under its new leadership, the CSAO demanded twenty-four changes in CECBA.[3] It began an effective $600,000 advertising campaign to bring its case to the public. The campaign slogan, "Free the Servants," was posted up throughout the province.

The contracts of some 19,000 workers in the operating category was due to expire at the end of December 1974. This category included correctional officers, stationary engineers, hospital maintenance workers, elevator inspectors, police radio operators, nursing and psychiatric assistants, and highway equipment operators, among others.

In September 1974 the CSAO announced its bargaining demands for this group. The association asked for wage increases amounting to 61.5 per cent over a one-year contract. An increase of 36.7 per cent was required, the union maintained, just to bring the government employees' incomes in line with those in private industry. An additional 4.3 per cent was needed to absorb the effects of inflation over the previous 18 months, and 3.75 per cent would take care of inflation for the first three months of the new contract. Additional cost of living payments would be made as lump sums at the end of each three-month period remaining in the new contract. Finally, the CSAO asked for a 16.75 per cent increase to account for higher productivity and the generally higher standard of living in the province.[4]

Other bargaining goals included the proposal that workers doing the same jobs be paid uniform rates, and that the number of steps required to reach the maximum pay level for any job be reduced.

The CSAO's biggest contract previously was a 12.5 per cent increase over 15 months for 8,000 members of its social service category. This was only three months earlier, and significantly, there had been no strike threat.[5]

The government waited a month before coming up with a counter-offer to the operating group's demands: increases ranging from ten to sixteen per cent. This was totally unacceptable to the union, and the CSAO began to talk of a possible illegal strike. "The CSAO is a sleeping giant that at last is coming awake," general manager Norman said. "If we strike, it will be [due to] a combination of the government's reluctance, if not total indifference, to our demands for cost of living adjustments and a change in the regressive, repressive legislation that governs our bargaining."[6]

Former CSAO president, George Gemmell, had resigned in June, feeling he could not support the new militant stance the association was taking.[7] His successor, Charles Darrow, thought that the CSAO might have to go on illegal strike to prove to the government that it was now dealing with a union:

> I don't think the government has bought it yet that we have not only assumed a union stance but we have the machinery to go with it. Maybe they don't realize that membership feeling is building up — every day our people are getting angrier.[8]

At the end of September, delegates representing the operating employees met and overwhelmingly endorsed a "no contract, no work" policy if agreement had not been reached by December 31.

A civil service strike in Ontario would have been illegal and unprecedented. Once again, as with the teachers and the hospital workers, legitimacy was overriding legality.

Concern with the consequences of such thinking by unionists was voiced by *The Globe and Mail* is an editorial written about the illegal four-day strike of Toronto's transit workers after they had been ordered back to work by the Ontario legislature:

> Most strikers do not see themselves as lawbreakers, as thieves are lawbreakers. They think they are free men resisting forced labour. Yet their kind of lawbreaking is far more dangerous to the rule of law in Canada than is the lawbreaking of thieves; for they are organized, they can put thousands of men behind the act of breaking the law, they can set an example for other organized groups to break the law.[9]

A few weeks later, Chris Trower, CSAO negotiator, provided labour's rejoinder to this view of illegal strikes when he told the Ontario government negotiating team:

> You may quote to us your law that makes such a strike illegal. But, by its enactment, you place yourselves above the law. If you seek to deal with us from a position above the law, don't be surprised if our members, in desperation, strike to spite that law....[10]

Darrow set the tone of the CSAO meeting:

> If there is no bargain by December 31 ... then we don't work.... That's the message we must send today.... This is the last year ever for compulsory arbitration. This is the end of CECBA. This is the beginning of free collective bargaining for all Ontario government employees.[11]

During October and November the association ran a series of "Free the Servants" advertisements in Ontario newspapers aimed at winning public support for their demands. The ads included such memorable slogans as "Bill Davis is a cheapskate," "Bill Davis, clean up your act," "The government has made 60,000 Ontarians second-class citizens," and "The government is discriminating against a typist at Queen's Park."

In November 1974 a province-wide meeting of the operational group was held where the old CSAO structure had to be bypassed. The meeting was set up in an unusual way. The main meeting took place in Toronto with 2,800 members attending. This was transmitted via a closed-circuit television hook-up to meetings of 450 members in Thunder Bay, 300 in Ottawa, 600 in Kingston, 275 in Sault Ste. Marie, 800 in London, and 400 in Sudbury. When CSAO negotiator Chris Trower presented the details of the government's offer, a chorus of "boos" and cries of "never" showed the workers' response. All of the meetings rejected the government proposals.[12] A province-wide ballot of the operating group showed 10,250 in favour of an illegal strike, and only 549 opposed: a majority of 94.5 per cent.[13]

A week later the annual general meeting of the association was held. To the apparent surprise of the executive, a motion came from the floor authorizing the union officers to call on all 60,000 provincial employees to strike if the operating group did not reach a satisfactory settlement by December 31. One of the delegates, OHIP worker J.D. Lindsay, spoke in support of the motion:

> Let's get together and act like a union. Let's have solidarity. This is the only way we'll stop the province right in its tracks.[14]

On a standing vote, a strong majority of the delegates supported this resolution. If the operating group did not settle by the end of the year a strike vote of the entire CSAO membership would be taken. President Darrow was asked whether this meant he had been given a stronger bargaining weapon. He replied that he had been given "a lot more responsibility".[15]

By the beginning of December the government had given up its attempt to negotiate a two-year agreement and was now offering increases of between fifteen and twenty-three per cent for 1975. The one-year contract was important to the CSAO because it meant all Ontario provincial civil servants' contracts would expire on December 31, 1975.

The association had by then cut its 61.5 per cent demand, first to 41 per cent and then, on December 19, to 29 per cent. But negotiator Trower warned that if the government moved no further, it would still face a strike.

The brinksmanship continued right up to the December 31 deadline. At the last moment, the government raised its offer. On Sunday, December 29, the operating group members voted to accept 21.5 per cent across the board, and 23 per cent for jail guards, in a one-year contract. The final vote tallied at 5,798 in favour of the settlement, and 1,361 opposed. This sizeable minority of the membership was still prepared for an illegal walk-out despite the considerable victory the union had won.[16]

The day after the government's offer to the operating employees was accepted the CSAO began another campaign. This time the target was Bill 179, the government's attempt to amend the Crown Employees Collective Bargaining Act. In response to the union's earlier campaign, the bill included changes in the composition of arbitration and grievance boards and gave the union the right to discuss job classifications. The new bill, however, excluded the right to negotiate over pensions or technological change. Most importantly, public employees were still denied the right to strike and to engage in political activity.

By the end of 1974 the union had organized forty-one committees across the province to press its campaign against CECBA. In the event of a provincial election, these committees could quickly be converted into political action groups.

About this time, ballots were out among the 18,000 workers in the general service category — clerks, stenographers and general office workers — on the question of whether the government's offer of a five per cent cost of living increase in 1975 would be acceptable. This vote carried the possibility of yet another "illegal" strike.

Ontario's public employees had joined the union movement. At their 1975 annual meeting, the Ontario Public Service Employees' Union was proposed as a new name for the CSAO, a name signifying their new role and their relationship to their employer, the Ontario government. When the June meeting also endorsed the earlier decision to join the CLC the transformation to unionism was complete. The new union became one of the big five unions in Ontario — along with the USWA, the UAW, CUPE, and PSAC.

The mid-seventies saw many strike actions among provincial and municipal public servants across Canada.

In October 1974, 18,000 Alberta civil servants held a two-day walk-out, charging that the provincial government had sabotaged contract negotiations.[17]

In November, 13,000 Saskatchewan government employees staged "study sessions" in their campaign for a special pay increase to offset inflation.[18]

In Calgary, 1,600 CUPE outside workers staged a four-day illegal walk-out. Seven union officers were charged with contempt of court for permitting CUPE Local 37 to strike in defiance of an Alberta Supreme Court injunction.[19]

In February 1975 some 400 civic workers were on strike in British Columbia. Another 1,500 had been locked out, while 500 were staging on the job action and 5,000 were working to rule. All these workers were CUPE members.[20]

Since the CLC convention there have been meetings of representatives of provincial public employee associations affiliated to the CLC to lay the basis of a national organization of provincial public workers. Debate over the degree to which such an organization should be centralized has delayed the date for the calling of the first national convention to launch the new organization.

Such a body would grow quickly into one of the big five of organized labour, joining CUPE, USWA, PSAC, and the UAW. Together the three organizations of public employees in Canada would have a membership of over half a million — a power to be recognized in the CLC and the Canadian labour movement.

1. *The Globe and Mail*, September 30, 1974.

2. Delegates Radio Report, Ontario Federation of Labour, Convention, October 29, 1974.

3. For details, see *CSAO News*, May-June 1974, p. 3.

4. *The Globe and Mail*, September 30, 1974.

5. *Ontario Report*, March-April 1975, p. s-11.

6. *The Ottawa Citizen*, September 18, 1974.

7. *The Toronto Sun*, July 23, 1974.

8. *The Ottawa Citizen*, September 18, 1974.

9. *The Globe and Mail*, September 3, 1974.

10. *CSAO News*, October 1974, p. 1.

11. *The Globe and Mail*, September 30, 1974.

12. *The Toronto Star*, November 18, 1974.

13. *The Globe and Mail*, December 2, 1974.

14. *The Toronto Star*, November 25, 1974.

15. Ibid.

16. *The Globe and Mail*, December 30, 1974.

17. *The Toronto Star*, October 3, 1974.

18. *The Globe and Mail*, November 13, 1974.

19. Ibid.

20. *Financial Times of Canada*, February 24, 1975.

CHAPTER 26
Federal Workers and the Right to Strike

The Public Service Alliance of Canada, the union which represents 168,000 federal government employees, has won public attention through actions by some of its affiliated groups, including strikes by shipping pilots and meat inspectors, and, in February 1975, 19,000 federal blue-collar workers in PSAC's General Labour and Trades group.

The Alliance was formed in 1966 when the Civil Service Association of Canada merged with the Civil Service Federation of Canada.[1]

Both were old-style "staff associations" organized on company-union principles.

In 1889 the Railway Mail Clerks Association held its first convention. This association, the earliest component of PSAC, later affiliated to the Civil Service Federation, and eventually became the postal section of the Public Service Alliance.

The Civil Service Federation was formed in 1909 following the enactment in 1908 of the Civil Service Act. The initiative for forming the Federation came from an earlier organization, the Dominion Civil Service Association of Western Canada. Under the name of the Civil Service Association of Canada, a committee was formed whose recommendations led to a meeting of staff associations in Ottawa in 1909. A total of 23 associations, comprising 5,223 members, were represented. They set up the Civil Service Federation, which in time became the largest organization of federal government employees. By the time of the merger which created PSAC the Federation had almost 80,000 members.

The Civil Service Association of Canada was the result of a 1958 merger between the Civil Service Association of Ottawa — one of the founding members of the 1909 meeting, which later broke away from the Federation over a jurisdictional dispute — and the Amalgamated Civil Servants of Canada, representing some 21,000 members. However, by

1958 the postal employees and letter carriers had withdrawn to set up their own, more militant unions.

When the Public Service Alliance of Canada began a series of rotating strikes in February 1975 its situation differed from that faced by Ontario hospital workers, teachers and civil servants. Public employees in the federal civil service have had the right to strike, with the exception of certain "designated" workers whose services are deemed to be essential.

The walk-outs in February and March of 1975 involved most of the 19,000 "blue-collar" workers in the federal civil service, members of the General Labour and Trades (GLT) group of PSAC. By a margin of five to one, GLT workers across the country rejected a majority conciliation board report offering a 27 per cent increase over two years. Initially, the union had demanded a 42.5 per cent raise in one year which, they said, would bring the public employees' pay to within 90 per cent of that received by workers in similar private sector jobs.[2]

A series of strikes developed which had a marked effect across the country. Airports were shut down because their runways were not cleared, despite the fact that forty per cent of the runway cleaners were "designated" employees without the right to strike. Post offices were closed in Ottawa, Montreal, Toronto and Edmonton when maintenance workers' picket lines were respected by members of the letter carrier and postal worker unions.

Federal grain weighers and checkers struck elevators in northern Saskatchewan, Edmonton, Vancouver, Prince Rupert and Victoria, halting grain shipments. Civilian defence employees were out at armed forces bases in Saskatchewan, Alberta and Nova Scotia, as well as Ottawa and Toronto. Prairie farm rehabilitation administration employees in southern Saskatchewan, and maritime service workers at Quebec City were also on strike at one time or another during the series of rotating walk-outs. About 1,200 workers in Newfoundland and Labrador joined the strikes, many of them at the U.S.-run military base at Goose Bay.

The impact of these selective strikes by about 11,000 of the 18,000-member GLT group went beyond the highest expectations of union negotiators and strategists. The GLT workers finally won a 29.25 per cent increase over a 26-month period.[3] The strikes and Parliament Hill demonstrations boosted the morale and solidarity of the group.

In these activities, the GLT group was using the militant tactics which had previously been used by federal postal workers. Beginning with the work-to-rule campaign initiated in January 1969, the postal workers have engaged in roughly thirty significant job actions and strikes, mainly over issues of pay, job security, and technological change, in a six and a half year period.[4] The postal workers have sustained their series of militant actions within the past few years without the support of an international head office. With memberships of some 16,000 (LCUC) and 20,000 (cupw) they showed that even relatively small Canadian unions can be viable both organizationally and financially.

One of their greatest victories came in 1970 when the postal workers broke through the wage guidelines established by the Trudeau government. They were under tremendous pressure to settle the strike and accept the government guidelines, not only from the government, but from newspaper editorials, business organizations and the leadership of the federal NDP.

During the postal strike, NDP member for North Winnipeg David Orlikow rose in the House of Commons in August to urge the postal workers to accept an offer below their own demands — but above the government's 6.0 per cent guidelines. Orlikow argued that the postal workers would surely accept an increase of 6.3 per cent, recommended in a conciliation board report.[5]

The strike continued, however, and finally the government changed its "maximum" guideline to 7.0 per cent. The final settlement represented a major breakthrough for the union. According to the union, the final settlement amounted to 7.2 per cent, but the government insisted it was 6.8 per cent. As *The Globe and Mail* report put it:

> Apparently, the government laid great stress on the importance of keeping the annual increase below 7 per cent. A source indicated that the Cabinet balked when [mediator Thomas] O'Connor's proposal was laid before it, with a 7.2 per cent annual price tag on it. It was only when government negotiators checked the arithmetic and produced a figure of 6.8 per cent that agreement at the bargaining table became possible.[6]

It did not matter that the government called the increase 6.8 per cent, for the union had broken through the guidelines the government had set for its own workers.

More recently, postal workers confronted the post office over issues centred on technology and automation. The 1974 round of militancy began in February when there was a wild-cat strike in the Toronto post office over the firing of a union steward.

In April 1974 postal workers in Quebec walked off the job after three hundred of their number were suspended for protesting the introduction of the postal code. Another hundred were suspended for demanding the firing of their supervisor at Montreal's main postal station. Several hundred workers were involved in the work stoppages there.

The day after the work stoppages in the Montreal post office began, Mr. Justice R. Ouimet of the Quebec Superior Court issued an injunction ordering the strikers back to work. The strike continued. Marcel Perrault, president of the Montreal local, explained the protests against the postal code:

> We have nothing against modernizing the postal system, but we do not accept automation unless the government will negotiate the

change with the workers concerned and remove the atmosphere of worry and confusion that has surrounded the question of declassification.[7]

The whole problem was rooted in the automatic mail-processing system, based on the postal code, which was by this time in operation at the Ottawa and Winnipeg postal terminals. Workers in the automated process were receiving fifty cents an hour less than manual sorters. Although Postmaster General André Ouellet had indicated that the Montreal terminal would not be automated for another two years, workers there wished to have the wages issue settled in advance.

One of the main complaints was that a joint management-labour committee to discuss the automation problem, provided for in a 1973 arbitration award, had not yet met to consider the issue. The 2,000 Montreal-area workers decided to continue their work stoppages until they got a written promise from Postmaster General Ouellet that negotiations over the issue of technological change would be held.[8]

The strike spread across the country. Ouellet responded by telling the House of Commons that the government would not discuss technological change with the postal union until regular mail service was restored. Although he indicated that he was ready to discuss automation plans with the union, he side-stepped the critical question of whether the post office would actually negotiate on the matter of technological change.[9]

On April 18 picket lines were set up at the Victoria post office and, four hours later, at Vancouver. In Calgary 550 CUPW members set up picket lines, and mail carriers and evening shift sorters refused to cross their lines.

That same day, the postmaster general repeated his previous remarks, telling the Commons that "the strike is illegal and infinitely regrettable because the permanent employees of the post office department are guaranteed jobs and salaries under their collective agreement".[10]

The following week, the Canada Post Office ran full-page advertisements in newspapers across the country giving its point of view on the situation. After noting that none of the workers in the mechanized Ottawa or Winnipeg terminals had lost their jobs or had their wages reduced due to automation, the advertisements continued:

Our conclusion must be, then, that irresponsible elements of the Canadian Union of Postal Workers are seeking to disrupt the mail service for reasons known only to themselves. While we understand that union leaders have a mandate to protect the interests of their members, it is their responsibility to do so by lawful means. If they think that the current collective bargaining agreement does not meet their needs, they will have an opportunity to table new demands at the time of renegotiations of the collective agreement at the end of the year.[11]

Except for the reference to "irresponsible elements," this was simply a reiteration of official government labour policy, which prohibits action during the life of a contract. The old idea that a contract is sacred and must not be interferred with by strike action was becoming a thorn in the side of the whole labour movement.

Eric Taylor, an industrial relations specialist, was appointed by the post office on April 21 to help settle the national strike. Subsequently, a labour-management committee was established to deal with the automation and job classification issues.

Taylor further recommended that there be written assurances guaranteeing that disciplinary measures such as the suspensions would be lifted, and that no reprisals or legal proceedings be undertaken in connection with the dispute. On April 26 these recommendations were accepted by both sides.[12]

Seven months later, Bryce Mackasey — who had replaced Ouellet as Postmaster General following the summer federal election — told the House of Commons that the postal dispute had been resolved. Under a formula initiated in the negotiations with Eric Taylor, the gap between manual and automated coders was to be narrowed and finally eliminated.[13]

Mackasey's announcement was overly optimistic. The post office was still fraught with problems relating to automation, supervision and other working conditions. Work-stoppages and slow-downs continued to occur in the first months of 1975. And new, sharp confrontations seemed inevitable when, in March 1975, the CUPW announced its bargaining goals, amounting to increases of seventy-one per cent in one year, plus a thirty-hour week.[14] With new disputes over the hiring of casual employees as mail sorters, and many of the old problems still unresolved, the sources of conflict and worker militancy remained.

-----

1. "Public Service Alliance marks 80 years of Progress", *PSAC*, October 1969, p. 6.

2. *The Globe and Mail*, February 18, 1975.

3. *The Globe and Mail*, March 20, 1975.

4. Recorded in *The Toronto Star*, April 26, 1975.

5. During the 1970 postal strike, David Lewis, then NDP Deputy Leader, urged the union's negotiating consultant, Bill Walsh, to advocate acceptance of the government's offer. Lewis believed that the government intended to stick to its six per cent maximum wage guidelines. For the workers to hold out for more would seriously hurt the image of the labour movement and his party. Walsh convinced Lewis not to take a position contrary to the postal workers' demands in the House of Commons. With Lewis away on a trip, however, David Orlikow spoke for the NDP in the House: Canada, House of Commons, *Debates*, June 26, 1970, p. 8862.

6. *The Globe and Mail*, September 4, 1970.

7. *The Globe and Mail*, April 12, 1974.

8. *The Globe and Mail*, April 17, 1974.

9. *The Globe and Mail*, April 19, 1974.

10. Canada, House of Commons, *Debates*, April 19, 1974, p. 1579.

11. Canada Post, André Ouellet, public letter to *The Globe and Mail*, April 22, 1974.

12. *CUPW*, May-June 1974.

13. *The Globe and Mail*, December 21, 1974.

14. *The Globe and Mail*, March 15, 1975.

CHAPTER 27

Industrial Unions Catch the Mood

Canadian unions in the public sector have not been alone in rejecting the bargaining practices of American business unionism in favour of a new militancy. Canadian industrial workers faced similar economic circumstances, and in the mid-seventies some of their unions were breaking out of the pattern of *pro forma* bargaining, with its avoidance of high expectations, "extravagant" demands and strikes. Other international unions, while they bent to the pressure of the new Canadian militancy, managed to sustain their pattern of low demands and secret negotiations.

Some of the biggest pay increases in 1974 and the first part of 1975 were won by construction workers organized in the international building trades unions. Construction workers receive the highest rates of pay among blue-collar workers, and in Canada they have traditionally been assertive in defence of their position. Several factors have contributed to maintaining their leading position among blue-collar workers. Among these factors are their high skill level, requiring years of union-supervised apprenticeship; their strong bargaining power deriving from the scarcity of workers with their skills; their willingness to respect the picket lines of other building trades unions and hence their ability to shut down the construction sites; and their often seasonal and sometimes dangerous work which has tended to encourage militancy and higher wage claims.

Thus in August 1975 construction workers in Alberta signed new two-year agreements. Plumbers, who had been receiving about $9.35 hourly, were to get $13.75 under the new contract; carpenters, who had been working for $8.68, were to receive $11.73; and labourers in the northern part of the province were to rise from $6.80 to $9.80 an hour by the end of the contract. In the same month, Toronto carpenters accepted a settlement that would yield increases of about $3.45 an hour in wages and benefits over a 30-month contract. All of these settlements were made following strikes.[1]

But construction workers' bargaining historically has not been the pattern setter for the industrial workers. Traditionally the pattern has been set by the two largest industrial unions — the UAW and the USWA — in their negotiations with the major auto and steel corporations. But by 1975 a new potential model had emerged in the shape of the Canadian Paperworkers Union.

Having signed three-year agreements with the four major firms in the auto industry in 1973, the UAW was largely out of the bargaining picture in 1974-1975. The USWA, on the other hand, began to bargain with the major steel industry pace-setters — Stelco and Algoma, and Inco in nickel mining — in the spring and summer of 1975. Before these major negotiations were under way, the steel union had been involved in bargaining at a number of smaller and medium-sized plants throughout 1973 and 1974. One of these is particularly interesting because it represented a break with typical USWA tactics.

As noted earlier in chapter twenty, after a majority of the workers at the Trail plant of Cominco had opted for an independent Canadian union, their break-away attempt from USWA was quashed through a legal technicality. When the contract between the USWA and Cominco expired in 1974, the union demonstrated a new militancy to local members and conducted a three-month battle in the old tradition of CIO unionism. The 4,200 strikers were demanding a $3.60 hourly wage increase over two years, with a wage re-opener in the second year. The final settlement provided for an immediate increase of $1.22 plus a cost of living adjustment of one cent for every .35 rise in the consumer price index, along with a new pension programme and early retirement at age 55 with twenty years' service.[2]

Following this settlement, Lynn Williams told the Cominco workers:

> The strike showed that if you want to be effective in bargaining, good strong and militant locals are an absolute necessity. This strike has demonstrated that we are both strong and effective.[3]

But Cominco proved to be an exception in the USWA's general bargaining strategy. In negotiations on behalf of 37,000 Stelco, Algoma and Inco workers, the USWA opted for cautious wage demands and the avoidance of "raised expectations". Despite the decision of the 11,500-member Hamilton local to go for a two-year agreement, the union signed a three-year contract. In working out its negotiating strategy, the USWA decided not to issue wage demands in advance, but to leave it to the negotiating teams to work out the best settlement possible.

In this settlement the Canadian section of the USWA avoided the ENA model of the U.S. locals, insofar as they made no advance pledge to avoid striking, but their approach differed significantly from that of Canadian public sector bargaining in 1974 and 1975 — and from the industrial pattern established by the Canadian Paperworkers Union as well.

In January 1975, 4,200 CPU members in the Abitibi chain stunned the business community by turning down a pre-negotiation offer of 25 per cent over one year.[4] In March, the CPU announced its wage demands: a $2.00 hourly wage increase for Ontario and Manitoba amounting to a 41 per cent rise, over one year, together with a cost of living adjustment of one cent for every .25 rise in the consumer price index.[5] The paper union's negotiations differed from the Steelworkers in these crucial aspects: substantial wage demands, short contracts and advance public calls for increases.

The significance of long rather than short contracts is substantial. Government statistics indicate that one-year contracts have tended to yield better wage increases than longer contracts. Federal Department of Labour figures showed that in the second quarter of 1975, there were 114 settlements covering 500 workers or more across Canada. Of these, 43 were for one year, 62 for two years, and 9 for three years. The one-year contracts yielded an average annual increase of 24.5 per cent, compared to an average for all contracts of 18.8 per cent. Taking only the first year of all contracts, one-year contracts yielded 24.5 per cent in comparison to 22.2 per cent for all contracts. Two-year contracts yielded an average of 20.8 per cent in the first year and 10.8 per cent in the second year. Three-year agreements yielded 19.5 per cent in the first year, 11.4 per cent in the second year and 2.5 per cent in the third year.[6] Since the second and later years of long contracts yielded much lower increases on average than their first years, there appeared to be considerable cumulative advantage to locals that typically bargained annually if this pattern persists.

Shorter contracts have other implications as well. Annual bargaining has meant more frequent opportunities for rank and file involvement in union decision making, and has had the potential to increase the interest of the membership in union affairs.

In its negotiations with Stelco, Algoma and Inco, the steel union never publicly announced a wage demand that had been decided on and backed by its membership. The union negotiators conducted prolonged closed sessions with management during the last few weeks before reaching tentative settlements in July. With no announced wage demands to consider, the local members had no advance guidelines with which to assess the offers finally recommended to them by union negotiators.

The tentative agreements reached by the negotiating teams were presented to the local members at the very last minute before the strike deadlines. At Inco in Sudbury, the offers were presented too late to forestall a short-lived strike which the rank and file enforced against the advice of the top union leadership.[7] At Stelco in Hamilton, the 11,500 basic steel workers did not hear details of the tentative agreement until July 30, while the contract was to expire at midnight on July 31. The vote was held on the 31st, less than 24 hours after many of the members had first heard the terms. In general, the USWA members at the Inco, Stelco and Algoma plants had to decide within a matter of hours — at the most, a few days — whether to accept or reject an agreement whose terms, having been arrived at privately, were new to them.

Thus, for instance, the membership of Local 1005 of the USWA at Stelco in Hamilton first heard reports of the proposed three-year agreement at two meetings on July 30, 1975 — one in the morning and another in the evening. The time between the end of the evening meeting and the balloting, which began the next morning at 6:00 a.m. was ten hours — a short time for workers to consider fully the proposed hourly rate and many other details of the proposed agreement.

On July 30 *The Hamilton Spectator* reported that "The Steel Company of Canada's contract offer received an angry reception from many of the Steelworkers at a meeting in Ivor Wynne stadium today ... Members of the union's negotiating committee ... explained the contract offer against a barrage of jeers and insults from some members."

The newspaper also reported that three-quarters of the way through the two-hour meeting, many of the men walked out, protesting that one member of the negotiating committee was not being allowed to speak. The member was Cec Taylor, chairman of the grievance committee, and the only member of the negotiating team to oppose the contract offer.

> He had been allowed to speak against the contract earlier in the meeting and was greeted with a tremendous cheer when he urged members to vote against the contract offer tomorrow.
> Later he walked away from the rest of the committee and tried to speak at one of the microphones set up for members to voice questions. The microphone was turned off. Some members rushed onto the playing field to protest but Mr. Taylor indicated he would rather leave and communicate with members by means of leaflets rather than disrupt the meeting.
> [During the previous evening the steward body had] rejected the offer at a meeting at the Steelworkers Centre ... The stewards claimed that the contract which gives workers a $1.30 an hour wage hike over three years, was a rush job and said it was inadequate.
> Another major grievance was that the cost of living allowance without upper limit, or cap, would only come into effect in the second year of the contract instead of immediately.

The Spectator reported that Taylor had claimed that the uncapped COLA was insufficient to allow an average employee to keep up with inflation.

"A class eight employee has lost $1.60 an hour or $4,489.00 in inflation over the last three years," Taylor said. He told the meeting that "the average guy in the plant needs at least $1.50 in the first year just to keep up with inflation". One union member, George Gilks, urged members to reject the offer and send the negotiating committee back to Stelco to get a two-year agreement. "We have suffered three-year contracts in the past and felt the results in our pockets," Gilks said.[8]

The outcome of the next day's ratification vote was close — fifty-two per cent in favour, forty-eight per cent against.

The 1975 bargaining procedure of no advance wage rate demands and no reporting back to the membership on developments in negotiations represented a significant break with the practice of the union in its early days. Then, bargaining was begun with rank and file participation in formulating a set of demands for a one-year contract. The object of this had been not only to come up with a set of demands that would be acceptable to the membership, but also to build the militant mood necessary to convince the company that the union was determined to back its demands with action. In the old days, too, early preparations for a possible strike, involving the election of various committees and readying workers for the picket line, were used to create maximum rank and file participation and militancy and to put full pressure on the company.

But this pattern of preparation for a possible confrontation was missing from the 1975 negotiations. From the point of view of union strategy, the absence of rank and file involvement and of preparations for a picket line confrontation let management know, in advance, that the union leadership was eager to avoid a strike. The object was for the company and union negotiating teams to arrive at a package sufficiently attractive to win the support of a majority of a membership which had received little advance information on the negotiations.

If union negotiators had as their goal the avoidance of "excessive" demands, high expectations and a strike, then their efforts would be focused on reaching the minimum settlement that could be presented to the membership with the appearance of an impressive, or at least a "realistic" gain.

The companies' foreknowledge that this was likely the union leaders' goal would probably serve as a bargaining counter for the top union negotiators. The companies had to recognize that the avoidance of a strike would require visible concessions to the union. The three-year wage increase formula which was presented to USWA members by all three sets of negotiators — 90 cents, 20 cents, 20 cents — seemed to meet the criteria for a settlement the membership would buy.

From the point of view of the workers, the first year offer would have to be large enough to improve their pay appreciably over their income before the settlement. An increase of 90 cents an hour in the first year was expected to be sufficiently large for this purpose, although if it was considered to include an annual productivity increase of 3 per cent, it was not large enough to cover losses due to inflation over the term of the previous three-year contract. There would also have to be other benefits, including a modest improvement in pension rates, an increased differential between classifications and some increase in holidays. Added up by optimistic calculations this could be made to amount to an overall package of $3.00 over three years. Calculating the value of the package involves a certain amount of juggling since unions and companies seldom agree on what the monetary value of the various benefits amounts to.

From the point of view of the company, the second and third year increments would have to be sufficiently low to enable them to keep real wages from rising in 1976-1977 and 1977-1978. There would have to be a visible increase, but an illusory one for all that. Assuming a 10 per cent annual rate of inflation, the 20 cent increase in the second year in this agreement would hold real wages more or less constant. It would result in a real drop in purchasing power in the third year. Of course, if the annual inflation rate was to top 10 per cent, the workers would fall behind in purchasing power sooner.[9]

The policy of avoiding strikes and "excessive" demands which the USWA successfully pursued in 1975 through the strategy of secret bargaining and no advance wage demands to involve the rank and file bore little resemblance to the approach of another industrial union, the Canadian Paperworkers Union.

The CPU's call for a basic $2.00 hourly increase, amounting to 41 per cent, came only a few hours after the International Woodworkers of America, representing 45,000 forest and sawmill workers in B.C., had decided on a demand of $1.00 hourly.[10] The independent PPWC, with 5,500 B.C. members, was calling for $1.50.[11] With only 7,300 of its 52,000 members in B.C., the CPU decided to lower its demand to the PPWC figure in the interests of joint bargaining in that province. Based on the call for a one-year contract with a basic increase of $1.50, the three forest products unions set up a joint liaison committee in May, although this broke down during the course of negotiations.

The Canadian union's long-term strategy had been unveiled in March, when Henri Lorrain called for eventual industry-wide bargaining in the pulp and paper industry in Canada.[12] Bernard O'Reilly, Domtar's industrial relations director, rejected this proposal, commenting that "the advantage of group bargaining flows to the unions".[13]

In July, CPU and PPWC members struck twenty pulp and paper mills in B.C. In the same month, CPU members struck Abitibi's Ontario plants. These strikes, according to CPU president Lorrain, were "somewhat in advance of plans set forth in our union's national strategy".[14] The union had hoped to co-ordinate a national confrontation for mid-August in order to present the strongest front and to take advantage of a projected improvement in the industry's economic position.

The CPU had moved into its negotiations with only $440,000 in its newly-established strike fund, "not enough to pay the postage", according to Region 3 vice-president Thomas Curley.[15] Nevertheless, he described the mood of the membership in Ontario, Manitoba and western Quebec as "pretty militant, in spite of the problems in the industry and in spite of the fact that we do not have an adequate strike fund". There's more than one way to skin a cat, he added.[16]

In sharp contrast to the CPU's stance, its former international union in the United States, the UPIU, was adopting the "mature" collective bargaining model of the Steelworkers' ENA. Early in 1975 it had signed what president Tonelli called a "landmark" agreement on behalf of the 200 employees of the Garden State Paper Company, tying the union to a ten-year no-strike pact with wage increases on a productivity formula.[17] In the event of a wild-cat strike, the wage increase for that year would be forfeited.

At the Boise Cascade Corporation plant at International Falls, Minnesota, the UPIU accepted a three-year contract providing for 9 per cent in the first and third years and 10 per cent in the second. At American Can's Marathon, Ontario plant — the international still represented some 3,500 Canadian members who had rejected the formation of the CPU — the union accepted a two-year agreement with a 19.3 per cent increase in the first year and 11 per cent in the second.[18] This was lower than Abitibi's offer of 25 per cent in one year, which had been rejected by the CPU.

In the paper and forest industry, the new CPU was leading the departure from the policy of avoiding demands that would "raise expectations". Lorrain had estimated that since the 1973 agreement, his members had lost about $1.25 per hour to inflation. That portion of the $2.00 proposed increase, therefore, was merely "catch-up".[19] The 41 per cent demand, according to Curley, "is not a cynical, screw-them posture. Rather, it represents an honest appraisal of where we stand and where we have to go if we are to get our fair share."[20]

The CPU unveiled its new strategy under circumstances that were not favourable. In the summer of 1975 the pulp and paper industry was relatively depressed in Canada and the United States so that the economic pressure on the companies to settle would not become strong without a prolonged strike. The CPU, as a new union, was extremely short of strike funds — a condition that would tend to weaken the resolve of the membership to stay out as long as was necessary to win a substantial increase. That the union went ahead with strike action in spite of these handicaps showed the growing gulf between the new Canadian unionism and the "no-strike" strategies of most American unions.

By October 1975 the CPU was involved in widespread strike action across the country without the participation of the IWA in B.C.[21]

In mid-1975 it seemed that while the Canadian public sector unions had changed the bargaining mood of many Canadian workers, the practices in negotiations of many internationals in the industrial sector had hardly been affected. However, the fifty-two per cent majority which won the settlement at Stelco in Hamilton suggested that the business union strategy might be losing some of its appeal. The Canadian unions in the public sector, and the CPU in the industrial field, were opting for a different kind of strategy in their negotiations.

1. *The Globe and Mail*, August 6, 1975.

2. *The Searcher*, October 1974; *Canadian Tribune*, October 23, 1974.

3. *Canadian Tribune*, October 23, 1974.

4. *Financial Times of Canada*, January 13, 1975; *The Globe and Mail*, January 28, 1975.

5. *The Globe and Mail*, March 25, 1975.

6. *The Globe and Mail*, July 31, 1975.

7. *The Globe and Mail*, July 9, 10, 14, 1975; *The Toronto Star*, July 12, 1975.

8. *The Hamilton Spectator*, July 30, 1975.

9. An example of the sleight of hand involved in packaging an agreement was the way the new cost of living adjustment (COLA) was presented to the membership in the basic steel industry in July-August 1975. The August issue of the Canadian edition of *Steel Labor*, the official paper of the USWA, reported the expected increases in hourly rates from the COLA in the second and third years of the contract, based on a 10 per cent annual rise in inflation. The figure for the second year was given as 48 cents, for the third year as 53 cents. While the increase in the last quarter of the second year of the contract would be 48 cents, through the year it would average 30 cents. The same is true for the third year, where the average for the third year would be 33 cents, not 53 cents.

10. *The Globe and Mail*, March 25, 1975.

11. *The Globe and Mail*, April 15, 1975.

12. *The Montreal Star*, March 26, 1975.

13. *The Globe and Mail*, March 28, 1975.

14. *The Globe and Mail*, July 16, 1975.

15. *The Financial Post*, March 29, 1975.

16. Ibid.

17. *The Globe and Mail*, February 12, 1975.

18. *The Financial Post*, May 31, 1975.

19. *Financial Times of Canada*, April 14, 1975.

20. *The Financial Post*, March 29, 1975.

21. On October 7, 1975, the NDP government under Premier Dave Barrett introduced and had passed in the B.C. Legislature a bill which ordered striking paper workers and three other groups of strikers back to work for a 90-day period. This ended the paper strike in B.C.

PART VI
Unions and Political Action

CHAPTER 28
Labour Politics in Canada

... it is impossible to secure adequate representation of the working class on the floor of Parliament, until we are represented by men of our own class; ... this Congress pledges itself to use all legitimate means in its power to secure the election of working men to Parliament ...

Resolution adopted by Canadian
Labour Union, 1877 Convention[1]

[In April 1958] the second convention of the CLC reached the momentous decision ... to bring into being a new political party in Canada. This decision ... by the CLC was a rallying cry for ... persons who realized that Canada could never reach its potential greatness while its future lay in the hands of political parties which were the puppets on the end of the corporate string.
The 1958 decision ... followed from meetings which were begun prior to 1955 and which grew naturally out of the merger talks between the old CCL and the TLC.

Joe Morris
President, CLC
Federal NDP Convention
July 1975[2]

Although unions have directed their primary energies toward improving the economic and working conditions of their members, they have also established a tradition of political activity to achieve social legislation and economic policies for Canada and its working people.

Shortly after local unions became established, they began to organize labour councils and federations such as the Toronto Labour Council, established in 1871.

National and provincial federations and congresses of unions also have a long history. The Canadian Labour Union was established in 1873, and the Trades and Labour Congress of Canada in 1886.

These organizations, which grouped together separate unions or locals, were formed for at least three purposes.

The first was to provide effective machinery for unions to assist each other during disputes with employers. For example, in 1872 the striking Toronto *Globe* printers received the support of large groups of organized and unorganized workers culminating in a march of ten thousand to the provincial legislature. This show of solidarity was instrumental in convincing the federal government under John A. Macdonald to pass legislation legalizing the formation of unions.[3]

The second reason was to aid and encourage other workers to organize, thus increasing the power of the labour movement as a whole. Campaigns for the nine-hour working day in the 1870s, and for the forty-hour week after 1945, became broad social movements and led to a substantial increase in union membership.

The third purpose, and the subject of this chapter, was to give unionized workers an organization through which they could express themselves collectively on a wide range of social, legislative and political issues. It became increasingly evident as the union movement developed that employers' interests were represented at a level broader than just the particular company.[4]

Demands for legislative reforms, such as minimum wages, shorter hours, and pension and welfare schemes came early in the history of Canadian trade unionism. In addition, socialists in the labour movement urged the unions to challenge the very existence of private enterprise. This required that the working class take an active role in politics.

In the 1870s and 1880s the question of how workers should enter into political action was frequently debated in the union movement. The exploitation of workers by the newly-established factory and resource industries prompted many unionists to seek an alternative kind of society. John Hewitt, president of the Toronto Trades Assembly, expressed these desires and visions in what he called the governing principles of the new system:

> The system of employers and employees would be superseded. Labour would be lightened individually. Men would enjoy the fruits of their labour and not the dregs of their production. The kind of unjust system that gives men undue advantage over men would cease to exist.[5]

He called for workers to develop their own political institutions rather than try to work within the old parties:

> Let us remember that neither of the existing parties are parties of labour, and neither will give reforms the workers need, except in compliance with the tactics and with the demands of well-directed and united agitation.[6]

In 1872 the Toronto Trades Assembly called for the formation of "labour reform leagues" in each city ward, to be made up of workers "using their united efforts to advance the interests of labour". In the same year, the Ontario Workingmen's Progressive Political Party had a programme of electoral reform in London.

During these years, two opposing philosophies of labour political action emerged, one based on the British example and the other on the American. Until about 1900, the British model of a separate labour party supported by the trade union movement held sway. However, as the international unions came to predominate in Canada — especially after 1902, when the American unions took over control of the Trades and Labour Congress — the American model, based on Samuel Gompers' notion, "reward your friends and punish your enemies," became more widespread. This notion held that unions should support those candidates of the existing parties who seemed most willing to make concessions to labour's legislative programme. The first philosophy held out the possibility of a thorough-going transformation of society; the second accepted the status quo. As Gompers put it, "the American union movement should fit into the American system . . ."[7]

Despite the increasing strength of American business unionism and its political philosophy in the Canadian labour movement, the idea of a labour party always remained alive in Canada. This has been an important difference over the last hundred years between the Canadian and the American union movements. In various parts of the country, organizations such as the Dominion Labour Party (which received a modicum of support from the TLC in the 1920s), the Social Democratic Party of Canada, the Socialist Party of Canada, and the Socialist Labour Party appeared in the early decades of the twentieth century. British Columbia, whose labour movement was relatively free of business unionism, was especially significant as a centre of "third party" support.

In the early 1920s the Communist Party of Canada was organized, and a decade later (1932), the Co-operative Commonwealth Federation (CCF). Both organizations had substantial influence in the labour movement in the 1930s although neither of them had official labour sponsorship at the time. During the thirties, activists in both of these parties were deeply involved in industrial union organization. The Workers Unity League (WUL) brought some 25,000 unorganized workers into industrial unions before 1935; it was organized primarily by members of the Communist Party. The new industrial unions of the Congress of Industrial Organizations (CIO), which displaced the WUL in the second half of the 1930s, were largely organized by Communist Party and CCF members.[8]

These two parties contended for the leadership of the industrial union movement until 1941. At that time, the Canadian Congress of Labour was formed and the CCF group achieved dominance. Its position was cemented in 1948 and 1949 when the Congress expelled such Communist-led unions as the United Electrical Workers, the Mine, Mill and Smelter Workers, the Fur and Leather Workers and the Fishermen's Union.[9]

By 1949 the top unionists allied to the CCF — men like Charles Millard of the Steelworkers and Aaron Mosher of the CBRE — had begun to back the foreign policies of the U.S. government and of the international unions' American headquarters. Largely because of its close association with the foreign policies of the Soviet Union, the Communist Party lost, and has never since regained, its influence in the labour movement. By contrast, the CCF and its successor, the New Democratic Party, became the strong political influence in the unions.[10]

The fact that the NDP received the official endorsement of the Canadian Labour Congress did not mean that the American philosophy of union "neutrality" in politics had disappeared in Canada. Even in 1975, after seventeen years of CLC sponsorship of the NDP, the American political model still guided many unions in Canada.

The American business unionist approach to politics had had as long a history in Canada as the labour party approach.

In the 1870s and 1880s, the Conservative and Liberal parties vied for union support as true "friends of labour". For almost two decades Macdonald campaigned on the strength of the Tories' 1872 labour legislation, while in the 1887 election Liberal leader Edward Blake criticized the Conservatives for having done nothing in the labour field for fifteen years. Both parties tried to recruit labour leaders as their candidates in elections. In Ontario the Conservative party established links with the craft unions over the years, while in Quebec it was the Liberals who were more successful in wooing labour. In 1965, for instance, Jean Marchand went straight from the general-presidency of the Confederation of National Trades Unions into the Liberal Cabinet.

There are similar examples from earlier periods. Gideon Robertson, the Conservative labour minister in 1919, had been a senior Canadian officer of the Commerical Telegraphers' Union. Another trade union official, Humphrey Mitchell, became minister of labour in the Mackenzie King government, where, following the traditions of the prime minister, he led the campaign to break the Canadian Seamen's Union in the late 1940s.[11]

The continuing conflict between the two philosophies is illustrated in the history of the Trades and Labour Congress of Canada. In 1899 when the TLC went on record in favour of forming a labour party, it acknowledged the British roots of the idea. The resolution urged that unionized workers should "have direct representation in the various Houses of Parliament on lines similar to organized workers in Great Britain".[12] Despite the international unions' take-over of the TLC in 1902 this remained the official policy of the Congress, at least on paper, into the 1920s. But when the Dominion Labour Party was formed with official TLC sponsorship its development was undermined by top officers of the international unions in the Congress. By 1923, the TLC had formally adopted a policy of political neutrality. At the Congress convention that year, John Bruce of the Plumbers' Union spoke against "the Congress becoming part of any political party".[13] Gustav Francq of the International Typographical Union and Quebec vice-president of the Congress, spoke of the "difficulties of mixing trade union and political action".[14] The convention decided that the Congress was to "act as the legislative mouthpiece of organized labour in Canada, independent of any political organization".[15]

In the 1930s the question of the Dominion Labour Party arose again but a resolution of support was defeated by the votes of the internationals' representatives. In 1931 the TLC declared again that it "must confine itself to the legislative field".[16] This meant lobbying the two established parties for concessions to labour, rather than trying to elect a labour government that could make laws in labour's interest.

The question of a labour party was not dead, however. At the 1932 Congress Convention, the Calgary Trades and Labour Council pressed again for a nation-wide labour party supported by the TLC. In reply, the AFL representative for Ontario, IBEW member John Noble, insisted: "It was not the duty of the Congress to interfere in politics; to turn it into a political movement would destroy it."[17] Humphrey Mitchell also argued that the political and industrial movements must be kept separate.

The only prominent union leader to be involved in the formation of the CCF in 1932 and 1933 was Aaron Mosher. As president of the Canadian Brotherhood of Railway Employees and of the All-Canadian Congress of Labour, he was outside the sphere of influence of the TLC.

A new move toward independent political action by labour followed the organization of the mass industrial unions in the late thirties. Grouped in the Canadian Congress of Labour after 1940, the industrial unions were increasingly attracted toward the CCF. In 1942 the CCL endorsed the CCF and maintained that stance until it merged with the TLC in 1956 to form the Canadian Labour Congress.[18] With the Steelworkers, under Canadian director Charles Millard, taking the lead, some unions began to affiliate directly to the party.

These events marked the beginning of a new form of labour politics in Canada — a form which blended elements of both the British and American approach. This was to be the model of the emerging New Democratic Party in the 1960s and 1970s.

The British Labour Party, in common with many European social-democratic parties, had traditionally relied on the union membership for electoral support. It had been independent both of the business parties and of control by foreign organizations. The British and European social-democratic parties have been generally recognized as working-class parties, and there had been a greater consciousness of the relationship between social class and politics in those countries than there had traditionally been in Canada. This kind of awareness, in turn, has been much greater in Canada than in the United States where the "American

Dream" of the classless society has shaped workers' perceptions of their social status.

The CCF was not strictly a labour party since much of its support and electoral success came from western Canadian farmers. It had little official support in the labour movement until the 1940s. Nevertheless, it adopted a programme that was clearly different from those of the two business parties, advocating labour's broad programme of reforms and being in the van of a movement for a co-operative commonwealth. As it developed its policies in the 1930s, the CCF remained independent of any significant organizational influence from Britain, the United States, or any other foreign country (although it was influenced by ideas of other social-democratic parties, particularly the British Labour Party).

In its 1933 Regina Manifesto, the CCF declared that it would not "rest content until it has eradicated capitalism and put into operation the full programme of socialized planning which will lead to the establishment in Canada of the Co-operative Commonwealth".[19] The manifesto called for public ownership of industries and banks.

In 1956 the Regina Manifesto was replaced by the Winnipeg Declaration. "The CCF," said the new statement of principles, "will not rest content until every person in this land and in all other lands is able to enjoy equality and freedom, a sense of human dignity, and an opportunity to live a rich and meaningful life as a citizen of a free and peaceful world."[20] This was a change in the basic political direction of the CCF, and it was typical of the new philosophy of labour politics that was being developed in Canada.

After 1945, under the leadership of M.J. Coldwell and national secretary David Lewis, the CCF began to move toward the political centre. International union endorsement and affiliation exerted a pressure to change the CCF programme.[21]

In the United States, the AFL and CIO agreed to merge as a direct consequence of their support for the U.S. war effort in Korea. The CCF, too, supported the Korean War.[22] It also supported the formation of NATO, another key element in American foreign policy, which had the support of the international unions.[23]

Just prior to and after the formation of the CLC in 1956, top union and CCF leaders tried to negotiate a marriage between the CCF and the international unions in Canada.[24] Since the international unions with their Canadian members were committed to supporting American policies, any official political arm of labour in Canada had to respond to at least some of those policies to win the unions' official support. The irony of the situation was that the CCF could only become formally a labour party by discarding some of the traditional labour and socialist content of its programme.

The Winnipeg Declaration displaced the old CCF commitment to "eradicate capitalism". Significantly, too, it did not make American control of Canada its central concern, although the statement was

passed in the year of the parliamentary debate over the financing of a
U.S.-controlled Trans-Canada natural gas pipeline routed through the
United States which the CCF had dramatically opposed.

The formation of the CLC and the passage of the CCF's Winnipeg
statement in 1956 set the stage for the realization of a long term objective
— the creation of a model for a new party, the NDP, which would be
largely shaped in policy-making, finances and organization by direct
union affiliation. This plan of union affiliation and financing proved quite
successful in the 1960s.

By 1975, however, the two and half million union members in Canada
continued to support the whole range of political parties. Although the
CLC and provincial federations of labour had officially backed the NDP in
federal and provincial elections since its formation, most union locals in
Canada had been either inactive in electoral politics, or had given limited
or perfunctory support to the NDP.

Of the two and a half million union members in Canada in 1975, some
eleven per cent were formally affiliated to the NDP.[25] Approximately
275,000 unionists had a ten cent monthly deduction from their union dues
going to the party.

Union affiliation to the NDP increased slowly but steadily over the
years. From the end of 1966 to the end of 1974, it grew from somewhat
less than 200,000 to about 275,000; an increase of 40 per cent, roughly the
same as the increase in the size of the union movement over the same
period.

In 1975, as earlier, the largest union affiliation came from the USWA
and the UAW. These two unions contributed about half the total monthly
payments made by Canadian unionists to the NDP. Other unions
affiliated on a substantial scale included the Canadian Food and Allied
Workers, the Rubber Workers, the CBRT, the United Textile Workers,
the International Woodworkers of America and the Retail, Wholesale
and Department Store Union.

The New Democratic Party has operated similarly to the British
Labour Party insofar as the party leader and caucus — the group of
elected NDP members — have been able to control party policy in
practice. There is a significant difference between the two, however. For
instance, Prime Minister Harold Wilson's campaign to keep Britain in
the European Economic Community succeeded in 1975 despite a two-
to-one vote against that policy at a special Labour Party Conference and
the strong opposition of most British unions and union leaders. The
position of the Labour Party as either government or official opposition
enabled the caucus to treat the unions and the membership more as
advisory and electioneering supporters than as a policy-directing group.
The fact that a minority of Labour's MP's have been trade unionists has
faciliated this relationship. A parallel situation exists in Canada in the
provincial NDP parties in the three provinces where the NDP is in power.

At the federal level, however, the NDP party leader and caucus have relied on the top union leaders to preserve their control over party policy. As a relatively weak party federally, the NDP could not offer the immediate possibility of forming a government or even the official opposition. This was in contrast to some provincial party organizations where practices were similar to the British Labour Party. Where the NDP formed the government, as in Saskatchewan, Manitoba and British Columbia, caucus and party leaders could appeal to party loyalty to win support for policies that otherwise would have been unpopular among the membership. This appeal was used, for example, to defeat a resolution on public ownership of the oil industry at the Saskatchewan NDP's 1974 convention, despite the overwhelming support of NDP members and, according to Gallup polls, the public in general, for such a measure.

Union officers usually control many convention delegateships which are turned over to them by locals which cannot afford to send representatives to party conventions. Often, these delegateships have been given to union staff representatives, and their votes used to outweigh the votes of delegates from constituency organizations. This alliance between the caucus and the top trade union leadership also operates in Ontario where more than half of the union affiliates to the NDP are located.

From the beginning, the dual nature of the NDP as a party made up of individual members in constituency associations and block membership through union affiliation created a set of contradictions which grew more acute by the mid-1970s. At the 1969 and 1971 federal NDP conventions the combined forces of the international union leadership and the party caucus defeated the attempts by many party members, some of them involved in the Waffle group, to move the NDP in the direction of left-nationalist positions. These attempts were mainly expressed through the Waffle which had appeared on the political scene in 1969 when a group of NDP members prepared a statement, "For an Independent Socialist Canada". At the core of this and subsequent statements was concern over the increasing American control of the Canadian economy and public policy. Accompanying this was the central demand for public ownership of the resource industries as a vital step in the direction of a new industrial strategy for Canada.

In 1970 a resolution calling for public ownership of the energy resource industries won overwhelming support at the Ontario NDP convention. At the federal convention in 1971, the resolution on public ownership of resource industries won over one-third of the vote.

The Waffle became a highly charged issue in the NDP during the early seventies. In 1972, the Ontario Provincial Council ordered the Waffle to disband as an organized group in the NDP. A year later, the Waffle withdrew voluntarily from the NDP in Saskatchewan.

Waffle supporters claimed that they had been ordered to disband in Ontario primarily because their left-nationalist polices were unacceptable to top international union leaders. The NDP leaders, and many party activists, responded with the claim that the Waffle had been so tightly organized as a group within the party that it took on a separate existence, and that it was intolerable for an organized group within the party to make public policy statements at variance with those of the leadership.[26]

Another factor in the situation was the difference in style and language between generations within the NDP. Some Waffle supporters, influenced by the American "new left" of the 1960s, were disrespectful of the old CCF traditions of many party members and union stalwarts. This made belated efforts at accommodation more difficult.

In the area of social and labour reforms and civil rights the CCF-NDP, along with the union movement, made a substantial impact federally and provincially over the years. After the introduction of unemployment insurance federally in 1940, the outcome of several decades of demand from the labour movement and CCF members of parliament like J.S. Woodsworth, perhaps the most important national reforms were those of public hospital insurance and, later, medicare. The CCF government of Saskatchewan, which was in office from 1944 to 1964 with T.C. Douglas as premier for all but the last year and a half, was the pioneer in these reforms. The CCF government in Saskatchewan, and later NDP governments in Saskatchewan, B.C., and Manitoba introduced legislation which met some, although not all, of the unions' programmes.

A dramatic moment for the NDP caucus in the federal parliament came in October 1970 when, for the first time in Canada's peace-time history, the federal government passed and enacted the War Measures Act in an attempt to halt an alleged "apprehended insurrection". The NDP headed in parliament by T.C. Douglas as leader and David Lewis as deputy leader, led the majority of their caucus into vigorous opposition to this act.[27]

After the 1971 federal convention, at which he was elected party leader, David Lewis led the NDP in two election campaigns. The 1972 campaign in which Lewis stressed his attack on "corporate welfare bums", was moderately successful, resulting in thirty-one members elected and the NDP holding the balance of power in parliament. The success was more evident in the number of seats won than in the percentage of the vote, since the relative popular vote for the NDP did not differ substantially in 1972 from that won by the party in 1965 or 1968.[28]

During the 1972-1974 parliament in which the Liberals formed a minority government, the NDP's balance of power position in the Commons enabled it to press the Trudeau government toward increases in old age pensions, some reductions in taxes and the establishment of a two-price structure for oil to protect Canadian consumers. The NDP's conditional support of the Trudeau government, followed by its decision to defeat that government eighteen months later, became a subject of controversy among its members and union supporters. The controversy became acute after the 1974 election which was a serious set-back for the NDP.

With only sixteen members elected, it was the worst showing since the
CCF's 1958 campaign.[29] Labour's role in Canadian politics again became
a matter for debate.

1. Charles Lipton, *The Trade Union Movement of Canada 1827-1959* (Toronto:
   NC Press, 1973), 3rd edition, p. 48, from Canadian Labour Union, *Proceedings*, August 1877.

2. *Address to the Eighth Convention of the Federal New Democratic Party*, Joe
   Morris, president, CLC, Winnipeg, Manitoba, July 1975, p. 2.

3. H. A. Logan, *Trade Unions in Canada* (Toronto: Macmillan Company of
   Canada, 1948), pp. 40-41.

4. Ibid., pp. 55-60.

5. Lipton, op. cit., p. 53, from Canadian Labour Union, *Proceedings*, August
   1877.

6. Ibid., p. 46.

7. J. C. Goulden, *Meany* (New York: Atheneum, 1972), p. 61.

8. Logan, op. cit., pp. 340-341; Gad Horowitz, *Canadian Labour in Politics*
   (Toronto: University of Toronto Press, 1968), pp. 66-68; Walter D. Young,
   The Anatomy of a Party: The National CCF, 1932-1961 (Toronto: University
   of Toronto Press, 1969), p. 273.

9. Horowitz, op. cit., pp. 85-131.

10. Ibid., pp. 132-161.

11. Lipton, op. cit., p. 277; Mackenzie King, who was Prime Minister of Canada
    for more than twenty years between December 1921 and November 1948,
    was prominent in establishing the modern pattern of industrial relations in
    Canada. The model of government intervention in labour disputes which
    King helped introduce was a factor in the triumph of American business
    unionism over more militant forms. Along with the modern type of corporate
    expert on labour relations, a body of parallel experts in government labour
    departments and boards is essential to the viability of business unionism.
    King was the prototype of such government labour experts.
        King was made first editor of the *Labour Gazette* — the federal government's labour publication — in 1900, and rose rapidly to become Canada's
    first Deputy Minister of Labour. When the labour department became an
    autonomous ministry in 1909, King became its first Minister. During this
    period, he served on numerous investigative and conciliation boards and
    drafted the Industrial Disputes Investigation Act of 1907. This act provided a
    "cooling off" period before strikes in public utilities, coal mines, and railroads by outlawing strikes until after an investigative board had made its
    report. King was personally involved in breaking railway strikes in 1903,
    1907, and 1908, as well as other disputes, particularly in the Quebec cotton
    industry.

King emphasized the difference between militant unionism and conservative business unionism, urging employers that the latter was in their own interest. His opposition to international unionism was restricted to militant American unions outside the AFL. King became a special consultant to the Rockefellers during the First World War, helping to introduce company unionism into their Colorado mining companies in opposition to the militant Western Federation of Miners. See H. S. Ferns, B. Ostry, *The Age of Mackenzie King* (London: Heinemann, 1955); Lipton, op. cit., pp. 103-116, 144, 182.

12. Lipton, op. cit., p. 86, from Trades and Labour Congress, *Proceedings*, 1899.

13. Ibid., p. 235, from TLC, *Proceedings*, 1923, p. 99.

14. Ibid.

15. Ibid.

16. Ibid., p. 258, from TLC, *Proceedings*, 1931, p. 179.

17. Ibid., from TLC, *Proceedings*, 1932.

18. Horowitz, op. cit., p. 77.

19. Walter D. Young, *The Anatonomy of a Party: The National CCF* (Toronto: University of Toronto Press, 1969), p. 44.

20. Ibid., p. 129.

21. Horowitz, op. cit., pp. 171-175.

22. W. E. C. Harrison, *Canada in World Affairs, 1949 to 1950* (Toronto, 1957), p. 285.

23. Young, op. cit., p. 243.

24. Horowitz, op. cit., pp. 162-199; Young, op. cit., pp. 132-133.

25. Donald MacDonald, MPP, Federal NDP President, NDP Symposium, University of Toronto, March 4, 1975.

26. Desmond Morton, *NDP, The Dream of Power* (Toronto: A. M. Hakkert, 1974), pp. 130-135.

27. In 1974 Conservative leader Robert Stanfield acknowledged that he had envied the NDP leaders in 1970 for their courageous stand and that he had been unable to follow their example because of the sentiments of his party, in spite of his own serious doubts about the need to apply the War Measures Act.

28. In 1965, the percentage of the popular vote won by the NDP was 18 per cent with 17 per cent and 18 per cent in 1968 and 1972 respectively. *The Globe and Mail*, November 1, 1972.

29. *The Globe and Mail*, July 10, 1974.

CHAPTER 29

Labour's Political Arm—1974 and After

> The time may have come for the unions to revive their own political education machinery on a broader base and insist upon setting their own political priorities.
>
> Murray Cotterill
> Former director of public relations
> in Canada, USWA, 1972[1]

The New Democratic Party had been labour's official "political arm" since its creation by the Canadian Labour Congress and the Co-operative Commonwealth Federation in 1961, and its electoral fortunes were of deep concern to many thousands of union activists. Thus the 1974 federal election results came as a shock to the labour movement. The NDP entered the election with thirty-one seats in parliament and emerged with only sixteen, while its share of the popular vote dropped from eighteen per cent to fifteen.[2] The results produced a crisis of confidence about the potential of the party to become a serious rival to the Liberals and Conservatives in federal politics.

Joe Morris, president of the CLC, expressed this concern over the NDP's future when he told its leadership convention in July 1975 that "the new leader will be confronted immediately with the responsibility of guiding this social movement out of the political morass in which it has become mired . . ."[3]

Gallup polls from 1968-1974 had suggested that about twenty-five per cent of Canadian union members, on average, voted for the NDP in federal elections. New Democrat support in union households had increased substantially between 1963 and 1968. In the 1972 and 1974 federal elections the percentage of unionists intending to vote NDP declined. In 1968 about twenty-seven per cent of union households said they intended to vote for the NDP; in 1972 the figure was twenty-five per cent; in 1974, twenty-two per cent, a drop almost to the 1963 level of twenty-one per cent.[4] For non-union households, the figures were thirteen per cent, fourteen per cent, and thirteen per cent respectively in 1974, 1972, and 1968.[5]

In 1974 the Liberals apparently received about twice as many votes as the NDP in union households, whereas in 1972 the Liberals and Conservatives had each received about one-third more votes from unionists than had the New Democrats.[6] It appeared that the Liberals won a majority government in 1974 largely because of increased unionist support. The Liberals managed to increase their share of the union vote in the middle of a period of rising union militancy which was concentrated in the highly unionized provinces of British Columbia and Ontario. Between them, these two provinces accounted for about seventy per cent of organized labour in English Canada.

In British Columbia, the NDP federal representation dropped from eleven seats in 1972 to two in 1974. Whereas the New Democrats had received thirty-four per cent of the B.C. popular vote in 1972, they managed to garner only twenty-three per cent in 1974.[7] This was the lowest share of the popular vote in B.C. recorded by the CCF-NDP in any federal election since 1957.

In Metropolitan Toronto, the centre of the new wave of militancy among hospital workers, teachers and public employees, the NDP lost three of its five seats in solid working-class constituencies. The most serious blow came in the Metro Toronto riding of York South. Federal NDP leader David Lewis had held this seat for nine years, retaining it even in the face of the "Trudeaumania" of 1968. Now he was defeated by a relatively unknown Liberal.

The simple explanation for the NDP's losses was that unionists did not really vote pro-Liberal, but anti-Conservative. The Tories had campaigned on a programme of wage controls which many workers, it was argued, saw as a threat to their purchasing power on top of the already rampant inflation. In this situation, assuming that the New Democrats would not receive enough seats to form a government, workers switched their votes to the Liberals to prevent the Conservatives from taking office.

This explanation seemed credible in the immediate sense. But it failed to explain the key fact that despite twenty years of huge investments of time, money and organization by trade unions on the NDP's behalf, and despite the wave of labour militancy and dissatisfaction with inflation, only 22 per cent of Canadian unionists supported "labour's political arm". In particular, it failed to explain why the NDP was not able to increase its credibility as a potential federal government. In 1945 the CCF, with little formal backing from the labour movement, had won more seats than the NDP, officially supported by a 1.9-million member Canadian Labour Congress, was able to win in 1974.

The labour leaders who strongly supported the NDP viewed the election results with dismay. The reaction of UAW director Dennis McDermott was that, the people of York South ought to be ashamed of themselves. "The people of York South have made their bed and I hope they lie in it ..."[8] McDermott's angry comment seemed to imply that the working people in York South were too backward to appreciate the NDP, and that they deserved what they would get from a Liberal government. But this assumed that the NDP had provided a clear alternative to the Liberals in 1974 — clear enough, at least, to override the immediate concern over Tory wage policies.

The party strategists and union leaders had spent the previous two years bringing the NDP closer to the Liberal Party by rejecting increasing Canadian concern over American control as a major policy issue and by moving the party to the cautious political centre to attract "middle class" votes.

The NDP had been supporting the Liberals in a minority government situation for eighteen months prior to the election. It had tolerated policies like the unprecedented concessions to the oil companies, raising prices from $3.70 to $6.50 a barrel, because the Liberals were considered preferable to the Tories and because the NDP government in Saskatchewan had pressed for the higher price. Those eighteen months had also narrowed the popular perception of differences between the two parties.

In June 1974 Mc Dermott told the UAW that Canadians had never done so well as under the 1972-1974 minority Liberal government, pressured by the NDP,[9] even though this contradicted those labour leaders who claimed that Canadian workers had suffered their first major loss in puchasing power since the Second World War.

The narrowing difference between the NDP and the Liberal Party was not altogether new. In 1949 Louis St. Laurent had described the supporters of the CCF in Saskatchewan as "Liberals in a hurry".[10] But the process had taken a new turn, especially following the 1971 Ottawa convention. The move toward the centre was coupled with a rejection of Canadian nationalism at the time that rank and file workers were becoming increasingly militant and nationalistic. This move affected the image of the party among significant sections of the electorate, particularly younger voters. The NDP leadership was increasingly out of step with public opinion.

This crisis in the NDP had its roots in the marriage between the CCF and the international unions. International union leaders did not expect the NDP to take a strong nationalist line. Joe Morris, president of the CLC, reiterated this position at the NDP's 1975 convention when he declared that "the majority of the labour leaders do not believe that nationalism is a solution to the problems created by the growth of multinational corporations".[11] Earlier he had referred approvingly to the NDP's "rejection of inner organizations with leaders who have particular positions and

policies to pursue and who wish to thrust the party in other directions".[12] This was presumably a reference to the left-nationalist debate of
1969-1972 and the Waffle.

Morris reminded the party of its financial dependence on the unions,
which had enabled some provincial NDP sections to "contemplate spending one million dollars in an election campaign". (Most of the contributing unions had been international unions.) By this reference to the NDP's
dependence on union financing, Morris made it clear that continued
financial and other backing of the CLC for the NDP would depend in the
future on a continued rejection of nationalism as the answer to the threat
of the multinational corporations in Canada.

In effect, the NDP is two parties. In Saskatchewan, B.C. and Manitoba
where it forms the provincial governments, it is relatively free of international union control. Riding association members hold the balance of
power, In Ontario, on the other hand, the international unions have
considerable power.

At the federal level, discouragement had become particularly acute
over the question of a successor to David Lewis. Morale became low
with the realization that constituency delegates no longer had the power
to decide the outcome of federal conventions. Constituency delegates
and elected delegates from affiliated unions were, by and large,
nationalists, at least at the gut level. The internationals' staff representatives, on the other hand, had already shown their willingness to stop any
drift toward nationalist programmes.

In addition to the existence of these conflicting forces within the party
over the nationalist issue, there were also organizational reasons for the
decline of the NDP federally. When the architects of the new party
discarded the CCF structure, where ultimate control rested with individual members organized in riding associations, in favour of direct
union affiliation, they created a potentially serious problem of morale.
The individual riding association members have been the main support
for the party at election time, in terms of canvassing and related work.
Their growing feeling of impotence over the policy direction of the NDP
undermined the party's fighting strength.

On the other hand, the drive for direct union affiliation only partially
succeeded in its objective to turn the NDP into the "political arm of
labour". The fact that most unions, particularly the old AFL organizations, are still not affiliated to the party is a consequence of the business
unionist philosophy that continued to hold sway in many internationals.

The depth of the crisis within the NDP prior to the July 1975 leadership
convention was illustrated in an almost desperate approach by some
party strategists to Eric Kierans, former member of the Trudeau
Cabinet, asking him to run for the leadership. Kierans reminded them
that he could not consider running for the top slot in the NDP since he was
not even a member of the party.

Since the crisis in the party was linked to the weight of international union influence opposing nationalist policies in the NDP, it appeared that one possible solution to these difficulties lay in the rapidly-emerging move toward Canadian unionism.

If one or more of the powerful industrial unions affiliated to the party were to move strongly in the direction of independence, it could break through the anti-nationalist barrier in the NDP. The party could unite its disparate forces around a programme such as public ownership of largely foreign-owned resource and energy industries and the possibility of an alternative industrial strategy for Canada. Such a programme could channel the nationalism of the riding association and local union membership toward immediately realizable objectives. It could make the NDP a clear alternative to the continentalist and business strategies of the old-line parties. The NDP could reach out to win the support of unions not yet affiliated and become for the first time truly the political arm of labour. With basic agreement over the left-nationalist direction of the party, a new formula could eventually be worked out for a sharing of power between membership groups in the NDP.

It is even conceivable that the NDP could undergo a basic change in policy without a major international affiliate moving toward independence. If the fully Canadian unions in the CLC were to assume a much more prominent role in the Congress and the party, they could conceivably apply sufficient pressure to tip the balance toward a left-nationalist policy.

The time-table for such a change appeared critical in 1975. To overcome the crisis in the federal NDP the party would have to begin to pick up momentum by the end of the 1970s — and perhaps even by the 1978 federal election. Should the process be delayed appreciably beyond this point, other organizations could emerge with the kind of programme that would unite nationalists in the union movement and outside. The NDP would be left without a genuine alternative to offer Canadians, and might become increasingly irrelevant. If international union leaders in the party were determined to make a last-ditch fight to preserve American unionism in Canada they could conceivably delay the transformation of the NDP beyond hope of recovery.

The key to the situation may be the convergence of the parallel movements of growing labour militancy and nationalism in the context of political action. The Quebec labour movement has provided one model for such convergence through its actions and manifestos. The Quebec model sees labour as the decisive force in nationalist politics. This implies wide participation of workers in shaping policies and political activities.

The important factor is the recognition by workers that narrow bread-and-butter unionism severely limits the possibility of real gains in a corporate economy. The treadmill of repeated negotiations with individual employers will not achieve the basic working-class goals of security, well-being and dignity. Ultimately, the issue is one of economic and political power. The American corporations and their English and French-Canadian counterparts have the federal and provincial governments on their side. Working people have to rely on organization and the widest possible democratic participation. This approach to politics is a new one, differing greatly from the American, and to a lesser degree from the concepts of labour political action in English Canada. The Quebec model differs vastly from the American model because it emphasizes that labour should be deeply involved in independent politics leading ultimately to a political party where labour is dominant. Within this model, working-class nationalist politics are at the core of labour's interests.

The Quebec model resembles the NDP model in that it advocates that organized labour must be an independent political force. But it differs from the current NDP model by escaping the contradiction between the official disavowal of nationalism while the membership is basically nationalist. Even the QFL, most of whose affiliates are international unions, has participated in the movement toward nationalist labour politics under the influence of the other two Quebec centres and its own rank and file.

A second basic difference between the Quebec model and the model of the NDP as labour's political arm is the extent of grass-roots involvement called for. Within the NDP, while union leaders have participated actively in formation of policy at the federal level, rank and file workers have been largely uninvolved. Affiliation to the NDP has been largely a top-down arrangement.

For top union leaders in English Canada, political action has often meant the avoidance of militant action. Instead of organizing mass demonstrations or work stoppages against legislation attacking labour, for example, they have called for the election of an NDP government.

There were at least two fallacies in the simple call for the election of an NDP government in the mid-seventies. First, the NDP was not about to elect a government in many parts of Canada — such as Quebec, in the Atlantic provinces or Alberta.

The second fallacy was that an NDP government which had not been elected as a consequence of mass democratic participation by labour — in other words, as a consequence of labour militancy and political activity of the very kind that some of the leadership discouraged — would not necessarily heed labour's demands for legislative changes.

Organized labour in British Columbia had not been fully satisfied with the Barrett government's labour legislation. In Manitoba, NDP Premier Ed Schreyer had even advocated wage controls.

Joe Morris acknowledged these differences between labour and NDP provincial governments when he said that "there have been obvious and important issues of confrontation between sections of the labour movement in Canada and elected New Democratic governments in some of the provinces".[13] Electing an NDP provincial government had not solved all or even most of labour's political problems.

There was some evidence in the mid-seventies that unionists in English Canada were beginning to recognize the limitations of confining their political action to formal support of the NDP. The UAW, in its mass lobby in Ottawa in February 1975, and its promise of stepped-up actions in the future, was seeking some new form of political expression. Following the 1974 election, Morden Lazarus, former director of political education for the OFL, suggested that labour leaders should, "perhaps ... consider a five-year moratorium on resolutions in support of the New Democratic Party and spend time in more active endeavours. Perhaps they should take a penetrating look at political action."[14]

Ironically enough, another union spokesman had made a similar proposal in 1972, as part of an attack on what he saw as dangerous nationalism in the NDP.[15] Murray Cotterill, retired USWA public relations director, and long-time party activist, recognized that there was a dilemma inherent in the relationship between the NDP and the unions. He called for a reassessment of the CCF-union merger which had created the NDP, saying that it had "obliterated the unions' own political education machinery, surrendered issue-resting to the full-time politicians and provided those politicians with an automatic supply of union funds".

Cotterill's statement shed light on the further possibilities of labour political action:

> One obvious answer for both the unions and the NDP is to simply admit that they have both tried to climb too high, too soon on a too shaky foundation. The time may have come for the unions to revive their own political education machinery on a broader base and insist upon setting their own political priorities. They can still support the NDP indirectly through encouraging membership participation on an individual basis and by financial support from special union political action funds.

Cotterill was advocating a return to the type of relations which existed between the CCF and CCL prior to 1956 when several CCL-affiliated unions had local, provincial, and national political action committees.[16]

An alliance between unions and the NDP which did not rely entirely on formal affiliation, or see political action exclusively in terms of supporting the party at election time, could be a step toward broad unionist participation in politics. Cotterill's suggestion that unions "revive their own political education machinery" could be a move toward the Quebec model. This would depend on the proviso that "political action" not become a formula for substituting the American model of union lobbying, neglecting the building of an independent political party and movement where working people decided programmes and strategies.

Discouragement with the NDP's set-back in the 1974 federal elections could lead unions in one of two directions. Unions could move out of fully independent labour politics by disaffiliating from its "political arm" into an American model of lobbying the parties of business, or unions could strengthen their independent role in labour politics by greater unionist activism and an even closer relationship to the NDP. Adoption of a substantially modified NDP model would offer at least three new avenues for political action by labour.

First, it would permit all unions — not just those formally affiliated to the NDP — to become involved in political and legislative actions organized by the CLC, provincial federations of labour, local labour councils or other trade union bodies. Such actions would include events like the UAW's Ottawa demonstration in February 1975, or the QFL's 80,000 strong one-day strike in support of the United Aircraft workers.

Second, the unions would have to provide their political education or political action committees with specific programmes for involving the membership. Whereas they have merely been receiving and distributing NDP literature, they would have to initiate campaigns and actions, prepare materials, in short, become actively involved in the political work themselves.

Third, organizations like the CLC would be thrown back on their own resources in developing and carrying through campaigns on the political or legislative issues they wish to support. For instance, the CLC's policy in favour of a seventy-five per cent pension for all Canadians could be translated into real political action at the national level, involving the whole range of actions from petitions and lobbying MPs, all the way to nation-wide work stoppages. [17]

The NDP model has tended to emphasize a distinction between the unions, which are supposed to act on economic issues, and the party, which is supposed to deal with political questions. The unions themselves, in this model, are not seen as potential centres for rallying workers to action on specific legislative or political issues. By contrast, both the CNTU model and a modified NDP model which would emphasize independent labour political action combined with active support for the party would achieve active involvement of unionized workers on a broad range of political, social and economic issues.

It should be stressed as well that there has been a fundamental distinction between all three of these Canadian models and the American model of labour neutrality, since all three Canadian models have emphasized an independent and key political role for organized labour in determining Canada's future.

This difference between the union movement in Canada and the

American union movement was underscored by David Archer, president of the OFL, in a speech to the Graphic Arts International Convention in August 1975. "The union movement in Ontario," Archer said, "is determined to play an active role in the coming [Ontario] election." After explaining that "all fifty Labour Councils have been alerted to co-operate with the NDP," he commented that "the American union movement is perhaps the last union body in the world to pay the compliment of hypocrisy to non-partisan political participation". Archer contrasted this with "the European union groups [which] have all accepted the proposition of partisan politics. Many of them were the outgrowth of political philosophies".[18]

In the context of continuing serious problems in the Canadian economy and the prospect of further crises resulting from Canadian dependence on a weakening American economy, organized labour is seeking new channels to express itself politically. This is true in the area of energy policy. It is true in the fight against lay-offs in manufacturing, resulting from the export of jobs to the United States. It is true as well in the need for nation-wide labour actions to counter the attempts by corporations and governments to make workers bear the brunt of economic restraints.

Unionists may decide they can no longer afford simply to await the election of New Democratic governments, important as those would be to labour's cause.

The latter half of the 1970s and early 1980s promise a paradox. Some of the very unions whose leaders opposed the NDP becoming the major political expression of the nationalist movement in Canada might themselves be transformed into independent Canadian organizations. In this they could add their weight to a labour movement which is moving toward Canadian union predominance. With this accomplished, the transformation of the NDP into a major force to challenge the rule of the foreign and domestic corporations in Canada could become a reality.

---

1. *The Toronto Star*, June 22, 1972.

2. *The Globe and Mail*, July 11, 1974.

3. *Address to the Eighth Convention of the Federal New Democratic Party*, Joe Morris, president, CLC, Winnipeg, Manitoba, July 1975, p. 2.

4. *The Gallup Report*, July 24, 1974; July 13, 1968.

5. *The Gallup Report*, July 24, 1974.

6. Ibid.

7. *The Globe and Mail*, July 10, 1974.

8. *The Globe and Mail*, July 9, 1974.

9. *Solidarity Canada*, June 1974, p. 6.

10. Dale C. Thomson, *Louis St. Laurent: Canadian* (Toronto: Macmillan Company of Canada, 1967), p. 266.

11. *Address to the Eighth Convention of the Federal New Democratic Party*, Joe Morris, President, CLC, Winnipeg, Manitoba, July 1975, p. 7.

12. Ibid., p. 5

13. Ibid., p. 8.

14. *OFL Labour Review*, September-October 1974, p. 2.

15. *The Toronto Star*, June 22, 1972.

16. Gad Horowitz, *Canadian Labour in Politics* (Toronto: University of Toronto Press, 1968), pp. 134-140.

17. CLC, *Information*, March 23, 1975. The CLC's *Memorandum to the Government of Canada* called for Canada and Quebec Pension Plan changes that would result in benefits equalling 75 per cent of earnings at age 60 by 1996.

18. Speech to the Graphic Arts International Convention, *OFL Press Release*, August 18, 1975.

PART VII
Canada's Unions in Historical Perspective

CHAPTER 30

One Hundred Years of National Unionism

A federation of American unions represented by a national union, and a federation of Canadian unions represented by a national union, each working with the other in special cases, would be a great advantage over having local unions in Canada connected with the national unions of America.

Ralph Smith
President, TLC, 1901[1]

Co-operation, yes! Domination, no!

Executive Council, TLC, 1949[2]

Since Confederation there has been a continuing tradition of nationalism among organized workers in Canada. Alongside feelings of solidarity with American workers, there has been the awareness that the powerful republic to the south posed a certain challenge to the survival and well-being of Canada as an independent nation.

The Canadian labour movement voiced concern over American economic domination almost as soon as Confederation was accomplished. In 1874, with negotiations for a reciprocity, or free trade, agreement between the United States and Canada in the air, the secretary of the Canadian Labour Union warned convention delegates:

If there is anything calculated to make this country more dependent than it is now, it is the passage of the proposed treaty.
. . . Let's manufacture our own iron, wool, etc. I do not think we ask too much when we claim the right to set a foothold upon our own soil, without being pushed down by foreigners.[3]

The reciprocity agreement never came about. But the far-larger American economy, protected by tariffs, still had an adverse effect on the young Dominion. In 1877 J. S. Williams pointed this out at the CLU convention: "To a very great extent, the present depression of trade in Canada results from the excessive importation of foreign manufactured goods."[4]

Working people's convictions that their country's future depended on its economic independence led naturally to a desire for a Canadian trade union centre.[5] The Canadian Labour Union was formed in 1873, thirteen years before the formation of the AFL in the United States. In 1886, the year Samuel Gompers founded the AFL, the TLC was formed, including among its affiliates the Canadian locals of the Knights of Labour, an early industrial union-oriented group. This attempt to form a united trade union centre in Canada contrasted with the AFL, which excluded the industrial unionist Knights from its exclusively craft-oriented membership.

The rise of the AFL meant the decline of the Knights of Labour in the United States. In Canada, however, they maintained a strong existence, particularly in Quebec. Emphasizing the organization of unskilled workers from different trades into district assemblies, the Knights in effect became a Canadian organizing centre and played an important role in the early days of the TLC. The majority of the delegates to the 1890 TLC Convention were Knights, and one of their number, Urban LaFontaine, was elected to the presidency of the Congress.

This situation was not to last. When the tariff came into effect with John A. Macdonald's National Policy, many American companies found it profitable to open branch plants in Canada.

In the wake of the branch plant factories came organizers of the AFL craft unions. The AFL's founder Samuel Gompers had a vision of a continent-wide union movement based on AFL principles.

These principles stood in sharp distinction to the organizing philosophy of the Knights of Labour, on the one hand, and the political philosophy of many of the British immigrants to Canada, on the other. These immigrants had brought with them traditions of militant working class unionism, and a commitment to political action. The latter meant either running workers as independent candidates in elections, or forming a labour party.

The business unionist philosophy of the AFL also ran counter to the radical syndicalist unionism of miners in British Columbia and Alberta. There, the Western Federation of Miners had made extensive organizing gains in the coal and metal mines of western Canada. The WFM was unlike the AFL in that it organized on industrial lines, and expressed a syndicalist political philosophy.

The special environment of the B.C. mines, where workers often lived in company-owned houses and bought their supplies at company stores, together with the extreme anti-labour activities of the mine owners, many of whom were provincial government politicians, gave rise to the radicalism of the WFM and similar organizations in British Columbia.

Socialist and anarcho-syndicalist labour traditions were built in B.C. to an extent unequalled elsewhere in Canada.

AFL penetration into the Canadian labour movement occurred especially in Ontario where widespread manufacturing, increasingly centred in American branch plants, was predominant, as compared to the resource-based company towns of B.C. The AFL pressed the Canadian sections of the internationals to adopt the policies of U.S. labour headquarters and this resulted, among other things, in the American-exported conflict with the Knights of Labour in Canada.

Conflict between the craft and business union orientation of the AFL and the broader industrial tendency of the Canadian labour movement led to a debate about the role of the TLC. Members of the Congress who favoured Canadian union independence pressed the TLC to become a union centre with authority to conduct organizing drives, charter new unions, and speak for Canadian workers as a whole. Members who favoured Gompers' plan wanted to reduce the TLC to the functions of a state federation of labour in the United States.

Gompers and the AFL executive were determined to restrict the Canadian Congress to this limited role. The TLC leadership thought differently, however, and shortly began to issue charters to new unions in its own name. The object was to create new Canadian unions organized in a national union centre.

At the 1901 convention, TLC president Ralph Smith explicitly called for the TLC to become the Canadian equivalent of the AFL in the United States. He wanted the TLC to become a Canadian Federation of Labour, and argued that the AFL should not take over this function in Canada:

> A federation of American unions represented by a national union [centre] and a federation of Canadian unions represented by a national union, each working with the other in special cases, would be a great advantage over having local unions in Canada connected with the national unions of America.[6]

Smith's actions resulted from at least two independent factors. In his stance there was a clear expression of the genuine Canadian nationalism of active unionists. However, as a supporter of the Laurier government he may also have been providing indirect support for the Liberal strategy of damning strikes under the claim that "Yankee agitators" were responsible for them. Whether or not this was the case, events soon made it clear that the unity of the Canadian labour movement depended on limiting AFL control. Ironically enough, the failure of the Liberal strategy to weaken the trade union movement was the best guarantee that labour would be split and set against itself.

The death-blow to Smith's proposal, and to the goal of an independent and united Canadian union centre, came at the 1902 convention of the TLC in Kitchener. The majority of the delegates came from AFL craft locals, and many of them had advance instructions about how to vote on the issue of national versus international unionism. A proposed amendment to the constitution of the TLC ended with the following condition: *no national union be recognized where any international union existed.*[7] (emphasis added) The passage of this amendment meant that the Knights locals, together with other fully Canadian unions which organized workers in the same crafts as AFL unions, lost their affiliation to the Congress. The TLC, the voice of Canadian labour, passed into the hands of the international craft unions, and of Samuel Gompers.

The Canadian union ousted from the TLC immediately set out to build the National Trades and Labour Congress of Canada. Founded in 1903, the NTLC was dedicated to "organization along national lines".[8] It demonstrated how, in Canada, working class nationalism merged with an awareness of the difference between workers' interests and those of business — two things lacking in the AFL-TLC's business unionist philosophy.

Thus the NTLC Executive Committee for Ontario denounced the "paid officers of internationals" in its 1908 report, saying that:

> [they sought] to retain the allegiance of Canadian workers to a cause which is at best bound to keep Canada in a position of subservience and is preventing its working class from adopting a more progressive and modern policy.[9]

The report went on to suggest steps to help Canada "avoid the mistakes which have allowed the United States to become the plutocracy and oligarchy which at present it represents socially and industrially".

The NTLC supported tariffs and other measures which would promote the development of industry and jobs in Canada under the slogan "Canada for Canadians".[10] In 1904 it protested the import of boots and shoes from the United States, and in 1906 called for a Canadian shipbuilding industry. By 1906 it claimed to have a membership of twenty thousand — a respectable size for the time. In 1908, seven years after Ralph Smith's ill-fated proposal, it changed its name to the Canadian Federation of Labour.

The NTLC-CFL, beset by organizational problems, was not a long-lived success. But the movement it represented, opposed to American economic and union domination of Canada and AFL-style craft unionism, and in favour of a united fully-Canadian union movement, lived on in other organizations. Most important among these were the All-Canadian Congress of Labour, established in 1927, and the Confederation of National Trade Unions, which has played a prominent role in Quebec unionism into the 1970s.

Even within the TLC the voice of Canadian nationalism could not be stilled. The TLC refused to submit to the status of a state federation of labour completely dominated by the AFL. Thus the American federation's fraternal delegate to the 1911 TLC Convention was shocked to hear discussions that ranged far beyond the limited local legislative concerns of the state federations in the United States:

> I imagined that I was attending the convention of the American Federation of Labor, where all sorts of disputes are expressed and acted upon.[11]

At that convention, the Alberta provincial executive had proposed a policy that doubtless contributed to the AFL observer's uneasiness:

> We are of the opinion [that] . . . the Trades and Labour Congress must declare for absolute supremacy, not merely on legislative matters alone, but also in all economic questions which concern the welfare of Canadian trade unionists as a whole.[12]

In addition the TLC convention passed a resolution which struck at the heart of AFL dogma:

> Whereas craft unions have proved inadequate to successfully combat present-day aggregations of capital, . . . therefore be it resolved that this convention endorse the principle of industrial unionism.[13]

The AFL had the offending policy sufficiently watered-down at the next TLC convention so as to be practically meaningless. But this experience of interference by Gompers in TLC policy was a further spur to nationalist feelings among some Canadian unionists.

These feelings were further intensified during the First World War. The TLC had a policy of opposition to military conscription. The AFL, by contrast, was strongly in favour of the war, denouncing as unpatriotic any pacifist or anti-conscriptionist position. With the Americans' entry into the war in 1917, AFL pressure on the TLC over the conscription issue mounted.

Toward the end of 1917 Gompers himself came to Canada to boost support for the war. He told a large Toronto audience that he had no desire "to interfere" in Canadian affairs, and then went on:

> The people of Canada ought to stand united without regard for religion or any other difference to bring victory and glory to the Dominion.[14]

Canadian workers, he said, should abandon their opposition to conscription:

> I . . . hold it to be the duty of every Canadian and American citizen in time of war to obey that decision, rightfully and lawfully reached. . . .

Gompers' appeal received a strong reply in the House of Commons. Alphonse Verville, member of Montreal Plumbers' Local 144, past president of the TLC, and MP for Hochelaga since 1906, denounced conscription:

> There are two major views on the war, that of the exploiter and that of

the exploited. .... Is it patriotism to manufacture implements of war at scandalous profits?[15]

While many trade union activists in Canada retained their opposition to the war and to conscription, there were some who bowed to Gompers' view. Prominent among these were Canadian officials of international unions. Five days before the United States entered the war, Gompers convened a special conference of the AFL in Washington. Several Canadian officers, in a fit of misplaced patriotism, signed the AFL statement, proclaiming loyalty to "the Republic of the United States against enemies, whomsoever they may be".[16]

The First World War raised the level of Canadian workers' anger against the system which had brought it about.[17]

One prominent unionist, James Simpson, then vice-president for Ontario of the TLC, and later mayor of Toronto, expressed in 1917 the feeling of impotence which many Canadian unionists experienced in their relations to the AFL:

> It is just as well at this time that I should point out that the organized workers of Canada stand in a position that has no parallel in any other country of the world. This Congress can only exert its moral influence in the enforcement of decisions. .... This is because economic power necessary to support legislative demands is not vested in our movement, but is under the control of the international officers of our representative unions. .... [Our Congress] does not have the same powers as the AFL. When the executive council of the American Federation of Labor reaches a decision, members of that council, being the heads of powerful international unions, can use their influence effectively. .... [In Canada, however,] we cannot use our economic power without the sanction of the heads of our international unions ... in cases where our decisions are at variance with decisions taken by the American Federation of Labor regarding important national issues, it is difficult to secure that sympathy, that support in the exercise of our economic powers, as we otherwise would receive if the executive of the Congress were composed of the heads of powerful economic organizations.[18]

Shortly after the Armistice, two important Canadian conferences expressed the new level of militancy and working class consciousness.

The British Columbia Federation of Labour met in March 1919, and launched a campaign for the six-hour working day. The campaign was to take the form of a nation-wide general strike effective not later than June the first. A vote was to be held among all Canadian locals to decide on the general strike. When some delegates suggested that the vote include U.S. locals, the convention voted them down. One of the delegates said, "we are seeking to break away from the bucket-shop of the international officers of the AFL".[19]

The Western Canada Labour Conference also took place in March 1919. The 250 delegates, representing most of the important locals from Winnipeg to Victoria, called for organization along industrial lines.[20]

They resolved that the issue of disaffiliation from the "internationals" be settled by a referendum among the Canadian membership. The Canadian members, once separated from the American craft organizations, would form an industrial organization of all workers.[21] This new body came to be known as the One Big Union (OBU).

Six weeks later the Winnipeg General Strike became the focus of attention of the union movement, particularly among supporters of the OBU.

Much has been written about the Winnipeg General Strike of 1919. Most significant in this context is the role played by the international unions in helping to break the strike, illustrating their conservative and often reactionary influence on the Canadian labour movement.

In the middle of the strike Gideon Robertson, minister of labour in Prime Minister Borden's cabinet, and one-time international vice-president of the Commercial Telegraphers Union (AFL), wrote to Gompers to enlist his aid in breaking the Winnipeg strike and urged:

> Serious consideration of the executives of the various [international] organizations concerned ... the motives are undoubtedly support of the One Big Union movement.[22]

In connection with this letter, Ernest Lapointe later told the House of Commons, "this is an appeal clamouring for help by a Canadian Minister of the Crown to a foreign labour leader".[23] Several years later Mackenzie King's labour minister, Peter Heenan, told the House that an inquiry into the 1919 strike had shown that:

> ... the Minister of Labour (Robertson) did, ... prolong the strike by refusing to declare in favour of collective bargaining. ... I think he said himself it was in the interests of the international unions. ...[24]

The U.S. headquarters of the internationals lost no time in moving to break the strike. When the Toronto street railway local met on June 1 to decide whether to offer support to the Winnipeg strikers, international representatives of their union told them to desist. When Canadian locals of the railway unions asked their U.S. superiors what they could do to help the Winnipeg strikers, headquarters replied that their constitutions forbade sympathy strikes, and that all strikes required international consent.

There was at least one case in which a U.S. headquarters specifically instructed its Canadian members to act as strike-breakers. The international office of the Brotherhood of Railway Trainmen in Cleveland, Ohio, sent the following orders to its Canadian members:

> In view of illegal strike of members of the Winnipeg lodge ... it is deemed necessary that our organization use every effort to furnish members of the brotherhood willing to accept positions made vacant by the illegal strikers. ...[25]

Some Canadian officers of internationals chimed in. James Murdoch,

Canadian international representative of the Brotherhood, warned members of his union who defied head office's instruction that they would be stricken from the membership list, and that locals who supported the Winnipeg strikers would lose their charters.[26]

Even more harm was done when the internationals decided to intervene directly. In mid-June senior Canadian officers of the railway running trades internationals offered to mediate in the strike. Their offer was accepted by Winnipeg's Central Strike Committee. But the mediating group entered into direct negotiations with the metal trades employers, behind the backs of the strike committee. On June 16, about twenty-four hours before the large-scale arrests of strike leaders began, the mediators and the employers issued a joint statement. They announced that the employers would recognize the unions on a craft basis, but would not accept strikers' demands for a metal trades council.[27] Thus, at a critical moment the Canadian leaders of international craft unions stabbed the strikers in the back.

This was not lost on the Winnipeg strikers. Shortly after the end of their strike, OBU organization resumed. On July 8 the Winnipeg Trades and Labour Council decided to vote on the report of the Western Canada Labour Conference. Winnipeg trade unionists voted 8,841 to 705 in favour of breaking away from the internationals and the TLC to join the OBU.[28]

The Vancouver Trades and Labour Council followed suit, severing its links with the AFL and the TLC. A vote within the B.C. Federation of Labour showed a large majority in favour of seceding from the internationals.

By the end of the year, the OBU had 41,000 members. Despite its ill-considered tactics — particularly the self-imposed split with the TLC — which led to its decline shortly afterwards, the place of the OBU in Canada's labour history was assured. It stood as the symbol of militant, industrial and independent Canadian unionism in rejection of the AFL's craft, business and continentalist policies.

In the space of less than twenty years, two great show-downs — the 1902 Berlin convention of the TLC, and the Winnipeg General Strike — had taken place between Canadian and international unionism. More were to come.

The Canadian Brotherhood of Railway Employees, the only major Canadian union in the railway industry, had been organized in 1908.[29] Originally, it had been affiliated to the old Canadian Federation of Labour. Later on, after the decline of the CFL, the CBRE joined the TLC. In 1921 it came under attack from another TLC railway affiliate, the Brotherhood of Railway and Steamship Clerks (AFL). The BRSC charged that the CBRE had an overlapping jurisdiction with the international and thus violated the Berlin amendment to the Congress constitution. Responding to pressure from the TLC leadership, officials of the Canadian union began negotiations for a merger with the international. But the BRSC refused to guarantee democratic control and election of officers by the Canadian membership. The talks were stalemated.

A few months later the TLC executive council, without waiting for a regular convention of the Congress, decided the matter by cancelling the CBRE's charter. For the Congress to continue to recognize the CBRE, it declared, would mean "recognition of a dual organization, which policy the Congress had emphatically declared against at its annual convention in the City of Berlin".[30]

When the next TLC convention met, president Tom Moore reported this decision to the delegates, insisting that the Congress, "will uphold the right to restrict its membership to supporters of the international trade union movement. . . .[31]

The secretary-treasurer of the TLC, P.M. Draper, referred to the Congress as "the mouth-piece of international trade unionism".[32]

A.R. Mosher, president of the CBRE, and later president of the All-Canadian Congress of Labour and then the Canadian Congress of Labour, replied: "The CBRE is going on in spite of you as it did before it became affiliated to the Congress."[33]

The 1920s, marked by a renewed flow of American investment to Canada and relative prosperity, particularly for the craft workers who dominated the Canadian union movement, was a low point both in union militancy and in national union conflict with the internationals. Canadian unionism had by this time been seriously weakened. All the same, the voice of independence continued to be heard within the councils of the TLC.

At the 1923 convention the Toronto lodge of the International Association of Machinists called on the TLC to become "the real centre of a virile, active, powerful trade union movement".[34] The following year, the Edmonton local of the Brotherhood of Railway Carmen (AFL-TLC) appealed to the Congress to secure Canadian autonomy so that "mass action by the Canadian working class may become a reality".[35] The 1925 convention saw resolutions from Trades and Labour Councils in Halifax, Winnipeg and Vancouver all calling for the amalgamation of craft unions. In 1926 there was an attempt, actively opposed by the TLC leadership, to call a conference of all trade union bodies in Canada, regardless of affiliation.

The defeat of this last proposal, which was in effect a renewal of the old dream of a strong and united Canadian labour movement, led to the formation of the All-Canadian Congress of Labour in 1927. Despite the efforts of the TLC leadership, and the generally low ebb of the movement for Canadian unionism during this period, by 1928 one out of every three trade unionists in the country belonged to Canadian organizations.

Then came the Great Depression. By 1933, one out of every five members of the labour force was out of work and looking for a job. The business unionist policies of the craft internationals and the TLC emphasized protecting the jobs of their skilled membership and protecting the status of their unions, often without regard for the unskilled, the unorganized and the unemployed. With so many out of work, the TLC withdrew into a protective shell of international craft exclusiveness and business unionism.[36]

At the same time, Canadian workers in various parts of the country were engaging in a series of actions under the leadership of the Workers Unity League. The initiative for this organization came from members of the Communist Party. With a minimum of finances and no previous union base, the WUL organized at least 25,000 workers between 1930 and 1935.[37]

Among its better known actions was the strike of coal miners in Estevan, Saskatchewan, in September 1931. In 1933 furniture and packing house workers went on strike in Stratford, Ontario, supported by some locals of the internationals in the immediate area. The militia was called in to discourage the strikers. The TLC's president condemned the strike, but partially retracted his statement, following pressure from local TLC affiliates.[38]

In 1934 the WUL-affiliated Lumber Workers Industrial Union led a strike of about 3,500 workers on Vancouver Island. In 1935 the WUL policy of organizing unemployed workers as a hedge against strike-breaking bore fruit in the "On to Ottawa" trek of single unemployed men, most of whom had struck the relief camps. The trek was halted and dispersed by the RCMP in the Regina riot of July 1, 1935.

The ability of the WUL to organize workers during the depths of the depression illustrated the strength of militant Canadian unionism. The League folded after 1935, not as a result of any internal weakness — although it did have some organizational problems — but because of other external interference in Canadian union affairs. Against the wishes of some top WUL organizers, the League was disbanded on the decision of the Seventh Congress of the Communist International in Moscow to organize "popular fronts" in all countries.[39]

The late 1930s and the 1940s saw the model of industrial unionism, already embraced by the Knights, the TLC and the WUL coming into its own in Canada and the United States. Organization of industrial unions among unskilled workers in Canada began after 1935. Much of this organization was carried out under the CIO banner, but the actual work of organization was carried out by Canadians themselves. At least in the early years of the industrial union drive, some Canadian locals were affiliated to the international centre only after the organization was under way. The bulk of this work was carried out by unpaid organizers, often members of the CCF or the Communist Party, in the plants, mines and forests.[40]

There were instances of Canadian workers being in a stronger position to organize themselves than workers in the United States. Philip Murray, president of the Steelworkers' organizing committee in the United States, acknowledged that in its early years his organization was substantially funded by the local in the Dosco plant at Sydney, Nova Scotia.[41] The argument that Canadians needed American help to build their unions was reversed in this instance.

Outside the CIO, Canadian workers demonstrated once again their ability to form their own industrial organizations without U.S. intervention. Thus the Canadian Seamen's Union was born in 1937 and remained strong until it was destroyed in 1949.

The experience of the industrial union period did not prove that Canadian workers needed American organizations to form unions. It demonstrated, instead, a deep-seated colonial mentality among labour leaders and activists — including people who considered themselves in the left-wing of labour — who found it necessary to affiliate their home-grown organizations to an American labour centre. But the deeper commitment of Canadians to the old dream of a united labour movement was illustrated in the refusal of the TLC for three years to expel the industrial unions following the split between the AFL and the CIO in 1936.

Once again, in this dispute the international executives of the craft unions found it necessary to intervene in the Canadian labour movement. If the craft and industrial unions were to split in the United States, the same had to happen in Canada. Pressure on the TLC built up until, in 1939, representatives of the craft unions were powerful enough to expel the new industrial unions from the Congress.[42] Just as the Knights of Labour and the Canadian locals had been driven out in 1902, now, almost forty years later, the U.S. union leaders were repeating their success. The new industrial unions had to go.

The war years temporarily stilled the debate between Canadian and international unionism. Canadian labour was busy fighting the war and organizing its ranks. The trade union movement grew more rapidly than at any previous time. But once the war was over, the old debate emerged again and another major confrontation was waiting in the wings.

The story of how the SIU came to Canada has already been told.[43] When the top TLC leadership of president Percy Bengough and secretary-treasurer John Buckley proclaimed the autonomy of the Canadian labour centre, the AFL leaders proposed (as was noted in chapter twelve) that the TLC constitution be amended. This would allow "each international union to deliver a block vote at the convention"[44] through its international representatives. The TLC council denounced this proposal:

> [as] nothing less than an audacious attempt to disenfranchise the Canadian members and to make the Trades and Labour Congress of Canada a special appendage of the American Federation of Labor.[45]

In reply to threats by international unions to disaffiliate from the TLC, the Congress statement warned that:

> if any international union decided . . . to sever their affiliation, then we will have no other choice than to take over jurisdiction of that inter-

national union and issue national or federal charters to cover those that remain loyal to our cause.[46]

This was the moment of truth. The TLC leadership had risen to the challenge of the "internationals" and was on the brink of establishing a fully-Canadian labour centre uniting most organized workers. But this did not come about. The American unions mounted an unprecedented assault on the TLC, and the Bengough-Buckley executive folded under the pressure. Another great confrontation had ended, and American domination of the Canadian movement seemed assured once again.

Twenty-five years later, in the period whose developments have been described in earlier chapters, the theme of Canadian vs. American unionism was once again to play a central part in the thinking of many Canadian unionists.

1. H. A. Logan, *Trade Unions in Canada* (Toronto: Macmillan Company of Canada, 1948), p. 71.

2. Charles Lipton, *The Trade Union Movement of Canada 1827-1959* (Toronto: NC Press, 1973), 3rd edition, p. 279, from *Trades and Labour Congress Journal*, March 1949, pp. 12-13.

3. Ibid., p. 45, from Canadian Labour Union, *Proceedings*, August 1874.

4. Ibid., from Canadian Labour Union, *Proceedings*, August 1877.

5. Eugene Forsey, "Insights into Labour History in Canada", *Relations Industrielles*, Vol. 20, No. 3, July 1965, pp. 445-465.

6. Logan, op. cit., p. 71.

7. Logan, op. cit., p. 73; Lipton, op. cit., p. 137.

8. Logan, op. cit., pp. 370-371.

9. Lipton, op cit., p. 146, from National Trades and Labour Congress of Canada, *Proceedings*, 1908, p. 10.

10. Ibid., p. 146.

11. Ibid., p. 151, from Trades and Labour Congress of Canada, *Proceedings*, 1911.

12. Ibid., p. 150, from Trades and Labour Congress of Canada, *Proceedings*, 1911, pp. 38-40.

13. Logan, op. cit., p. 356.

14. Lipton, op. cit., p. 178, from Samuel Gompers, *American Labor and the War* (New York, 1919), pp. 141-158.

15. Ibid., p. 170.

16. Ibid., p. 173, from Canada, Department of Labour, *Annual Report on Labour Organization in Canada*, 1917.

17. Logan, op. cit., pp. 303-306.

18. Lipton, op. cit., p. 177, from Trades and Labour Congress of Canada, *Proceedings*, 1917.

19. Ibid., p. 188, from B.C. Federation of Labour, *Proceedings*, 1919, pp. 28-36.

20. Logan, op. cit., p. 310.

21. Ibid.

22. Ibid., p. 209, from W. H. Crook, *The General Strike*, p. 522.

23. Ibid., from Canada, House of Commons, *Debates*, June 2, 1919.

24. Ibid., p. 211, from Canada, House of Commons, *Debates*, June 2, 1926.

25. Lipton, op. cit., p. 209, from *Western Labour News*, June 28, 1919.

26. Ibid., p. 210, from *The Gazette* (Montreal), June 16, 1919.

27. Ibid., p. 210, from *Western Labour News*, June 20, 1919; H. A. Robson, Royal Commission . . . General Strike . . . 1919, *Report*, p. 23; D. C. Masters, *The Winnipeg General Strike*, p. 102; *The Gazette*, August 1, 1919.

28. Logan, op. cit., p. 322.

29. Ibid., p. 141.

30. Lipton, op. cit., p. 231; Logan, op. cit., pp. 368-369.

31. Lipton, op. cit., p. 231.

32. Ibid.

33. Ibid.

34. Ibid., from Trades and Labour Congress, *Proceedings*, 1923.

35. Ibid., p. 232, from Trades and Labour Congress, *Proceedings*, 1924, p. 101.

36. Logan, op. cit., p. 342.

37. Ibid., p. 341.

38. *Ontario Report*, January-February 1975, pp. 19-20.

39. Logan, op. cit., p. 342; Irving Martin Abella, *Nationalism, Communism, and Canadian Labour* (Toronto: University of Toronto Press, 1973), p. 3. Unions affiliated with the WUL were instructed to join the TLC "to strengthen the trade union ranks and to lay a solid foundation for a broad united front movement against fascism and against another imperialist war". Communist Party of Canada, *Canada and the VII World Congress of the Communist International*, (Toronto, 1935), pp. 16-18.

40. Logan, op. cit., pp. 251-253 and 340-341; Walter D. Young, *The Anatomy of a Party: The National CCF, 1932-61* (Toronto: University of Toronto Press, 1969), p. 273; Abella, op. cit., pp. 5-22; Gad Horowitz, *Canadian Labour in Politics* (Toronto: University of Toronto Press, 1968), pp. 66-68, 85.

41. Abella, op. cit., p. 55.

42. Logan, op. cit., p. 82.

43. See Chapter 12.

44. Lipton, op. cit., p. 279, from *Trades and Labour Congress Journal*, March 1949, pp. 12-13.

45. Ibid.

46. Ibid.

CHAPTER 31
The Internationals: Seven Problems

For decades Canada occupied a relatively privileged place in the American economic empire. For most of the 20th century, Canadian workers have experienced one of the highest standards of living in the world. While this usually remained some twenty-five per cent lower than that of workers in the United States, it was high enough to cement the allegiance of most of the organized sections of the Canadian work force to the policies and practices of international business unionism. Until the late 1930s only skilled workers tended to be organized in both countries. The status and prestige of these conservative craft unions was founded on the large differences in pay between skilled craft unionists and unskilled, unorganized industrial workers.

During and after the Second World War, the labour movement in Canada underwent a substantial change with the organization of the mass industrial unions. With the unprecedented world-wide expansion of U.S. business between 1945 and the late 1960s, Canadian workers in both craft and industrial unions experienced a degree of affluence derived from Canada's special status in its relations with the United States.

In the early 1970s, as the American economy lapsed into a period of decline, Canadian prosperity and passivity were both being undermined. Short-term privileges began to disappear. Canadians generally, and Canadian workers in particular, responded to this situation as we have seen with a growing nationalism. For the younger, more militant members of the Canadian labour movement in particular, the call for Canadian unionism followed.

By 1975 American business unionism represented a declining force in Canada. Linked to the era of the American economy's rise to world ascendance, it had opposed Canadian nationalism in favour of continentalism and continued Canadian integration into the American economic domain. But Canadian workers were increasingly rejecting these practices and philosophy.

Summarizing the discussion of this book, the problems which Canadian workers have identified with international unionism as it is practiced by U.S. unions fall under seven headings:[1]

1. *Economic Factors*. American style business unionism lost a good deal of credibility in Canada during the early 1970s because it failed to deliver the goods.

In the 1950s and 1960s, Canadian workers found little fault with American control of their unions as the living standards they experienced improved during the period of U.S. expansion. Nevertheless, some of the American unions' bargaining practices which were imported into Canada, had a deleterious effect on the economic position of Canadian workers. The most important of these were the lengthening of union contracts and the avoidance or limitation of strikes.

Most Canadian leaders of the international unions accepted legislative restrictions on the right to strike during the life of a contract. In most countries workers had the right to strike on a number of issues, including grievances, during the life of a contract. In Canada, during the previous thirty years, there had been no serious challenge from the labour movement to these restrictions. In June 1975 when the Ontario legislature considered amendments to the provincial labour laws that would further restrict the right to strike, most top union leaders did not protest seriously. They were implicitly accepting one of the basic tenets of American business union philosophy — that there is an essential harmony of interests between workers and corporations so that strikes are basically harmful to all Canadians.

Long contracts are another way of avoiding strikes. The living standards of Canadian workers in the early seventies were seriously undermined because they had signed long-term agreements containing inadequate provisions for unexpectedly rapid increases in living costs. Yet the American head offices of unions like the Steelworkers and Paperworkers were calling for even longer ''no strike'' periods, and tying wages to increased productivity.

2. *Protectionism and Job Security*. The decline in the world-wide power of the American corporations gave rise to a new spirit of protectionism in the American labour movement in the late 1960s and the 1970s. Canada was already experiencing a shift of skilled jobs in manufacturing to the United States, particularly in the automobile industry. American labour's support of protectionist policies such as DISC and the Burke-Hartke Bill amounted to a threat to Canadian jobs.

Every time an American union leader advocated the return of production from U.S. branch plants abroad to the metropolitan United States, or called for his members to "Buy American" at an international union convention, he lost the allegiance of some Canadian members. In economic terms, American protectionism made sense for unions in the United States. But such protectionism showed the Canadian worker that he was really a foreigner in his own union.

3. *Politics and Canadian Sovereignty.* American business unionism has had two key tenets related to questions of politics and sovereignty. The first has been that labour must avoid any direct political action in its own right, restricting itself to short-run lobbying or support for one or another business party.

The consequences of this for Canadian workers have been manifold. On the broadest level, many Canadian members have heard their top union leaders advocating political philosophies that they themselves considered counter to the interests of labour. This was perhaps most pronounced in the hawkish support of international union leaders like Meany, Abel, and Fitzsimmons for the American war in Viet Nam.

The American leaders of international unions have been unstinting in their praise for American capitalism and the benefits they consider it offers for working people. This philosophy has been expressed economically in the signing of long no-strike agreements and tying wages to productivity. Politically, it had been expressed in the rejection of independent labour political action by U.S. unions.

In Canada, many American unions, notably some of the craft organizations, have followed this philosophy. Some international unions in Canada, particularly the steel and auto unions, have taken a different course through their support of the New Democratic Party since its inception. This was an outgrowth of Canadian labour's traditional support for independent political action. However, leaders of the international unions in Canada have generally used their positions of influence within the NDP to steer that party's policy away from such fundamental issues as Canadian nationalism — a nationalism which would attack not only the American corporations for which business unionism has such respect, but also control of Canadian unions by American unions.

4. *"Internationalism".* The "international solidarity of the working class" has been a traditional aspiration of the labour movement worldwide, dating back to the middle of the nineteenth century. It has been based on the idea that working people the world over should make common cause in their attempts to build a world liberated from the rule of big business and in which equality and humanism would be the guiding principles.

American business unionism, however, had applied the notion of labour internationalism in many cases to offer support abroad for U.S. foreign policy. American union leaders and their Canadian representatives have often used the label of internationalism to attack Canadian nationalism and the movement for a fully independent Canadian union movement.[2]

Their "internationalism" was summarized in the claim that "multi-national unions are required to deal with multinational corporations". But American unions are not international unions at all — they exist in only two countries, the United States and Canada, and they are controlled to a greater or lesser extent by their U.S. head offices. Second, the philosophy of these unions has been such that they did not in any case provide a real alternative to the power of the multinational corporations. Finally, the experience of the 1970s has shown that in an economic crunch American unions will act in the interests of their American membership before their Canadian membership. This was demonstrated in strike situations like that of the rubber workers, Douglas or United Aircraft and more generally in the U.S. unions' protectionist movement.

Rejecting this version of the idea of internationalism of American business unions has not meant that Canadian workers reject international labour solidarity. On the contrary, in its original meaning internationalism was as necessary in the mid-seventies as it had ever been. In practice, even with the limitations of American union control in Canada, it has been the CLC and not the AFL-CIO which is affiliated to a world trade union body, the ICFTU. Canadian labour's ability to contribute to world-wide union solidarity within the ICFTU and in world industrial federations of metal and chemical workers or miners has been restricted, not assisted, by U.S. union domination of Canada's unions. This suggests that independent unions can be more truly internationalist than subordinate branch organizations.

True internationalism would seem to require that the labour movement of every country be strong and independent; that each has a sovereign power to determine for itself the part it will play in building a better world for working people. Ironically, Canadian workers cannot participate fully in working-class internationalism until they are freed from the "internationals".

5. *Structure, jurisdiction, and finances.* Apart from these broad philosophical and policy constraints on the ability of Canadian workers to bargain in their own interests and develop their political role, there have been a number of structural limitations that have followed from American unionism in Canada. These include lack of control over finances, restrictions on the ability of unions in Canada to merge, and the import of jurisdictional disputes from the United States into Canada. The subordinate role of Canada in international labour organizations, the issue of rights over union property in Canada, and the imposition of trusteeships have also been important.

Several of these problems occur simultaneously in the issue of mergers and proposals for a more rational union structure in Canada. In 1973 there were more than forty American unions with Canadian memberships under five thousand — some had fewer than one thousand members.[3] In place of this multiplicity of small, and consequently weak, organizations, there could have been a structure of fifteen to thirty organizations so that no union in Canada had fewer than 50,000 members. In 1975 there were serious obstacles to such a rational union structure in Canada.

In 1970 CLC secretary-treasurer William Dodge told an international union convention that mergers of unions in Canada should be encouraged:

> What concerns us is that very few of these internationals with small Canadian memberships are able to maintain the kinds of operations Canadian union members are insisting upon more and more — education programmes, research facilities, social action programmes and publications — all designed to operate within the framework of Canadian economic and social trends.[4]

The problem was that the Canadian sections of the internationals were prevented from merging unless a similar merger was taking place in the United States. Ed Finn of the CBRT has suggested that a campaign for mergers in Canada could only gain impetus if it was supported by the top Canadian leadership in the internationals.[5] Such support was not likely to be forthcoming, he pointed out, because most of the officials in question were appointed by their international presidents. They were expected to maintain "peace in the colonies," he wrote, and not to "stir up the natives". Finn noted, in addition, that were Canadian union independence to be achieved — partly through a series of mergers in Canada — these officials would have to stand for direct election by their Canadian members.

Some supporters of the internationals have rejected the argument that Canadian labour's organization is fragmented because of the multiplicity of American unions with small Canadian memberships. They have argued that the American affiliates are no more splintered than the all-Canadian unions. This claim deserves examination.

In 1973 there were some 96 international and 93 national unions in Canada. Nine of the national unions were in the CNTU, with a membership of 163,928. Of the remaining 84 Canadian unions, 60 were very small independent bodies, many of them having only one local with perhaps a few hundred members.[6] Some of these were affiliated to the CCU. They were out of the mainstream of labour because they felt they could find no satisfactory independent Canadian union in which to belong. Their existence, therefore, was itself a consequence of international unionism in Canada.

The large Canadian unions affiliated to the CLC included provincial public employees' organizations, CUPE, PSAC, CBRT and the two postal unions. Between them, they represented over 500,000 workers in 1975.[7] CUPE alone had over 200,000 members in 1975, and PSAC had more than 150,000. These unions were themselves the products of mergers between smaller national unions. The national union of provincial public employees, expected to be organized in 1976, was to have well over 100,000 members.

Canadian unions faced the problem that, if they were affiliated to the
CLC, they were not permitted to organize unorganized workers in industries where American unions had jurisdiction. Ed Finn pointed out
that his union, the CBRT, had had to refuse membership to workers within
the jurisdiction of American unions, as laid out by the CLC.[8]

Aside from mergers and jurisdictional problems, there had been a
great deal of debate about the availability of international funds to
Canadian locals. In the 1970s some U.S.-based unions were investing all
of their Canadian revenues in Canada. In 1970 their Canadian assets
amounted to almost $100 million.[9] With few exceptions, however, these
funds were administered from the U.S. head office. Union locals which
required funds for other than routine pre-arranged expenses had to seek
special authorization from their international boards.

Financial control by American head office has had serious implications for the success of Canadian strikes. Canadian unions could usually
respond more quickly than the internationals to requests for financial
support.[10]

Another aspect of the financial issue is the recurring question of
whether international unions receive more money in the form of dues
than they spend on benefits and support in Canada. Ed Finn summarized
the arguments pointedly in 1970:

> ... American unions, in the aggregate, are now taking considerably
> more out of this country in dues than they are putting back. In 1967, 35
> million dollars in Canadian members' per capita dues were paid to
> U.S. headquarters, while the internationals' expenditures in Canada
> for salaries, strike benefits, and pension and welfare payments
> amounted to 18 million dollars. In the six years, 1962 to 1967, for
> which records have been kept, the internationals were reported to
> have collected $166.3 million in Canada while pumping back $98.3
> million. Granted, there are other expenses not recorded in the
> COLURA [sic] reports that some internationals incur in this country:
> the costs of education and research services, for example, and the
> publication of separate Canadian journals. But, with the exception of
> the large industrial unions, few internationals provide extensive ser-
> vices of this kind to their Canadian members. [For] their total expen-
> ditures for such purposes ... in 1967 ... [a] most liberal estimate
> would be about seven million dollars. So it can safely be assumed that
> the internationals collectively made a "profit" that year of at least
> ten million dollars on their Canadian operations, and over the six-year
> span approximately forty-five million dollars.[11]

John Crispo, professor of economics and management studies at the
University of Toronto, had a business-like comment on the net outflow
of Canadian unionists' dues to the United States. The internationals
"could not immediately be accused of engaging in a kind of profiteer-
ing," he wrote, "At least, an economist would not take that view."
Crispo argued that international unions have a right to a fair return on
their past investment, and that the return had to be comparatively large

to compensate for the risks involved.[12] Crispo's argument may have made good economic sense in the context of business unionism. But it had nothing to do with the interests of Canadian union members. What the figures do show is that if the internationals could make a net benefit of ten million dollars back in 1967, the Canadian labour movement overall has had the potential to be financially self-supporting. In 1975, with a membership of three million (if teachers and all organized public employee were included), the financial base for Canada's unions was powerful.

Another structural problem has been the existence of trades councils such as the Maritime Trades Department, and councils of buildings trades unions. These are AFL-CIO bodies which bring together craft unions in a given industry for common bargaining and policy-making. The Canadian branches of the international crafts unions were directly chartered to these trades organizations without going through the CLC. In the past, these trades departments had included in Canada unions that had been expelled from the CLC, such as the Teamsters and the SIU.

The building trades councils which were chartered directly by the AFL-CIO restricted their membership to American unions, refusing to admit any purely Canadian organizations. This has given rise to serious organizational and jurisdictional problems, particularly in Quebec where there had been fierce struggles between AFL-CIO and CNTU construction unions. In many cities, contractors had been forced by the internationals to employ only members of American unions.

Trucks driven by members of the CBRT had often been harassed by American construction unions when they attempted to make deliveries to building sites. The craft unions insisted that all such deliveries be made by members of the Teamsters union. The Teamsters is not affiliated either to the AFL-CIO or to the CLC — but it is an American union. In several cases the CBRT which is affiliated to the CLC had been forced to resort to court injunctions against the craft union boycott in order to protect its members' jobs, after appeals to the CLC and provincial federations had proven futile.[13]

Other structural problems have been related to the international constitutions which gave the American head offices the right to approve or disapprove of any contract, and to exercise their power by taking over control of a local through trusteeship. Many American head offices had vetoed agreements arrived at by their Canadian members or had insisted that locals accept settlements which the membership had rejected.

Most international union headquarters reserved the right to approve strike actions by their locals as an extension of their power over strike funds. If Canadian workers went on strike without the permission of the top union leadership in the United States, they might have found themselves without financial support; if they refused to settle an approved strike, they might have had their strike pay cut off.

International union constitutions typically grant the president or the

executive board control over strike pay, pensions, welfare benefits,
jurisdiction over union agreements, and the right to hold union property
and other assets through the imposition of a trusteeship. In 1967 twenty-
six internationals put twenty-six of their Canadian locals under trusteeships. In addition, the international constitution provided for the U.S.
headquarters to establish total control over the Canadian sections. This
right has been upheld in Canadian courts when it has been challenged.
The decision of the courts had usually been that a local of an American-
based union was not a separate legal entity. American unions had used
their right to seize local property and funds as a way of discouraging
break-aways by Canadian locals.[14]

6. *Organizing the Unorganized.* One of the most telling criticisms of the
international unions in Canada during the past two decades has been
their failure to organize the millions of unorganized workers in their own
jurisdictions, particularly in some of the manufacturing and service
industries. Growth of Canadian unions, most notably in the public sector, has been very rapid in the past decade, while there has been no such
growth of American unions in the industrial or private service sectors.[15]
The AFL-CIO's business union attitude that it didn't really matter that
three-quarters of American workers remained unorganized seemed to
have influenced Canadian leaders of the internationals in their laissez-
faire approach to non-unionized workers. This could be judged by their
performance.

The larger percentage of unionization in Canada compared to the
United States which became marked in the late 1960s was mainly accounted for by the growth of independent Canadian unions.[16] The failure
of the international unions to do relatively better in Canada than in the
United States, when the climate for union organization had been proven
to be more favourable in Canada, argues against their ability to serve the
needs of unorganized Canadian workers in the industrial and private
service sectors.

The vast potential in a concerted nation-wide drive in Canada to
organize the unorganized in thousands of small and medium-sized
manufacturing shops, retail stores, garages and auto sales outlets, service businesses, such as hotels, restaurants and cleaning operations, as
well as in the large and medium-sized financial institutions, like banks,
insurance and trust companies is shown by the recent spontaneous
moves of nurses, clerical and white collar workers, university professors, social workers, librarians, and engineers into the union movement.

The possibility of adding two million unionists to Canadian labour's
ranks within a decade — to a total of five million — would likely go
unrealized if it depended on the internationals.

The million-dollar drive to organize the unorganized in manufacturing
industries announced in 1973 by the CLC, and supported by the major
industrial unions when they were fearful of the inroads of Canadian
unions into their jurisdictions, died without a clear explanation.[17]

The inherent weakness of the CLC as a Canadian union central was revealed in its inability to act effectively in its own right to carry out a nation-wide drive to organize workers in industrial union jurisdictions because such decisions were ultimately dependent on the treasuries of the large international unions. The CLC was able to act strongly against CUPE's decision to embrace provincial employees because it was dealing with jurisdictions of Canadian unions; it has never shown the same clout in the area of organizing and merging industrial workers.

7. *Independence*. This chapter has dealt with some of the reasons why Canadian workers were questioning their affiliations to American unions in the 1970s. They amount to the *negative* argument for fully independent Canadian unionism: the argument against continuing American head-office control. The next chapter considers the *positive* side of the argument, by discussing the new possibilities that are opened up by the prospect of an all-Canadian labour movement. Before this, however, there is at least one other important factor in the negative argument.

Canada is the only country in the world without its own national labour movement. Even if the international unions in Canada could meet all the criticisms levelled against them the question remains as to why Canada should be in this unique position. There appears to be no overriding benefit for Canadian workers in belonging to American unions sufficient to overcome the natural aspiration for independence.

In fact, the most compelling rationale for the continued existence of international unions in Canada is that they are already here. For many years, they have had the allegiance of Canadian workers. In the past, the pressures to transform the Canadian sections of the internationals into independent national unions have not been sufficiently strong or long-lasting to become widely successful. The result has been typically passive acceptance, and occasionally local break-aways. In the first half of the 1970s, however, the pressures intensified. For the first time since the turn of the century, a fully independent Canadian union movement had become possible: a possibility which was moving toward realization because it was increasingly an economic, social, political, and national necessity.

---

1. General discussions of international unions are found in: Ed Finn, "The Struggle for Canadian Labour Autonomy", *Labour Gazette*, November 1970; John Crispo, *International Unionism: A Study in Canadian-American Relations* (Toronto: McGraw-Hill, 1967); Abraham Rotstein, Gary Lax, eds., *Getting it Back* (Toronto and Vancouver: Clarke, Irwin and Company, 1974) Chapter 10; Mel Watkins, "The Trade Union Movement in Canada", in R. M. Laxer, *(Canada) Ltd*. (Toronto: McClelland & Stewart, 1973), p. 178.

2. Discussed in Chapter 13.

3. Labour Canada, *Labour Organizations in Canada*, 1973 (Ottawa: Information Canada, 1974), p. xxviii.

4. Finn, op. cit., p. 771.

5. Ibid.

6. Labour Canada, op. cit., Table 3, p. xxvii.

7. Calculated from Labour Canada, op. cit., Table 3, p. xxvii.

8. Finn, op. cit., p. 772.

9. Ibid., p. 773.

10. Ibid. For instance, when the postal workers were trying to break through federal government wage ceilings in their 1970 strike, they sent out a call for support from other unions. Canadian unions like the CBRT, which had direct control over their own funds, were able to respond immediately. By contrast, response from the Canadian sections of internationals was slow. The Canadian officers sent the postal workers' appeal to their locals, asking them to give support from their limited treasuries, and then began the tedious process of appealing to their American head officers.

11. Ibid., p. 770.

12. Crispo, op. cit., p. 277.

13. Finn, op. cit., p. 773.

14. Ibid., p. 774.

15. International unions in Canada showed an increase in membership of 2.2 per cent from 1972-73 while national unions showed a growth rate of 23.1 per cent in the same period. (Labour Canada, op. cit., p.xii.)

16. The following table shows union members as a percentage of non-agricultural workers in the U.S. and Canada.

	United States	Canada
1965	28.4	29.7
1969	27.1	32.5
1970	27.5	33.6
1971	27.2	33.3
1972	26.7	34.4
1973		36.3

Source: U.S. Bureau of Labor Statistics, *Handbook of Labor Statistics*, 1974, p. 366; Labour Canada, op. cit., p. xxiv.

17. Discussed in Chapter 13.

CHAPTER 32
New Options for Canadian Labour

In the mid-1970s Canadian labour was moving steadily toward national unionism and away from dominance by the international unions of Canada's labour movement. This book has described the growth of this movement among Canadian unionists. Identifying the problems of the international union structure or pointing to this trend, is not, however, to downgrade the absolutely crucial role which these unions have played in the defence of the rights of working people in Canada. Businesses in Canada, whether American- or Canadian-owned, have rarely welcomed any bona fide unions into their operations, and the organizing and continued existence of Canada's unions have been of vital importance to Canadian workers.

The fact asserted in this book that Canadian unionism appears to be moving toward ascendancy in Canada in no way denies the value of the energies and sacrifices of tens of thousands of Canadian activists who built the internationals in Canada, often against determined opposition from corporate management and from their allies in government. Accounts of the big breakthroughs of industrial unions in the 1930s and 1940s deserve a proud place in Canada's social history. The very existence of international unions in most of the large industrial enterprises in Canada and the struggles in which these unionists were involved during the past four decades are a tribute to the Canadian union activists who first linked up with those union organizations which seemed most viable in their context. In most cases of industrial union organization in Canada, these were international unions.

To try, in 1975, to impose the wisdom of hindsight on Canadian labour's past would be to replace analysis with moralizing. It would produce, too, a blindness to the contemporary tenacity with which older Canadian workers have defended international unionism, while fully aware of its shortcomings. Whenever Canadian workers have faced what they believed to be a choice between an American-based union and no union, their decision was seldom in doubt.

This book has not presented a detailed historical account of the evolution and growth of unions in Canada for that does not belong in what is primarily a contemporary account of Canada's unions. The few specific historical chapters and references have been mainly confined to tracing the continuity in the movement for Canadian unionism during those many decades when the internationals were in the ascendancy. However, a broad historical perspective helps to explain the change from the period when American-based unions assumed control of Canada's labour movement to the 1970s when the internationals were beginning to lose that control. What is asserted in this book about the future of Canadian unionism arises from an examination of the changing historical relations between Canada and the United States, and recent changes in the economic and political position of the United States.

The recent growth of Canadian unionism has not been attributable to any single factor. The reasons summarized in the last chapter provide part of the story but additional factors have influenced the new labour militancy and national self-confidence. They include the necessity to respond to losses in purchasing power and substantial unemployment in the wake of the inflation and recession of the 1970s. An important factor, too, has been the rise of nationalist sentiments in Canada. All of these factors, in combination, have created a new set of options for Canadian labour — options which had already begun to be partially realized by 1975 and which appear to lead to an all-Canadian labour movement by 1985.

Ten or even five years earlier such a prediction might have seemed fanciful, but in 1975 it was little more than an optimistic but plausible projection of present trends. In this concluding chapter, the new options which Canadian labour has created for itself are discussed in the context of such a possibility.

The unions of public workers, overwhelmingly Canadian organizations, that have come to include provincial public employee associations, teachers' and nurses' federations, have taken on an entirely new role in the Canadian labour movement.

Joe Morris, president of the CLC, recognized the new role of the public sector workers. "With this influx of thousands upon thousands of employees from the public sector into the organized labour movement," Morris told the 1975 NDP Convention, "there may be a new emphasis placed on established policies but the strength and wisdom which these groups bring to organized labour will help us meet the challenges which lie ahead."[1]

The strategy and style of operation of these Canadian unions; their increasingly dynamic memberships and activists who have tended, on

the whole, to be younger and more flexible than those in the internationals; their pressure for a common front and other forms of labour
solidarity[2]; their dramatic successes in negotiations and confrontations
— all of these factors created a movement that has been infectious.

Between 1972 and 1975 this took the form of an unprecedented
social-political unionism marked by flexible strategies and new alliances.
The miniature — and not so miniature — 24-hour general strike was
developed. The Common Front strike of April 1972 was followed by
broadly-based strikes in Quebec in the following month, by the teachers'
walk-out in Ontario in December 1973, and by the Quebec one-day strike
in May 1975, protesting the Bourassa government's trusteeships over
construction unions and demanding an end to the 16-month strike at
United Aircraft, to name a few. Labour was beginning to act as a united
economic and political force, rejecting the business unionist notion that
each group of workers must basically bargain for itself or limit its
legislative activities to professional lobbying.

The Common Front model of the first half of the 1970s had the
potential to spread beyond Quebec and Ontario public employees,
where it began, to embrace all sections of organized labour.

The growth of the fully-Canadian unions, particularly those in the
public sector, together with the development of new national unions
such as the Paperworkers, reopened the debate over international
versus Canadian unions. The transformation of the Canadian sections of
international unions into fully independent national unions became a
legitimate topic of discussion within the councils of the entire union
movement, in spite of the resistance of some Canadian leaders of American unions. Increasingly the question became not *whether* such a transformation should take place, but *when* and *how*.

The issue became particularly meaningful to unionists in the internationals in the mid-1970s because the choice for them was no longer
between individual break-aways versus remaining in the U.S.-based
unions, but between retaining the status quo and deciding to opt for
greater Canadian autonomy and even full independence as a Canada-
wide organization.

For top Canadian leaders in international unions, the next five or ten
years promise to be a period of agonizing reappraisal. They will be
asking themselves whether they should maintain their resistance to
independent Canadian unionism in the face of mounting opposition to
the internationals, or provide the leadership that would take their
memberships into the ranks of an all-Canadian labour movement.

In important respects, the paper workers have paved the way. But the
tide will probably not turn in a definitive way until a major industrial
union in the manufacturing heart-land of Ontario takes a similar step.
Should a union leader like Dennis McDermott move in that direction,
leaders of smaller industrial internationals could not long continue to

look to Washington, Pittsburgh, Detroit, Chicago or Minneapolis for direction. Even the USWA, the largest and most influential of the internationals in Canada, could not long withstand its rank and file's opposition to remaining part of the American union.

Among the pressures for severance from the internationals, the demand for mergers of unions in Canada could probably play an important part and would thus strengthen the structure of the labour movement in Canada. The initial discussion for merging the URW and OCAW, later abandoned because of rivalries between the top American leaders, could have established a powerful industrial union in the chemicals industry, particularly if it had incorporated the International Chemical Workers' Union as well. Were the Paperworkers to join with all chemical workers or all wood industry workers, the result would in either case be a Canadian union numbering roughly 100,000 members.

The newly autonomous BRAC could work with the CBRT to realize the century-old dream of a single all-Canadian union on the railways — and then move beyond this to form a single Canadian transport union incorporating all transportation workers on air, land and sea. A new Canadian metal workers union, bringing together steel, auto, aircraft, electrical products and other metal workers now scattered in some two dozen different organizations could have perhaps half a million members — and the organizational power and commitment to undertake the unionization of the hundreds of small, as yet unorganized shops.

In the field of education, an industrial union of some 400,000 members in English Canada could result from the organization of all elementary, secondary, college and university teachers, together with the growing number of pre-school and nursery teachers and such other workers in the educational field as secretaries, librarians and maintenance staff. Similarly, a huge health-care union could be built, with nurses, technicians, maintenance staff and other hospital and medical workers.

The scope of Canadian union development was promising in 1975. The emergence of such powerful all-Canadian unions would mean the availability of a large financial base to support their own activities, those of fellow unionists, and those of unorganized workers in other fields in furthering a labour programme of economic and political action.

Canadian Labour Congress conventions would provide an important barometer of change. The alignment and polarization of forces which began to emerge in the CLC in 1974 at Vancouver would likely recur in the 1976, 1978 and 1980 conventions, especially as the relative size of the delegations from all-Canadian unions increased. If the national union delegates and their supporters in international unions were to develop a clear programme and strategy and a leadership committed to carrying it out, they might well force the pace of change within the CLC. The real changes that were required to transform the internationals could not occur mainly within the Congress since the CLC tended more to reflect than to initiate developments at the shop and office level. But it would be a focal point for the attempt by nationalists in the union movement to appeal to the rank and file of international unions to speed the process toward militant Canadian unionism within their own organizations.

The time-table for a cordial break with international unionism within the CLC appeared to be growing short. In large part the next three or four biennial conventions would reveal the degree to which a capable and determined Canadian union leadership had emerged in response to the ultimately irresistable force of membership pressure. But they would reveal, as well, the extent to which Canadian officers of the internationals were determined either to resist or to acknowledge that pressure.

Should developments in the CLC move too slowly, the arrangement which some CUPE leaders had considered in 1973 might be revived. This would amount to a new grouping of all independent Canadian unions in a labour central separate from the CLC. The more Canadian leaders in the internationals attempt to thwart the growth of Canadian unions, to forestall Canadian mergers outside international constitutions, or to block the nationalist demands of their own rank and file, the more likely such a development would become.

Some international locals affiliated to the Quebec Federation of Labour would perhaps be interested in such an all-Canadian centre. It might prove attractive, as well, to the new teachers' and nurses' organizations. With a membership of more than a million trade unionists, a national centre would provide a formidable rival to the American unions in Canada. Its existence would be a further spur to Canadian members of the internationals to move toward independent national unionism with a view to the reunification of all Canadian union members in a single central organization, free from any American control.

How likely such a development might be is difficult to assess since the range of possibilities within the CLC is still very large. From the point of view of labour's ultimate potential to become the major force for Canadian independence and broad social change, the course of staying within a single house of labour appeared to be the winning strategy. But this could be thwarted by an inflexible top leadership in the Canadian sections of the internationals.

A key to Canadian labour's development would be the rank and file coming into its own. In 1972, L.D. Hanley — then of Local 601, Pulp, Sulphite and Paper Mill Workers in St. John, New Brunswick — wrote:

> The labour movement as I understand it, originated to create a life worth living as a man, not as a servant or serf to an industry. Was it not meant to be a step or even a path to human dignity and rights? . . . We have created in our labour movement a highly centralized authoritarian administration: the same type of administration that industry and even government of today have perfected. We have created a

bureaucracy with its endless stream of red tape and consistent shirking of independent decision-making until the top of the bureaucratic ladder has been reached. . . . It will take a united effort to create a situation where man as an individual is the back-bone of the union as a whole.[3]

As Canadian unionists, especially the younger activists and stewards, apply mounting pressure for their goal of independent national unions, they will come into conflict with some of the entrenched bureaucracy Hanley criticized. Thus the movement for national unions would become a movement for greater union democracy and rank and file control as well. Already at the 1974 CLC Convention the tension between rank and file and union leadership on these questions was in evidence.

The prospect of a revitalized and much more effective reform movement developing before the 1976 or 1978 CLC Conventions rested on the newly-gained strength and self-confidence of the fully Canadian unions. The beginning for such a reform movement would be to broaden the terms of the 1970 and 1974 autonomy guidelines. Two of the policy recommendations by the reform leadership in 1974 — full Canadian control of union finances collected in Canada, and the right to merger in Canada regardless of events in the United States — would no doubt head the list of demands for compulsory guidelines.

Beyond this, it was likely that the far-reaching "autonomy" developments in BRAC and NABET would act as a goad to the other internationals which had traditionally boasted about the degree of autonomy enjoyed by their Canadian members. One area for experimentation in the direction of much greater autonomy would be to constitute separate Canadian conventions of international unions, replacing less influential Canadian section meetings such as the USWA's Canadian Policy Conference or the UAW's Canadian District Council. The establishment of Canadian presidents, vice-presidents and other executive officers, elected by a Canadian convention, would be another major step toward fuller autonomy, leading toward eventual independence.

Amendments to international constitutions, giving the Canadian sections the right to secede if they so decided by national referendum or convention, would probably be demanded. Such amendments, testing the waters of much fuller Canadian autonomy, would have to include the right of the Canadian membership to all international property in Canada, together with a pro-rata share of international treasuries and special funds. The passage of such constitutional amendments with a degree of cordiality such as that shown by the UPIU, NABET, UCWA or BRAC would obviate the need for the Canadian government to pass special legislation guaranteeing Canadian workers the right to opt for Canadian unions, without loss of union property, pensions or bargaining rights.

Reform movements in 1976, 1978, or 1980, however, would require a different quality of leadership than that displayed by the Canadian union

group in 1974. They would required a broadly-based, hard-headed programme, clearly committed to the goal of a fully-Canadian labour
movement, even if they compromised on the speed of its realization.
They would require leaders who are tough, articulate and able to carry
with them not only their own membership but also activists within
international unions. As the Vancouver convention showed, there were
many within the American unions who were looking for leaders with the
ability and imagination to help them pilot their way through the stormy
waters of entrenched business unionism.

Beyond the structure of the unions and their economic programmes,
the new developments in labour militancy and nationalism had opened
up the prospect of new forms of labour political action, including the
potential transformation of the New Democratic Party into a left-
nationalist party.

At the beginning of the 1970s, the first rumblings of change in the
Canadian union movement held out little hope that the transformation of
the NDP into a left-nationalist party would be possible. Many Canadians
had begun to look elsewhere for a political or cultural expression of their
developing nationalism. They had formed organizations such as the
Committee for an Independent Canada and the Waffle, or movements for
Canadian studies and Canadian school curricula and textbooks. They
engaged in actions to cut *Time* and *Reader's Digest* down to size, to halt
the Mackenzie Valley and James Bay resource projects, to support
Native Peoples and environmentalists in their resistance against the
American resource companies, or to restrict the flood of American
professors in Canadian universities. And, of course, many of them were
working to develop Canadian unionism.

These Canadian nationalists would not lightly give up these organizations and movements to place their trust in an unreformed NDP. But they
might begin to look at that possibility, as many had in the days of the
nationalist debate in the party between 1969 and 1972. The end of the era
of David Lewis as the dominant figure in the CCF-NDP could mark a new
chapter for the party. The Lewis leadership, in contrast to that of
Tommy Douglas, had accented the role of the international unions in the
party and moved the NDP away from some of the earlier nationalist tone
of the Douglas years. Even after he resigned the leadership of the NDP,
Douglas continued to reflect the nationalist sentiment in the party. By
mid-1975 the potential role of the new forces of Canadian unionism
within the NDP was hard to estimate, at least in the short run. But it
seemed likely that as its power grew, the Canadian union movement
would begin to tip the scales toward such policies as public ownership of
energy and resource industries and a Canadian auto industry — the very
policies that had been anathema to the NDP and the international union
leadership during the early 1970s.

The new labour and popular consensus in favour of public ownership, and the debate over a new industrial strategy for Canada that such a consensus implied meant that new dialogues would open between nationalists outside the NDP and those in the party who saw the issue of Canadian economic and cultural independence as central to Canadian politics.

Whether the NDP would rise to the occasion, or continue in the tradition of anti-nationalism and pro-continentalism, would depend largely on the pace of events in Canada's political economy. But it would depend as well on the hardihood and strategic sense of those who wished the NDP to play a nationalist role.

Other nationalists would no doubt consider alternatives to the NDP since the failure of existing political institutions to serve the Canadian interest would not be allowed to go unchallenged. Either the NDP would become a broadly-based left-nationalist party, or some other organization would arise to fill that void in the Canadian political spectrum.

In July 1975, Mel Hurtig, former national president of the Committee for an Independent Canada, after outlining the failure of all three major political parties to defend Canada's interests from American control, proposed the formation of a Canadian nationalist party. In asking his readers to suggest an alternative to his proposal he might have been hoping that some NDP members or supporters, unionists or non-unionists, would indicate how the NDP could still become the major political vehicle for Canadian nationalism.[4]

In the meantime, the key to Canada's future rests more with working people in general and organized labour in particular than with any other section of the population. As Canadian labour leaders and activists become increasingly conscious of that fact, they are likely to raise their sights so that labour's immediate economic demands are linked to a broader social programme. This could include such objectives as public ownership of oil and other resource industries to serve the needs not only of organized labour but of all working Canadians. It would include proposals for an alternative industrial strategy to increase processing and manufacturing in Canada, to provide more skilled and research jobs for Canadians, to meet their individual needs, but also to serve Canada's economic and social well-being. It would feature higher quality education and health care, to meet the needs of teachers and hospital workers, but more importantly the interests of all Canadians. It would include a programme for greater cultural and sport opportunities for Canadians to meet the needs of Canadian writers, artists, athletes and broadcasters, but even more, to serve Canada's future.

Labour's social programme would continue to be labelled "excessive" and "unreasonable" by the business organizations and press, because labour's ultimate goals are far-reaching. In July 1975 Joe Morris warned that labour would "become the target, for the cry has gone out for wage controls; curtail the right to strike; impose compulsory arbitration; jail the labour leaders". He explained that "the reason ... is that trade unions are highly visible; they are vulnerable and they operate in a liberal milieu which has been opposed to their growth and formation".[5]

By July 1975 federal government spokesmen were warning Canadian labour against the dire consequences of high wage demands. Some of the business press were urging wage (and price) controls. Trade Minister Gillespie advised unions in Canada to follow the example of organized labour in the United States, West Germany and Japan and their policy of making moderate demands.

In his budget speech of June 1975 Turner said: "As the United States economy begins to pull out of its present deep recession, . . . it is likely to experience a much greater improvement in productivity than our country. Under those circumstances, the gap between our unit labour costs and those in the United States will progressively widen and our competitive position progressively deteriorate."[6]

Labour, according to these views, was to take the brunt of the battle against inflation and bear responsibility if the Canadian economy was weakened by an export-import imbalance with the United States. Apart from the fact that these same spokesmen never objected to the record profits of corporations in 1973 and 1974, based on the inflationary prices they imposed on the public and on products for export, Canadian business and government spokesmen were continuing to assume that Canada would remain in a position of dependency and act primarily as a resource base for the United States. They ignored the possibility of an alternative economic strategy for Canada, with an accent on manufacturing key products at home, such as auto parts and machinery, thereby reducing dependency on exports of raw materials, and imports of finished goods from the United States. A home market in which most of currently imported finished goods were produced in Canada would make the factor of foreign competition less important. Even more crucial, such an economic strategy would reduce unemployment, extend the economic base for the service sector, and tend to increase incomes because of the higher skill component in secondary manufacturing and the service sectors.

Most references to the high costs of labour ignored the cost to the national economy of having over 750,000 unemployed — who could be contributing to the nation's production if Canada had a more developed industrial economy.

Such an alternative outlined briefly, for example, in the statements of the UAW (1975), of the Brantford teachers (1974) and of the B.C. Federation of Labour (1971),[7] exposed the precarious nature of the dependent economy which has resulted from the sale of the country's resources to the United States and other industrialized nations. These statements carried the implication that a new social-political grouping would have to take over Canada's leadership before there could be a turnabout in the country's economic prospects, away from a dangerous reliance on the sale of shrinking resources to the United States.

The business partners of the United States in Canada do not relish the prospect of their replacement in the country's leadership by people who are truly loyal to their country. They abhor the thought that working Canadians would determine the economic, cultural and political sovereignty of their society. They would cry "unreasonable" and "illegal" when labour presses for an ever-widening set of goals, hitherto the prerogative of corporate management and the élite.

In breaking out of the confines of anti-labour legalisms and entering the liberating arena of social legitimacy, much of organized labour has already experienced the zest of expanding expectations. It has begun to raise its sights to the realization that labour's potential in the life of the nation knows no bounds, except those imposed by its own hesitation or unwillingness to win the leadership in Canada.

The year 1986 will mark the centennial of the founding of the Trades and Labour Congress of Canada, the union central which, more than any other, has reflected the contest for supremacy between international and national unions over the years. That anniversary could be observed by the existence of an all-Canadian union movement of some five million members. Such a movement, committed to freeing Canada from American corporate control, wedded to Canadian labour's traditional humanism and devoted to the liberation of women, Native Peoples, immigrants, and all working Canadians, could be the base for a democratic nationalist political party which could lead Canada to a new social order.

In 1975 Canadian labour was in the unprecedented position of being able to combine its limited economic objectives with unlimited opportunities to prove that labour's future is the future of the country — to champion the cause of the millions of poorly paid, unorganized Canadians, to present its own economic and social goals within a broad national economic strategy for Canada, to serve the national interest first and by that token meet the needs of Canada's working people.

When organized labour speaks for the interests of the eighty per cent of Canadians who produce Canada's wealth but who are employed by a small corporate group that determines their daily fate, it speaks for Canada. When labour speaks out against U.S. dominance of the cultural and educational life of the country, it speaks for Canada. To speak for Canada, and for all who are not part of its corporate élite is to break out of the narrow confines of business unionism and range on the broad plateau of national, social and economic concerns of the overwhelming majority of Canadians. No other existing social institution can do that in Canada. No other force can appeal to the nationalism of Canadians so powerfully as Canada's most dynamic and growing institution — the union movement.

1. *Address to the Eighth Convention of the Federal New Democratic Party*, Joe Morris, president, CLC, Winnipeg, Manitoba, July 1975, p. 6.

2. For example, in *The Globe and Mail*, November 21, 1974, it was reported that representatives of Ontario teachers, civil servants, transit, OFL, CUPE, and other public employee organizations agreed to draft a bill of bargaining rights for all public sector workers.

3. *Canadian Pulp and Paper Worker Journal*, March 1972, Vol. 10, No. 1, p. 2.

4. *The Toronto Star*, July 1, 1975.

5. *Address to the Eighth Convention of the Federal New Democratic Party*, Joe Morris, president, CLC, Winnipeg, Manitoba, July 1975, p. 7.

6. Canada, House of Commons, *Debates*, June 23, 1975, p. 7023.

7. See Chapters 4, 23, and 9 respectively.

Postscript

As this book went to press in November 1975, one month after the introduction of the federal government's incomes control program, Canada's unions entered a new phase in their recently-evolved militance. In October-November 1975, organized labour challenged the wage restraint policies of federal and provincial governments with the threat of Canada-wide defiance. This stand reinforced the emerging pattern of a new Canadian unionism which differed substantially from the business union philosophy of international headquarters in the United States.

As Prime Minister Trudeau travelled across Canada to sell the government's decision to "kill this kind of expectation" among working Canadians for higher incomes, labour pointed to the absence of real restraints on prices and corporate income in the government's plan. The CLC and Quebec's national unions argued that the wage restraint policy had made labour the scapegoat and that governments were acting as protectors of the corporations.

Labour's initial response to Trudeau's economic arguments tended to be defensive since most unions seemed to accept or tolerate the federal government's assumption that Canada was destined to remain primarily a resource-based economy. Trudeau had argued that Canadians must "live within their means", that the economic "pie" had not been expanding to allow for increases in real income for most Canadians. Labour countered by demanding that the existing national product should be redistributed more equitably.

In the early stages of this national debate labour did not seriously propose the alternative of expanding Canada's gross national product through an independent Canadian industrial strategy aimed at increasing manufactured goods in Canada and reducing dependency on imports. This would accomplish at least two objectives. It would reduce the effect of inflation due to high costs of imported goods. More important, it would drastically reduce unemployment by creating jobs in manufacturing. It could eliminate Canada's adverse trade in manufacturing which was expected to reach ten billion dollars in 1975 and reduce the outflow of capital in dividends, patents and other costs, amounting to another five billion dollars. Such a shift in industrial strategy from dependence on the United States and its fifteen billion dollar annual cost to Canada could allow for increases in real pay for working people and a sizeable increase in capital available for investment in an expanding economy.

Labour will strengthen its position in the overall national debate when it combines its programme for a redistribution of existing national income with an emphasis on the need for a larger national product through a made-in-Canada industrial strategy. Such a strategy was partially enunciated in the UAW brief of January 1975 which stressed new manufacturing possibilities for Canada. Grace Hartman, in late October 1975, after her election as the new president of CUPE, called for more processing in Canada as essential to the economy. The B.C. Federation of Labour made a similar proposal in 1971.

The 1975 mood of labour was reflected in statements about the wage restraints by Canada's top labour leaders. The CLC argued that the absence of genuine price controls in the initial Trudeau proposals made the restraint policy purely and simply a "wage control" policy, and that the program was "unfair, unequitable and unworkable". Joe Morris, president of the CLC, was quoted as saying, ". . . this is one goddam law that I'm prepared to disobey no matter what the cost".

As its initial policy of persuasion foundered the federal government moved quickly toward intimidation. "We'll put a few union leaders in jail for three years and the others will get the message" the prime minister told a Toronto radio audience in October 1975. But labour leaders did not appear to be intimidated.

David Archer, president of the Ontario Federation of Labour, advised the 1975 convention of that body to "continue normal bargaining procedures and arrive at an agreement. If there is an attempt to roll back the negotiated wage increase or other benefits, then a confrontation should be expected. At that point, the trade union movement must stand solid, prepared to resist, and if necessary, to suffer whatever penalties that resistance entails."

Dennis McDermott, Canadian director of the UAW, even entertained a general work stoppage as one means for labour to challenge the government's incomes policy, although he expressed some uncertainty as to how effective a measure it would be. "I don't think it would be a panacea for everything, or even know if we have the capability of pulling one off in this country."

Characteristically, CUPE, Canada's largest Canadian union, spoke out strongly against the Trudeau wage restraint policy. On the floor of that union convention in October 1975 there was delegate demand for a general Canada-wide work stoppage to oppose the government's policy.

It was Canadian unions like the Canadian Paperworkers Union with 24,000 members on strike, the 22,000 striking postal workers, and the 8,800 striking Metro Toronto secondary school teachers which set the pace in union militancy after the federal government had announced its economic restraint policy.

The turn toward militant and independent unionism in the 1973-1975 period has strengthened greatly the ability of Canada's unions, now three million strong, to deal with the corporations and their government protectors. The response of Canada's unions to the wage controls imposed in late 1975 shows how far Canadian labour has moved from business unionism and dependence on American labour towards programmatic and organizational independence. This is laying the ground for a new role for labour in the economic and political leadership of the country.

Appendix

The Effect of Inflation on Real Wages
in Selected Manufacturing Industries 1972-1975

To illustrate the change in the economic position of unionists in Canada during the period of what has been termed "galloping inflation", eight contracts involving six unions in five manufacturing industries were selected for examination. The loss in real income over a two- or three-year period due to inflation (contracts were of varying lengths) between 1972 and 1975 is shown in the accompanying table. Essentially, the table shows the effects of inflation on actual wages.

The contracts selected include the following key manufacturing industries: auto, steel, electrical, textile and paper. They include a group of workers who are generally at higher levels of industrial pay, such as auto, steel and skilled paper workers. They also include workers, particularly women in the electrical and textile industries, who are generally at the lower end of the average pay in unionized manufacturing.

All calculations were based on a 40-hour week, without over-time or shift-differential pay. Workers on incentive pay were not included. The only exception to the 40-hour week was at Harvey Woods where a 42.5-hour week was in effect until September 29, 1974, then changing to 40 hours. The contracts chosen were of varying lengths but all fell within the highly inflationary period 1972-1975. All calculations began at the opening day of the particular contract, a date specified in the list of contracts following. All calculations were terminated in spring and summer 1975 although not all contracts had expired at that time. The closing date for calculations is also specified in the list of contracts.

Two sets of calculations were performed to arrive at the figures in the accompanying table. The first was the determination of actual pay received by workers in particular categories and classes in the specified period based on the terms of the contract plus any additional increase given for cost of living during that period. These figures were worked in consultation with the local union and/or the company involved. Some contracts, such as the auto and steel contracts, had Cost of Living Allowances (COLA) built into them. COLA payments were included in the figures of total gross pay and final hourly rate received by workers during the duration specified whether or not the COLA was fully folded into the base rate on which calculations for fringe benefits and pensions, for example, are based.

These calculations do not deal with "take-home" pay but rather with gross pay before numerous deductions, including graduated income tax deductions.

The second set of calculations for total pay over the duration specified was hypothetical; that is, it was based on the assumption that the hourly wage rate had been adjusted monthly to keep up exactly with the increase in the cost of living as determined by Statistics Canada's monthly Consumer Price Index (CPI). Two variations on the hypothetical calculations were used. One assumed that the hourly wage rate was simply indexed to the monthly change in the CPI. The other assumed a three per cent annual rise in real pay, as generally practised in key industries in the 1960s and early 1970s, in addition to the indexed hourly rate.

The two hypothetical figures described were then compared to actual pay received under the contract. The columns designated as loss of pay are based on a subtraction of total actual pay from the two types of hypothetical indexed pay. The last column shows that loss averaged for a twelve-month period.

The results of these calculations clearly illustrate a general lowering of real pay over the three-year period for all contracts examined and for both lower paid and higher paid workers.

Contracts Studied

Abitibi Paper Co.
Canadian Paperworkers
Union, Local 90
650 employees
May 1/73-April 30/75

Philips Electronics
Industries Ltd.
International Brother-
hood of Electrical
Workers, Local 1590
125 male, 125 female
employees
April 1/72-March 31/74

Abitibi Paper Co.
Canadian Paperworkers
Union, Local 109
260 employees
May 1/73-April 30/75

Stelco, Hamilton
United Steel Workers
of America, Local 1005
11,255 employees
August 1/72-July 31/75

Ford of Canada Ltd.
United Auto Workers
Locals 200, 584, 707,
1054, 1520
13,500 employees
Sept. 16/73-June 1/75

Wabasso Ltd.
United Textile Workers
of America, Local 155
299 male, 259 female
employees
August 4/72-August 3/75

Harvey Woods Ltd.
Textile Workers' Union
of America, Local 1300
90 male, 376 female
employees
Sept. 1/73-August 31/75

Westinghouse Canada Ltd.
United Electrical Workers
of America, Local 504
2,642 male, 327 female
employees
June 22/72-August 22/75

Contract and Duration	Job Class	Actual Total Pay Received	Initial Hourly Rate	Final Hourly Rate
Abitibi	Wood Room — Bark Sluice	$18,622	$4.21	$4.82
Paper	Core Machine Op.	20,016	4.53	5.17
May/73-	Utility Oiler	20,827	4.72	5.37
April/75	Journeyman 'A' Plus	25,320	5.76	6.49
Abitibi	JC-43 Sixth Hand	19,433	4.40	5.02
Paper	JC-61 Fourth Hand	23,552	5.35	6.05
May/73-	JC-25 Machine Tender	28,585	6.51	7.31
April/75	JC-43 Machine Tender	32,225	7.35	8.22
Ford	4.59*	20,122	5.23	6.11
Auto	5.25	22,590	5.92	6.81
Sept./73-	5.92	25,075	6.61	7.52
June/75	6.59	27,550	7.29	8.23
Harvey Woods	Cutting-Odds Operator	10,052	2.66	2.54
Textile	Knitter	11,041	2.95	2.77
Sept./73-	Dryer-Tender	11,944	3.21	2.98
August/75	Dyer's Helper	12,890	3.49	3.20
Philips	JC-2	11,312	2.67	2.79
Electrical	JC-6	13,784	3.27	3.39
April/72-	JC-13	19,305	4.61	4.73
March/74				
Stelco	JC-4	27,439	4.06	4.83
Steel	JC-8	30,284	4.45	5.40
August/72-	JC-12	33,146	4.84	5.98
July/75	JC-18	37,438	5.42	6.85
Wabasso	Bobbin Stripper	15,521	2.30	2.74
Textile	Yarn Hand	16,296	2.42	2.87
August/72-	Card Fixer Learner Gr. 2	16,998	2.53	2.99
August/75	Card Fixer	21,254	3.19	3.71
Westinghouse	JC-2-5	22,101	3.44	4.32
Electrical	JC-1-9	26,222	4.14	5.08
June/72-	JC-1-13	29,683	4.72	5.73
April/75				

*Regular hourly wage rate prior to increase

| Final Hourly Rate | | Loss in Real Pay | | Average Annual Loss | |
If Indexed to CPI	If Indexed + 3%	Indexed minus Actual	Indexed + 3% minus Actual	Indexed Pay	Indexed + 3% Pay
$5.15	$5.30	$ 744	$1,053	$372	$ 527
5.54	5.70	825	1,155	413	578
5.77	5.94	888	1,232	444	616
5.05	7.26	1,180	1,599	590	800
5.37	5.54	809	1,490	405	745
6.54	6.73	1,062	1,811	531	905
7.95	8.19	1,365	2,199	683	1,099
8.98	9.25	1,590	2,485	795	1,242
6.21	6.40	610	891	349	509
7.03	7.25	878	1,196	502	684
7.85	8.09	1,128	1,483	644	848
8.66	8.92	1,349	1,741	771	995
2.59	2.66	23	179	12	89
2.87	2.95	127	300	64	150
3.12	3.21	222	410	111	205
3.39	3.49	322	526	161	263
3.12	3.19	570	799	285	400
3.81	3.92	769	1,049	385	524
5.36	5.52	1,212	1,607	606	803
5.35	5.67	1,383	2,315	461	772
5.86	6.22	1,292	2,313	431	771
6.37	6.76	1,184	2,295	395	765
7.14	7.57	1,023	2,267	341	756
3.05	3.24	1,332	1,892	444	630
3.21	3.41	1,436	2,026	479	675
3.36	3.56	1,540	2,156	513	718
4.24	4.49	2,121	2,898	707	966
4.45	4.73	774	1,553	273	548
5.36	5.68	1,303	2,240	460	790
6.10	6.47	1,662	2,729	586	963

Glossary

Arbitration
The procedure by which a board or a single arbitrator, acting under the authority of both parties to a dispute, hears both sides of the controversy and issues an award, usually accompanied by a written decision, which is ordinarily binding on both parties. Arbitrators are usually appointed by the parties concerned, but under special circumstances, they are appointed by the government.

Break-away
In Canada in recent years the term break-away has referred to the end result of a process by which a labour relations board designates a trade union as the exclusive bargaining representative for a particular bargaining unit following a majority vote in a Canadian local of an international union to sever its connection with that international union in favour of independent local status or affiliation with an existing Canadian union.

Certification
The official designation by a labour relations board of a trade union as the exclusive bargaining representative for employees in a particular bargaining unit, following proof of majority support among employees in a bargaining unit.

Compulsory Arbitration
Compulsory arbitration is a procedure required by law usually used to settle contract interpretation disputes. Governments sometimes impose it to avoid a strike or to end one.

Conciliation
The process by which an employer and a trade union, bargaining for the employer's workers, attempt to achieve a voluntary agreement over

disputes arising in the course of negotiating a collective agreement, through the offices of a third party. The conciliator or conciliation board does not bring in a binding award. The conciliator is often a government official.

Continentalism
Continentalism, in its economic form, is the belief that the North American economy should be fully integrated.

Designated Worker
A designated worker is a federal government employee whose work has been designated by the Public Service Staff Relations Act as necessary for the "safety and security of the public". It is illegal for a designated worker to participate in a strike.

Dues Check-off
A clause in a collective agreement authorizing an employer to deduct union dues and, sometimes, other assessments, and transmit these funds to the union. There are four main types. The first three apply to union members only: 1) voluntary revocable, 2) voluntary irrevocable, 3) compulsory. The fourth type is the Rand formula under which dues are deducted from both union and non-union employees.

ENA
The Experimental Negotiating Agreement was signed between the USWA and the U.S. steel industry in 1973, and was founded on a no-strike pledge for three years. USWA president Abel said of the agreement in 1973 "... [it] will provide an opportunity for the companies to increase production through stability of operations and enhance the steel industry's competitive position".

Grievance
A complaint against management by one or more employees, or a union, concerning an alleged breach of collective agreement or an alleged injustice. Procedure for handling of grievances is usually defined in the agreement.

International Union
A union whose head office is normally in the United States and which charters locals in both the United States and Canada.

Mediation
A means of settling labour disputes whereby the contending parties use a third person — called a mediator — as a go-between.

National Union
A union whose membership is confined to Canada.

Sources used were Canadian Labour Congress, *Notes on Unions*. Glossary of Labour Terms, n.d.; CCH Canadian Limited, *Canadian Labour Terms 1975*. (Don Mills: CCH Canadian Ltd., 1974).

Abbreviations

Abbreviations used in *Canada's Unions* are listed alphabetically. These include central labour bodies, national and international unions operating in Canada and independent local organizations.

ACWA	Amalgamated Clothing Workers of America
AFL	American Federation of Labor
BRAC	Brotherhood of Railway, Airline and Steamship Clerks, Freight Handlers, Express and Station Employees
BRSC	Brotherhood of Railway and Steamship Clerks
CBRE	Canadian Brotherhood of Railway Employees
CBRT	Canadian Brotherhood of Railway, Transport and General Workers
CCCL	Canadian and Catholic Confederation of Labour
CCU	Confederation of Canadian Unions
CEQ	Corporation des enseignants du Québec Quebec Teachers Corporation
CFGEO	Canadian Federation of Government Employee Organizations
CFL	Canadian Federation of Labour
CIO	Congress of Industrial Organizations
CLC	Canadian Labour Congress
CLSU	Canadian Lake Seamen's Union
CMSG	Canadian Merchant Service Guild, Inc.
CMU	Canadian Maritime Union
CNTU	Confederation of National Trade Unions
CPU	Canadian Paperworkers Union
CSAO	Civil Service Association of Ontario

CSD	Centrale des syndicats démocratiques
CSN	Confédération des syndicats nationaux
	Confederation of National Trade Unions
CSU	Canadian Seamen's Union
CUPE	Canadian Union of Public Employees
CUPW	Canadian Union of Postal Workers
CWC	Communications Workers of Canada
FCWC	Federation of Catholic Workers of Canada
FTQ	Fédération des travailleurs du Québec
	Quebec Federation of Labour
IAM	International Association of Machinists and Aerospace Workers
IBEW	International Brotherhood of Electrical Workers
ICFTU	International Confederation of Free Trade Unions
ICW	International Chemical Workers' Union
ILGWU	International Ladies Garment Workers' Union
IUE	International Union of Electrical, Radio and Machine Workers
IUOE	International Union of Operating Engineers
IWA	International Woodworkers of America
LCUC	Letter Carriers' Union of Canada
NABET	National Association of Broadcast Employees and Technicians
NAME	National Association of Marine Engineers
NTLC	National Trades and Labour Congress of Canada
NUPE	National Union of Public Employees
NUPSE	National Union of Public Service Employees
OBU	One Big Union
OCAW	Oil, Chemical and Atomic Workers' International Union
OFL	Ontario Federation of Labour
OSSTF	Ontario Secondary School Teachers' Federation
OTF	Ontario Teachers' Federation
PPWC	Pulp, Paper and Woodworkers of Canada
PSAC	Public Service Alliance of Canada
QFL	Quebec Federation of Labour
QTC	Quebec Teachers Corporation
	Corporation des enseignants du Québec
SEIU	Service Employees' International Union
SIU	Seafarers' International Union of Canada
TLC	Trades and Labour Congress of Canada
UAW	International Union, United Automobile, Aerospace, and Agricultural Implement Workers of America (United Auto Workers)
UPIU	United Paperworkers International Union
URW	United Rubber, Cork, Linoleum and Plastic Workers of America (United Rubber Workers)

USWA	United Steel Workers of America
UTWA	United Textile Workers of America
WFM	Western Federation of Miners
WUL	Workers' Unity League

Index